CONTEMPORARY JAPANESE POLITICS

Contemporary Asia in the World

Contemporary Asia in the World

David C. Kang and Victor D. Cha, Editors

This series aims to address a gap in the public-policy and scholarly discussion of Asia. It seeks to promote books and studies that are on the cutting edge of their respective disciplines or in the promotion of multidisciplinary or interdisciplinary research but that are also accessible to a wider readership. The editors seek to showcase the best scholarly and public-policy arguments on Asia from any field, including politics, history, economics, and cultural studies.

CONTEMPORARY JAPANESE POLITICS

Institutional Changes and Power Shifts

TOMOHITO SHINODA

COLUMBIA UNIVERSITY PRESS   *New York*

COLUMBIA UNIVERSITY PRESS
Publishers Since 1893
NEW YORK   CHICHESTER, WEST SUSSEX
cup.columbia.edu

Library of Congress Cataloging-in-Publication Data
Shinoda, Tomohito, 1960–
     Contemporary Japanese politics : institutional changes and power shifts / Tomohito Shinoda.
          pages cm—(Contemporary Asia in the world)
     Includes bibliographical references and index.
     ISBN 978-0-231-15852-7 (cloth : alk. paper)—ISBN 978-0-231-15853-4 (pbk. : alk. paper)—
ISBN 978-0-231-52806-1 (ebook)
1. Japan—Politics and government—1989–   I. Title.
DS891.S546 2013
320.952—dc23

2013012145

Columbia University Press books are printed on permanent and durable acid-free paper.

This book is printed on paper with recycled content.

Printed in the United States of America

c 10 9 8 7 6 5 4 3 2 1
p 10 9 8 7 6 5 4 3 2 1

BOOK DESIGN BY CHANG JAE LEE, COVER DESIGN BY THOMAS STVAN

References to Internet Web sites (URLs) were accurate at the time of writing. Neither the author nor Columbia University Press is responsible for URLs that may have expired or changed since the manuscript was prepared.

To Gretchen and Erika

CONTENTS

FIGURES AND TABLES

ACKNOWLEDGMENTS

A FTER I COMPLETED my doctoral dissertation on the role of the Japanese prime minister in 1994, I focused my research on political institutional changes and their impact on leadership by the national leader. In my first English-language book, *Leading Japan*, I argued that the prime minister can make a difference by using his formal and informal sources of power. My second English-language book, *Koizumi Diplomacy*, described how the prime minister took advantage of newly strengthened political institutions to exercise top-down leadership on national security issues. *Contemporary Japanese Politics* is the most comprehensive book covering institutional changes and analyzing how and when the national leader can be effective.

This book would not have been possible without the support of many individuals. I am particularly indebted to George R. Packard and the late Sohei Nakayama, who both provided me with guidance throughout my academic and professional career. Without them, my academic career would not have even begun.

Over the past years I have had the opportunity to interview many important policy makers. Their comments provided significant insights into how the government functions and how decisions are made. My thanks go to Tatsuo Arima, Keiichirō Asao, Kenji Eda, Yasuo Fukuda, Motohisa Furukawa, Teijirō Furukawa, Masaharu Gotōda, Yoshihiro Handa, Yoshimasa Hayashi, Morihiro Hosokawa, Toshio Kitazawa, Yutaka Kobayashi, Keiichi Konaga, Tarō Kōno, Michihiko Kunihiro, Yoriko Madoka, Junzo Matoba, Jun Matsumoto, Raisuke Miyawaki, Tomiichi Murayama, Akihisa Nagashima, Mieko Nakabayashi, Yasuhiro Nakasone, Tetsuya Nishikawa, Yasutoshi Nishimura, Motohiro

Ōno, Nobumori Ōtani, Hiroshige Sekō, Masahiko Shibayama, Kaname Tajima, Takuya Tasso, Noboru Yamaguchi, Tsuyoshi Yamaguchi, and Kyōji Yanagisawa. I would also like to thank all the other interviewees in the Japanese government who preferred to remain anonymous. If readers feel that this work is unique and concrete, it is because of their invaluable comments.

In the final six months of my work on this book, I was also involved in a project organized by the Rebuild Japan Initiative Foundation to evaluate the government response to the Fukushima nuclear accident. In this project I heard insightful testimony while participating in a group interview with high governmental officials, including Naoto Kan, Yukio Edano, Banri Kaieda, Tetsurō Fukuyama, and Gōshi Hosono. I am grateful to Yōichi Funabashi for inviting me to participate in the project.

I would like to express my gratitude to many scholars for their valuable input. They include Robert Angel, James Auer, Kent Calder, I. M. Destler, Chihiro Hosoya, Carl Jackson, Glenn Hook, Takashi Inoguchi, Richard Katz, Ellis Krauss, Seigen Miyasato, Henry Nau, Robert Pekkanen, T. J. Pempel, Richard Samuels, James Schoff, Sheila Smith, Michael Smitka, Yoshihide Soeya, Akihiko Tanaka, Nathaniel Thayer, Akio Watanabe, and anonymous readers. I owe special thanks to two anonymous reviewers for the insightful suggestions on revising the introduction.

My sincere gratitude goes to Victor Cha, who recommended me to Columbia University Press's series of Contemporary Asia in the World, and to Anne Routon of the Press for her support of this book project. Research support for this study came principally from JSPS KAKENHI Grant Number 22530168.

Finally, I dedicate this work to the two most important women in my life—my wife Gretchen and daughter Erika, who brought new meaning to my life and motivation to finish this project.

A NOTE ON CONVENTIONS

JAPANESE WORDS AND PERSONAL NAMES are romanized according to the modified Hepburn system. Japanese personal names are normally presented in the Western order, with the exception of Japanese scholars whose Japanese-language publications give the author's name in Japanese order. Most monetary figures are given in yen and not translated into U.S. dollars.

ABBREVIATIONS AND JAPANESE TERMS

amakudari	institutional practice of placing Japanese senior bureaucrats in high-profile positions in the private and public sectors
APEC	Asia Pacific Economic Cooperation
CCS	chief cabinet secretary, *kanbō chōkan*
CEFP	Council on Economic and Fiscal Policy
Dōteki Bōeiryoku	Dynamic Defense Force
Dōmei	All Japan Labor Federation
DPJ	Democratic Party of Japan
DSP	Democratic Socialist Party
FRF	Futenma Replacement Facility
fuku daijin	senior vice minister
FY	fiscal year
GDP	gross domestic product
genrō	founders of modern Japan
gojūgo-nen taisei	1955 system under which the ruling LDP and the largest opposition party, JSP, were split ideologically
GRU	Government Revitalization Unit, Gyōsei Sasshin Kaigi
honebuto no hōshin	*Basic Policies at the CEFP*
ISAF	International Security Assistance Force
JCP	Japan Communist Party
JDA	Japan Defense Agency

jimujikan kaigi	administrative vice ministerial meeting
JNP	Japan New Party
JSP	Japan Socialist Party
jūshin	senior statemen
ka	division
kachō	division director
kaiha	caucus in the Diet
Kantei	prime minister's official residence
Keidanren	Federation of Economic Organizations
Keizai Dōyūkai	Japan Association of Corporate Executives
kōenkai	local support group for politicians
Kibanteki Bōeiryoku	Basic Defense Force
Kōmeitō	Clean Government Party
LDP	Liberal Democratic Party
MAFF	Ministry of Agriculture, Forestry, and Fisheries
MCA	Management and Coordination Agency
METI	Ministry of Economy, Trade, and Industry
MEXT	Ministry of Education, Culture, Sports, Science, and Technology
MHLW	Ministry of Health, Labor, and Welfare
MIC	Ministry of Internal Affairs and Communications
Minnanotō	Your Party
MITI	Ministry of International Trade and Industry
MLIT	Ministry of Land, Infrastructure, Transportation, and Tourism
MOC	Ministry of Construction
MOD	Ministry of Defense
MOF	Ministry of Finance
MOFA	Ministry of Foreign Affairs
MOT	Ministry of Transportation
MOU	Memorandum of Understanding
MPT	Ministry of Post and Telecommunications
Naimushō	prewar Ministry of Home Affairs
nemawashi	log-rolling
NISA	Nuclear and Industry Safety Agency
NFP	New Frontier Party
NHK	Nippon Hōsō Kyōkai
NPA	National Police Agency

NSC	National Security Council of the United States
NSO	National Strategic Office (Kokka Senryaku Shitsu)
NTT	Nippon Telegraph and Telephone
PARC	Policy Affairs Research Council (LDP)
PKF	Peacekeeping Force
PKO	peacekeeping operations
PMO	Prime Minister's Office
PNP	People's New Party, or Kokumin Shintō
PR	proportional representation
Rengō	Japan Trade Union Confederation, Nihon Rōdō Kumiai Sōrengōkai
Sakigake	Harbinger Party
SDF	Self-Defense Forces
SDP	Social Democratic Party
seifu shunō	top official of the government
seimukan	parliamentary secretary
seimu sanyaku kaigi	three-political-appointees' conference
seisaku kaigi	policy conference
Sōhyō	General Council of Japanese Trade Unions
Tachiagare Nippon	Sunrise Party of Japan
TEPCO	Tokyo Electric Power Company
TPP	Trans-Pacific Strategic Economic Partnership Agreement
UN	United Nations
zoku	policy tribe at LDP's Policy Affairs Research Council

CONTEMPORARY JAPANESE POLITICS

INTRODUCTION

WHEN THE DEMOCRATIC PARTY of Japan (DPJ) assumed leadership of Japan's government in September 2009, the country's political scene experienced a drastic change. Among Japan scholars there had been an ongoing debate in the 1990s whether Japanese politics was really changing. Scholars using the political culture approach saw changes in Japanese politics throughout the postwar period as less significant, given the backdrop of the continuing reign of the Liberal Democratic Party (LDP).[1] On the other hand, institutionalists predicted that the 1994 electoral reform would change the Japanese political scene. Proponents of change were in the minority.[2] The 2009 power shift effectively ended the debate, however, and the institutionalist argument prevailed.

In their 1993 study J. Mark Ramseyer and Frances McCall Rosenbluth advanced the theory of rational choice institutionalism of Japanese politics. They abandoned "any notion of a peculiar Japanese culture" and argued that the institutional framework of government decisively shapes the character of political competition in Japan, that the players in this competitive political market try to build organizations adapted to that framework, and that these players also try to manipulate the framework to their private advantage.[3] According to Ramseyer and Rosenbluth, under the old multiple-member electoral system, LDP members rationally developed factionalism and *kōenkai* (personal support groups of politicians) in order to be reelected.[4] The new single-member district (SMD) electoral system introduced in 1994 altered their electoral incentives and brought major revisions to Japanese politics. These authors can therefore be said to follow an electoral system approach to institutionalism.

Adapting such an approach, Masahiko Tatebayashi analyzed changes in LDP legislators' behavior after the 1996 general election. He concluded that the electoral change weakened the pork-barrel type of policy involvement and strengthened the involvement in nonpork policies such as national security and the judiciary system. Tatebayashi also observed the weakening of factionalism and the strengthening of the prime minister in policy making.[5] Similarly, Rosenbluth and Michael F. Thies argue that the electoral reform eliminated intraparty competition, which prompted the weakening of factions and the centralization of the prime minister's authority within parties.[6]

This book's scope is different from that of studies using the electoral system approach. The new legislative incentives are treated as merely one of the factors that set a new power balance between the government and legislators and their political parties. The book tracks the slow but steady structural changes under the LDP reign that were brought about by the 1994 electoral reform, just as the electoral system approach predicted. These structural changes led to the selection of Junichirō Koizumi, an antimainstream politician, as prime minister and resulted in the power shift to the DPJ that ended LDP rule. The book, however, goes beyond the impact of the electoral reform to shed light on other institutional reforms, such as the 1999 government reform, the 2001 administrative reform, and the 2001 LDP presidential election rule change. It explains how Prime Minister Koizumi took advantage of these institutional changes to exercise strong leadership in policy making, and it explores the alterations in political institutions that occurred under the DPJ administrations, which changed the structure of power within the government and vis-à-vis interest groups, the public, and the media.

The goal of this book is to explain how the institutional changes shifted the locus of policy making among bureaucrats, legislators, and the prime minister and cabinet, and how the new power balance among these main political actors affected the government's ability to coordinate diverse policy preferences and respond to political crises. First, let us examine how previous studies on Japanese politics have treated the role of these actors in policy making.

THE STRONG BUREAUCRACY

Until the 1980s the political culture approach dominated explanations of Japanese politics and supported the power elite model. According to a classic study by Kiyoaki Tsuji, the cultural heritage of the prewar bureaucratic supremacy over the people survived because the bureaucracy was the only national institution to maintain influence under the American Occupation. The bureaucracy, with support from the Occupation forces, could exercise relatively strong power vis-à-vis the Diet and thus established itself as pivotal in decision making.[7]

The individual ministries maintained and expanded their power after the Occupation authorities left Japan. Chalmers Johnson, in his best-selling book *MITI and the Japanese Miracle*, portrayed high-level Japanese bureaucrats as "the most prestigious in the society." He noted that although "it is influenced by pressure groups and political claimants, the elite bureaucracy of Japan makes most major decisions, drafts virtually all legislation, controls national budget, and is the source of all major policy innovations in the system."[8]

A corporatist argument is a variation of the power elite model. A typical argument is presented by T. J. Pempel and Keiichi Tsunekawa.[9] According to these authors, policies were made by the government and key organizations such as Keidanren (Federation of Economic Organizations) and the National Association of Agricultural Cooperatives. Although labor organizations act as a key group in European corporatist societies, such organizations are not active participants in Japanese policy making. Similarly, Karel van Wolferen described the Japanese power elite model as "the system" with a submissive middle class.[10] The system, made up of elites in the political, bureaucratic, and business worlds, somehow makes decisions as a unit: everybody within it tries to preserve the system. A similar monolithic view of Japanese society is described by the popular phrase "Japan Inc."[11] In this view, Japan is a country where the intimate ties between the government and industries dominate decision making in industrial and related policies. Bureaucrats are treated as pivotal players in policy making.

The Japanese bureaucracy, however, is not a single, solid entity. Each ministry has its own interests and client industry to protect. Career bureaucrats spend their entire careers in a single ministry and develop sectionalism. They resist policy changes that negatively affect their clients to effectively serve as veto players.

The Decentralized Party

In the 1980s many Japan scholars focused on the power shift between the bureaucracy and politicians, arguing for the pluralist model as structural change gradually took place under the LDP's long reign. Many LDP Diet members accumulated knowledge and experience in specific policy areas and became identified as *zoku*, or policy tribes. Some scholars, such as Akira Nakamura, Takashi Inoguchi, and Tomoaki Iwai, emphasized the role of the LDP's Policy Affairs Research Council (PARC) and saw its subcommittees as a key to policy making. According to their view, power shifted from the bureaucracy to the LDP committee after the oil shock. Lower economic growth brought a significant slowdown to the growth of budget size and made it impossible for the bureaucracy to make a political decision on budget allocation with limited funds. As a result, bureaucratic officials became more dependent on the mediation and political decisions of the ruling party members when reallocating funds among administrative programs.[12] It became part of the official process for bureaucrats to seek approval from the relevant zoku members before submitting budget proposals and other policy initiatives to the cabinet. The LDP government delegated considerable policy-making power on specific issues to these specialists within the party organization.

While LDP zoku members increased their influence and became veto players in the "iron triangle," the bureaucracy still played a pivotal role in drafting legislative proposals. Because the LDP headquarters had only a limited staff, LDP members could not turn to their party's policy staff for extra help, as their German counterparts did. With a limited personal staff (officially only two staffers for each Diet member prior to 1993, three thereafter), LDP members did not command the resources necessary to draft legislation by themselves, as many in the U.S. Congress did. The LDP had to continue to rely substantially on the bureaucracy in making policy on specific issues.

The increase of the LDP legislators' influence in policy making did not correspondingly increase the power of the prime minister or the cabinet. On the contrary, the cabinet's core executive role declined with the emergence of bureaucratic sectionalism in the party. Zoku members and ministries handled many specific policy issues, not only outside the Diet but also often beyond the reach of the cabinet. When the government tried to introduce a major policy change that a single ministry did not favor, zoku members and their related ministry would form an issue-specific alliance against such a change. On a broader issue that involved several ministries, they formed a smaller iron triangle in each policy arena, and these triangles would compete with each other for their sectoral interests. With the growth of zoku members' influence, the prime minister and cabinet faced stronger sectionalism, which had to be overcome in order to pursue policies initiated by the prime minister.[13]

The Weak Prime Minister and Cabinet

The Japanese prime minister was often considered weak, and a lack of leadership is a reoccurring theme in many analyses. The power elite model asserted that political leaders depended on Japan's strong bureaucracy for the formulation and execution of policies. Some even argued that the bureaucracy was so strong that political leaders, including the prime minister, had a limited role in policy making. Much policy making was highly decentralized and handled by the LDP zoku members. According to van Wolferen, Japan's system had no political center and thus no political leadership.[14]

The policy-making power of the prime minister and the cabinet depends on how many veto players exist in the political system. According to George Tsebelis, veto players are defined as "individual or collective actors whose agreement is necessary for a change in the status quo."[15] Tsebelis introduces two kinds of veto players: *institutional* players who are constitutionally or legally defined, and *partisan* players who are in the different parties and are specified by the political system.[16] Any policy change that alters the status quo requires the unanimous agreement of all the veto players. Therefore the more diverse veto players a political system has, the more difficult it is for the government to achieve agreement.

The Japanese prime minister faces many veto players. As in many parliamentary governments, the constitution vests executive power in the cabinet, not in the prime minister. The authority over administrative operations is divided among the various ministers. This institutional setting allows bureaucrats in each ministry with strong sectionalism to serve as institutional veto players when their interests conflict with the prime minister's policy initiative.

While the prime minister in a parliamentary system represents a majority of the legislative branch, this does not mean an automatic approval for government proposals. The short duration of Diet sessions, the bicameral system, and the committee system leave limited time for the government to pass legislation, which often makes the opposition parties effective partisan veto players, especially when the government cannot get public support for policy changes. Since the 1990s there have been a series of coalition governments instead of a single-party government. Coalition partners often act as veto players when they disagree with the government's policy initiatives. Under the LDP governments of Yasuo Fukuda and Tarō Asō as well as the DPJ governments of Naoto Kan and Yoshihiko Noda, the government coalition did not have a majority in the upper house, so the opposition parties served as very influential partisan veto players.

In addition to these institutional and partisan players, there are *intraparty* veto players in the Japanese political system. The longtime ruling LDP had developed strong factionalism within the party, just as its Italian counterparts did. To become prime minister, a candidate first had to form a coalition of factions for support and then had to maintain that support to be an effective leader. The prime minister had to form the cabinet considering factional balance. As a result, the national leader did not have strong control over the cabinet like the British leader enjoys. Ignoring or losing factional support could create veto players within the government party.

In addition to factionalism, various zoku members in the PARC could be another kind of intraparty veto player. LDP zoku group members specialized in specific policies and had their own interests and client industries to protect. Such members often allied with the related ministries to protect their client industries, forming a major obstacle to confront the prime minister under LDP governments.

Weakening the political influence of LDP factions was a major motive for introducing electoral reform. With the 1994 reform, the electoral system approach predicted that LDP factions would disappear when a strong party center was created, and the new single-seat electoral system would force LDP legislators to become policy generalists instead of specific policy specialists. Ellis S. Krauss and Robert J. Pekkanen, on the other hand, offer a different explanation based on historical institutionalism. They looked into the origin and historical developments of factions and the PARC and explained why these political institutions persisted even after the 1994 electoral changes.[17] Instead of disappearing, the LDP factional system reverted to that of the 1950s, when the party had more, smaller-scale factions. The PARC did not change in many aspects despite the electoral change. In other words, factions and zoku members might continue to serve as veto players.

With so many active veto players, the need to strengthen the power of the prime minister and the cabinet became a major focus of the administrative reform effort under the Ryūtarō Hashimoto administration. As a result of political battles over institutional reform, the 1999 government reform and the 2001 administrative reform were introduced. Based on the impact of these institutional reforms combined with the 1994 electoral reform, Margarita Estévez-Abe introduced the structural analysis approach.[18] The electoral reform created a more centralized and cohesive party, and the government and administrative reforms strengthened the cabinet and created a top-down decision-making council to carry out a series of major economic reforms. With these institutional changes, which weakened the intraparty veto players, Estévez-Abe declared that Japan was moving toward a Westminster system. After seeing the difficulty the Abe administration had in dealing with the loss of a majority in the 2007 upper house, Estévez-Abe added strong bicameralism as an obstacle to Japan's transformation into such a system.[19] Her analysis, however, does not explain why the DPJ administration under Yukio Hatoyama could not exercise strong, top-down leadership even with a majority in the both houses.

This book does not see the institutional changes as a sufficient condition like the electoral system approach and the structure analysis approach do, but as a mere necessary condition. Institutions do not produce leadership; they only enable it. A motivated and talented leader like Junichirō Koizumi could take advantage of institutional changes to exercise leadership, while others like Hatoyama and Naoto Kan failed to do so. This book's ultimate goal is to offer analysis of how and when institutions matter.

The LDP prime ministers before Koizumi relied heavily on the bureaucracy and the LDP zoku members in making policy. The policy-making process was slow, and drastic, controversial policy changes were very difficult to deliver. Policy outcomes usually ended up with political compromises among the veto players. Koizumi took advantage of the institutional changes that encouraged the establishment of a top-down, centralized policy-making style and successfully made the veto players, even if reluctantly, follow his direction. The post-Koizumi LDP leaders—Abe, Fukuda, and Asō—failed to take advantage of the new institutional arrangements to exercise strong leadership. Hatoyama introduced a series of institutional changes to establish political leadership by eliminating the influence of the bureaucracy and the government party. Without support from the other veto players as well as political determination to establish a centralized policy process, however, he could not effectively carry out policy changes, as seen in the relocation of the Futenma air base. Kan tried to reverse Hatoyama's antibureaucratic stance but failed to take advantage of bureaucratic support. To successfully exercise political leadership, the prime minister needs to balance centralized institutions and bureaucratic support.

Outline of the Book

The study begins with an explanation of Japan's political institutions and the political traditions under the LDP government that created veto players. The old multimember-district electoral system with malapportionment for the lower house significantly benefited the LDP as it maintained its power as the ruling party. The electoral system also contributed to the development of intraparty factions within the LDP as well as the growth of LDP legislators' private support groups, or *kōenkai*. These created a strong, decentralized nature in the party. Owing to the decentralized nature, factions served as strong veto players, and the power of the prime minister and the cabinet was limited. To run the government smoothly, the national leader had to maintain harmony within the party. LDP zoku members with growing political influence often allied with related ministries in policy making to serve as powerful veto players against the cabinet. Chapter 1 discusses how the development of factions and kōenkai also accelerated the aspect of money politics in Japan, leading to a movement toward political reform to change the electoral system.

Chapter 2 illustrates the process of institutional reform in the 1990s. Factionalism was seen as a cause of political corruption. A single-seat electoral system was expected to eliminate factionalism within the LDP. Two attempts at enacting electoral reform under the LDP failed because of opposition by veto players who wanted to preserve their kōenkai. Disappointed voters ousted the LDP, and the non-LDP government under Morihiro Hosokawa successfully introduced an electoral system with single-member districts. After bureaucratic scandals and natural disasters, the public wanted to see stronger political leadership. Prime Minister Ryūtarō Hashimoto conducted administrative reform against the opposition of the many veto players in the government and the government party. Although political compromises were finally made with these veto players, Hashimoto successfully reorganized the bureaucracy and strengthened the prime minister's power.

Chapter 3 analyzes the impact of these political institutional changes on the power balance between the government and veto players. The piecemeal institutional changes of the 1990s created a new environment within the Japanese government that encouraged top-down leadership by the prime minister. The redistribution of power between junior and senior politicians within the LDP that followed the 1994 electoral changes contributed to the creation of a more open electoral rule for the LDP presidency, which led to Koizumi's landslide victory in the 2001 presidential race. In addition, the 2001 administrative reform provided Koizumi with clear legitimacy to take stronger policy initiatives and empowered the Kantei, the prime minister's official residence (the Japanese equivalent of the Britain's 10 Downing Street or the U.S. White House), to carry out his policy objectives against veto players. Koizumi led a centralized, top-down policy process to enact important pieces of national security legislation and effectively utilized the newly established Council on

Economic and Fiscal Policy (CEFP) to deliver a series of domestic policy changes.

Chapter 4 focuses on the changes in political culture and elections that eventually led to the birth of the DPJ government. The 1994 electoral change had a significant impact on the political culture. All Diet members had to reorganize their kōenkai and needed to reach out to a wider spectrum of voters in their new constituencies. Although LDP factions and zoku members survived, their political influence as intraparty veto players was significantly decreased, especially under the Koizumi administration. The chapter describes the transition of the DPJ from a small opposition party to a viable opposition party. Finally, it provides analysis of the elections after the 1994 reform. Under the single-seat electoral system, the value of floating votes significantly increased, and the winner in each district became much more difficult to predict. This change brought a political power shift to the DPJ when the public became disappointed by the LDP's handling of the government.

Chapter 5 addresses the decision-making process under the Hatoyama government. The DPJ manifesto during the election campaign identified bureaucrats as unnecessary veto players for reform plans and called for reducing bureaucratic influence in the government. Prime Minister Hatoyama introduced a new set of rules to encourage the DPJ political actors in the government to take policy initiatives within each ministry. These DPJ members frequently met with each other and made policy decisions, deemphasizing the role of the bureaucrats. Hatoyama replaced the CEFP with the newly established National Strategy Office, but this office could not deliver any drastic policy changes. In a case study, chapter 5 explores the details of the Futenma air base relocation. Hatoyama rejected the existing plan and sought his own alternative without relying on expert advice from the bureaucracy. His failure on this issue led to his resignation.

Chapter 6 investigates policy making in the Naoto Kan administration. Prime Minister Kan felt that the institutional changes brought by his predecessor had caused problems. He tried to restore relations between political leaders and bureaucrats. But the networks of bureaucrats were not easily fixed. Then an earthquake of an unprecedented scale hit eastern Japan. Chapter 6 explains the government's response to the crisis, a process made increasingly difficult by weak links between politicians and bureaucrats, who were considered veto players.

Chapter 7 presents a concluding overview of this study. Japanese politics has changed significantly as a result of a series of incremental institutional changes. Under the DPJ government, institutional changes were introduced to strengthen political leadership, but the attempts weakened the policy-making power of the bureaucracy instead of strengthening that of DPJ politicians. The Noda government announced its intent to recover the relations between politicians and bureaucrats, seeking a new equilibrium. Chapter 7 concludes with an analysis of the changes in leadership style from the pre-Koizumi era to the Noda administration.

1 JAPANESE POLITICS UNDER THE LDP

J APAN'S POLITICAL TRADITIONS developed under the long reign of the Liberal Democratic Party. Some were rooted in Japanese culture before the Second World War, and many others were developed under the postwar political institutions to create veto players against the government's policy initiatives. To understand the veto players and how the government sought to change them after the 1990s, it is important to understand the initial logic of institutional choice and the developments under the LDP government.

The basic framework of Japan's political institutional setting was formed under the American Occupation. During World War II the U.S. government studied and planned policies for the occupation of Japan, producing numerous papers and guidelines. The two main goals of the Occupation were clear: the demilitarization and democratization of Japan. Demilitarization was completed in the early stages of the Occupation. Japan's military services were disbanded at home and abroad immediately after the war. Article 9 of the Japanese Constitution, a peace clause, turned Japan into a pacifist nation for a long time in the postwar period.

The second goal of democratization was institutionalized by the constitution and other laws. The prewar Meiji Constitution of 1889 was largely modeled after that of Prussia, with imperial sovereignty. The emperor was clearly the head of state and held national sovereignty and executive power, with strong control over the legislative branch. Statutorily there was no effective veto player against him. The U.S. Occupation authority wanted substantial changes in the constitution to remove the authoritarian aspects of the Meiji Constitution and to establish democratic political institutions that would be "responsible to the will of the people."[1]

The Occupation authority first asked the Japanese government to initiate revision of the Meiji Constitution in October 1945, just seven weeks after the end of the war. The government committee produced a draft revision of the constitution, which maintained the basic prewar framework of imperial sovereignty with just minor revisions. This draft, however, was unacceptable to the Occupation authority. On February 3, 1946, Supreme Commander Douglas MacArthur instructed Courtney Whitney, chief of the Government Section, to prepare a new constitution for Japan and handed him his own notes with three major points to be incorporated into the draft.[2]

The following day Whitney organized a steering committee and seven subcommittees to revise Japan's constitution.[3] After a weeklong discussion, these committees completed their work and jointly submitted their draft to MacArthur on February 10. Two days later he approved the draft with minor revisions and it was presented to the Japanese government with little room for changes in the basic principles and fundamental structure.[4] After a series of negotiations, the Japanese government draft was finalized on March 5. Although some concessions were made, the basic outlines of the American draft remained unchanged: to establish a more democratic, representative government. This new constitution is referred to as the Shōwa Constitution.

Japan's basic political institutional setting under the current constitution is largely modeled after the British parliamentary system. A majority of elected representatives in the national parliament, or Diet, select the prime minister. The selected national leader forms a cabinet, which is vested with executive power. The prime minister and the cabinet are responsible to the Diet and ultimately to the electorate. If there is disagreement between the executive and the legislative branches, the prime minister resigns or calls for a general election. While Japan's basic institutional framework is similar to that of many parliamentary democracies, its political experiences helped develop the practices and power structures in its own way. The following sections examine more closely the details of political institutions and customs surrounding the executive and legislative branches that shaped their roles.

Formal Institutional Setting and Postwar Developments

Stronger Institutions for the Prime Minister and the Cabinet

One of the political institutions that went through the most drastic change was the prime ministership. The postwar prime minister and cabinet are institutionally much stronger than their prewar predecessors. Under the Meiji Constitution of 1889, the emperor was the head of state and held national sovereignty and executive power. The prime minister and the cabinet were to assist the emperor in administering the government. The cabinet was not the only group that advised to the emperor: the Privy Council existed outside the cabinet's jurisdiction and, when instructed by the emperor, deliberated "upon the important matters of State." The Ministry of Imperial Household also assisted the emperor in an advisory role in policy matters. In addition, the extraconstitutional actors, such as *genrō* (founders of modern Japan) and *jūshin* (senior statesmen) had strong influence on the emperor's decision making.

Under the Shōwa Constitution, the emperor was reduced to a symbol of the state, with no political power. At subcommittee meetings of the Government Section, there was strong disagreement over whether executive power should be vested collectively in the cabinet or individually in the prime minister in order to strengthen the national leader's power. The steering committee eventually ruled that the prime minister should be empowered to appoint and dismiss cabinet ministers at will, and that executive power is vested in the cabinet, which is collectively responsible to the Diet.[5]

Article 66 of the Shōwa Constitution clearly defines the prime minister as head of the cabinet. This status is supported by his authority to appoint and dismiss cabinet members (article 68) and to protect cabinet members from legal actions during their tenure (article 75). However, his actual role as head of the cabinet is ambiguous. For example, article 72, which defines the prime minister's job, reads, "The Prime Minister, representing the cabinet, submits bills, reports on general national affairs and foreign relations to the Diet and exercises control and supervision over various administrative branches." The wording is not clear as to whether he represents the cabinet only when he submits bills or when he conducts all the duties described in the article. If representing the cabinet applies only to the submission of bills, the prime minister can control and supervise the ministries independent of the cabinet. This was the intent of the original English-language draft constitution proposed by the Government Section. Cabinet Legal Bureau officials, however, insisted on their interpretation of the cabinet's collective responsibility to the Diet and that the prime minister should not be able to control the executive independently from the cabinet.[6]

These officials wrote the Cabinet Law, which clearly limits the prime minister's executive power. First, article 5 defines the prime minister's role as a representative of the cabinet when reporting on general national affairs and foreign relations. The statements and actions of the prime minister are in theory limited by the cabinet decisions. Second, article 3 states that the executive authority is divided among cabinet members. This provides direct authority over administrative operations to the relevant minister, not the prime minister. The prime minister legally holds direct authority over the agencies under the Cabinet Office only (formerly the Prime Minister's Office). Over the other ministries, he has indirect authority through the relevant minister or collective decision by the cabinet. Third, although article 8 vests in the prime minister with authority to block administrative operations, the final decision must be made in cabinet meetings. Legally the prime minister cannot control or supervise each minister. Ministers do not receive individual direction from the prime minister unless his direction meets certain conditions.[7]

Even the prime minister's indirect authority is limited. Article 6 of the Cabinet Law does not allow him to hold executive power independent from decisions made in the cabinet. Thus the prime minister can control or supervise the executive branch only to the extent that he is authorized by the cabinet meeting. In policy making, the prime minister needs to build a consensus among different groups within the ruling party to ensure that the cabinet will approve the policy. This legal arrangement allows cabinet ministers and their ministries to become veto players.

This can be problematic, especially in the case of an emergency. During the administrative reform efforts under Prime Minister Ryūtarō Hashimoto (1996–98), this issue was repeatedly discussed in order to explore the possibility of reinforcing the prime minister's executive authority under the existing legal framework. An advisory council to the prime minister suggested that the cabinet preapprove a package of decisions to authorize the prime minister to act in emergency cases, and it also recommended a more flexible interpretation of the article. However, these proposals met strong opposition from the Cabinet Legal Bureau, which saw them as a threat to the principle of the collective responsibility of the cabinet.[8] In the end, no change in article 6 of the Cabinet Law was included in Hashimoto's administrative reform.

The Emergence of Bureaucratic Supremacy

Although the American Occupation authorities emphasized popular sovereignty and the supremacy of the legislature when drafting the constitution, they also helped the Japanese bureaucracy gain power vis-à-vis the legislative branch in actual policy-making procedures.[9] The Occupation authorities decided to maintain the bureaucratic institutions and to administer the Occupation indirectly through them. Planners originally intended to have a government directly administered by the U.S. military, but because of the sudden, unconditional surrender of Japan, they decided to use the existing governmental institutions to achieve the immediate and enormous task of governing an entire nation. As the Occupation reforms proved to be successful and popular, Japanese bureaucrats touted them as their own achievements.

The Occupation authorities conducted a large-scale purge that removed or excluded more than 200,000 people from public office. Many incumbent legislators became targets of the purge, which thus effectively eliminated most of the experienced politicians from the political parties. Of the legislators elected in the first postwar general election of April 1946, more than 80 percent (381 of 466 members) were newly elected. These inexperienced legislators had to rely completely on the bureaucrats to formulate legislation. The Diet became no more than a rubber stamp for legislation submitted by the bureaucrats. The ideal of legislative supremacy over the executive, held by the American reformers, was far from reality. After the Occupation authorities left, the bureaucrats continued to administer government programs developed under the Occupation. As a result, the bureaucracy became the primary political beneficiary in Japanese society in the immediate postwar period.

The bureaucracy did not escape from the Occupation reforms, however. The hardest hit government agency was the prewar Home Ministry (Naimushō), the most prestigious and powerful agency. In the Occupation authorities' view, the ministry "represented the heart and center of the internal administrative bureaucracy and exercised the controls which reached down through regional, prefectural, city, town, and village governments and to the ward offices and neighborhood association system to enter, influence and restrict every phase of every man, woman and child in Japan."[10] About 60 percent of the Home Ministry's high officials were purged, and its administrative authorities were divided among the new ministries of Construction, Labor, Health and Welfare, and Home Affairs, as well as the Police Agency. However, the purge did not cut deeply into the civil service of other ministries, where less than 20 percent of civil servants were removed, except in the Foreign Ministry, where about 30 percent were purged.[11] Overall, the purge helped bring new, younger officials to power in the government, and it had little negative impact on the efficiency of the bureaucracy, which promoted postwar reforms.

In the area of economic policy making, the relative power of the bureaucracy increased while the bureaucrats' rivals lost power. The Imperial Army and Navy, influential in prewar industrial policy making, were abolished. The influential *zaibatsu*, privately owned business empires, were dissolved into smaller business organizations, and many business leaders were purged. On the other hand, under the controlled economy during the Occupation period, the power of the economic bureaucrats in the Ministries of Finance (MOF) and International Trade and Industry (MITI) grew as they implemented a wide range of economic policies. After the Occupation the economic ministries retained "the emergency controls that they could effectively use, while endeavoring to dismantle other Occupation reforms that threatened to reduce or restrict their powers."[12]

The experience of the Occupation also helped to strengthen sectionalism among the different ministries and agencies in the Japanese government. The Occupation authority was a bureaucratic organization staffed by U.S. Army officials. Individual sections competed with each other to achieve reforms. American reformers began to cooperate with their Japanese counterparts in specific areas such as fiscal austerity, civil liberties, local sanitation, highway construction, democratization of the elementary and high school curricula, and revitalization of newspapers. Sometimes members of this cross-national alliance jointly stood up to their superiors in the Japanese government and the Occupation authority.[13] Although the cabinet was collectively responsible for overall administrative actions, the individual ministries grew in actual decision-making power during the Occupation.

The individual ministries maintained their power after the Occupation authorities left Japan. Each ministry is staffed by a group of highly competent, elite bureaucrats who have strong loyalty to their ministry. The majority of these bureaucrats are graduates of top national and private universities who have passed a highly competitive entrance examination for civil service. Although there are occasional interagency personnel exchange programs, the career patterns of the bureaucrats are dominated by service in a single ministry.[14] This strengthens their loyalty to their ministry and also promotes sectionalism in the different agencies.

Throughout their careers, elite bureaucrats learn to design, draft, implement, and interpret legislation under the jurisdiction of their ministry. As these bureaucrats prepare most of the legislation presented to the Diet, they have strong influence over the legislative branch. Their major interest is to protect their ministry's interests and expand its authority, and they tend to put their ministerial interest over national interest. In the postwar era individual ministries have created their own jurisdictions and empowered themselves through various laws. MITI, for example, worked to have a multitude of functions assigned to it by 175 separate laws as of April 2000. The authority for administrative interpretation of these laws is assigned to the relevant division of the ministry. Knowledge of the complicated network of laws is a great asset to the elite bureaucrats who can cite various legal restrictions to block policy initiatives of other political actors. In addition to their executive operations, they have strongly influenced the legislative branch through the drafting of legislation and the judiciary branch through administrative interpretation.

A top civil service official, the administrative vice minister, was in charge of coordinating the activities of the various branches of the ministry, preparing ministerial decisions, and supervising their implementation, just like the British permanent secretary. Although the minister statutorily held appointive authority, the appointments of the vice minister as well as other positions were almost always decided within the bureaucracy, with the minister rubberstamping the decision.[15] During his short tenure, the minister more often than not represented the interest of the ministry vis-à-vis the cabinet and the ruling party. As minister, the elected legislator had an excellent opportunity to build personal relations with the bureaucrats and staff at related industries. To gain trust and administrative assistance from elite bureaucrats, the minister was expected to be loyal to the ministry.

These developments supported the bureaucratic supremacy or power elite model, which perhaps was the most popular among explanations of the Japanese policy-making process until the 1980s. In this model there were characteristically three actors: bureaucrats, politicians, and business and other interest groups. Sometimes this was portrayed as the "iron triangle" model. Although there was significant disagreement among the supporters of this view on which actor was the most powerful among the three, the bureaucracy was often described as pivotal.[16]

With its central role, the bureaucracy developed the highly decentralized, bottom-up policy process. In this process, the main working-level officers were usually at the deputy director level and in their late thirties to early forties.[17] Their original proposals were discussed within the section. A proposal accepted at that level was brought to a working-level meeting with other sections within the same bureau. If the other sections approved the proposal, it was finalized as a bureau decision with the approval of all the bureau's directors. Before the decision was made, however, the officers in charge were expected to have completed the process of coordinating with officials in other ministry bureaus and related ministries, as well as examining legal and budgetary issues through the ministry secretariat.

Former administrative deputy chief cabinet secretary Nobuo Ishihara described the bureau meetings as "the actual decision-making organ within the bureaucracy."[18] Of course there were official meetings at higher levels: ministry meetings, administrative vice ministerial meetings, and ultimately cabinet meetings. The decisions made at the cabinet meeting represented the end of a long, formal process within the government. However, the steps in the policy process taken after the bureau meeting were really nothing more than confirmation. In this bottom-up policy-making process, the bureaucracy played a pivotal role, serving as an instrumental veto player in policy making.

Chalmers Johnson, in his famous book on the Ministry of International Trade and Industry, attributed Japan's economic success to the ministry officials' central role in industrial policy making.[19] This industrial success owing to the bureaucratic supremacy enabled the LDP, which had supported capitalism, to maintain its control over the government for a long time in the postwar period.

The Legislature and the Multimember-District Electoral System

Bureaucratic supremacy was not what the designers of the Shōwa Constitution envisioned. They set up political institutional arrangements to give substance to the principle of popular sovereignty and to ensure legislative supremacy over the executive. The Diet is defined as "the highest organ of the state power" in article 41. In addition to the cabinet's collective responsibility to the Diet, the prime minister must be a Diet member when elected. The prime minister must select at least half the cabinet ministers from among Diet members.

The Diet is also defined as "the sole law-making organ of the state." In prewar Japan the Diet enacted laws, but many of them were loose statements of general principles. The real legislation was effected in the form of imperial or ministerial ordinances, prepared and promulgated by the Privy Council and the cabinet.[20] The Shōwa Constitution, on the other hand, vests the whole legislative power in the Diet.

During the Occupation there was a discussion as to whether Japan should have a unicameral or a bicameral legislature. Based on MacArthur's preference, the Government Section draft provided only for a unicameral legislature with 300–500 members, largely because MacArthur believed the House of Peers should be abolished.[21] The prewar House of Peers was made up mainly of the hereditary nobility, whose function was to check decisions made by the publicly elected House of Representatives, also called the lower house. The Japanese government vigorously argued to preserve a second upper house. Under a unicameral system, one election result might provide a majority party with the authority to move too quickly and too passionately. Japan needed to have "a safety valve," a cabinet member stated in the Diet.[22] Compromise was reached to establish a popularly elected House of Councilors, or upper house, which would be subordinate to the lower house.[23]

The upper house comprises elected officials from different constituencies from those of the lower house. It has a fixed six-year term with no dissolution, with half of its members elected every three years. The upper house can stop decisions of the lower house in order to secure sober consideration, but with a slightly limited legal authority. The lower house can override the upper house by means of a two-thirds majority vote. In the case of disagreement between the two houses on the selection of the prime minister, on the budget, or on treaties, the decision of the lower house is final. While the lower house, through a vote of no-confidence, can force the cabinet to resign or to call a general election, the upper house can express its dissatisfaction only through nonlegally binding resolutions. However, the upper house has almost equal power to the lower house in the normal legislative process. This created an additional opportunity for the opposition parties to serve as powerful partisan veto players when the government party does not hold a majority in the upper house.

The electoral system for the upper house was set before the April 1947 election. To bring a more reflective and sober perspective to the upper house, the electoral system originally had 100 seats in a single nationwide constituency and 150 seats in prefecture-wide constituencies (originally 46 prefectures; 47 after the reversion of Okinawa in 1973: 146 seats in prefecture-wide districts and 96 seats in nationwide proportional representation districts after 2004).

On the other hand, the first postwar election of the lower house was held in April 1946, with 46 prefecture-wide constituencies; a total of 466 seats were allocated to each prefecture, with 2–14 seats in proportion to the population of the given prefecture. Large, prefecture-wide electoral districts encouraged small political groups to declare candidacy in many districts. In the 1946 election, 2,770 candidates ran, representing 258 political parties. The Socialists increased their seats from 17 to 95 and the Communists from 0 to 5, bringing the leftist representation up to 100 of the 466 seats in the lower house.

In February 1947, three months after the constitution was promulgated, the new Home Affairs minister, Etsujirō Uehara, stated at a press conference that the first lower-house election under the new constitution should be held under a revised electoral system with smaller constituencies. Uehara visited Chief Whitney of the Government Section and expressed his concern that the existing prefecture-wide constituencies would allow many more Communist members to be elected to the Diet. Whitney told Uehara that the existing electoral system had been tried only once and should be tested more to see the real effects. Prime Minister Shigeru Yoshida, however, directly contacted Mac-Arthur to gain his personal approval to revise the electoral law.[24] On March 14 Whitney wrote to Yoshida that "the National Diet should have a sole discretion" on the decision of its electoral system, allowing the Japanese government to change the law.[25]

Yoshida's Liberal Party submitted to the Diet a bill to introduce a new electoral system with a single, nontransferable vote for multimember constituencies with three to five seats.[26] This medium-sized, multimember-district system attracted the coalition partner the Progressive Party, as it would give a chance for both the Liberal and the Progressive candidates to be elected from the same districts while undermining smaller parties like the Communists. Indeed, this proposal was strongly criticized by the opposition parties, such as the Socialists, the Communists, and the National Cooperatives, which preferred a proportional representation system with large districts. At the end of March 1947, immediately after the two coalition parties forcefully passed the electoral reform in the Diet, Prime Minister Yoshida dissolved the lower house, calling for a new election.

Surprisingly, the Japan Socialist Party won 143 of the 466 seats in the April 1947 election and became the largest party in the lower house. While the Socialist-led government under Tetsu Katayama was established in coalition with the newly established Democratic Party (mostly former Progressives) and the National Cooperative Party, this government collapsed after just ten months because of a Marxist rebellion within the JSP. The same coalition formed another government led by a Democratic leader, Hitoshi Ashida. But this government lasted only seven months because of the prime minister's own political scandal. As a result, Yoshida again took over the government and called for a general election in January 1949.

The result of the 1949 election was a landslide victory for Yoshida's Liberal Party, gaining 269 of the 466 seats. The reign of the Liberal Party continued until February 1955, when the Democratic Party won 185 seats to become the largest party, led by Ichirō Hatoyama. One year later, owing to the escalation of intraparty fighting, the JSP was split into the Rightist Socialist Party, with centrist socialists, and the Leftist Socialist Party, with hard-line left-wingers and Marxist socialists.

LDP Dominance in the 1955 System

The two socialist parties were merged in October 1955, reunifying and recreating the JSP.[27] One month later the Liberals and Democrats joined forces to create the Liberal Democratic Party. With the mergers of the conservative and socialist camps, the so-called 1955 system (*gojūgo-nen taisei*) was established, under which the ruling LDP and the largest opposition party, the JSP, were split ideologically.[28] While the LDP favored maintaining the Self-Defense Forces (SDF) and promoting close security cooperation with the United States, the JSP was against this and maintained the hope to establish an unarmed neutrality. As for the constitution, the LDP was eager to revise it while the JSP wanted to defend it. This ideological cleavage long served as a major characteristic of Japan's party system.

In the first election (1958) after the four political groups merged into two camps, the LDP and the JSP together won 97 percent of the lower house seats.[29] Of the 467 seats, the LDP captured 287 while the JSP took 166. During the first five years of the period starting in 1955, a two-party system with an ideological cleavage settled in. The JSP was seen as an effective veto player on the Japanese political scene.

This situation was against the conventional wisdom on the relationship between the number of political parties and the electoral system. Maurice Duverger, in his classic study on the subject, argued a multimember-district system brings about a multiparty system, while a single-member district system leads to a two-party system. This happens because rational politicians will leave losing parties, and rational voters will not waste their votes on losers. Eventually an electoral system with M seats in a district will lead to the party system with M + 1 political parties, according to Duverger's law.[30] Steven Reed applied this law to the 1947 multimember system with 3 to 5 seats in a district and concluded, "Where *n* is the number of seats in the district . . . elections in simple plurality elections with multimember districts tend to produce competition among *n* + 1 candidates."[31] According to this theory, the multimember-district system encourages the establishment of a multiparty system.

As the theory indicates, Japan's two-party system did not last long. The year 1960 witnessed the breakup of the Socialist Party and marked the beginning of the multiparty system. While improvements in the standard of living weakened blue-collar workers' support for the left wing of the Socialist Party, some moderate socialist members supported the revision of the U.S.-Japan Security Treaty, which would make the bilateral relationship more equitable by removing the legacies of Occupation control. The left wing responded to these challenges by driving out the members who advocated the movement to modernize the party.[32] After the left wing managed to pass a motion to punish a leader of the structural reform movement within the party, the punished politician and fifty-two other moderate socialists left the party to form a centrist party, the Democratic Socialist Party (DSP).

The split of the Socialist Party also reflected the division of the labor unions. The JSP from its inception in 1945 had been a loose amalgam of labor unions with different political stances. The right wing of the labor union held the moderate view that workers' interests could best be pursued through cooperation between labor and management on the basis of an enterprise union structure. On the other hand, the left wing took a more confrontational position.[33] Sōhyō (General Council of Japanese Trade Unions), which represented public-sector unions, was a dominant group on the left and sustained a more militant Marxist stance. Four years after the formation of the DSP, the moderate labor unions formed Dōmei (All Japan Labor Federation) to support the DSP, while Sōhyō continued to support the JSP.

Further weakening the JSP were the rise of the Japan Communist Party (JCP) and the formation of another new centrist party in the 1960s. While public support for both the LDP and the JSP decreased, the JCP steadily increased its seats in the lower house, from 1 in 1958 to 3 in 1960, 14 in 1969, and 38 in 1972. Meanwhile, a Buddhist sect, Sōkagakkai, formed its own political party, the Kōmeitō or Clean Government Party, in 1964. Both the JCP and the Kōmeitō expanded in the rapidly growing urban areas that the LDP and JSP could not reach through their traditional networks to mobilize their support. In 1976 six Diet members defected from the LDP because of the Lockheed scandal to form a new party, the New Liberal Club.

As a result, the multiparty system developed by the mid-1970s. The LDP maintained constant rule, with the main opposition coming from the JSP. While the New Liberal Club merged back into the LDP in 1986, three other small parties—the DSP, the JCP, and the Kōmeitō—established themselves as stable actors by successfully demonstrating their ability to consistently win twenty to fifty lower house seats in the old electoral system. As Masaru Kohno argues, the 1947 electoral system, with multimember districts, allowed these smaller parties to enter the electoral race and steal anti-LDP votes from the JSP.[34] The electoral system eventually led to the decline of the JSP and brought about the multiparty system, as Duverger's law suggests.

The JSP never became a viable opposition party that threatened to replace the LDP as the ruling party. Since the 1960s the appeal of Marxist ideology had continued to decline. The number of JSP lower house seats peaked at 166 in the first election (1958) after the party's reunification. Since then the numbers had steadily decreased, widening the gap with the LDP. Some argue that there was never a two-party system but a "one-and-one-half party system," reflecting more accurately the seat allocation of the two major parties. The JSP never had enough candidates to win a majority of the lower house, indicating that it did not have the potential muscle to rule the government single-handedly. It also failed to ally with other opposition parties to challenge the LDP's dominance in a coalition arrangement. With the decline of the JSP, the LDP became a "predominant political party," in Giovanni Sartori's terminology.[35]

In contrast, through the 1980s the LDP successfully increased the number of its lower house seats. Many scholars observed that the ruling party strengthened its predominant status, while the JSP became "the permanent opposition." Gerald Curtis, for example, called the LDP's status "perpetuating dominance" and argued that the ruling party entered a new phase in which it could "act in disregard of opposition party views."[36] Partisan veto players in the opposition parties were seen as less significant than those within the ruling party and the government. This view gained popularity especially after the 1986 general election, in which the LDP captured the largest majority ever, with 304 out of 512 seats in the lower house.

Many factors contributed to the LDP's success in retaining power. Japan's postwar economic prosperity and the LDP's success in promoting it is the obvious one. After the 1960 revision of the U.S.-Japan Security Treaty, which ideologically divided the Japanese public into two opposing camps, the ruling party swiftly shifted its focus to economic development, while the leading opposition party was left stuck with the ideological issue. A group of scholars, including Takashi Inoguchi and Kent Calder, emphasized that the LDP's strength came from its ability to use the government to serve its special, long-term clients. When the LDP's traditional supporting groups, such as small businesses and farmers, were in trouble, the ruling party made timely, client-targeted, and effective use of its public policy tools to help them.[37] Another group of scholars, including Gerald Curtis and Yasusuke Murakami, had a somewhat contradictory view. According to them, the LDP's strength came from its ability to adjust its policies in accordance with changes in Japan's socioeconomic environment. Over its long reign the LDP successfully shifted the target of its concern by reducing favors to special interest groups and providing more public goods to a broader range of constituencies.[38]

Ikuo Kabashima, on the other hand, spotlighted the high political participation in the rural sector. One of the LDP's main political goals was the redistribution of wealth from the urban to the rural areas in order to narrow income inequality between the two areas. Voter turnout in rural areas had constantly been higher than in urban areas. Support of the rural sector for the LDP in the election provided Japan with political stability and continuity, which was an important political source of economic growth. In return, farmers received preferential treatment in the budgetary system, which successfully equalized income distribution among the areas and assured the continued support of rural areas for the ruling party.[39]

Institutional Explanations for LDP Dominance

Instead of political participation, some experts emphasize the multimember-district electoral system as the cause of LDP dominance. The LDP consistently received a higher share of lower house seats than its share of votes. According to Raymond V. Christensen and Paul E. Johnson, the LDP received an average 7.3 percent "seat bonus" in the twelve consecutive lower house elections from 1958 to 1990.[40] This bonus had a great impact. In the 1990 election, for example, the LDP captured less than a majority of the total votes (46.1 percent), but a 7.6 percent seat bonus allowed the party to capture 53.7 percent of the lower house seats to control the government.

Many factors contributed to the LDP seat bonus. As stated earlier, the old electoral system allowed the smaller opposition parties, such as the DSP and the Kōmeitō, to survive. The fragmentation of the opposition parties split the anti-LDP votes.[41] This also prevented the JSP from becoming a viable opposition party to challenge the LDP's dominance.

Japan's multimember districts with relatively small magnitude (seat number in each district) also gave a large advantage to the LDP. The 130 districts (after 1975) were almost evenly divided between three-, four-, and five-seat constituencies. As the smaller parties were less likely to win a seat in the three-seat districts, they were discouraged to field candidates.[42] As a result, seats were usually divided between the LDP and the JSP, and the LDP had much better chances to win two seats in many of these districts. In five-seat districts, the smaller parties had their own candidates to gain the anti-LDP votes, which gave a disadvantage to the largest opposition. After examining the results of the lower house elections between 1958 and 1990, Christensen and Johnson argued that district magnitude was "the largest positive contribution to the LDP seat bonus and LDP victories."[43]

On the other hand, Taku Sugawara argues that the multimember districts allowed vote-dividing strategies based on geography, benefiting the LDP. As each of the multiple candidates from the LDP represented a different region within the same district, they could focus their election campaigns on more geographically specific voters. Meanwhile, the opposition parties with one candidate had to appeal to the entire constituency. As Japanese voters felt a stronger affiliation with their regional representatives, they voted for the LDP candidates.[44]

As Kabashima points out, the LDP's major economic policy was the redistribution of wealth from urban to rural areas. This policy focus made LDP candidates in rural districts very strong. Masumi Ishikawa and Michisada Hirose analyzed the seats acquired by the LDP in the lower house elections between 1947 and 1986 by dividing the electoral districts in terms of population density into four categories—rural areas, local cities, cities, and metropolitan areas. While the LDP's share of the lower house seats in metropolitan districts fluctuated between 30 and 60 percent, that of the rural constituencies constantly stayed between 68 and 86 percent.[45] Japan's rapid economic growth in the postwar period, however, created a massive population shift from the rural to the urban areas, which should have been disadvantageous to the LDP.

The population shift grew especially in the 1960s. In 1955, 5.1 million people moved between municipalities, and by 1969 more than 8 million people shifted.[46] According to Yoshiaki Kobayashi's calculation, the percentage of the electoral districts that were categorized as rural decreased from 80 to 35 percent in the period between 1960 and 1975.[47] As a result, the malapportionment of the lower house became a political issue. But the LDP refused to reapportion the lower house completely and offered only partial adjustments by adding nineteen seats in urban districts in 1964 and an additional twenty seats in 1975.

These minor adjustments, however, did not solve the problem. In the 1972 general election, it took 4.99 votes in the most underrepresented district to have a voice in the Diet equal but only 1 vote in the most overrepresented district. In 1976 the Supreme Court ruled that the allocation of the lower house seats in that election was unconstitutional as it denied urban voters' equal rights, which are guaranteed by the constitution. Just before the 1986 lower house election, for the first time, Prime Minister Yasuhiro Nakasone reduced eight seats in rural districts against political opposition within the LDP while adding seven seats in urban areas to correct disproportional allocation. Although the largest disparity was still as high as 2.92 times in the election, the Supreme Court ruled in October 1988 that the situation was constitutional. According to the ruling, a disparity within 3.00 times was considered constitutional. But in the following general election in 1990, the gap again widened to 3.18 times, making the allocation unconstitutionally imbalanced.

The rural overrepresentation in the Diet significantly benefited the LDP. Sadafumi Kawato examined the correlation between the number of voters in each district and the share of acquired votes of the LDP, the JSP, and the JCP in ten consecutive lower house elections between 1958 and 1990. The results show that the LDP benefited from the malapportionment at a relatively high degree, illustrating the party's rural orientation. On the other hand, the JCP was at a constant disadvantage, showing its urban orientation. While the JSP had an urban orientation in 1958–67, it gained a rural orientation in 1969–86.[48]

Malapportionment made the LDP very rural oriented.[49] As a large proportion of LDP Diet members represented rural areas, the party constantly pushed through the redistribution of wealth from urban to rural areas in the form of subsidies and public works. By providing such political pork, the ruling party members won reelection in the rural constituencies more easily than in the urban areas. LDP members from the rural areas therefore had better chances to rise in the hierarchy within the ruling party than their fellow Diet members from urban areas. Most of the prime ministers since Eisaku Satō, for example, were from rural areas. The many LDP political leaders from the countryside ensured that the government would continue the wealth redistribution.

In addition to the electoral system, the constitutional authority of the prime minister to dissolve the lower house also gave advantage to the LDP. This authority allows the ruling party to choose the timing for a general election. During the LDP's reign from 1955 to 1993, there was only one time that the lower house lasted to the end of the four-year term: when Prime Minister Takeo Miki could not call for an election owing to his weak leadership.[50] In all other cases the ruling party did not wait for the term to end and often tried to choose the best timing for an election. Takashi Inoguchi points out that the LDP often based the election timing on the business cycle.[51] On the other hand, Masaru Kohno and Yoshitaka Nishizawa suggest that the LDP manipulated public works spending based on the election timing.[52] Either way, the LDP took advantage of its ability to choose the election timing and to provide rewards to its constituency to maximize its election results.

The old electoral system lasted until 1994, when the non-LDP coalition government under Prime Minister Morihiro Hosokawa introduced a new electoral system with a combination of single-member and proportional representation constituencies. Under the multimember-district system for nearly half a century, LDP members developed their own local support group, or *kōenkai*, and factionalism within the party.

Growth of Informal Institutions and Political Culture

Need to Organize Kōenkai

The multimember-district system of the lower house encouraged multiple candidates from a single party. To gain or maintain an LDP majority in the lower house and control the government, the party needed to win two to three seats in the three-to-five-seat districts. Because LDP candidates shared a similar voting base, the competition among them was usually more intense than was the competition with candidates from opposition parties.

The LDP had local branches at the prefectural level. While they became very active for prefecture-wide campaigns for the election of the governor or upper house members in the prefecture district, these local branches avoided involvement in electoral competition among LDP candidates in the lower house elections.[53] In addition, the LDP headquarters and prefectural branches did not develop centralized control over election finances or campaigns for lower house candidates. Each candidate was therefore forced to organize individual support groups.

Kōenkai were legally defined as "organizations whose main political activity is to recommend or support a certain candidate for a public position," such as a Diet member.[54] Such organizations allow a candidate to create offices to handle administrative tasks, to locate signboards with the candidate's name in the constituency, and to contact voters and conduct constituency services during the noncampaign period.

At a shop in the LDP headquarters in Tokyo, a handbook entitled *Guide for Practical General Election* for LDP candidates is sold.[55] This book urges candidates to organize kōenkai to gain committed votes and helpful support.

According to the book, under the umbrella organization of kōenkai are regionally based "horizontal organizations" in each municipal unit and "vertical organizations" such as business groups and corporations. Within these organizations, candidates are encouraged to form a "youth department" and a "women's department."

A typical LDP politician had fifty to eighty constituency organizations, ranging from hobby and sport clubs to women's activities and social groups for older people. These groups organized tours to hot springs and to the Diet to visit their representatives. LDP politicians attended many of their supporters' meetings and ceremonies. According to a 1989 survey by the *Asahi Shimbun*, the average LDP Diet member attended 116 year-end or new-year parties annually and 6.6 weddings and 26.5 funerals monthly.[56] In return for these services, at election time these groups formed the core of the politicians' electoral constituencies for the campaign. Thus elections became expensive contests between candidates to win local support through pork-barrel politics and other constituency services.

Targeting specific groups was a very important and effective strategy under the multimember-district system. In a five-member electoral district, for example, candidates were guaranteed to win if they could get 20 percent of the total votes cast. The average vote share of election winners receiving the least number of votes in five-member districts was 8–14 percent over the course of the 1947–86 lower house elections.[57] It was possible for candidates to be elected with less than 10 percent of the votes in many districts. Under such an electoral system, candidates tried to develop personal networks and create strong ties with specific groups and companies in order to build their own solid voting base, instead of appealing to a broader base of voters. For example, candidates who received support from the local agricultural co-op could expect a couple percent of the total votes. With support from major construction companies, candidates could add another couple percent. If the supporting group represented more than 10 percent of the total votes, candidates could win the next election by adding several more percentage points. Instead of appealing to a politically inactive majority, candidates thus tried to solidify support from active minority groups.

Kōenkai developed in a couple of stages. The purge of the old political leaders under the American Occupation broke their political monopolies in most of regions. When more than 80 percent of the winners were newly elected in the first postwar general election, however, there were no established party organizations to help them. This situation continued in subsequent electoral campaigns during the first postwar decade because of the high fluidity of conservative parties. Therefore candidates were left to their own resources. "By 1952, most of the Dietmen had created *kōenkai* for themselves," according to Nathaniel Thayer's study.[58]

Kōenkai began to boom among conservative Diet members after the Liberal and Democratic Parties merged to form the LDP in November 1955. The merger was designed to solidify conservative camps in the face of the merger of the right and left wings of the Socialist Party. In many districts former Liberal and Democratic candidates now had to run the next electoral campaign under the same banner, that of the LDP. Conservative candidates began building their electoral bases to compete with their new fellow party members rather than with Socialist candidates.[59] As a result, kōenkai became central organizations for electoral mobilization.

In the early 1960s the LDP aimed to strengthen the central party and local branches while kōenkai of the individual Diet members were expanding. In January 1961 the LDP announced the organizational activities guidelines, which included the plan to convert the members of individual kōenkai, who reportedly totaled ten million, to LDP party members.[60] In October 1963 the LDP's Organization Research Council, led by Takeo Miki, announced that because the focus of kōenkai was on supporting a certain individual Diet member, there was often conflict with party activities, and that in the future these groups needed to be merged into the party organization. As it was impossible to abolish kōenkai immediately, the council requested that individual LDP Diet members arrange for some five hundred of their kōenkai members to register with local LDP branches.[61] Strong opposition came from LDP Diet members, however, and the request was rejected.

The LDP then came up with a backup plan to establish liaison offices between kōenkai and the LDP branches. The liaison offices would distribute the party's public relations materials and serve in some election activities. This was a major setback for the people who aimed to centralize party control. The LDP conducted no further major reform efforts to strengthen the national network of the party organization; as a result, the party remained "a loose association of individual Diet members" instead of becoming "an organized party of members with various rights and obligations."[62]

An important institutional change came in the form of a reform of the LDP presidential elections. Prime Minister Takeo Miki originally proposed a plan to introduce a primary election in which nonparliamentary party members would vote. Miki wanted to replace the behind-the-scenes factional politics of LDP Diet members with an open election by nationwide party members to choose a party leader.[63] Although Miki's proposal was rejected, he asked his successor to bring about the reform. Under the administration of Takeo Fukuda, in April 1977 the party accepted the reform to set a primary election for the LDP presidency.

Ironically, Miki's original plan to remove the influence of LDP factions actually accelerated factional competition and division in the presidential race. LDP factions competed to recruit the individual Diet members' kōenkai members as LDP members to help elect their leader as party president. In Kagawa prefecture, home of Masayoshi Ōhira, one of the candidates in the 1978 presidential race, 49,603 new members registered, amounting to the highest rate of recruiting in proportion to the population. Gunma prefecture, which was home to two candidates, Takeo Fukuda and Yasuhiro Nakasone, recorded the second highest rate, with new membership of 76,041.[64] The number of LDP members swelled from some 400,000 to nearly 1.52 million running up to the days before the election.[65]

Although Miki's scheme in the 1960s to integrate kōenkai into the party organization was fulfilled, it did not achieve the original goal of centralizing party control. On the contrary, the recruiting campaign for the LDP presidential race served to expand the kōenkai of individual LDP members and to strengthen their ties with LDP factions in Tokyo.

In sum, the multimember district electoral system discouraged central control by the government party. The weak local branches and the lack of electoral support from the party center encouraged LDP Diet members to develop their own personal support groups. The 1955 LDP merger and the 1978 LDP presidential primary race further contributed to the expansion of kōenkai.[66]

The Emergence of LDP Factions

The electoral system of the lower house also contributed to the development of intraparty factionalism within the LDP. As discussed in the previous section, the competition among multiple LDP candidates was usually fiercer than the competition with candidates from opposition parties. The LDP's lack of central control over election finances and campaigns increased each candidate's reliance on factions and kōenkai rather than on the party.

Some scholars argue that factions within political parties are the product of the characteristics of a Japanese society that puts more emphasis on vertical relations, such as leader-follower and superior-junior relations, than on horizontal relations among colleagues. According to sociologist Chie Nakane, Japanese communities are usually organized in a pyramid-shaped hierarchy of ranks consisting of many very personal relationships between superiors and juniors, the basis of human relations in Japan. Japanese leaders are therefore directly supported by subleaders, who themselves have their own followers.[67] Formal, institutional group organizations are often eroded and subsumed by the unity of subgroups with the traditional values of human relations. Nakane's description of the way the Japanese organize themselves fits perfectly with the structure of Japanese political parties, with a formal party leader and members grouped into factions.

Culture and social behavior, however, cannot be a single explanatory factor, as factionalism is not unique to the Japanese political system. Although their forms and functions vary depending on political institutions and environments, factions exist in the politics of many democratic states. Generally factionalism is weaker in nations with a single-seat electoral system, such as Great Britain, where party affiliation is the dominant factor in elections. On the other hand, nations with an electoral system of proportional representation or multi-member districts, like Italy, have developed strong factionalism.[68]

In addition to the cultural explanation, the development of LDP factions has been attributed to the electoral system. While the electoral incentive under the multimember district system was not necessarily the cause or origin of factionalism, it significantly contributed to its development. Ramseyer and Rosenbluth assert that "the electoral system alone is sufficient to explain the survival of LDP factions. . . . LDP party members join factions out of self-interest. Faction leaders help members . . . to improve their reelection chances."[69] Krauss and Pekkanen, on the other hand, deemphasize the influence of the electoral system and focus more on the impact of internal power struggles among LDP leaders and between leaders and rank-and-file representatives as the determinant that defined the nature and role of factions under LDP rule.[70]

Factions competed in recruiting new candidates and supported reelection campaigns of existing members. As Masaru Kohno points out, owing to the institutional arrangements, LDP candidates with factional affiliation had several advantages over those with no affiliation.[71] First, the LDP aimed to limit the number of party-endorsed candidates in order to maximize winning seats with the votes cast under the multimember-district system. The major factions had dominant power to arrange party endorsement for their candidates. As a result, many new LDP candidates already had factional affiliation before the official campaign even started. Second, as the prime minister usually dissolved the lower house before its four-year term ended, it was important for new candidates to have information on the political schedule from their factions for when the next election was expected. The timing of general elections was determined by many different factors within the political climate, such as pressure from the opposition, interfactional negotiations, and economic conditions. With inside information from the senior members of the faction, candidates could schedule their election campaigns effectively. Third, the short official campaign period created disadvantageous conditions for relatively unknown LDP candidates without a factional affiliation. Candidates with a factional affiliation could receive the campaign visits of nationally known senior politicians from their faction as well as financial assistance and tips for the campaign.

Factions within the LDP were not formed for ideological reasons or around a specific policy position. The Liberal Democratic Party was originally formed by combining different conservative political groups, some with roots in prewar political parties. Therefore from the start the LDP had been highly fractional with several intraparty factions, each with its own leader. These might even be considered mini parties within the parent party. Their primary goal was to make their leader the prime minister.[72]

Although the first LDP presidential race, in April 1956, was won by Ichirō Hatoyama almost unopposed, the second one, eight months later, became an intense battle among three candidates—Tanzan Ishibashi, Kōjirō Ishii, and Nobusuke Kishi. During the election eight senior members of the LDP competed to form their group of supporting members in order to choose the leader they preferred. In addition to his own faction, Kishi was supported by groups led by Ichirō Kōno (Kishi's colleague from the former Democratic Party) and Eisaku Satō (Kishi's real brother). Ishibashi was supported by the three groups led by himself, Banboku Ōno, and Takeo Miki. Ishii was supported by his own group and the Hayato Ikeda group. Although Kishi received the most votes in the first round, he did not achieve a majority (223 of 511 votes). In the final round between Kishi and the candidate with the second largest vote count, Ishibashi, the latter received Ishii's support to win.[73] It was after this election that the LDP factionalization of eight major groups took hold.[74]

As the size of their faction was a vital factor in their eventually becoming prime minister, faction leaders maintained and tried to expand their factions despite the high cost of supporting faction members. In the words of Tsuneo Watanabe, a politically astute journalist, "To become the prime minister, [an LDP politician] must become 'the boss' of a faction. Becoming 'the boss' of a faction means to be on the short list of the [LDP] presidential candidates."[75] Being a faction leader was considered necessary to becoming LDP president. During the LDP's continuing reign between 1955 and 1993, with two extreme exceptions in the party's waning years of control,[76] every LDP president who automatically became the prime minister was a faction leader. By 1972 the number of LDP major factions had decreased to five, and until 1993 the prime ministership was rotated among these five major factions. This rotation was not only inevitable but also justifiable because factions could effectively provide necessary alternatives for the leadership position.[77] The leadership change usually enhanced the public image of the party and improved public support for the government.[78]

Because no faction alone had enough members or votes to secure the prime ministership for its leader, factions had to cooperate and form coalitions to challenge other intraparty coalitions. The faction leader who successfully formed a coalition of a majority of LDP Diet members won the LDP presidential race and thus acquired the premiership. The prime minister then had to maintain that support to be an effective leader.

As the LDP had been a loose organization with a high degree of factionalization, the political dynamic among the factions often caused friction. Factional competition had existed from the inception of the LDP, first between the former Liberals and Democrats, and later between the mainstream and the antimainstream.[79] Political rivalries, policy confrontation, and unequal allocation of power all led to severe interfactional fights, and sometimes to the resignation of the party leader.

Prime Minister Nobusuke Kishi (1958–60), for example, faced strong opposition from factions within the LDP during the policy process related to revising the U.S.-Japan Security Treaty in 1960. One of the anti-Kishi faction leaders repeatedly demanded that Kishi resign once the bill was passed. Kishi indeed sacrificed his premiership to secure support for the security revision within the ruling party and resigned after his opponents agreed to vote for the motion and it passed.[80] Kishi later lamented how unfortunate it was for a political leader to be forced to spend much more energy on party affairs than on conducting his task as prime minister.[81]

Two decades later Kishi in turn led a factional conflict to force Prime Minister Zenkō Suzuki (1981–82) to resign. After Suzuki met U.S. president Ronald Reagan at the 1981 summit, the two leaders announced a joint statement. Prenegotiated by diplomatic officers, the statement included the word "alliance" for the first time. In an attempt to deny that the use of the word implied Japan's newly increased military role, Suzuki at a press conference and again at a Diet committee meeting repeated that the "alliance" did not connote a military component for Japan.[82] After Suzuki's statement, the vice minister of foreign affairs commented to reporters that an alliance without a military context would make no sense, especially with the bilateral security pact, and Foreign Minister Masayoshi Itō fully supported the vice minister. The media reported this incident as a disagreement within the cabinet. After Suzuki denounced the Ministry of Foreign Affairs (MOFA) at the cabinet meeting, the foreign minister and the vice minister submitted their resignations to the prime minister as a form of protest.[83] Kishi, who had sacrificed his administration to revise the bilateral security treaty, was very disappointed by Suzuki. Under fear of worsening relations with the United States, Kishi and his faction followers began an anti-Suzuki movement within the LDP, which led to Suzuki's resignation.

The problems of interfactional conflicts were evident in the length of the national leader's tenure. The twenty-two LDP prime ministers in the periods 1955–93 and 1996–2009 served an average of 2.3 years. This short tenure was partly due to the two-year term of the LDP presidency,[84] but the primary reason was pressure from the other LDP factions whose leaders were waiting in line for election to the office.

Factional competition was exacerbated during the 1970s by the fight between faction leaders Kakuei Tanaka and Takeo Fukuda. The battle began in the 1972 LDP presidential election to succeed Prime Minister Eisaku Satō. As the factional conflicts grew fierce, Prime Minister Fukuda announced the party reform plan, which included a proposal to abolish factions. By April 1977, when this proposal was accepted by the LDP party conference, all the major factions had officially declared that they would dissolve themselves. By the beginning of 1978, however, LDP factions restarted their activities.[85]

The July 1976 indictment of Kakuei Tanaka in the Lockheed scandal, in which he accepted a bribe to urge a major Japanese airline to select Lockheed planes, also contributed to the worsening of factional competition. Tanaka's trial opened in January 1977, and the Tanaka faction lost ten seats in the July 1977 upper house election, decreasing its membership from eighty-six to seventy-six members. To recover his political influence, Tanaka further extended factional battles to local politics and the electoral districts over the 1978 primary election for the LDP presidency between Takeo Fukuda and Masayoshi Ōhira.[86] Tanaka provided massive funds to his faction members and their kōenkai to vote for Ōhira.[87] Ōhira's electoral victory, achieved with the assistance from Tanaka, enabled Tanaka to maintain his influence in the political world.

As Tanaka's trial continued, he tried to further increase his political influence by expanding his faction. He recruited former members of the minor factions, which had lost their leaders.[88] In the 1980 double election for both the upper and lower houses, the Tanaka faction increased its members to 92.[89] After these elections, Tanaka recruited several independent Diet members to expand his factional membership to over 100. In October 1983 the Tokyo District Court found Tanaka guilty in the Lockheed bribery case and sentenced him to four years in prisons. As the opposition party pressured the government, Prime Minister Yasuhiro Nakasone dissolved the lower house. As a result, while the LDP decreased seats, the Tanaka faction boosted its membership to 120.

During the LDP reign it was often said that "power exists in numbers." It was relatively easy for a large faction to take political initiative and to build consensus within the party. In selecting the prime ministers from Ōhira to Nakasone, the largest faction, led by Tanaka, had the decisive power. After Noboru Takeshita replaced Tanaka as the faction leader, maintaining most of Tanaka's faction members, the Takeshita faction, now with the largest number of members, boasted its dominant control in selecting LDP party leaders. The factional control over leadership selection continued until 2001, when Junichirō Koizumi won the LDP presidency outside the framework of a factional balance.

The magic number was the equivalent of one-fourth of the LDP members, according to the theory of political journalist Masumi Ishikawa.[90] If the LDP had more than half the total of Diet members, it remained the ruling party. If a coalition of factions was larger than a majority of all LDP Diet members, it could have decisive power over the selection of the prime minister and the execution of major policies. If one faction had a majority within the coalition, that faction controlled the coalition, and thus the party and the government. By this rule of "a majority of a majority," a faction with more than a quarter of LDP members could demonstrate strong influence on the political scene.

Institutionalization of Factions

During the LDP rule, factions became more institutionalized as they served as channels to allocate cabinet posts, subcabinet seats, Diet committee chairmanships, and party posts. In the early period of LDP rule, the party had weaker unity and was divided between the mainstream and antimainstream, as the battle for party leadership was fierce. The important cabinet posts were dominated by the mainstream factions, who supported the prime minister in the LDP presidential election. During the long tenure of Eisaku Satō (1964–72), however, cabinet posts were allocated in proportion to factional size.[91] By the latter half of the 1970s, allocating cabinet posts based on factional balance became a norm under LDP rule.[92]

By the 1980s most of the LDP members who had won at least six lower house elections were listed in the recommendation letter for cabinet posts, which was prepared by faction leaders, and were appointed as cabinet ministers.[93] Seizaburō Satō and Tetsuhisa Matsuzaki, in their influential book, described a career path for LDP member. Before reaching a cabinet position, the average LDP lower house member experienced the post of either vice minister, executive of a Diet committee, or vice chairman of the subcommittee of the LDP Policy Affairs Research Council during the member's second term (or after the first reelection). Chairmanship of the PARC subcommittee was given during the third term, and the post of deputy secretary general and bureau director was awarded during the fourth term. The hierarchy of seniority within the LDP was thus institutionalized.[94]

While cabinet posts and chairmanship of the Diet committees, as well as some executive positions within the party, were allocated based on factional balance, there were also posts filled to represent factions. These included the LDP deputy secretary general, vice chairman of PARC, the LDP General Council, and the LDP House of Councilors Members Committee. These representatives served as information providers to the faction and briefed other faction members on current policy and political developments. In turn, they also served as channels through which members could voice their opinions on government and party decisions. Thus factions became a primary source of political and policy information for their members.

Factions also served as a distributor of political funds. Faction leaders raised money by collecting from corporations, organizing fund-raising parties, and receiving from senior members within the faction. Junior members received money from faction leaders for annual operating funds and election campaigns. Senior members expanded their influence within the faction by contributing money. Thus a hierarchy was established based on financial contributions within the faction.[95]

Ultimately LDP factions took over the political party's functions: recruitment of new candidates, campaign support, provision of information, post allocation, and fund raising/distribution. Factions were developed largely because of two institutional factors: the multimember electoral system of the lower house and the LDP presidential races. Factions acted as powerful veto players when they desired to be. As a result, factions became distinctive characteristics of the LDP and Japanese postwar politics.

Weak Cabinet and Prime Minister

As the influence of factions expanded during the LDP reign, the prime minister's constitutional authority to appoint cabinet members was eroded. Prime Minister Shigeru Yoshida (1946–47, 1948–54), for example, enjoyed total appointive power and frequently changed cabinet members to reward loyal members and punish disloyal members. During his seven years, Yoshida appointed over eighty people to cabinet posts. Yoshida's frequent reshuffling of his cabinet was carried on by his successors, and this significantly affected the power structure of Japanese politics. Critics argued that Yoshida's frequent reshuffling lowered the prestige of cabinet positions and weakened the ruling party's control over the bureaucracy.[96]

While many observers of Japanese politics criticize Yoshida for this political custom, Nobusuke Kishi (1957–60) may well be more responsible for it. Kishi reshuffled his cabinet three times, replacing almost all cabinet members during his three-year tenure. Cabinet reshuffling before Kishi was on a small scale, with just a few members replaced at a time. Kishi observed that Yoshida's manner of removing individual cabinet members created antipathy toward the prime minister. By reshuffling the entire cabinet at the same time, Kishi avoided the situation in which cabinet members could lose face.[97] This practice became a tradition under subsequent LDP governments.

After Kishi, cabinet reshuffling became almost an annual event, further weakening the power of ministers over their ministries. The political career ladder within the LDP became more institutionalized in the 1970s. Regardless of their ability, almost all the LDP lower house members were entitled to be appointed to the cabinet after their sixth term. As factionalism grew stronger, the prime minister had to appoint cabinet members carefully, considering factional balance and requests from faction leaders. Cabinet members who obtained their position because of factional recommendation actually felt stronger loyalty to their factional leader than to the prime minister. Thus the cabinet was often a group of politicians who represented their individual

factions and the interests they promoted, allowing them to become veto players within the highest policy-making organ in the government.

Confrontation between factions therefore often resulted in disharmony in
the cabinet. On the other hand, disagreement among cabinet members often
caused disharmony within the party. To maximize effectiveness in formulating and executing policy, the prime minister had to maintain harmony in
both the cabinet and the party. Careless cabinet appointment instantly created resentment from the other factions.

As the prime minister has the constitutional authority to dismiss cabinet
members, he can have direct control over the cabinet and administrative operations by choosing cabinet members and by dismissing members who do not
agree with him and replacing them with somebody who agrees with him. If he
desires, the prime minister theoretically can dismiss all cabinet members and
appoint himself to hold all the positions. In 1947 Prime Minister Tetsu Katayama, for example, appointed himself to all the ministerial positions until he
finally formed a cabinet eight days later.

In reality, however, the prime minister cannot freely exercise the appointive and dismissal authority without endangering majority support in the Diet
and thus his premiership. Because most cabinet members hold Diet seats and
remain leading ruling party members, the political implication of dismissing
a member from the cabinet is very strong. As Masaharu Gotōda writes, the
dismissal authority "would also hurt the prime minister" who implements it.[98]
Under the current constitution there were only five cases of exercising this authority.[99] Usually the prime minister prefers to accept a voluntary resignation
rather than dismiss a cabinet member.

Although Yoshida initiated frequent cabinet appointments to better control the bureaucracy by ensuring ministers' loyalty to the prime minister, this
tradition weakened the control of the prime minister over the bureaucracy
in the long run. During a minister's short tenure, there was generally little time
to accumulate the experience and knowledge necessary to become influential
in actual decision making within the ministry. Given this lack of experience
and expertise, many ministers had to rely completely on the civil servants in
their ministry. All their official statements in the Diet were prepared in advance by career bureaucrats. When ministers could not answer the questions
of other members at a Diet meeting, the high-level bureaucrats answered on
behalf of the minister. This differed from the situation in the British Parliament, where nonelected government officials cannot attend a session. The Japanese system allowed even incompetent ruling party members to be appointed

as cabinet members. This custom over the long run weakened the influence of the minister over civil servants.

Although the cabinet holds the executive power and is the highest decision-making organ in the government, actual decisions were rarely made in cabinet meetings but instead were made long before the meetings took place. The agenda for a cabinet meeting was prepared and approved at a subcabinet meeting (*jimu jikan kaigi*) usually held the day before and attended by the administrative vice ministers, who were top bureaucrats at the administrative ministries. The agenda included a proposed decision. According to a former cabinet member, the cabinet meetings under the LDP reign were where the necessary cabinet members signed official documents; actual discussions rarely occurred.[100] Although the subcabinet meetings did not have any legal authority for their existence, the cabinet had never repealed the decisions of such meetings. Therefore any actual influence of the cabinet meetings on decision making was quite limited.

This does not mean, however, that all the policy decisions were made by the bureaucracy. Cabinet decisions generally reflected the interests of the prime minister. He and his staff introduced their ideas to the lower ranks in the government. The Kantei, including the chief cabinet secretary and deputies who served the interests of the prime minister, worked to build consensus among various agencies and the ruling party before an issue was taken to the subcabinet meeting. Still, building such consensus with a functionally weak cabinet was a very difficult task for a political leader.

The limited number of staffers at the Kantei (the prime minister's supporting staff) exacerbated the situation. Although the Kantei listed nearly two hundred officials, many of them were on loan from other ministries. Their loyalty usually belonged to their home ministry rather than to the prime minister, and they often served as hidden veto players by sabotaging the prime minister's policy initiatives. Former prime minister Tomiichi Murayama (1994–96) lamented to the author, "There were only three politicians, including myself, at the Kantei. We were surrounded by bureaucrats."[101] As a result, it was very difficult for the prime minister to establish a centralized policy-making system.

Decentralized Policy-Making Power in the LDP

Decentralization of policy making was also developed within the ruling party. From its 1955 inception, the LDP had a policy-making organ, the Policy Affairs

Research Council. The PARC had seventeen subcommittees (*bukai*) and more than thirty research commissions.[102] Commissions were designed to deal with broader issues rather than specific legislation. On the other hand, the subcommittees were set up corresponding to administrative ministries and used by the LDP to influence policy decisions and budget making in each policy area.

Although the PARC existed from the birth of the LDP, its role in actual decision making was limited at the beginning. Most of the policy making was done within the government. Under the cabinet of Hayato Ikeda (1960–64), some LDP members boycotted the deliberation of a cabinet-sponsored bill in the Diet. It was an embarrassment to the Ikeda cabinet as well as to the LDP General Council, which was the highest decision-making organ to build a party consensus. In February 1962 LDP Executive Council chairman Munenori Akagi sent a memo to Chief Cabinet Secretary Masayoshi Ōhira requesting the approval of cabinet-sponsored bills by the LDP General Council prior to approval at the cabinet meeting.[103] Prior approval by the LDP would avoid turmoil in the Diet operation, so Ōhira accepted this request in order to make the prior party approval a political custom. The LDP's influence in policy making, however, was still somewhat limited in the 1960s.

The power shift from the bureaucracy to the LDP policy committees became more evident after the two oil shocks of the 1970s. In the rapid growth that symbolized the 1950s and the 1960s, government revenue increased significantly each year. A majority of policy decisions involved the allocation of extra revenues to different programs. However, after the oil shocks the lower economic growth slowed down government revenue increases and thus decreased the money available to these programs. With funds limited, bureaucratic officials became more dependent on the mediation and political decisions of the ruling party members when reallocating funds among administrative programs.[104]

LDP Diet members accumulated knowledge and experience in specific policy areas by attending PARC subcommittee meetings and became identified as *zoku*, or policy tribes. Those who earned the zoku label increased their influence vis-à-vis bureaucrats in the same policy field. As a result they became instrumental in policy making. It became part of the official process for bureaucrats to seek approval from the relevant zoku members before submitting budget proposals and other policy initiatives to the cabinet. The LDP governments delegated considerable policy-making power on specific issues to these specialists within the party organization, while the prime minister concentrated on broader issues.

The PARC subcommittees served as the first forum the government consulted regarding a proposal. Members of these subcommittees served as the ultimate arbiters of political power on a specific issue and became instrumental in policy making. They examined government policies and often made amendments to them. According to Nobuo Ishihara, who served as deputy chief cabinet secretary for seven and a half years, the subcommittees dominated policy making within the ruling party: "Since the LDP controlled the government for a long time after the war, an approval at the subcommittee level was virtually the same to the bureaucrats as a de facto approval in the Diet."[105] The typical bottom-up, decentralized policy process was established within the LDP as well, making LDP zoku members powerful veto players.

Once the subcommittee approved a policy, it was brought to the deliberation council of the PARC, and finally to the LDP General Council, where the decision had to be unanimous. Under a coalition government, agreement from the coalition partners is necessary. But when the LDP was stable and in charge, Ishihara testifies, "We only needed to seek approval from the powerful figures within the subcommittees and the party. The deliberation at the Diet was close to a ceremony."[106]

Each LDP Diet member in both houses was assigned to up to four PARC subcommittees. LDP Diet members were appointed to one or two committees in their house, and they were automatically assigned to the corresponding PARC subcommittees. In addition, they were allowed to belong to two more subcommittees.[107]

The three most popular subcommittees were Construction, Agriculture and Forestry, and Commerce and Industry, to which nearly half of the LDP Diet members belonged.[108] The first two subcommittees were involved with the most political pork in the form of public works and subsidies that LDP Diet members, especially in rural districts, could offer to their constituencies. The affiliation with the Commerce and Industry helped Diet members build connections with the business world, which would provide funds to them and their factions. In contrast, the subcommittees that did not offer the pork or ties to industries were unpopular.[109]

The multimember-district system allowed LDP Diet members to be policy specialists. With multiple representatives from the same electoral district, there was often a division of labor among LDP members. Masahiko Tatebayashi conducted an extensive data analysis on policy specialization of LDP members in the same district, finding two patterns of vote-dividing strategies: one based on geography and the other on policy specialization. In districts without geographic divisions, LDP members were likely to have different policy specializations with their membership in different PARC subcommittees.[110]

The division of labor based on policy specialization also existed within the LDP factions. Kakuei Tanaka, for example, once referred to his own faction as a "general hospital" because there were many experts and fixers in many specific policy areas within the faction who would be able to help their fellow faction members with constituency demands and requests. The Tanaka faction boasted that it had a total of 150 zoku members who formed a network of policy expertise to cover almost all policy issues.[111] Policy expertise enabled the LDP Diet members to provide constituency services and to establish ties with industry for political funds.

Money Politics

The longtime one-party dominance by the LDP changed the essence of Japan's elections. Elections are supposed to be the means by which a political party gains power in the government to achieve its policy goals. Under the LDP's long reign, however, the reelection and the expansion of its members became the party's goal. Faction leaders competed to recruit candidates who would join their faction and then supported their election campaign. With assistance from their factions, individual members organized their kōenkai as the LDP headquarters did not provide extensive campaign support to individual candidates.

LDP factions and kōenkai were developed as informal political institutions under the multimember-district system. As all LDP candidates ran election campaigns with the same party platform, the lower house election became more candidate oriented than policy or party oriented. To compete with each other for votes from a similar political base, LDP candidates focused on constituency services, including providing pork and promoting kōenkai activities. Such activities became a major part of LDP Diet members' political schedules.

Factions and kōenkai were very costly to maintain for individual LDP members and faction leaders. Many LDP members saw these as the source of money politics and corruption and tried to reform these informal institutions in the 1970s. As described earlier, Miki's effort to integrate kōenkai into the party organization failed. Similarly, though factions were once formally dissolved, they came back shortly thereafter. Although they were costly institutions, they became the hallmark of LDP politics that many LDP members needed to maintain in order to maximize their chance of reelection and eventually play leadership roles.

A veteran journalist vividly describes how a faction leader raised funds for a new faction member. Shin Kanemaru was the powerful leader of the large Takeshita faction and was often referred to as a big boss among the construction zoku. When the faction recruited a new candidate for a Diet seat, Kanemaru requested that an industry organization make contributions to the candidate. The organization then asked its member corporations to provide funds. These corporations did not offer money without any return. Kanemaru successfully lobbied the government for a budget for these industries and corporations to get government work. The larger the faction, the more influential it was in the budget-making process and the more effective its leader could be in raising funds for new members. This was how the Takeshita faction expanded.[112]

As LDP factions and kōenkai became more and more institutionalized, the cost for political activities constantly increased in the 1970s and 1980s. According to the political fund reports published by the Ministry of Home Affairs after the 1975 Political Fund Control Law was enacted, the total political funds reported to the ministry amounted to 110 billion yen in 1976. This amount nearly tripled by 1988 to 307 billion yen. Of this total, 172 billion yen was raised for national-level politics, factions, and individual Diet members. This amount did not include secret political funds, bribes, and profits from stock trading, which were not reported to the government. Some people suspected that by the end of the 1980s the real size of Japan's political funds was nearly a trillion yen.[113]

Among the political funds, the fastest growing were those raised by factions. In 1976 the political revenue of factions and individual Diet members was 25.5 billion yen, compared with 43 billion yen for political parties and related organizations. This amount more than tripled in 1988 to 88.2 billion yen, surpassing the amount raised by political parties. Factions became major fund-raising bodies and fund distributors.

Money politics became the focus of criticism in the late 1980s. Ten LDP first-term Diet members who shared a common interest in political reform formed the Utopia Political Study Group. They had fifty-nine study meetings with guest speakers from academia, the media, and the political world. This group attracted significant media attention when its members disclosed their revenue and expenditures regarding political funds. The average revenue of the ten members was 126.5 million yen. They raised nearly 60 percent of their

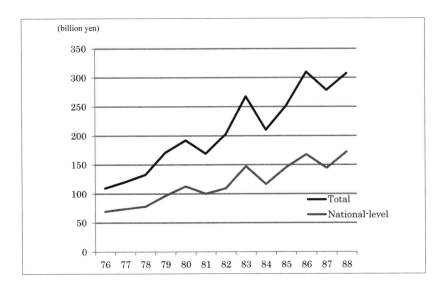

FIGURE 1.1. Political Funds Revenue, 1976–88
Source: Ministry of Home Affairs, Political Fund Control Law, Political Fund Reports.

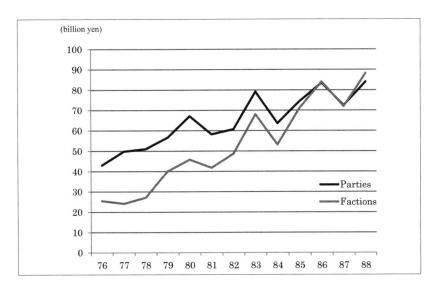

FIGURE 1.2. Revenues of Political Parties and Factions, 1976–88
Source: Ministry of Home Affairs, Political Fund Control Law, Political Fund Reports.

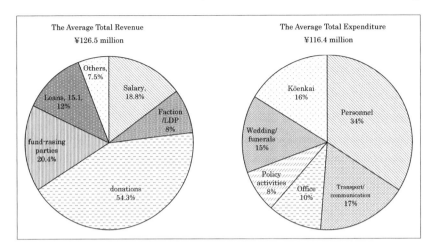

The Average Total Revenue
¥126.5 million

Others, 7.5%
Salary, 18.8%
Loans, 15.1, 12%
Faction /LDP 8%
fund-raising parties 20.4%
donations 54.3%

The Average Total Expenditure
¥116.4 million

Kōenkai 16%
Personnel 34%
Wedding/ funerals 15%
Policy activities 8%
Office 10%
Transport/ communication 17%

FIGURE 1.3. Average Revenues and Expenditures of Ten LDP Diet Members
Source: Utopia Political Study Group, March 3, 1989.

income from political contributions and fund-raising parties. The average expenditure was 116.4 million yen. More than 60 percent of the spending was to maintain their offices (personnel, office, and transportation/communications). In addition, they spent an average of 17 million yen on funerals and weddings, and 19 million yen on other kōenkai activities. This report revealed that even many first-term Diet members spent more than a million dollars a year to finance their political activities.

Regulations on corruption under the 1975 Political Fund Control Law were full of loopholes. A clear distinction was made between political parties and other political organizations. While political parties were required to report all expenditures and revenues, including contributions over 10,000 yen, other political organizations did not have to report contributions under a million yen. Although the law limited contributions from a single source to 1.5 million yen, it allowed politicians to evade maximum limits by setting up several separate funding organizations. The maximum limit encouraged politicians to throw many fund-raising receptions. Corporations bought hundreds of tickets (usually at 10,000–30,000 yen per ticket) to these parties, which allowed them to make unofficial contributions beyond the legal limits.[114]

Money politics is often viewed as associated with political corruption. In Japan's postwar political history, there were major corruption scandals in each decade: the Shōwa Denkō scandal in the late 1940s, the shipbuilding scandal in the mid-1950s, the "black-mist" scandals in the 1960s, and the Lockheed scandal in the 1970s.[115] The late 1980s saw the Recruit scandal, which resulted in a step toward political reform as well as other institutional reforms and will be discussed in the next chapter.

2 THE POLITICS OF INSTITUTIONAL

REFORM

I N JUNE 1988 the *Asahi Shimbun* carried a story about the corruption involving the vice mayor of Kawasaki City, who profited from dealing the unlisted stocks of Recruit Cosmos, a subsidiary of the Recruit Corporation, the prices of which were destined to inflate when the stocks were listed in the market. A couple of weeks later, the newspaper reported that former prime minister Yasuhiro Nakasone, LDP secretary general Shintarō Abe, Finance Minister Kiichi Miyazawa, and Prime Minister Noboru Takeshita had also received stock, either in their own name or in the name of their secretaries. Later it was found that the scandal involved about 160 of Japan's political, business, media, and bureaucratic elites.

The Recruit scandal resulted in the indictment of twelve people and forced many recipients out of office. Two politicians were found guilty of receiving bribes, along with the former vice ministers of education and labor.[1] The approval rating of the Takeshita cabinet sank to a humiliating historical low of 3.9 percent by mid-April 1989.[2] On April 24 the prime minister announced his resignation. The following day Takeshita's secretary, who was responsible for his political finances, committed suicide. Public anger and distrust of politics spurred political reform.

THE POLITICS OF ELECTORAL REFORM

Political Reform Efforts Under the Kaifu Cabinet

Political reform efforts started under the Takeshita cabinet, when the LDP established the Political Reform Committee in December 1988. It was led by former chief cabinet secretary Masaharu Gotōda. Gotōda had experience planning the single-member district (SMD) system in 1973 under the Tanaka administration and had expressed in his 1988 book that much of Japan's political corruption was rooted in expensive political activities under the multimember-district system, and that an SMD system should be introduced to reduce political corruption.[3] On May 23, 1989, the LDP approved a reform package presented by Gotōda's committee. It included a requirement for all Diet members to disclose their financial assets and sources of income, restricted fund raising and expenditures on political activities, strengthened the Diet Ethics Committee to impose tougher punishments, banned political funds received from stock trading or speculation, and, most important, proposed a shift from multimember- to single-member electoral district system. The proposal also suggested that the LDP should consider adding a proportional representation element to reflect minority opinion.[4] This was the first LDP official scheme to propose a mixture of SMDs and proportional representation districts.

Meanwhile, Takeshita was acting as a kingmaker on behalf of the largest LDP faction and was in search of his successor. He picked Sōsuke Uno, who did not receive a contribution from the Recruit Corporation and was considered to be Mr. Clean. But this turned out to be a disastrous choice for the LDP. Soon after Uno assumed office on June 3, a weekly magazine implicated him in a sex scandal. This "Mr. Clean" was not as decent as Takeshita had hoped, and the public was again disappointed.

The first test for Uno was the June 25 supplementary election for an upper house seat in the conservative prefecture of Niigata. The LDP candidate lost to the Socialist candidate by a significant margin of 80,000 votes. The following day, the *Nihon Keizai Shimbun* published its public opinion survey. Only 16 percent of respondents supported the Uno cabinet, while 52 percent expressed their disapproval. On the Recruit scandal, 85 percent felt that the issue was still not settled, but 74 percent had little or no hope for the Uno cabinet to carry out political reform.[5] Obviously voters had strong distrust and very low expectations of the government.

In the July 23 upper house election, voters expressed their anger against the Recruit and Uno scandals in addition to the unpopular introduction of a 3 percent consumption tax by the Takeshita government. The LDP had a comfortable majority of 142 seats in the 252-seat house before the election. As only 36 of the 69 LDP members who faced reelection survived, the party's share in the upper house shrank to 109 seats, compared with the opposition's 143. Uno took political responsibility for the defeat and resigned as prime minister after sixty-nine days in the post.

Takeshita again had to search for a superclean party president and prime minister. His pick was Toshiki Kaifu, a political disciple of "Mr. Clean prime minister" Takeo Miki. When Kaifu took office on August 10, he set "political reform" and "election victory" as his mission.[6] Ichirō Ozawa, a young leader of the Takeshita faction who was eager to introduce an SMD system, was posted into the powerful position of LDP secretary general. Ozawa told Kaifu, "For political reform, we need to form a special committee and seriously tackle this issue even if we have to forcefully push it through."[7] The public received the Kaifu cabinet with a moderate approval rating of 39 percent, which was slightly higher than its disapproval rating of 35 percent.[8] This, however, was a significant improvement over the ratings of the Takeshita and Uno cabinets.

The first test for Kaifu and Ozawa was the October 1 supplementary upper house election for the conservative Ibaragi prefecture seat. LDP secretary general Ozawa led the election campaign, and Kaifu paid three campaign visits to Ibaragi, which was very unusual for a prime minister. With strong support from the party leadership, the LDP candidate defeated the Socialist candidate by a comfortable margin of 70,000 votes. Many LDP leaders saw that the peak of the public resentment against the party was over, and they began expressing their reservations regarding political reform.

On October 31 Kaifu was uncontestedly reelected to serve as LDP president for another two years. When Kaifu declared his candidacy, he set as his highest priority political reform. Masaharu Gotōda and Masayoshi Itō, two senior LDP members who were also proponents of reform, expressed their support.[9] The LDP was split between proreform and antireform groups.

The opposition from the antireform LDP members was largely due to strong resistance from their own kōenkai. The shift from the relatively wider multi-member districts to the geographically smaller districts under the SMD system would inevitably force drastic realignment of kōenkai. Individual LDP Diet members had developed their own kōenkai throughout their districts to maximize their reelection chances and had put a significant amount of energy and financial resources into this effort. Those investments could be significantly, if not entirely, lost because of a realignment of districts. Also, for the members of kōenkai, it was important to maintain their own existence. An electoral system change would eliminate a major portion of a kōenkai's members after the new constituencies were given to its LDP Diet member. The bond between the Diet members and their kōenkai members could be seriously crippled, and the role of kōenkai could be significantly reduced.[10] LDP Diet members and their kōenkai members began acting as intraparty veto players against the electoral reform.

In the February 1990 general election, the LDP ran its election campaign with political reform as the highest-priority issue and won 286 out of the 512 lower house seats. Confident after this electoral victory, Prime Minister Kaifu in his March 2 policy speech stated that he would promote political reform "with an indomitable resolve."[11] On April 26 the Electoral System Advisory Council announced its first proposal, which called for an electoral system in which three hundred members of the lower house would be elected in SMDs and two hundred would be elected in eleven regional proportional representation (PR) districts. Voters would have two votes to cast—one to write the candidate's name in an SMD, and the other to write the choice of the party in their PR district. Dual candidacy would be allowed. A candidate in an SMD could also be included in the party's PR list. This could create situations in which a defeated candidate in an SMD was elected through the party vote in a PR district. The proposal also called for public funding of the political parties to avoid corruption. Prime Minister Kaifu stated at a press conference on May 10 that he would "stake his cabinet's fate" on carrying out this political reform plan.

The Gulf Crisis of August 1990 changed the political agenda of the Kaifu cabinet and delayed its political reform effort. To provide a personnel contribution to the multinational forces, Kaifu introduced legislation to dispatch the Self-Defense Force (SDF) to the Gulf area. But this bill was killed in the Diet session in November.[12] Meanwhile, the LDP Headquarters for Political Reform recommended a minor reform to the council's proposal, which would reduce the total seats of the lower house to 471 by cutting the number of PR seats to 171. Based on this recommendation, the LDP officially approved the political reform plan on December 25.

However, intraparty veto players then became active. Junichirō Koizumi, for example, officially established the Political Reform Union to promote political reform under the existing multimember-district system. As a member of the Mitsuzuka faction, Koizumi was frustrated by the political situation of the long dominance by the Takeshita faction, and he tried to remove Kaifu, who was personally selected by and under the strong influence of Takeshita. Koizumi formed an interfactional alliance with his personal friends Taku Yamasaki of the Watanabe faction and Kōichi Katō of the Miyazawa faction. (This group was later called the YKK group based on their last-name initials.) As the battles over political reform within the LDP heated up, Ozawa resigned as LDP secretary general on April 5, 1991, taking responsibility for the LDP loss in the Tokyo gubernatorial election. As Ozawa's resignation changed the power balance over political reform within the LDP, Diet policy chairman Seiroku Kajiyama, another powerful member of the Takeshita faction, suggested postponing the submission of legislation to the Diet. Kajiyama himself was against the introduction of an SMD system.

The Kaifu government formulated three pieces of legislation: the revision of the Public Office Election Law to introduce the SMD system; the revision of the Political Fund Control Law to limit corporate funds; and the new Political Party Grant Law to provide government funds to political parties. However, because of the strong opposition of veto players within the LDP, party approval of these political reform proposals did not take place until June 29, after months of political maneuvering.

Soon after, the YKK group began asking LDP Diet members in their respective factions for signatures to petition for the reversal of the party's decision. On July 9 the LDP General Council decided to maintain the party decision while allowing LDP members to express their opposition in the Diet deliberations. While the political reform bills were introduced in the Diet in early August, the veto players within the LDP and the opposition parties successfully delayed deliberation on these bills. Deliberation finally began on September 10 and was referred to the lower house Special Committee on Political Reform. Originally former LDP secretary general Ichirō Ozawa had volunteered to be the chairman, but his heart condition prevented him from taking the appointment.[13] Ozawa's replacement for the committee chairman, Hikosaburō Okonogi, himself had reservations about the political reform plan and was persuaded by Kajiyama to kill the legislation.[14] After having only six meetings to consider the reform package, the chairman suddenly declared that the bill had been discarded in the Diet.

Kaifu was very upset to hear the news that Chairman Okonogi, with no prior consultation with party leadership, had terminated the bill on which Kaifu had staked his cabinet's destiny. Kaifu met with LDP top executives and stated that he would act with "serious determination."[15] Kaifu's statement was taken as his determination to dissolve the lower house. The YKK group, seeking to replace Kaifu with their own faction leader, publicly opposed the dissolution, thinking it might help Kaifu's reelection as a party leader. As they formed an anti-Kaifu coalition of the three major factions to become powerful veto players, the Takeshita faction, which Kaifu had relied on for support, could no longer form a majority within the LDP. Shin Kanemaru, the leader of the Takeshita faction, decided to join the veto players and withdrew the faction's support for Prime Minister Kaifu. Powerless, Kaifu had to give up dissolution. This action accelerated the anti-Kaifu campaign, which led to his resignation.[16]

The Miyazawa Cabinet and the Breakup of the LDP

To succeed Kaifu, the leaders of three major LDP factions—Kiichi Miyazawa, Michio Watanabe, and Hiroshi Mitsuzuka—declared their candidacy for LDP president. As all of them now competed to seek support from the Takeshita faction, the three-faction coalition, which the YKK group had formed to conduct the anti-Kaifu campaign, was dissolved. The Takeshita faction once again became the kingmaker. Shin Kanemaru, chairman of the Takeshita faction, asked his deputy Ichirō Ozawa to interview the three candidates. Ozawa invited them to his private office for interviews in order to make his final recommendation to the faction. The Takeshita faction's pick was Miyazawa.

Immediately after the Miyazawa cabinet was formed on November 5, 1991, the new prime minister stated in a press conference that his cabinet would work on political reform based on the Kaifu government's proposal. However, Miyazawa himself did not personally support the introduction of SMDs or the injection of government funds into the political party.[17] He appointed Kanemaru to the LDP vice president post and Kajiyama as the LDP Diet policy chairman. These two LDP leaders were against the introduction of the SMD system. Among the cabinet members, Foreign Minister Michio Watanabe, MITI Minister Kōzō Watanabe, Home Affairs Minister Seijūrō Shiokawa, Chief Cabinet Secretary Kōichi Katō, and Director General of the Defense Agency Sōhei Miyashita used a television program to express their hesitation about introducing an SMD system. On the other hand, Finance Minister Tsutomu Hata and Health and Welfare Minister Norio Yamashita supported the drastic reform outlined by Kaifu's proposal.[18] The split among cabinet members reflected disagreements within the LDP.

Yet another bribery scandal involving a secretary general of Miyazawa's own faction came up in December. On January 13, 1992, the former minister in charge of development of Hokkaido, Fumio Abe, was arrested for receiving a bribe from a steel-frame company, Kyōwa, in return for helping the company with its projects in Hokkaido. Facing public outrage over a new scandal involving his faction member, Prime Minister Miyazawa at the beginning of his January 24 policy speech apologized for Abe's scandal and stated that he would do his best to carry out political reform.[19]

In the July 1992 upper house election, the LDP won 69 of the 127 seats contested. Although the LDP decreased its share by 6 seats and did not gain a majority of the house, it almost doubled the number of seats it had won in the previous upper house election of 1989. Thus this was considered a victory. Many in the LDP felt that this result meant that the public had forgiven the party for the Recruit and Kyōwa scandals, and that a drastic political reform was no longer necessary. LDP Diet policy chairman Kajiyama, in a meeting with the opposition party, presented a reform plan with a minor reapportionment of the lower house districts: an increase of nine seats in urban districts coupled with a decrease of ten seats in rural areas.

However, another scandal broke out, this one involving LDP vice president Kanemaru. On August 22 the *Asahi Shimbun* carried a story that Kanemaru had received an illegal political contribution of 500 million yen from Tokyo Sagawa Kyūbin, a large parcel-delivery company. Kanemaru acknowledged accepting the illegal funds and resigned as vice president, following the advice of his protégé Ichirō Ozawa, who persuaded him to admit receiving the funds since the prosecuting authority would not charge Kanemaru himself but his assistant who handled financial affairs.[20] A month later, however, the Tokyo District Public Prosecutor's office charged Kanemaru himself for violating the Political Fund Control Law, which prohibited receiving a contribution of more than 1.5 million yen from any one company. Kanemaru filed a statement admitting his guilt to the prosecutor's office and paid a fine of 200,000 yen.[21]

The media and the public were upset by this deal, with Kanemaru only having to pay 200,000 yen for receiving 500 million yen. His political opponents, who had been frustrated by the control of the Takeshita faction, voiced their anger against Kanemaru and demanded his resignation as a Diet member. Even an incumbent cabinet member, Construction Minister Taku Yamasaki, publicly called for Kanemaru's resignation. Finally, on October 14, Kanemaru resigned as lower house member as well as the leader of the Takeshita faction.

This triggered a fierce battle over his successor as faction leader. Ozawa formed a group with thirty-five lower house members (more than a majority of sixty-seven members) within the faction to support Finance Minister Tsutomu Hata for faction leader. He also requested several upper house members in the faction to stay neutral. Former prime minister Takeshita was astonished to see Ozawa's action and persuaded the rest of his faction members to support his protégé, Keizō Obuchi, instead.[22] On October 28 the Takeshita faction officially announced that Obuchi was the new faction leader. On the same day, Ozawa and Hata held a press conference to announce that they had formed a new political group, Reform Forum 21, with thirty-five lower house members and eight upper house members. They said that the purpose of the new group was to promote the introduction of an SMD system.[23] With this move, the Takeshita faction broke apart into two groups: one led by Obuchi and one led by Hata.

On December 10 the LDP Headquarters on Political Reform submitted its proposal to Prime Minister Miyazawa. This proposal included provisions concerning political fund transparency and government funding of political parties, as well as the introduction of a pure SMD system without proportional representation districts. As a pure SMD system would not gain support from the opposition parties and would not pass in the upper house, where the LDP did not hold a majority, the decision in actuality was to abandon the electoral system reform.

The following day Prime Minister Miyazawa reshuffled the cabinet and the LDP leadership. To the powerful position of LDP secretary general he appointed Kajiyama of the Obuchi faction, who was the leading opponent of political reform. The Hata group members officially announced they would break off from the former Takeshita faction and demanded that Miyazawa propose a politically acceptable mixture of SMD and PR systems in order to realize the electoral system reform. Miyazawa, however, chose to proceed with the unrealistic LDP plan of a pure SMD system.

On March 6, 1993, Kanemaru and his secretary were suddenly arrested for income tax evasion. A search of Kanemaru's house found about several billion yen worth of cash, bearer bonds, and gold bars. Ironically, further revelation of the scandal involving Ozawa's former mentor strengthened public support for political reform and thus provided stronger backing for Ozawa's call. Ozawa and Hata said publicly they would quit the party if Prime Minister Miyazawa did not see political reform through.

The break-off of the Hata faction was a serious threat since it meant that the LDP would lose a majority in the lower house. However, the antireformers in the LDP, led by Kajiyama, persuaded Miyazawa to stick with a pure SMD system even though it had no chance to pass in the Diet. Between April and May Kajiyama tried to sell a new political reform package with a pure SMD system for the lower house and a PR system in the upper house. The LDP conducted an opinion survey of its Diet members on political reform, which was released on June 2. Roughly one-third of LDP members supported Miyazawa's pure SMD system to effectively kill the reform move. Another third preferred a small-scale compromise with the opposition party to bring about a mixture of SMD and PR systems. The last third demanded that political reform be achieved even if it meant further compromises.[24] The LDP was totally split, and there was no consensus to be formed.

On June 13 Miyazawa asked Kajiyama to make concession to the proreform-ers. But the LDP secretary general told the prime minister that it was impossi-ble to build a consensus over political reform. Two days later the LDP General Council decided to call for voting on the current LDP proposal with a pure SMD system, officially giving up the political reform plan.

On June 17 the opposition parties submitted a no-confidence resolution against the Miyazawa cabinet. Thirty-nine LDP lower house members (thirty-six from the Hata group and three others) joined them to pass the resolution, and eighteen other LDP members abstained. As a result, the resolution passed on June 18, forcing Prime Minister Miyazawa to call for a general election.

The Hosokawa Cabinet and Political Reform

On June 21 ten LDP lower house members broke off from the party to form a new party, Sakigake. The Hata group also followed them, breaking off from the LDP to establish another new party, the Renewal Party. In addition, an-other new conservative party, the Japan New Party (JNP), was formed, with no incumbent lower house members, under the leadership of the former gov-ernor of Kumamoto prefecture, Morihiro Hosokawa.

A general election was called. Issues for the July 18 election focused on the political reform pursued by the Hata group pursued. The reformist image won the Renewal Party fifty-five lower house seats, up from the original break-off membership of thirty-six. Sakigake and the JNP also did remarkably well, with Sakigake gaining thirteen seats and the JNP thirty-five seats. As these three new parties captured a significant number of lower house seats by attracting anti-LDP votes, the LDP did not achieve enough seats to form a majority. For the first time since its 1955 inception, the LDP was bounced out of power. The new conservative parties, with the help of long-established opposition parties, formed a non-LDP coalition government. This coalition of eight political groups,[25] which together held 260 of the 511 lower house seats, chose Hosokawa as its leader. The leaders of the eight groups met on July 29 and announced their policy agreements, including the introduction of a new electoral system with a mixture of SMD and PR systems.[26]

On August 9 Prime Minister Hosokawa labeled his cabinet "the political reform administration," and the following day at his first press conference he stated that he would take political responsibility if the cabinet could not pass the political reform bill by the end of the year.[27] The public, who had been disappointed by the failure of LDP prime ministers Kaifu and Miyazawa to deliver political reform, strongly supported Hosokawa. He received an unprecedented 71 percent public support rating.[28]

On August 27 the Hosokawa government decided the outline of political reform, which included the new electoral system with 250 single-member districts and 250 seats in a nationwide PR district. To create an SMD system to correct malapportionment, the maximum disparity between the most overrepresented and most underrepresented districts had to be within the ratio of 1:2.

On September 21, in his policy speech in the Diet, Hosokawa following his predecessors' example and declared political reform as his administration's highest priority, reiterating his determination to see the reform through.[29] Deliberation on the political reform bills began in the lower house's Special Committee on Political Reform on October 14. By the time the committee finished public hearings on the bill, deliberations had reached a total of 117 hours, the second longest deliberation time under the current constitution.[30] The coalition parties held a conference with the opposition LDP, who proposed a new electoral system with 300 SMDs and 200 seats in a PR district. The government coalition offered a concession with 274 SMDs with 226 seats in a PR district, but the conference did not reach an agreement, and the coalition parties decided to vote on the bills without the LDP's endorsement.

On November 18 the political reform bills passed the lower house, even achieving supporting votes from thirteen LDP members. In addition, seven LDP members avoided voting. Five Socialist members voted against the bills. Violating party discipline by casting a vote different from the party line reflected the individual Diet members' electoral conditions as well as the complicated power structure surrounding political reform in both the coalition parties and the LDP.

The stage for political reform now shifted to the upper house. The LDP upper house members demanded a concrete schedule for deliberation on a supplementary budget as a delaying tactic. As a result, deliberations on political reform did not start until November 26. This delay made it impossible for the Hosokawa government to enact the political reform bills by December 15, the original closing date of the current Diet session. On December 5 Hosokawa decided to extend the Diet session by forty-five days. The prime minister made up his mind to call for a general election if he could not pass the bill in the upper house by the end of January 1994.[31]

On January 21, 1994, the leftist faction of the Japan Socialist Party acted as veto players by voting to kill the political reform bills in the upper house.

Negotiations in the joint committee between upper and lower house representatives subsequently broke up on January 27. This meant that Hosokawa had only two more days to achieve political reform in the 128th extraordinary session of the Diet.

Hosokawa publicly restated his willingness to step down from the prime minister's post if political reform could not be realized under his leadership, and he called for a meeting with President Yōhei Kōno of the opposition LDP. Hosokawa asked Ichirō Ozawa, who was in charge of political affairs as a member of the Council of the Coalition Parties, to handle the situation. Ozawa saw Hosokawa's determination and realized a threat to dissolve the lower house would make it possible to get some political concessions from the LDP.[32] Behind the scenes, Ozawa had lobbied many LDP members for political reform. Some of them expressed their willingness to leave the LDP if their party blocked Hosokawa's political reform package. Ozawa then called on LDP Secretary General Yoshirō Mori to set up the Hosokawa-Kōno meeting. Fearing the possible breakup of the LDP, Mori agreed.[33] In the negotiations with Kōno, Hosokawa accepted the LDP's requests to change the number of electoral districts and to ease the reporting requirements for political finances.

With those compromises, an agreement was reached. Although many LDP members opposed the political reform measures on the table, they did not want to be blamed for blocking bills that were popular with the public. The compromise enabled the Hosokawa coalition government to pass the political reform bills in both the upper and lower houses by March 4, 1994.

The final political reform package ended up to be quite similar to the one the Kaifu government had proposed. The Public Office Election Law was revised so that the lower house electoral system would have 300 SMDs and 200 seats in eleven regional PR districts. Voters would have two votes to cast—one to write the candidate's name in an SMD, and the other to write the choice of the party in their PR district. Dual candidacy would allow a candidate in an SMD to be included in the party's PR list, making it possible for a defeated candidate in an SMD to be elected through the party vote in a PR district.

The 1994 revision of the Political Fund Control Law was designed to plug some of the loopholes of the 1975 law. Previously politicians had been allowed to set up several political organizations in order to evade the maximum donation limit from a single source. Now an individual politician was allowed to form only a single political funding body. Corporate contributions to an individual candidate were limited to 500,000 yen, while an individual could donate up to 1.5 million yen. All contributions of more than 50,000 yen had to be reported. In case of infringement of this provision, both the contributor and the receiver of funds were liable and could be punished, including suspension of civil rights, which would force a politician to stay out of public office. Under the old law, punishment was usually imposed on the politician's assistant responsible for his finances. But the new law established the principle of complicity so that politicians themselves could be penalized for illegal funding activities conducted by their secretarial staff or family members.[34]

While the new Political Fund Control Law restricted financial activities of politicians, the Political Party Grant Law provided government funding to the political parties in order to avoid corruption. The total amount of government funding was calculated on the basis of 250 yen per capita annually, which amounted to 30.9 billion yen in 1994. This money was distributed to political parties that had five or more Diet members or that received more than 2 percent of eligible votes in the most recent upper or lower house election. The amount of money each political party received depended on the number of Diet members in the party as well as the share of votes they received in the most recent national election.[35]

In April 1994 the government formed a consultative council to draw the constituency boundaries for the 300 SMDs. When the council was ready with its proposal, it was under the government led by Socialist leader Tomiichi Murayama in August 1994. The Murayama government swiftly moved on the SMD proposal and enacted it as a revision of the Public Office Election Law three months later. This finalized political reform efforts that had lasted for six long years. The politically difficult reform was achieved with public support, which was maintained at a high level owing to a series of political corruption scandals.

Politics of Administrative Reform

The LDP Returns to Power

As soon as Hosokawa completed these reforms, he took on the issue of raising the consumption tax from 3 to 7 percent.[36] The prime minister, who had used public support to achieve his political reforms, did not make much effort to persuade the public on this tax issue. At the press conference Hosokawa was asked how the government came up with the 7 percent figure. He answered that it was "a ball-park figure." Obviously he was not deeply involved in the policy-making process.

Hosokawa no longer was seen as a leader who enthusiastically communicated national goals to the public. The public was disappointed to see him acting like a puppet leader who was controlled by the Ministry of Finance (MOF).[37] With public resentment apparent, Hosokawa was forced into a retreat on the tax plan the very next day. Public support for Hosokawa further eroded in the aftermath of this event, and the prime minister suddenly announced his resignation in April 1994 amid allegations of personal financial impropriety.

When Hosokawa left office, Tsutomu Hata of the Renewal Party took over. The Hata cabinet faced political difficulty from the beginning. On the same day that Hata was elected prime minister, four of the eight coalition parties, excluding the JSP, formed a new political group within the Diet. As the largest group among the coalition parties, the new group would gain political advantages, including the acquisition of the chairmanships of Diet committees that would have gone to the Socialist Party. Upset by this treatment, the Socialist Party broke away from the coalition, leaving the new government in a vulnerable minority status. The Hata cabinet was doomed from the beginning and lasted only two months, without achieving any political results except passage of the 1994 budget.

Prime Minister Hata failed to persuade the Socialist Party to return to the coalition. Instead, the minority coalition supported as the next premier candidate former prime minister Kaifu, who had defected from the LDP with thirty-four other members. Meanwhile, suffering from its opposition party status, the LDP contacted the Socialist leader, Tomiichi Murayama, regarding the possibility of a cooperative relationship between the LDP and the Socialist Party.[38] In the following election in the lower house, an unexpected new three-party coalition was formed by the LDP, the Socialist Party, and Sakigake to elect Murayama as the national leader.

The new coalition was quickly criticized by the media as a marriage of convenience. Many Japanese doubted whether Japan's new leader would be able to depart from the traditional Socialist stance against the will of many other Socialist members to support the U.S.-Japan security alliance and Japan's Self-Defense Forces. Murayama's determination to support the alliance and the SDF was firm, however. In July 1994 the Socialist prime minister, breaking from the past, officially declared in the Diet that the Self-Defense Forces were constitutional, a stance much to the contrary of the traditional party line. Two months later the Socialist Party approved Murayama's position, abandoning its traditional goal of unarmed neutrality. This historical policy shift of the Socialist Party in effect put an end to the 1955 system, the political framework under which the LDP and the Socialists, as the government and the main opposition party, remained ideologically split over the constitutionality of the SDF.[39]

As the biggest policy gap between the Socialist Party and the LDP was thus filled, Murayama introduced a new process to deal with policy differences within the coalition. He formed eighteen different issue-specific project teams for major policy issues where the three government parties could exchange their views and find agreeable solutions. Murayama remarked in an interview, "Clearly, policy differences existed among the three parties. In many cases, we could not reach an agreement. But through serious discussions, I believe, we developed mutual understanding and trust."[40]

When the special interests of the three parties agreed on the direction the policy would go, they constituted an even more powerful lobbying body than the LDP zoku did under the system of single-party dominance. Under the LDP government between the 1960s and the 1980s, for example, agricultural zoku members always sought a realistic compromise while calling for a higher rice price to protect farmers. On the other hand, when the coalition government was planning to reduce the rice price for FY1994, the agricultural interests of the Socialist Party took advantage of being a government party to secure electoral bases in rural areas. They insisted on a higher price more stubbornly than their peers in the LDP did. As a result, while the rice price was kept at the same level as the previous year, the agricultural subsidy for rice farmers was nearly doubled in July 1994. The media criticized the revival of LDP zoku and the emergence of the Socialist zoku.

To deal with such criticisms, the policy committee chairmen of the three coalition parties announced their policy on September 7. To curb zoku activities, the government parties would increase the transparency of the policy process and strengthen anticorruption measures. But this policy had little actual impact on the decision-making process. Agricultural zoku members of the three parties pressured the Murayama cabinet to increase the government subsidy to compensate farmers for the opening of Japan's rice market. The Ministry of Finance proposed a total amount of 3.5 trillion yen, but zoku members were not satisfied with this figure and threatened to kill the World Trade Organization–related bills that would enable the opening of the rice market unless the number was drastically increased.[41] The Murayama government had to nearly double the amount of agricultural compensation to a total of 6.1 trillion yen. This victory by zoku marked their resurgence as powerful veto players under the coalition government.

On the other hand, crisis management, which requires top-down leadership for timely actions, revealed the limitations of the inexperienced prime minister when he faced the Great Hanshin-Awaji Earthquake. At 5:46 a.m. on January 17, 1995, an earthquake measuring 7.2 on the Richter scale struck Hyogo prefecture in the Hanshin region. Prime Minister Murayama first learned about the earthquake on the NHK news at 6 a.m. but did not take any action. His secretary from the Police Agency, who covered natural disasters, was in Kyushu because of his father's death. The secretary found out about the quake, contacted several agencies to collect information, and then telephoned the prime minister around 7:30 a.m., but with no more information than the television news had delivered.[42] This was the first official contact with Murayama that morning.

Thirty minutes later Murayama went to his office. No emergency meeting was called. Several cabinet members held a meeting on the monthly economic report as scheduled. At 10:04 the regular cabinet meeting was opened, but the most important agenda item was how to deal with former Socialist leader Sadao Yamahana's move to form a new party. Only after this discussion did the cabinet decide to form a headquarters for emergency disaster relief, instructing its head Kiyoshi Ozawa to visit the Hanshin area. Still, the top government officials did not realize how serious the earthquake situation was.[43]

All morning Murayama went through his scheduled meetings. At noon he had a meeting with the leaders of the coalition parties, during which Chief Cabinet Secretary Kōzō Igarashi slipped him a memo informing him that 203 people had been killed. Murayama was taken aback. Finally, at 3 p.m., six hours after the earthquake, Murayama held a press conference and told reporters that the government would take all possible measures to support the victims. Three hours later the top government officials learned that more than 1,000 people had been killed in the earthquake. By the end of the day, 2,300 SDF troops were dispatched to conduct rescue activities.[44]

At 10 o'clock the following morning, the cabinet decided to send 13,000 SDF troops to conduct rescue operations. But these troops could not reach the damaged region in a timely manner because of a traffic jam. In the end the death toll reached 6,434 people. The media criticized the lack of an immediate response by the Murayama cabinet. Murayama himself admitted his unpreparedness in a Diet session: "It was my first experience, and it happened early in the morning. Therefore, there was much confusion."[45] This statement only brought further criticism.

According to a public opinion poll taken by the *Asahi Shimbun*, 53 percent of respondents were critical of the government's actions in dealing with the earthquake. Among these, 41 percent pointed out the problem with the rescue system, 29 percent criticized the judgments immediately after the earthquake, and 19 percent accused the prime minister of lacking leadership.[46]

Two months after the earthquake, the Tokyo subway system was attacked by terrorists from the Aum Shinrikyō, a new religious cult headed by Shōkō Asahara. They released sarin gas into the subway, killing thirteen and injuring more than six thousand innocent people. As the government had been strongly suspicious that the cult was producing sarin gas even before the attack, the opposition parties criticized Murayama for not having taken any action to prevent the incident.[47]

The media also criticized Prime Minister Murayama for his incapability of dealing with the crises. Ten years later Murayama made a very honest statement in a press interview: "When I became the prime minister, nobody mentioned crisis management. I never even thought about it."[48] Strengthening the functioning of the cabinet, especially for crisis management, became an important topic of interest in the political community thereafter.

Hashimoto and the *Jūsen* Problem

By January 1996 Murayama resigned, and LDP president Ryūtarō Hashimoto was endorsed by the same coalition to succeed him. Hashimoto promised that he would maintain the decision-making system that comprised project teams and committees for policy discussion among the three coalition parties.

The new Hashimoto government had the immediate task of resolving the *jūsen* problem, which involved seven housing loan companies with bad loans. The Ministry of Finance calculated the total amount of outstanding loans by the seven companies at 13.2 trillion yen and identified about half the loans as the initial loss. To liquidate these bad loans, creditors had to bear the cost.

The MOF drew up its *jūsen* liquidation scheme. In accordance with this scheme, the so-called parent banks, the *jūsen* founding financial institutions, which included city banks, regional banks, life insurers, trust banks, and security firms, agreed to give up their rights to all 3.5 trillion yen worth of loans to the *jūsen*. Other banks promised to do likewise, giving up 1.7 trillion yen worth of loans of the remaining 4.2 trillion yen. The proposal also requested the agricultural financial institutions, which had invested 5.6 trillion yen in the housing loan companies, to bear 1.2 trillion yen of loss. This scheme was generous to the agricultural institutions, reflecting their strong political influence. They were asked to cover about 20 percent of their investments, while the parent banks gave up 100 percent and the other banks 40 percent.

The agricultural institutions, however, rejected the MOF's request, stating that they were not able to pay that much. They lobbied the zoku politicians of the LDP and successfully bargained down their payment to less than half the original request, or 530 billion yen. Agricultural experts in the Socialist Party (by this time, the party had officially changed its name to the Social Democratic Party, or SDP, but it will be referred to as the Socialist Party for the rest of the book) also supported the lessening of the burden of the agricultural institutions. With the small amount from the agricultural institutions, the Japanese government rewrote the bailout plan to use 685 billion yen of public funds from the 1996 fiscal budget. This marked another victory for LDP zoku members as veto players.

The *jūsen* crisis, however, sparked heated debates about the need to reform the MOF and divide its functions among independent agencies. Critics argued that the MOF's authority was too strong, and that its use of fiscal authority for the financial market distorted government policy, creating problems such as the *jūsen* crisis.

There was strong public sentiment about the MOF's *jūsen* liquidation scheme, which would require the use of taxpayer money. The public protested, fueled by the Diet's release of documents that contained the names of the top one hundred borrowers of housing loans, against the MOF's opposition. The information revealed that corporate borrowers were responsible for more than 95 percent of the nonperforming loans, and that many of the borrowers had loans with more than one housing loan company. The MOF had been aware of these practices and the size of the bad loans but had done nothing to correct the problems.

By this time Ichirō Ozawa had formed a new conservative party, the New Frontier Party (NFP), with 187 Diet members who were the members of the former non-LDP coalition parties. The NFP adamantly criticized the use of public funds to bail out the *jūsen*. Its members began a sit-in, blocking entry to the Budget Committee room to protest the ruling coalition's budget proposal that contained such a bailout plan. The Economic Planning Agency expressed concerns that a delay in approval of the budget could slow down Japan's economic recovery. Although the public as a whole was critical of the government plan, more and more people expressed their concern for Japan's economy as the sit-in extended into its third week. According to a poll conducted at the time, more than 70 percent of respondents wanted the politicians to pay more attention to prosperity and economic issues.[49] The sit-in ended with a compromise agreement between the ruling coalition and the NFP, which ensured time for sufficient debate over the budget bills in the Diet. The Hashimoto government managed to resolve the politically difficult *jūsen* problem, but the public continued to expect the prime minister to reform the bureaucracy.

Underlining the need for bureaucratic reform was the filing of a lawsuit over the transfusion of HIV-tainted blood. The Ministry of Health and Welfare was blamed for failing to take appropriate measures when an American authority issued a worldwide alert that all blood should be heated before infusion, to kill HIV. The ministry did not take the advice, and nonheated blood was kept in general use for transfusion, resulting in a number of HIV infectors. In February 1996 Minister of Health and Welfare Naoto Kan made an official apology, and the following month the victims and the government settled out of court. But public distrust of the national bureaucracy was stronger than ever under the Hashimoto government.

Lack of political leadership also became a focal issue for Japanese politics. Crisis management in particular arose as an immediate issue after the disastrous experience of the Hanshin earthquake and Aum Shinrikyō sarin gas attacks in 1995 under the Murayama government. The government had received heavy criticism over the lack of timely, decisive, and appropriate actions. Strengthening the cabinet thus became a major issue in the administrative reform effort.

In the summer of 1996, entering the final year of the lower house's four-year term, election pressure grew among Diet members. Observing the rising popularity of his cabinet in September, Hashimoto dissolved the lower house to call the first election under the new electoral law, which had introduced single-member districts.[50] During the campaign virtually all political parties, including the LDP, pledged to carry out administrative reform, reflecting public distrust of government agencies. While Hashimoto's rival, Ichirō Ozawa of the NFP, proposed the reduction of government agencies from the current twenty-three to fifteen during the campaign, the prime minister pledged that his government would cut the number in half. In the October 20 general election, the LDP gained 239 seats, up from 211, in the 500-seat lower house. The result, generally seen as a victory, strengthened Hashimoto's power base in his party. The LDP, however, still came up short and was unable to form a majority in the lower house.

Hashimoto approached the two other government parties to maintain the same coalition. However, the election results for these two parties were a disaster—the Socialist Party decreased to fifteen seats from a preelection total of thirty, and Sakigake won only two seats, losing seven. Their participation in the coalition government with the LDP might have been the reason liberal voters withdrew their support. The two parties decided to stay out of the cabinet to maintain their independence while agreeing to support the LDP government to form a majority in the lower house. Thus Hashimoto had to pursue administrative reform with a minority-led cabinet surrounded by very powerful, partisan veto players.

Hashimoto Starts Administrative Reform

One month after the October 1996 general election, Prime Minister Hashimoto inaugurated the Administrative Reform Council without any legislation, as he felt the immediate need to get going on administrative reform efforts. Even the ruling LDP did not officially approve of the establishment and membership of the council, which left room for the ruling party members to freely attack its recommendations. To suppress potential veto players, Hashimoto appointed himself council chairman, thus forcing his government to act on its recommendations.

In addition to Hashimoto, there were two representatives of the political community.[51] Among the twelve other members were three business leaders who had headed the existing government advisory councils on administrative reform-related matters.[52] Other members included six scholars, two media representatives, and one labor leader.[53] It is important to note that Hashimoto chose no bureaucratic representative for the council to discuss administrative reform, to avoid any influence of institutional veto players.

On November 28, 1996, Prime Minister Hashimoto called the first meeting of the council. He asked the members for recommendations on three issues: what functions the state should fulfill in the twenty-first century; how the government should be restructured to perform these functions better; and how best to strengthen the cabinet's functions. The following day he stated in his policy speech before the Diet, "Although resistance and difficulties are inevitable, I am fully committed to the cause of administrative reform." The public saw Hashimoto's determination, and his popularity rate in a *Kyodo News* poll rose to 58.3 percent, up from 43.4 percent at the beginning of his term.[54]

Between January and March 1997, with public attention focused on it, the council held a series of hearings with scholars and experts to exchange views on administrative reform.[55] In the early stage of the reform efforts, crisis management was an immediate issue. In addition to the disastrous experience of the 1995 Hanshin earthquake and the Aum Shinrikyō sarin attack, the ongoing hostage crisis in Peru, which began in December 1996, and the oil spill disaster in the Sea of Japan in January 1997 made better crisis management a priority. The council decided to separate this from other issues and to draft proposals by May 1997 that would provide the prime minister greater control over government ministries in emergency cases. According to the government interpretation of the Cabinet Law at the time, the prime minister could never instruct ministries without the unanimous consent of the entire cabinet. On May 1 the council announced recommendations for setting a package of cabinet decisions that would allow the prime minister to directly instruct ministries in times of crisis and for establishing a new cabinet position of deputy chief cabinet secretary for crisis management. Although the new director would interfere with the jurisdiction of existing agencies such as the Defense Agency, no strong opposition from the bureaucracy was observed. (The new position was created in April 1998.)

The council secretariat provided information materials that were used as a basis for debate and summary of previous arguments in the council. The bureaucratic executives of the secretariat sneakily changed wording in the information materials. For example, there was an argument for the establishment of "the Economic Advisory Council" that would give the prime minister strong leadership power in outlining the national budget. Although this proposal appeared in the first version of the information materials on "Reinforcing Cabinet Functions," it was removed from the third version.[56] Obviously this change reflected the intention of the MOF officials, who did not want their budget-making power weakened and thus acted as veto players within the government.

The MOF had been the center of public criticism against the national bureaucracy. On June 16, 1997, one year after the political turmoil over the *jūsen* scandal, the Diet enacted legislation to establish the new Financial Supervisory Agency. As a result, the inspecting and supervising authority over financial institutions would be removed from the MOF. MOF officials managed to maintain influence over the financial industry, however, by keeping the planning function of financial policy. The proud officials of the MOF could not endure any further erosion of their power and desperately sought influence over administrative reform planning.

Another example of veto players' action was in the establishment of the powerful Cabinet Office, which would be in charge of coordinating different interests among ministries on behalf of the prime minister. It was not desirable for many ministries to have such a powerful new office directly under the prime minister. The bureaucratic officials in the secretariat listed an alternative plan, which would combine the Prime Minister's Office (sōrifu) and the Management and Coordination Agency without giving it coordinating power. According to this plan, the new office would have an equal status with other ministries. In an attempt to manipulate the direction of deliberations, the secretariat leaked the plan to some of the media as the council's "original plan."[57]

Between July and August most of the substantial discussions of administrative reform were moved to two subcommittees. While the Subcommittee on Plans and Institutions mainly dealt with plans to reinforce cabinet functions, the Subcommittee on Organizational Issues dealt with reorganization of the national bureaucracy. Hashimoto asked these subcommittees to prepare the original draft for the interim report.[58] As a result, the Economic Advisory Council and the Cabinet Office were back in the proposal for the interim report. The public saw Hashimoto as exhibiting strong leadership in his administrative reform efforts against veto players and rewarded him with a popularity rating as high as 59.2 percent.[59]

Battles over Administrative Reform

On September 3, 1997, after a four-day series of intense meetings, the council presented an interim report that included rather drastic plans to streamline the bureaucracy.[60] The plan called for reinforcing the cabinet, privatizing postal saving and insurance services, dividing the politically powerful Ministry of Construction (MOC), and decreasing the number of government agencies from twenty-three to thirteen, including a newly created, powerful support organ for the prime minister, the Cabinet Office.

The limited influence of veto players on the council made it possible for its members to come up with ambitious plans. At the same time, this was a weakness. With the council's relative independence, the plans did not go through any policy approval process of the three ruling parties—the LDP, the Socialist Party, and Sakigake.[61] Therefore Hashimoto, when presenting the council's interim report to representatives of the coalition parties, had to bow and ask them to "respect the proposal to the furthest extent possible," leaving the plan in a vulnerable position.

Media and political attention focused mainly on the reorganization of government ministries and not much on reinforcing the cabinet and other proposals. The reduction of the number of agencies would clearly create winners and losers among government agencies. Potential losers became veto players, attacking Hashimoto's plan.

The LDP's zoku members argued that there was no need to respect the recommendations of the council because it did not have legislative approval. LDP members who were seeking to maintain voter support in the postal industry, for example, adamantly opposed the idea of privatizing the postal saving and life insurance services. Special post offices, which made up 80 percent of Japan's 24,600 postal outlets, served as a solid support base for many LDP members in election times. Hashimoto's privatization plan and the absorption of the telecommunication function into the proposed Industry Ministry would effectively dissolve the Ministry of Post and Telecommunications (MPT), an unpopular move among those who naturally wanted to protect their positions. On September 5 LDP Telecommunications Subcommittee chairman Keiji Furuya met with LDP secretary general Kōichi Katō and PARC chairman Taku Yamasaki and told them that he would oppose the postal service privatization scheme. Yamasaki publicly stated that the LDP would begin talks with the two other coalition parties on postal services and start from scratch.

The mass media criticized such veto players and supported the council's plan to privatize postal saving and insurance services. These services provided a large financial resource for quasi-governmental organizations that many economists had blamed for inefficient investments. The postal saving service attracted as much as 35 percent of the nation's individual savings by offering a higher interest rate, made possible by the injection of tax money.[62] Many economists argued that this created a major distortion in Japan's financial market.

Most members of the public, however, did not feel this was a problem and were satisfied with postal saving services. According to an *Asahi Shimbun* survey, 54 percent of those polled said they were against the privatization of these services.[63] The poll showed that people who lived in less populated areas with no commercial banks desperately needed the services, and that those who lived in urban areas were not particularly dissatisfied with them. This was completely different from the national railway reform situation in the 1980s, in which the dissatisfied, angry customers formed a strong political support base for privatization. The public supported the veto players on the postal saving services issue.

The council, already weak without legal backing, met with trouble when Hashimoto's popularity declined over the appointment of Kōkō Satō, who had a criminal record following the Lockheed scandal, as a cabinet minister. According to a *Kyodo News* poll, 74 percent of respondents said that they were against Satō's appointment. Subsequently Hashimoto's popularity rating dropped dramatically, from 60 percent to 28 percent.[64] After a week of political turmoil, Satō "voluntarily" resigned. At a press conference Hashimoto bowed deeply and expressed his apologies to the public, saying he "had not considered public opinion enough."

As Hashimoto's popularity eroded, the LDP's zoku members took the opportunity to attack the prime minister's administrative reform. In addition to the postal zoku members, other zoku members also joined the movement against Hashimoto's reform plan. The powerful construction zoku members, for example, publicly opposed the plan to divide the function of the Ministry of Construction into two newly created ministries. Against their campaign pledges for administrative reform, LDP veto players swarmed to attack Hashimoto's reform plan in order to protect their special interests, an old habit the ruling party had developed under the one-party dominance system.

After the interim report was announced, political-level committees on administrative reform were held among the three coalition parties and within the LDP. Virtually all the government agencies asked for help from their patron LDP members to acquire a better deal in the reform scheme. The opinions of these committees were reported at the council meetings. Besides such political pressure, many interest groups lobbied the members of the council hard. Workers at local post offices and construction companies were organized and requested to write letters to the members. Bureaucratic officials stepped on each other's toes as they struggled to secure appointments with council members to explain their standpoints.[65] As the council members began considering their opinions, Hashimoto's administrative efforts were no longer independent of political and bureaucratic veto players.

Over controversial issues, such as the privatization of postal saving and life insurance services and the division of the MOF and the MOC, there were widening gaps in the opinions of council members. At the September 17 meeting, for example, five different members stated their opposition to the privatization plan, and three members questioned the division of the MOC. As one council member described it, "That was the birth of 'zoku iin' [zoku council members]."[66] Hashimoto now had to face veto players within the council as well. On September 27 the LDP Headquarters on Administrative Reform presented its proposal to reform the postal service, instead of the privatization plan in the interim report.[67] As political pressure mounted, a major reworking of the interim report seemed more and more inevitable.

As Hashimoto's public support eroded, lobbying activities of interest groups and their patron LDP zoku members were so widely reported in the media that nearly 80 percent of voters in a poll found that lobbying by zoku members was problematic.[68] At the council meetings members found Prime Minister Hashimoto under strong political pressure and avoiding a decisive statement on controversial issues.[69] Hashimoto no longer exhibited strong determination for drastic reform.

Because the LDP, the Socialist Party, and Sakigake representatives were determined to refuse any privatization plan, Hashimoto proposed compromises. The services would remain government run, but they would be separate from the ministry and conducted under a new government corporation in five years. The coalition parties hesitated to accept Hashimoto's proposal because the government corporation plan might be a step toward privatization. To acquire an agreement with the coalition parties, Hashimoto promised that the government would not privatize the postal services. In return, the coalition parties also agreed to allow private companies to enter the postal service, and none of the three postal services would receive subsidies.

As the most controversial issue of Hashimoto's administrative reform efforts was resolved, the council issued its final report. While Hashimoto managed to keep the framework of thirteen agencies and the plan to strengthen the cabinet's function, he had to yield in several areas because of the pressure of veto players in the LDP and the two coalition parties. As described above, the privatization plan for the postal service was abandoned. The service would be continued as a governmental operation under the Postal Service Agency for five years and would later be run by a newly created, government-run corporation. All functions of the Ministry of Construction would be continued under a new Ministry of Land and Transportation.[70] In the final report an agreement was not reached among the coalition parties on separation of the fiscal and financial functions of the MOF. Sakigake strongly pushed for a total separation, which the LDP was hesitant to support. But later a political compromise was reached. The MOF would keep its influence over financial policies by maintaining its authority over financial crises.

On June 9, 1998, the Hashimoto government successfully passed the legislation in the Diet. After the passage the prime minister formed the Headquarters of Central Government Reform to design the revisions of the existing laws. To oversee and check the proceeding of administrative reform, Hashimoto formed the Advisory Council, chaired by Keidanren chairman Takashi Imai.[71] While new institutional settings were organized, Prime Minister Hashimoto could not continue his reform efforts. In the July 1998 upper house election, voters demonstrated their discontent with Hashimoto's handling of economic policy and his lack of leadership. The LDP lost 17 seats, leaving it 23 seats short of a majority in the 252-seat chamber. This historic loss forced Prime Minister Hashimoto to resign in the midst of his administrative reform efforts. But the seventeen pieces of administrative reform legislation did pass in the Diet under the government led by Keizō Obuchi in July 1999, bringing drastic organizational change to the central government in January 2001.

Obuchi and the 1999 Diet/Government Reform

The newly elected premier, Obuchi, faced the difficult position of having to run the government with majority control of only the lower house.[72] The Diet operations were more difficult than expected. In the fall session the LDP had to team up with different partners to pass important bills. To enact the Financial Renewal Bills, the government party had to cooperate with the opposition parties.

By this time the Democratic Party, established by former Sakigake members Yukio Hatoyama and Naoto Kan in 1996 with an aim of a more "citizen-centered" society, had become the largest opposition party, with 140 Diet members (93 lower house, 47 upper house). As for the bills for an early reconstruction of the financial system, the LDP forwent teaming up with the Democrats. It sought cooperation with the Liberal Party, which was led by Ichirō Ozawa and had 54 members (42 lower house, 12 upper house) with ideologies of political conservatism and economic liberalism, to pursue a smaller government. To pass the budget bills, the LDP had to cut a deal with Kōmeitō by agreeing to issue consumption coupons to children under sixteen and selected older people. These tough Diet operations made Prime Minister Obuchi and his cabinet realize the need to form a coalition government to secure the passage of the bills to revise the U.S.-Japan security guidelines during the 1999 ordinary Diet session.

Obuchi's choice for a coalition partner was Ozawa's Liberal Party. It was surprising and realistic at the same time: surprising in consideration of the strong animosity against Ozawa among LDP members, and realistic if considering the Liberal Party's policy line on strengthening U.S.-Japan security ties. The Liberal Party set immediate government and Diet reform as the conditions for its participation in the coalition. The reform was to include an immediate reduction in the number of cabinet ministers, gradual downsizing of civil servants by 25 percent over ten years, and an end to the government commissioner system, which allowed civil servants to answer questions at the Diet on behalf of cabinet ministers.

Before the coalition was officially formed, the LDP agreed to reduce the number of cabinet posts from twenty to eighteen and to form five project teams between the two parties: (1) abolition of the government commissioner system and introduction of senior vice ministers, (2) reduction of the number of Diet seats, (3) establishment of basic national security principles, (4) reorganization of the central government and downsizing of civil servants, and (5) economy and tax systems. The two parties agreed on the detailed scheme for the abolition of the government commissioner system and on the number of senior vice ministers to be introduced. These agreements were incorporated in the administrative reform bills that the Obuchi cabinet approved on April 27, 1999. The LDP and the Liberal Party also agreed to reduce by 50 the 200 proportional representation seats in the 500-member lower house. This agreement, however, later met political opposition and was not implemented in the 1999 Diet sessions. For policy discussions on items other than the five areas, the LDP and the Liberal Party agreed to hold regular monthly meetings between Obuchi and Ozawa.

While the LDP–Liberal Party coalition strengthened the Obuchi government, problems remained. Although the two-party coalition held a secure majority in the lower house, it was still ten seats short of a majority in the upper house. To secure a majority in the upper house, the Obuchi administration sought cooperation from the opposition Kōmeitō. The Kōmeitō at that time was seeking a new political stance by keeping its distance from the opposition Democratic Party. Cooperation with the LDP would make the party more politically influential in actual policy making. The Kōmeitō agreed to cooperate with the LDP-Liberal coalition government in Diet operations.

The 145th regular Diet session (January 19–August 13, 1999) was portrayed as the "LDP-LP-Kōmeitō session." Kōmeitō's cooperation was crucial for the passage of politically controversial bills such as the U.S.-Japan Defense Guidelines bills, the National Flag-Anthem bill, and the Anti–Organized Crime bills.[73] In the Diet session, the Obuchi cabinet was able to pass 110 of the 124 government-sponsored bills under the three-party cooperative framework.[74]

At the end of the Diet session, Prime Minister Obuchi invited the Kōmeitō to officially form a coalition. The policy gap between the Kōmeitō and the Liberal Party, however, was substantial in the fields of welfare and national security. The Kōmeitō, with strong support from the women's subgroup, was traditionally liberal, supported a larger government welfare program, and opposed an increase in the defense budget. On the other hand, the Liberal Party called for a larger role for Japan in international politics and less government involvement in welfare programs. The biggest gap between the two parties was on electoral reform. The reduction of 50 seats out of the 200 proportional representation lower house seats that the LDP agreed on with the Liberal Party was unacceptable for the Kōmeitō, for 29 of its 48 lower house members were elected in PR districts. To form the three-party coalition, the LDP had to renegotiate over electoral reform with the Liberal Party.

Meanwhile, Obuchi faced a presidential election in his own party. To retain the premiership, he had to be reelected as his own party's leader. Two other candidates, former LDP secretary general Kōichi Katō and former chairman of the LDP's Policy Affairs Research Council Taku Yamasaki, were both critical of forming a coalition with the Kōmeitō largely owing to its relationship with the religious group Sōkagakkai. In the September 20 election, however, Obuchi received 350 of the 514 total votes. Prime Minister Obuchi interpreted his reelection as party approval for the three-party coalition and further accelerated his efforts to conclude an agreement with the Liberal Party and the Kōmeitō.

On October 4 the three parties finally reached an agreement over electoral reform. They agreed to submit an electoral reform bill to reduce twenty of the proportional representation seats and postponed a decision over the remaining thirty seats. They also reached policy agreements, which included reforms in education, welfare, the tax system, and national security. On the following day Prime Minister Obuchi formed a new cabinet with one member each from the Liberal Party and the Kōmeitō.[75] For policy coordination, the three-party Policy Council (Yotō Sekininsha Kaigi) was formed with three members from each party.[76] Major policy issues were expected to be brought to this council for building consensus among the three parties. The three-party coalition totaled 356 lower house members (71.2 percent of the 500 seats) and 143 upper house members (56.7 percent). This overwhelming majority made the Obuchi administration's Diet operation productive. During the 146th extraordinary session (October 29–December 15, 1999), the Obuchi cabinet managed to pass all seventy-four government-sponsored bills.

Downsizing the lower house remained a thorny issue among the three parties. While the electoral reform bill was submitted to the Diet as agreed, the LDP and the Kōmeitō refused to call a vote for the bill during the Diet session. Thus Liberal Party president Ozawa threatened to leave the coalition. The three parties finally reached a compromise that the bill would be called for at the beginning of the following Diet session. In accordance with this compromise, the three parties introduced the electoral reform bill in the 147th ordinary Diet session. The opposition parties, however, refused to attend the Diet session, arguing that the passage of such an important bill should not be determined by only the government parties. Without the presence of all opposition parties in the committee and floor meetings of both houses on February 2, 2000, the three ruling coalition parties passed the electoral reform bill to eliminate twenty proportional representation seats in the lower house.

Although the three coalition parties enacted the electoral reform, the political climate changed after the Osaka gubernatorial election, which was generally regarded as a litmus test for the coming general election. In the February 6 election, Fusae Ōta, a former senior official of the Ministry of International Trade and Industry who was supported by the three-party government coalition, defeated her two major rivals to become Japan's first female governor. The election result was generally seen as approval for the Obuchi government.

At this point Obuchi no longer had a desperate need to maintain the coalition government with Ozawa's Liberal Party, as the LDP and the Kōmeitō could form a majority in both houses. Ozawa requested Obuchi to form a new party as the two parties had competing candidates in nearly thirty electoral districts for the forthcoming general election. In seven districts the incumbents of the two parties would have to battle over one seat. On April 1 Ozawa met with Prime Minister Obuchi and threatened to leave the coalition unless a new party was formed. Obuchi told Ozawa he could not accept his demand.[77] Once the breakup was decided, it became apparent that the Liberal Party was not a solid entity. More than half the Diet members saw a political advantage in staying in the coalition, as they could expect electoral cooperation with the Kōmeitō.[78] Twenty-six Liberals broke off from Ozawa to form the new Conservative Party and remain a coalition partner with the LDP and the Kōmeitō. Ozawa's party was left with only twenty-four Diet members and was out of the coalition.

Several hours after the three-party leaders' meeting, tragedy struck Obuchi. The sixty-two-year-old prime minister suffered a stroke and was hospitalized in a coma. On April 5 the Obuchi cabinet resigned en masse in accordance with article 70 of the constitution, which stipulates the cabinet's resignation "when the prime ministerial post is vacant." When LDP secretary general Yoshirō Mori was elected the fifty-fifth prime minister in the Diet, the Obuchi administration officially ended its 616-day history. One month later, Obuchi passed away.

During the 1990s three major institutional changes were created for the purpose of political reform: the 1994 electoral system reform under the Hosokawa government; the 1999 Diet and government reform under the Obuchi cabinet; and Hashimoto's administrative reform efforts, most of which became effective in January 2001. The next two chapters illustrate the impact of these changes on the political scene.

INSTITUTIONAL CHANGES AND KOIZUMI'S LEADERSHIP

FOLLOWING THE INSTITUTIONAL CHANGES in the electoral system, the Diet, and the government in the 1990s, Japanese politics observed significant structural modifications. These circumstances brought about the birth of the Junichirō Koizumi administration. Koizumi would have had little chance to become prime minister under the traditional LDP factional politics. By taking advantage of the changes introduced by Hashimoto's administrative reform, he altered the Japanese government decision making.

During the five and a half years of his term, Koizumi successfully streamlined the public sector; privatized special public corporations, government financial institutions, and, most important, the postal services; and resolved the nonperforming loan problems. He also changed the fiscal policy-making system, which had been dominated by the powerful Ministry of Finance. In the area of foreign and national security policy, Koizumi also took advantage of the newly strengthened political institutions. After the 9-11 incident, he expressed full support for U.S. military action and said Japan would do everything possible within the framework of its constitution to help. Koizumi kept his promise by passing antiterrorism legislation in an unprecedentedly short period of time and dispatching Japan's Self-Defense Forces overseas under wartime conditions for the first time in the country's postwar history.

This chapter first explains how the new electoral system modified the power balance within the LDP to weaken factions and allow the choice of such an unorthodox leader. Then it explores how the institutional changes brought about by the administrative reform helped set the playing field for Koizumi against other veto players. To examine how Koizumi exercised top-down decision making, concrete examples are introduced in the areas of fiscal and foreign policy. Finally, the chapter discusses developments in the post-Koizumi era.

THE NEW ELECTORAL SYSTEM OPTS FOR KOIZUMI

The impact of the 1994 electoral system changes eventually brought the power shift from the LDP to the Democratic Party of Japan in September 2009.[1] But it took five elections of the lower house, and the alterations at the beginning were subtle and slow (see the following chapter). One of the first impacts on the Japanese political scene was a significant shift in the power balance within the LDP, which indirectly weakened factional influence over the prime minister.

In the old system constituents generally brought their casework to more senior and politically powerful politicians in their district if there were two or more representatives of the government party. This reinforced the seniority hierarchy within the LDP. However, in the new era young LDP members in the single-seat electoral districts received virtually all the requests from their constituency and found themselves in a political position more equal to that of the party elders.

These young politicians became more vocal in criticizing the government and older LDP members. For example, LDP lower house member Tarō Kōno (age thirty-seven) openly criticized Secretary General Hiromu Nonaka for the LDP's "defeat" in the 2000 general election and called for his resignation from the party's number two position. "It would have been a politically suicidal action in old days," Kōno told the author.[2] Under the old electoral system, with multimember districts, such criticism was often stifled because the powerful factions could get rid of troublesome younger Diet members by supporting a rival candidate in the same district in the next election. The single-seat district system neatly eliminated this threat, as no LDP candidate was allowed to challenge an incumbent. As a direct result of the 1994 electoral reforms, empowered young LDP members from across the different factions, including Kōno, formed the Group to Build a Japan for Tomorrow and called for drastic reform of the LDP.

The power of younger Diet members to act independently of the factions helped Koizumi come to power in 2001. For the April 2001 LDP presidential race, the younger members demanded that the president be chosen not only by LDP diet members but also by local party members. At the March 2001

LDP meeting, Kōno presented a plan that allocated 346 votes to local, public elections by LDP members on top of the 346 votes from Diet members. This move came in response to the closed-door selection of Yoshirō Mori as prime minister by party leaders following Keizō Obuchi's sudden death, a move that generated widespread public and media disapproval. Although the LDP faction leaders did not want to allocate so many votes to nonelected LDP members, which would take the election out of their own control, they were forced to make the election more transparent and democratic. A compromise agreement increased the votes of each LDP prefectural chapter from 1 to 3, giving local LDP members a total of 141 votes, less than half the number of lawmakers' votes. But this still allowed more avenues for reform than before.

The largest LDP faction, with 101 LDP Diet members led by former prime minister Ryūtarō Hashimoto, looked on this electoral change optimistically. This faction, previously led by former prime ministers Kakuei Tanaka, Noboru Takeshita, and Obuchi, had played a decisive role in the selection of party leader for more than twenty years and boasted connections with local chapters. However, several younger members of the faction openly stated that they might vote against the faction's decision to support Hashimoto in the election. Younger members of the other LDP factions also called for voting rights independent of factional lines. They strongly requested an open forum to question the four LDP presidential candidates and held a two-day session with them before the election. Many of them went back to their district and expressed their personal support for Koizumi.

During the LDP presidential election campaign, Koizumi publicly vowed his determination to carry out structural reform of various aspects of the Japanese economy. In the end he earned a landslide victory, with 298 out of 487 votes, by capturing nearly 90 percent of the 141 local chapter votes. Hashimoto received only 155 votes, garnering support from his faction and the Horiuchi faction. Five younger members of the two factions voted for Koizumi, crossing factional lines. This underlined the weakening power of LDP factions.

Indeed, Koizumi was the first party president and prime minister to be selected outside of the traditional factional power struggles. He was elected by an overwhelming majority of LDP local branches, thus earning enough of a mandate to pick his own party leaders and cabinet without consulting faction leaders. As evidence of his independence from the old party chieftains, Koizumi's new cabinet had an unprecedented number of women (five), including Makiko Tanaka as foreign minister, and three civilians. In a press conference Koizumi boasted, "LDP members finally understand what 'appointments without factional intervention' is. They realized that I am serious."[3] Koizumi also stated that he would not conduct frequent cabinet reshuffles so as not to create an opportunity for factional influence. Polls taken by major newspapers immediately after the establishment of his first cabinet showed that Koizumi's initial support rate had skyrocketed to the highest in the history of collecting such data: 78 percent in the *Asahi Shimbun* poll, 85 percent in the *Mainichi Shimbun*, and 87 percent in the *Yomiuri Shimbun*. According to the *Asahi* poll, the biggest reason for people's support was that Koizumi had rejected factional influence.[4] He was standing on his own.

INSTITUTIONAL CHANGES TO STRENGTHEN THE KANTEI

When Koizumi became prime minister, the institutional changes brought about by Hashimoto's administrative reform were already set up.[5] The central government reform began in January 2001, reducing the number of central government agencies from twenty-three to thirteen by merging several ministries and agencies. The media paid much attention to the organizational change. More important changes enhanced the power of the prime minister and cabinet.[6]

The Cabinet Law was revised to improve the policy initiative of the prime minister. While the national leader's authority at a cabinet meeting was unclear under the old law, the revised article 4 clarified his authority to propose important, basic policies at such meetings. Technically under the old law it had been possible for the prime minister to propose a policy as a member of the cabinet. But cabinet members, including the prime minister, had rarely taken such initiative. As a result, the cabinet dealt with policy issues that had been discussed and preapproved at the vice-ministerial level. This practice had strengthened the bottom-up style of Japanese government decision making and weakened the political initiative of the prime minister. With the revision, institutional arrangements were clearly established for the national leader to initiate policies at the top.

The authority and function of the Cabinet Secretariat to support the Kantei were also reinforced. The revised Cabinet Law provided it with the authority to plan and draft important national policies. This was one of the major points that bureaucrats had strongly resisted during the deliberation of Hashimoto's Administrative Reform Council. The existing ministries did not want the Cabinet Secretariat to plan and draft bills that covered their own jurisdiction. The revised law allowed the Kantei to develop concrete plans under the direction of the cabinet and prime minister. Theoretically the prime minister and the cabinet could now initiate and proceed with policy processes independent of the relevant ministry.

Another significant move within the Cabinet Secretariat was the increase in the number and size of its supporting body. The prime minister was now allowed to appoint up to five assistants rather than just three. To assist the chief cabinet secretary (CCS) and his three deputies, three assistant CCSs were newly created as special career officers at the vice-minister level. At this career ranking the revised law also listed the cabinet public relations officer and the cabinet intelligence officer. In addition, the prime minister was also entitled to increase the number of secretaries even more with an executive order. This expanded body was expected to strengthen the functions of the Cabinet Secretariat as a supporting organ of the prime minister.

Pivotal to the operations of the Kantei are two high officials, the CCS and the administrative deputy. Former CCS Masaharu Gotōda summarized his job as "to mediate and settle disputes" between various government agencies participating in the policy-making process."[7] Policy coordination requires political skill, experience, and connections as well as knowledge of the content and an understanding of the implications of specific policies. The CCS must work with other members of the ruling party and the bureaucracy to coordinate policy. According to Gotōda, the task depends on "the power balance between the CCS and the relevant ministers of state. Thus it involves competition over their individual political power and character."[8]

As well as being a policy mediator, the CCS acts as spokesperson for the prime minister and his cabinet, holding official press conferences twice a day. Unofficial comments the CCS makes outside of these conferences are frequently quoted as statements by "the top official of the government (*seifu shunō*)." In a sense, the CCS position combines the duties of the U.S. vice president, the White House chief of staff, and the White House spokesperson. The CCS's role is probably much more influential than any of these, though, since the person holding the position is also directly involved in the decision-making process for most of the government's important policy decisions. The CCS must vet decisions even when not directly involved. It is no exaggeration to say that the CCS is much more involved in the policy-making process than the prime minister.

Until recently the CCS was relatively low in the hierarchy of cabinet ministers. The prime minister often appointed a close associate from his own faction to support his administrative goals. This situation changed in the 1990s when prime ministers began appointing political heavyweights to the post. Prime Minister Ryūtaro Hashimoto, for example, selected former LDP secretary general Seiroku Kajiyama in 1996. The Hashimoto administration analyzed the lessons from the 1995 Hanshin earthquake and examined scenarios in which a prime minister is unable to perform his duties. The Hashimoto cabinet decided to designate the CCS as acting prime minister in those cases. This decision, however, applied only in the event of natural disasters such as the Hanshin earthquake.

That limitation caused a major legal and political debate in April 2000 when Prime Minister Keizō Obuchi fell into a coma and CCS Mikio Aoki was appointed acting prime minister. The selection was supposed to be based on article 9 of the Cabinet Law, which stipulates that "if the prime minister is absent or has an accident, a state minister designated by him in advance shall assume the duties as prime minister as a tentative measure." However, since Obuchi had not given Aoki clear and explicit prior instructions, the latter's appointment sparked protests in the Diet.

To avoid such confusion in the future, since the first Mori cabinet was formed in April 2000 it has become customary for every new cabinet to make a list of five cabinet ministers in line for succession to the premiership.[9] The CCS has been always on top of the list and will continue to be so unless the position of the deputy prime minister is officially introduced. In principle, when the prime minister is out of Tokyo, the CCS is expected to stay in town. The fact that two former CCSs, Shinzō Abe and Yasuo Fukuda, became prime minister without any other cabinet experience symbolized the elevated status of the CCS. The CCS has in effect become a deputy prime minister in all but title.

As the status of the CCS rose, his deputies also began to play increasingly crucial roles. There are three deputy CCSs—one administrative and two parliamentary; the latter two are appointed from among Diet members. The administrative deputy CCS is often called the top post of Japan's entire bureaucracy. This individual serves as the liaison between the prime minister and the bureaucracy and frequently consults with the prime minister.

This post became pivotal during the lengthy tenures of two administrative deputy CCSs: Nobuo Ishihara, who held the job for seven years and three months (1987–95), and Teijirō Furukawa, who held it for eight years and seven months (1995–2003). Before Ishihara was selected, prime ministers had traditionally appointed someone new to the post when they took office. However, Ishihara and Furukawa combined to serve eleven prime ministers during their nearly sixteen years on the job. Their institutional memory proved invaluable to Japan's legion of short-lived prime ministers, especially those with limited cabinet experience. For example, Ishihara played a key role in the administration of Toshiki Kaifu, who was so unprepared to become the nation's leader that the media jokingly reported that the government was run by "Prime Minister Ishihara with assistance from Kaifu."[10]

The administrative deputy CCS plays a critical role as chair of the administrative vice-ministerial meeting. While the cabinet is the Japanese government's highest decision-making institution, actual decisions are rarely made in cabinet meetings, as described in chapter 1. The agenda for a cabinet meeting is prepared at the subcabinet meeting, usually held the day before, and the agenda goes to the cabinet meeting with a proposed decision. Although the subcabinet meeting has no legal authority or basis for its existence, the cabinet has seldom repealed decisions made at this meeting.

According to Deputy CCS Teijirō Furukawa, the subcabinet meeting served as the first stage of the top-down decision-making process under the Koizumi administration. Prime Minister Koizumi frequently instructed the Kantei on policy matters through CCS Yasuo Fukuda. Fukuda ordered Furukawa to take action, and the latter revealed the prime minister's intention to let the entire bureaucracy know about the policy directions. Furukawa then assigned officers in the policy unit to the task. The assigned officers consulted and coordinated with the related ministries and reported back to Furukawa (see fig. 3.1).

Another important task has become to screen the appointments of high officials (bureau chiefs and above) for all the ministries. As a result of Hashimoto's administrative reform, these appointments must be approved by the cabinet. The administrative deputy CCS checks the list of candidates on behalf of the cabinet prior to cabinet approval to ensure that the appointees will help promote the prime minister's policy goals. On several occasion in the past, the ministries' choices were rejected. But quite often the CCS is privy to early information from the ministries and removes some appointees from consideration. This gives the position de facto appointive power over high officials of all the ministries. This has changed the power balance between the Cabinet Secretariat and the ministries.

Further improving the supporting organ of the cabinet was the establishment of the Cabinet Office. This office is headed by the prime minister and administered by the chief cabinet secretary and the secretary's deputies. In addition, the prime minister can appoint cabinet ministers for special missions at the Cabinet Office. It is located in the cabinet and therefore ranks higher than other ministries. Its main task is to assist the cabinet and its

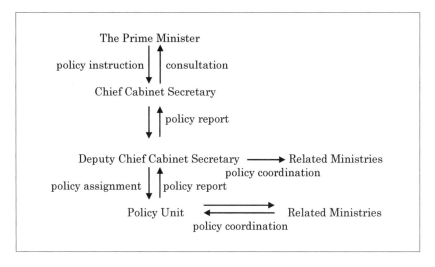

FIGURE 3.1. Conceptual Lines of Top-Down Decision Making
Source: Presented by Teijirō Furukawa, October 30, 2003.

secretariat in planning and drafting policy proposals and coordinating among other ministries.

Under the Cabinet Office Establishment Law, fiscal and budget policies were identified as an important national issue. The law also authorized the prime minister to form the Council on Economic and Fiscal Policy as an advisory organ independent of the bureaucracy. The council is supposed to advise the prime minister on macroeconomic and fiscal policy issues. The new Cabinet Office, which subsumed the functions of the old Economic Planning Agency over macroeconomic policy, provides administrative assistant to the council and the prime minister. Based on the recommendation of the council, the prime minister can initiate the budget process by proposing the total size of the budget and prioritizing major spending items. According to former deputy CCS Nobuo Ishihara, this change was designed to "shift the essential function of budget formation from the MOF to the Cabinet Secretariat."[11] Indeed, the change took place under the Koizumi government.

NEW FISCAL POLICY-MAKING PROCESS

The Council on Economic and Fiscal Policy was inaugurated in January 2001 with the major reorganization of the central government.[12] As defined by the Cabinet Office Establishment Law, it was officially chaired by the prime minister (article 21). The operational regulations of the CEFP give strong authority to the chairman. The council cannot reach any decision without the attendance of the chairman. The chairman is required to build a consensus among the members but can make a decision based on the discussion at the council.[13] Whether the prime minister can demonstrate strong leadership at the CEFP depends on how strong his determination is.

Besides the prime minister, there were ten other members of the Council— five other cabinet members, the governor of the Bank of Japan, as well as four experts from the private sector. In the beginning it was uncertain whether the new council would actually change the budget-making process. Six months ahead of the council's inauguration, Prime Minister Yoshirō Mori had established the Fiscal Leadership Council, with a membership of five cabinet members and nine executives of the coalition parties but excluding outside experts. It was MOF officials who persuaded Mori to form this council in order to block the CEFP's influence over the budget process. Former prime minister Hashimoto, who became the minister for administrative reform in January 2001, knew the MOF's intention and quickly moved to abolish the Leadership Council. As this event highlighted, Prime Minister Mori had no intention of taking advantage of the CEFP as a forum to demonstrate his leadership in budget formation.

During the four months of the Mori administration, the CEFP held seven meetings. Finance Minister Kiichi Miyazawa requested that council members bring up important issues at the meeting to lead discussion on the budget, but without any concrete figures.[14] Miyazawa obviously spoke on behalf of the MOF officials who did not want the council to come up with concrete proposals.

The situation surrounding the CEFP totally changed when Junichirō Koizumi took over the premiership. As Koizumi was selected outside of traditional factional power struggles, he had a mandate to form his own cabinet without consulting faction leaders. He appointed Heizō Takenaka, an economics professor at the Keiō University, as minister of economic and fiscal affairs at the Cabinet Office to take charge of the CEFP. Koizumi publicly promised that he would promote "reform without sanctuary" and received an unprecedented level of public support.

Backed by his high popularity, at the press conference after the first cabinet meeting Koizumi declared his determination to follow through with structural reform by stating, "I am resolved to make this cabinet 'a ceaseless reform cabinet' that would boldly undertake reforms in Japan's social and economic structures." To carry out reforms, he stated, "I am resolved to fully bear my responsibility as prime minister and head of the cabinet through direct leadership of forum such as the Council on Economic and Fiscal Policy, and to make thorough use of the strengthened functions of the cabinet resulting from the reform of central government implemented earlier this year."[15] Koizumi knew from the beginning the significance of the CEFP and other stronger institutions provided to the national leader by the Hashimoto reform, and he was prepared to take advantage of them.

In his first policy speech, on May 7, 2001, Koizumi publicly declared that his cabinet would conduct structural reform in the spirit of "no fear, no hesitation, and no constraint." As concrete reform plans, he presented three main schemes: (1) financial disposal of nonperforming loans within the coming two to three years; (2) creation of a competitive economic system that is appropriate for the environment of the twenty-first century; and (3) fiscal and structural reform. For the fiscal reform, the prime minister announced that the new government bond issues would be targeted at less than thirty trillion yen in the FY2002 budget.[16]

To achieve such reforms, he told members at the first CEFP meeting he attended:

> It is no exaggeration to say that the Council on Economic and Fiscal Policy is the most important council for providing more substance to the broad principles introduced in my policy speech. . . . Following the belief that "there will be no economic recovery without structural reform," the essential point is that we strive to carry out structural reform holding nothing sacred and to establish a society where people can move toward new goals with confidence and hope for the future development of Japan.[17]

Under the Mori administration, council members had repeatedly debated whether the government should choose to induce an economic recovery by continuing fiscal expansion or introducing structural reform. Koizumi's statement allowed the council to focus on structural reform. One of the private-sector experts responded to Koizumi's determination for reform by stating, "Today, I am so happy to be able to discuss essential matters."[18]

While the council was officially chaired by the prime minister, its proceedings were moderated by Economic Minister Takenaka. According to his memoirs, Takenaka had two important goals for the council. The first was to drastically change the framework of macroeconomic management. Throughout the 1990s the Japanese government had conducted a series of fiscal expansion policies, which resulted in an inflated government debt without significantly contributing to economic recovery. Takenaka wanted to reduce the public investment and to focus on disposal of nonperforming loans. The second goal was to present a scenario of structural reform with concrete figures in order to avoid a shock to the financial markets.[19] To improve the transparency of the council's proceedings, Takenaka told members that a summary of discussions would be posted on the Internet three days after each meeting.

At the first meeting Takenaka presented his idea of creating the Basic Policies, or *honebuto no hōshin*, to control fiscal policy formulation. He suggested making it the Koizumi administration's goal to limit deficit financing bonds to thirty trillion yen. Finance Minister Seijūrō Shiokawa supported Takenaka's proposal, reflecting the thinking of the austerity-minded MOF officials. He also suggested that the basic plan should include a bold plan to reallocate the budget by cutting wasteful expenditures and increasing spending for priority programs.[20]

To form the Basic Policies, Takenaka frequently met with the four private-sector experts of the council—Tadashi Okuda (chairman, Toyota Motors), Jirō Ushio (chairman, Ushio Electric), Masaaki Honma (professor, University of Osaka), and Hiroshi Yoshikawa (professor, University of Tokyo). The outline of the policies was presented at the second meeting, on May 31.

The council held two more meetings and finalized the Basic Policies at the fourth meeting, on June 21. In the introduction to the thirty-three-page document, the main items of Koizumi's reform were displayed—the privatization of postal services and special public corporations and the thirty-trillion-yen ceiling on debt-financing bonds. The first section identified the disposal of nonperforming loans within a few years as the highest-priority issue. The second section, which dealt with establishing a new social infrastructure, declared the intention to revise the traditional fiscal policy that focused on public investments, suggesting a substantial budget cut. The third and fourth sections offered the council's plan to tackle politically difficult issues, including the reform of the medical insurance and pension system, changing the boundaries of national and local taxes.

Before finalization of the policies at the council, CCS Yasuo Fukuda called for an informal discussion meeting of cabinet members on the Basic Policies on June 8. Each minister presented priority policy issues of their own ministry, which would be potential veto players within the government. Takenaka promised their opinions would be reflected in the final draft. This discussion meeting made it politically possible to acquire cabinet approval on June 28. The Basic Policies were approved by the cabinet without going through the administrative vice ministers' meeting, against the long tradition. This symbolized the political initiative of the new fiscal policy making.[21]

Throughout the process Takenaka and his staffers formulated policies without consultation with LDP policy subcommittees. It was Prime Minister Koizumi who had instructed them to ignore the traditional log-rolling process and not to contact zoku members of the relevant subcommittees, even if demanded. An explanation should be provided only to the chairman of the Policy Affairs Research Council, and it would be the chairman's responsibility to persuade fellow LDP members.[22]

LDP zoku members, who had served as powerful intraparty veto players before the Koizumi government, strongly criticized this process. For example, former Deputy CCS Muneo Suzuki stated, "The council does not understand the parliamentary system."[23] According to many LDP members, including Suzuki, prior consultation with the ruling party members was essential for policy making under the parliamentary system. But LDP zoku members did not choose to challenge the popular prime minister on this issue in the face of the forthcoming July 29 upper house election.

In that election, Koizumi's high popularity brought a victory for the LDP, with 64 out of 121 reelected seats. With the seats won by the LDP's coalition partners, the Kōmeitō and the Conservative Party, the government coalition gained a stable majority of 140 of the 247 upper house seats. At a press conference after the election, Prime Minister Koizumi reconfirmed his determination on economic reform and declared that his administration would introduce a detailed, three-step reform schedule: the first schedule by the end of August; the second during the fall Diet session; and the third during the year-end budget forming process.

On August 3 the first CEFP meeting after the election was convened, and the MOF budget bureau chief reported that to achieve Koizumi's thirty-trillion-yen limit on debt-financing bonds, the government needed to reduce spending by three trillion yen. One of the private-sector members, Chairman Okuda of Toyota, stressed that the first CEFP budget overview should show a clear difference from the past fiscal policy-making style so that the public would know the significance of the policy changes. Another member, Prof. Yoshikawa, then suggested increasing the priority policy areas by two trillion yen while cutting five trillion in nonpriority areas of expenditures to reach the goal of a three-trillion-yen reduction. Finance Minister Shiokawa, who had stated the need for drastic reallocation of the budget at the previous meeting, expressed his support for this suggestion. Then Prime Minister Koizumi stated, "This is right after the election [victory]. Let's go for the idea of a five-trillion-yen cut with a two-trillion-yen increase. . . . Otherwise, the people would not have a strong impression of change. . . . We need to 'strike while the iron is hot.' There certainly will be opposition from [the LDP]. But we had better show our determination that the CEFP will make the decision."[24] This became the decision of the council.

On the following morning, senior MOF officials visited the prime minister's office and expressed their concern about making a budget proposal with a drastic budget cut of five trillion yen without any consultation with the LDP. Koizumi did not yield, however, and instructed MOF officials to draw up a detailed proposal that followed the CEFP decision. Koizumi's assistant Isao Iijima declared that "this was a historic moment when the budget formation initiative shifted from the MOF to the Kantei."[25] On August 10 the Koizumi cabinet officially approved the budget overview with a two-trillion-yen increase in the seven prioritized policy areas and a 10 percent cut in virtually all other areas of spending, including public works investment and official development aid.[26]

After the cabinet approved the budget overview, Koizumi instructed cabinet ministers to come up with their own reform initiatives in their respective ministries to meet the overall goal of his reform. The ministers attended the CEFP meetings to present their reform plans. Koizumi's assistant later testified, "One minister stated that this is 'the evaluation' of each minister by the prime minister. Ministers are judged by their reform plans to see how much power they have over the bureaucracy and the vested interest groups. He was exactly right."[27] As the ministers were required to show their commitment to Koizumi's reform, they had to cooperate with the budget cuts in their ministries' spending programs.

Between August and November 2001, MOF officials had to negotiate with spending ministries and LDP subcommittees to draft the basic principles of budget formulation for the CEFP. The basic principles were presented at the November 27 CEFP meeting and approved by the CEFP and the cabinet on December 4. As a result, in the FY2002 budget new bond issuance was kept under thirty trillion yen, expenditures in nonpriority areas were reduced by five trillion yen, while two trillion yen was reallocated in the priority areas. Among the key areas of reduction, public works, which often became the pork barrel for LDP politicians, were reduced by 10.7 percent. Fiscal expenditures for public corporations were cut by 21.1 percent, with a reduction amounting to more than one trillion yen. This became strong fiscal pressure for the forth-coming privatization of many special public corporations, including the four highway-related public corporations and the postal service. On December 24 the cabinet approved the FY2002 budget to implement Koizumi's structural reform.

After the budget was officially approved, the CEFP began to work on me-dium-term economic and fiscal management. This was a very important task to connect medium-term macroeconomic conditions and fiscal policy. Eco-nomic Minister Takenaka pointed out the problem of the old decision-making system: "Fiscal policies were considered by the MOF, and macroeconomic policies were dealt with by the Economic Planning Agency. But there was nobody to check the relations between fiscal policy and macroeconomic pol-icy."[28] Takenaka analyzed the reason why the government had not established such a function much earlier and explained that two opposing powers existed: MOF bureaucrats, who did not want to be responsible for achieving fiscal goals, and LDP politicians, who wanted to play an instrumental role in final-izing fiscal policies. Medium-term perspectives by the CEFP would include concrete fiscal policies and targets for the forthcoming years; neither MOF officials nor LDP politicians wanted the council to establish these policies.[29]

Takenaka persuaded CEFP members to compile a report titled "Structural Reform and the Medium-Term Economic and Fiscal Perspectives" (hereafter, "Reform and Perspectives"). In the report he intended to "show desirable eco-nomic and social conditions, and the medium-term policy framework focusing on structural reforms for that end."[30] When Takenaka presented the idea of preparing a report at the LDP General Council on December 18, he heard many strong opinions against the plan. But the report was approved by the General Council on January 18, 2002. As a result, a new system was estab-lished to coordinate macroeconomic conditions and fiscal policies.

After the first year under the Koizumi administration, a new, nine-step schedule for fiscal policy making was established:

1. By the end of January, the CEFP would produce "Reform and Perspec-tive" to present the medium-term macroeconomic outlook and policy goals.
2. At the end of June, the CEFP would formulate the Basic Policies, which described major fiscal policies for the next fiscal year.
3. In July the Cabinet Office would provide the updated economic out-look and forecast for the detailed budget formulation.

4. At the end of July or in early August, based on this forecast, the CEFP would produce the Budget Overview to clarify budget allocation to priority areas and budget cuts in nonpriority areas.

5. By the end of August, initial budget proposals were to be submitted by spending ministries.

6. Negotiations and coordination between the MOF and spending ministries as well as LDP politicians would take place between September and November.

7. By the end of November or early December, the CEFP would announce the Basic Principles for Budget Formulation to present the basic principles of the budget in advance of the actual budget proposal.

8. By the end of December, the MOF would finalize the budget proposal for the next fiscal year for cabinet approval.

9. Finally, in late December or early January, the Cabinet Office would provide an economic outlook for the next fiscal year based on the basic stance on economic and fiscal management (see table 3.1).

As a result of fiscal policy reform initiated by the CEFP, the annual budget balance was significantly improved. The deficit in the primary balance (the budget balance excluding interest payment and debt redemption from expen-

TABLE 3.1 Changes in the fiscal policy schedule

	BEFORE 2001	SINCE 2001
End of January		"Reform and Perspectives" by CEFP
End of June		Basic Policies decided by CEFP
July–August	Budget ceiling by MOF	Budget Overview by CEFP
End of August	Budget proposal by ministries	Budget proposal by ministries
September–December	Examination and negotiation period	Examination and negotiation period
November–December		Basic Principles for Budget Formulation by CEFP
Late December	MOF proposal and Cabinet decision	MOF proposal and Cabinet decision

ditures and bond revenues from the revenue side) of the central and local government combined reached a high level at 5.7 percent of nominal GDP in FY2002. In FY2005 it was reduced to 3.3 percent. The expenditures of the central and local government decreased from 23.2 percent of GDP in FY2002 to 21.6 percent in FY2004.[31] The bond dependency ratio (bond revenue to the total revenue) of the central government significantly decreased from 44.6 percent in FY2003 to 30.7 percent in FY2007.[32]

The budget allocation had been inflexible because of sectionalism among the ministries and their bureaus. For example, the public works budget allocation was almost unchanged among the major categories for at least a couple of decades. The CEFP's scheme to prioritize the budget totally changed this situation. Between FY2001 and FY2006, expenditures for public works were reduced by 22.6 percent. Two other major budget categories that experienced significant cuts were Official Development Assistance (25.1 percent) and energy-related projects (23.3 percent). On the other hand, expenditures in the priority areas, such as social security (28.5 percent) and science and technology promotion (19.7 percent), were increased during the same period.

The CEFP's approach—tackling economic structural reform through setting budget outlines—worked well and created successful results in many areas. The reallocation of the budget brought significant advances in streamlining the public sector. It forced reforms and privatization of the special public corporations, government financial institutions, and, most important, the postal service. The council also successfully injected government funds into major banks to settle nonperforming loan problems. It raised the burden of patients for medical expenditures in order to relieve the deficit situation in social security. Furthermore, the council played an important role in bringing about tax reform to shift revenue sources from the central government to local governments.

The CEFP became a forum at which the prime minister, the economic minister, and private-sector members presented their reform agenda under the Koizumi cabinet. The economic minister and the private sector led the discussion to form the Basic Policies. This policy report became a "public roadmap for reform to the people."[33] In the spring of 2002, spending ministries and industry representatives began to lobby CEFP members so that their projects would be included in the Basic Policies. Deputy CCS Teijirō Furukawa told the author, "It was at this time that I realized the budget-making power had truly shifted from MOF into the hands of the Kantei."[34]

By forming the Basic Policies, the council not only built a broad framework and budgeting priorities for the next fiscal year budget but also created momentum for major structural reform, such as the disposal of nonperforming loans and the privatization of special public corporations. As the ministers of the economic ministries had to respond to the council's reform requests, all decision-making processes were open to the public. Council deliberations were available on the website soon after the meeting, improving the transparency of policy making. The new institutional arrangement surrounding the CEFP became a tool for Prime Minister Koizumi and his economic advisers to set their domestic policy agenda and fiscal policy to pursue their goals despite opposition from career bureaucrats and their patron LDP zoku members. The MOF, which used to monopolize the traditional cumulative budget process, had to formulate budgets following the instructions given by the CEFP under the Koizumi government.

Cutting Road Construction

Another wave of administrative reform was going on in parallel to fiscal policy reform. The Headquarters for Administrative Reform had been established under the Mori administration. Prime Minister Mori appointed former prime minister Hashimoto as the first cabinet minister for administrative reform to deal with three major areas of reform: (1) special public corporations, (2) the civil service system, and (3) administration-commissioned public service corporations. Hashimoto, who had led major reform efforts as prime minister, was well aware that the reform of special public corporations and public service corporations would require fundamental structural changes within Japan's political and economic system as institutional complementarities had formed over many years. During his tenure as cabinet minister, Hashimoto focused much of his efforts on the civil service system reform.[35]

A major policy shift in the headquarters took place when Koizumi became prime minister in April 2001. Koizumi had promoted reform of special public corporations and privatization of postal services throughout his political career. He appointed Nobuteru Ishihara as minister for administrative reform and instructed him to focus on reform of the special public corporations. The headquarters secretariat swiftly drafted reform legislation to establish the Special Public Institutions Reform Promotion Headquarters to make decisions on each public corporation by March 2006: whether they would be abolished, privatized, or allowed to continue after the review process. The bill was approved by the cabinet and submitted to the Diet. After a short deliberation, it was enacted on June 20, 2001.

The political battles began after the law was passed as the newly established headquarters now had to review and decide on the future status of each corporation. The seventy-seven special public corporations were originally established to efficiently rebuild Japan's infrastructure after World War II. They played instrumental roles in helping Japan's economic growth by overseeing state loans and construction projects. Over the years, however, inefficiency within such quasi-governmental corporations had developed, costing Japanese taxpayers 5.3 trillion yen a year. These funds were allocated to sixty-six special public corporations through subsidies or government endowments. With mounting fiscal pressure, the media and the public called for drastic reform of the special public corporations.

In August 2001 Prime Minister Koizumi publicly expressed his firm decision to cut a trillion yen out of the 5.3 trillion yen allocated to special corporations in the FY 2002 budget. This statement resulted in the December 2002 cabinet decision to reform special public corporations, including the abolition or privatization of the four highway-related public corporations, the Urban Development Corporation, the Japan National Oil Corporation, and the Government Housing Loan Corporation.

Among the most heavily criticized by the media were the four highway-related public corporations, especially the Japan Highway Public Corporation. This organization accumulated a total debt of 24 trillion yen as of 1999 by building 7,000 kilometers of highways all over the nation. If it tried to complete the original government plan to build an additional 2,342 kilometers of highways, it would have required 300 billion yen of government funds annually, and its debt would have swelled to 44 trillion yen. To formulate a privatization policy regarding the controversial organizations, the Koizumi cabinet formed the Promotion Committee for the Privatization of the Four Highway-Related Public Corporations directly under the cabinet in June 2002. In the committee deliberations there was a series of heated debates on whether to freeze the plans for the remaining 2,342 kilometers of highway.

As road construction was highly integrated with local politics, this attracted much media and public attention. In December 2003, based on the recommendation of the Promotion Committee, the Ministry of Land, Infrastructure, and Transport announced the final plan to privatize the public corporation. Although the plan did not include the freezing of construction on the remaining highway that the Promotion Committee had strongly recommended, it would substantially cut construction costs by scaling down the original scheme. Throughout 2003 the cabinet committee led the debate on privatization and pressured the vested interest groups, highlighting the cabinet initiative in the highly political issue of road construction.

As seen in the case of the reform of special corporations under the Koizumi administration, the Kantei often led politically difficult policy issues. The secretariat initiated the drafting of three pieces of domestic policy legislation—the Urban Renaissance Special Measures Law, the Basic Law on Intellectual Property, and the Law on Special Zones for Structural Reform—and established ad hoc policy offices to deal with these issues. The Office of Urban Renaissance planned drastic measures to advance urban redevelopment for future environmental needs, disaster prevention, and internationalization that would require deregulation in many policy areas. The Office of Intellectual Property Strategy Promotion planned measures for the creation, protection, and exploitation of intellectual property by clarifying the responsibilities of the state, local governments, universities, and business enterprises. The Office of Special Zones for Structural Reform promoted the creation of specified deregulation zones based on voluntary plans by municipal governments and private-sector enterprises. In each area the plans were advanced by initiative of the Cabinet Secretariat. Former deputy CCS Furukawa proudly told the author, "These plans required intensive policy coordination among several ministries. If it had not been handled by the Kantei, the policy advancement would not have moved in such a swift manner."[36]

BATTLES OVER POSTAL REFORM

Among Koizumi's reform efforts, the most politically dramatic event was his postal reform. This was a longtime political goal for Koizumi for more than twenty years and attracted significant media attention involving the 2005 general election. As mentioned in the previous chapter, the post offices formed a solid support base for many LDP Diet members. Prime Minister Hashimoto, during his administrative reform efforts, met with strong opposition from LDP postal zoku members and finally gave up the privatization of postal services.

Koizumi had long regarded the privatization of the postal services as the core of Japan's reform. When he was vice minister of finance in the late 1970s, he was concerned about the increasing fiscal deficit, which was in large part financed by the fiscal investment and loan program with revenues from postal savings. In addition, the huge share of postal savings, which accounted for about one-third of the total household savings, distorted Japan's financial market.[37] When Koizumi became the minister of post and telecommunications in 1992, he talked about the future privatization of the postal services. Many LDP postal zoku members strongly criticized Koizumi for his plan.[38]

Koizumi again had his chance during the campaign for the April 2001 LDP presidential election, in which he publicly promised that he would promote "reform without sanctuary" and privatization of the postal services. When Koizumi formed a coalition government, he secured an agreement from the Kōmeitō and the Conservative Party to promote postal reform, including its privatization.

The first political hurdle was to pass the legislation that would shift the provision of postal services from the Postal Service Agency for five years to a new government-run corporation, the Japan Post, as decided by Hashimoto's administrative efforts. In April 2002 many LDP members who opposed the reform publicly criticized Koizumi's legislative initiative as a step toward privatization and were prepared to block it. Koizumi publicly announced that he would pick a fight to see "whether the LDP crashes the Koizumi cabinet or the Koizumi cabinet crashes the LDP."[39] The highest policy-making organ within the LDP, the General Council, wanted to avoid a fierce political confrontation and came up with an unusual compromise. The council approved the cabinet's action to submit the legislation without approving the content of the bill. Without full approval from the LDP, the Koizumi cabinet managed to pass the legislation in July 2002.

After Koizumi was reelected as LDP president in September 2003, he decided to initiate a postal reform policy in the Kantei and take advantage of the CEFP to promote the reform. At the September 26 CEFP meeting, he proudly declared that the privatization of postal services was finally an official cabinet agenda, and he asked the council to draft the reform plan.[40] Heizō Takenaka, minister in charge of the CEFP, fully supported Koizumi's privatization plan and came up with the basic principles for privatization on October 3.[41] As a result, the postal privatization plan was included in the LDP's manifesto, or policy platform, for the November 2003 lower house election.

The media portrayed the election as "the manifesto election." The old Public Election Office Law had prohibited political parties from handing out policy pamphlets. The 2003 revision of the law finally changed this. Virtually all the political parties prepared their own manifestos. All the LDP candidates ran election campaigns with the policy platform in their hands, which supported the government's postal privatization plan. Koizumi saw the ruling coalition's victory, with 271 out of 480 lower house seats (LDP 237; Kōmeitō 34), as a popular mandate to proceed with the postal privatization.

While discussion continued at the CEFP, Koizumi established the secretariat to prepare the postal privatization in order to support Takenaka. But Takenaka found that the secretariat was just pretending to cooperate, only to sabotage his efforts. It was staffed with seconded officials from the Ministry of Internal Affairs and Communications and the Japan Post, as well as other ministry officials who were against the postal reform. These officials leaked information to their home organizations to block Takenaka's initiative.[42] Takenaka thus began forming policies totally independent of the secretariat.[43]

Between February and October 2004, the CEFP held eighteen meetings to discuss the privatization of postal services. Most of discussion focused on the three bottom lines that Takenaka proposed: (1) establishment of separate corporations for each postal service (postal service, postal saving, and postal insurance); (2) application of commercial laws to the new postal corporations; and (3) establishment of an oversight organization. Takenaka met with then-minister of internal affairs and communications Tarō Asō and Japan Post president Masaharu Ikuta to ask for their support. Asō and Ikuta, however, expressed strong concern on these points, especially the separation of postal services.

Takenaka patiently persuaded Asō and Ikuta. After the August 6 CEFP meeting, Takenaka and Asō jointly announced the outline of postal reform, which included a plan to form a holding company and separate corporations for four types of services (window services, postal services, postal savings, and postal insurance).[44] The media pointed out that the holding company might tightly control all four service corporations and make the separation obsolete.[45]

At the August 6 CEFP meeting, the outline was formally approved, and Prime Minister Koizumi declared that "the summer battle now begins." The Koizumi government needed to get approval from the ruling parties. The LDP formed a special committee on postal services. At the September 2 committee meeting, overwhelming opposition was expressed toward the CEFP privatization plan. On September 6 the secretaries general and the Policy Committee chairmen of the LDP and Kōmeitō held a meeting, but no agreement was reached owing to the opposition of these veto players. What Takenaka saw there was "the strongest political power of the postal service."[46]

On September 7 Koizumi personally met with President Ikuta of Japan Post and persuaded him to accept the CEFP plan to form a holding company and four separate service corporations by April 2007. This was a final step in decision making within the government. The government then held a meeting with representatives from the LDP on September 8, but these representatives did not accept the CEFP plan. Koizumi expressed his determination to make a cabinet decision without approval from the LDP. The following day the LDP representatives decided not to accept the plan but abstained from making a party decision on it, thus allowing the Koizumi cabinet to officially approve the plan.[47] On September 10 the outline of the postal privatization was finally approved as a cabinet decision without party approval.

On September 27 Koizumi reshuffled his cabinet and appointed Takenaka as minister in charge of postal reform to give him authority to coordinate reform policy with different ministries. He also named Tsutomu Takebe, a strong supporter of the reform plan later nicknamed "Koizumi's Greatest Yes Man," to the powerful position of LDP secretary general. On October 5 the Koizumi government held a meeting with all the cabinet ministers and approved three guidelines for postal privatization: (1) accurately follow the outline, (2) create simple and consistent institutions, and (3) keep the process transparent. On October 15 the LDP held a joint committee to combine three policy subcommittees—on post and communications, land and transport, and finance.[48] This joint committee was headed by Hiroyuki Sonoda. Takenaka perceived that only 10 percent of LDP Diet members actively supported the privatization plan, while the rest split into nearly two equal groups: one with strong opposition, and the other with a wait-and-see attitude.[49]

President Ikuta of Japan Post came back with opposition to the government plan. He argued that the April 2007 deadline could not be met because of the difficulty in constructing a computer system, which would take at least three to five years. Takenaka sent his assistant, Yōichi Takahashi, to Japan Post for discussions with its system engineers. After many meetings about system designing, Takahashi convinced its eighty engineers that a new computer system could be built within eighteen months.[50] Ikuta then had to accept the privatization scheme.

On January 21, 2005, Prime Minister Koizumi made a policy speech in which he publicly announced the privatization, with a holding company and four service corporations. LDP PARC chairman Kaoru Yosano requested Koizumi to cut the details of the privatization plan in the speech, but Koizumi flatly refused.[51]

On January 26 the government and the LDP held the first joint meeting on postal reform. Additional joint meetings were held twelve times over the next three months, in which the LDP consistently demanded changes to the

CEFP plan. Koizumi found two high officials at the Ministry of Internal Affairs and Communications circulating documents against the privatization to LDP members. He summoned them to his office, where they told him that they would follow his instruction to advance the reform plans, but they continued their antireform activities. Minister Asō finally removed them from the policy-related posts.[52] After removing the antireform elements within the government, the Koizumi cabinet finally came up with a government draft for postal reform legislation on April 3.

Now it was the LDP's turn to respond to the government proposal. On April 19, after a heated debate, LDP joint committee chairman Sonoda suggested delegating the decision to top executives of the LDP and received approval, though against strong opposition. The issue was then sent to the LDP's highest decision-making organ, the General Council, which traditionally made decisions on a unanimous basis. On April 27 Chairman Akio Kyūma, against the LDP tradition of forming unanimous consent, took votes to approve the postal privatization bills, thus keeping the antireformists in the LDP from exercising their veto power.

The Koizumi cabinet submitted the privatization bills to the Diet on the same day. The DPJ and the Socialist Party, which had solid ties with the postal labor union, expressed strong opposition to the privatization and boycotted Diet operations. On May 20 the ruling parties voted to establish a special committee in the lower house without the presence of the two parties. Koizumi was not shaken. The prime minister stated, "They will come back. Boycotting will not receive public support."[53] He was right: on June 1 the Diet deliberations began, with the DPJ and the Socialists in attendance. In addition to these opposition parties, the antireform members within the LDP criticized the government proposal. The heated debates continued in the special committee for over a hundred hours.

On June 28 the LDP General Council decided on a minor revision to the bill and confirmed that party discipline required all LDP members to vote for the bill. But even so, Koizumi expected resistance from a couple dozen LDP lower house members. In the July 5 lower house floor voting, the bill passed with a slight margin of 233 to 228 votes. Contradicting party discipline, 37 LDP members voted against the bill, including four subcabinet members. Koizumi immediately held a cabinet meeting to remove these four officials.

The bill was then submitted to the upper house. In an interview Koizumi implied that he was determined to dissolve the lower house if the bill did not pass the upper house. A rebellion of eighteen or more LDP members could kill the bill. Postmasters from all over the nation gathered in Tokyo to lobby LDP upper house members to oppose the privatization. Several LDP upper house members publicly declared that they would vote against the bill. Two major newspapers, the *Asahi Shimbun* and *Nihon Keizai Shimbun*, ran supportive editorials urging the enactment of the privatization plan.[54] In the August 8 upper house floor voting, twenty-two LDP members voted against it and eight abstained, effectively killing the bill.

An hour after the voting, Koizumi quickly held an executive meeting at LDP headquarters. He stated, "I will dissolve the lower house. Those who rebelled will not receive party endorsement. [The LDP] will send candidates to all the districts. . . . I will destroy the old LDP and create a new LDP."[55] Then Koizumi held a cabinet meeting to collect the signatures of cabinet members to call for a general election. Several cabinet members expressed opposition, but Koizumi persuaded all except one to sign. When Agriculture Minister Yoshinobu Shimamura refused to sign, Koizumi without hesitation invoked a rarely used constitutional authority of the prime minister to dismiss him as a cabinet member. That evening the lower house was dissolved.

Soon after the dissolution, Koizumi held a press conference. He told voters:

> About 400 years ago Galileo Galilei was convicted [for heresy by the Spanish Inquisition] for his theory that the Earth revolved around the sun. He replied, "Still, the Earth is moving." The Diet rejected the postal privatization. But I would like to ask the people whether the postal services must be operated by public servants. . . . If the LDP and the Kōmeitō do not get a majority of seats after the people's judgment [on this issue in this election], I will resign.[56]

Koizumi denied party endorsement of the thirty-seven rebels and chose high-profile competing candidates who were labeled by the media as "assassins" to run in their districts. He appealed to voters to give him a mandate to press ahead with the postal reform. Some political experts saw the election as disadvantageous to the LDP as pro-LDP votes would be split between former and new LDP candidates.[57] DPJ leader Katsuya Okada saw a chance to take over the government: "It has been seven years since the DPJ's inception. We have been working hard for today, and we can take over the government."[58] But the media coverage focused on the battles between the rebels and the assassins and paid little attention to DPJ candidates. The Koizumi cabinet's approval rating surged from 41 percent before the dissolution to 46 percent immediately after the dissolution, and a week later it further rose to 51 percent.[59]

In the September 11 general election, Koizumi won an overwhelming majority of seats, with 296 LDP seats and 31 Kōmeitō seats in the 480-seat lower house. Only 17 of the 37 rebels retained seats. Koizumi told reporters, when asked about the winning factor, "It was that we made the postal services an election issue. In the Diet, the privatization was regarded as a wild plan, but the public saw it as a sound plan. The people in the anti-Koizumi camp always make mistakes."[60] With this election victory, the Koizumi cabinet finally enacted the legislation on October 14. Koizumi's strong determination and willingness to take political risks finally realized the politically difficult postal privatization.

National Security Policy Making Under Koizumi

In addition to fiscal policy and postal reform, Prime Minister Koizumi had many major achievements in the area of foreign and national security policy.[61] After the 9-11 incident his cabinet smoothly prepared antiterrorism legislation to dispatch Japan's Self-Defense Forces overseas under wartime conditions for the first time in the country's postwar history.

This successfully removed Japan's passive image created during the 1991 Gulf War, over which Japan was heavily criticized by the international community as offering only "checkbook diplomacy." Subsequently the Koizumi cabinet enacted emergency legislation to provide a legal framework for the SDF to defend Japan, as well as legislation to send SDF ground troops for the reconstruction of Iraq. In addition, in September 2002 the prime minister visited Pyongyang to receive Kim Chong Il's apology for the abduction of Japanese nationals by North Korea and arranged for the return of five abductees and their families. The Koizumi government also submitted a UN Security Council resolution for the first time, which was successfully passed, to condemn North Korea's missile test in July 2006. Throughout his term, Koizumi had strong control over policy making related to foreign policy issues.

In the area of national security, the Cabinet Secretariat initiated three major pieces of successful legislation. The first was the antiterrorism legislation. After the 9-11 incident, Deputy CCS Teijirō Furukawa quickly organized a task force in the Cabinet Secretariat to design the Japanese government's response. The task force was formed under the leadership of the assistant CCS from the

Japan Defense Agency (JDA). Ministry of Foreign Affairs officials had earlier dominated foreign policy making but now found themselves forced to play subordinate roles on the task force. The new institutional arrangement of the Cabinet Secretariat avoided interagency conflicts between the JDA and the MOFA, which could have acted as troublesome veto players, and enabled smooth operations in the task force. As a result, on September 19 Koizumi was able to announce his plan to actively support American reprisals for terrorist attacks in a timely manner.

The plan included the dispatch of SDF vessels to help the United States in collecting intelligence, shipping supplies, and providing medical services as well as humanitarian relief. Koizumi also pledged to strengthen protective measures for U.S. bases in Japan. In addition, he announced nonmilitary measures that included the provision of ten million dollars to help fund rescue and cleanup work after the attacks in the United States, a plan to provide emergency economic aid to Pakistan and India to help solicit their cooperation, and economic measures to avoid confusion in the international economic system. In developing the plan, task force members carefully examined lessons from the 1991 Persian Gulf War and recognized that financial contributions alone would not be highly appreciated by the international community. On September 25 Koizumi visited the United States to meet President George W. Bush and pledged to implement his plan as quickly as possible. Koizumi's plan elicited much praise from U.S. policy makers as it was more than many experts in Japan and the United States had expected and was presented in a timely manner. The White House even provided a press release to show their appreciation.[62]

Koizumi was keenly aware of the importance of timeliness in Japan's response to the campaign against terrorism. A normal political process might delay the implementation and again invite international criticism. As previously described, government policies were usually vetted first with the relevant policy subcommittee of the LDP's Policy Research Affairs Council. After approval at the subcommittees, policies moved to the LDP's General Council to build a party consensus and then became the party's official policy. Under the coalition government, policies further required agreement with LDP's coalition partners the Kōmeitō and the Conservative Party before cabinet approval.

In the case of the antiterrorism legislation, however, Deputy CCS Furukawa came up with a novel idea to save time by reversing this political procedure.[63] The Koizumi cabinet acquired agreement from the coalition partners before consulting the LDP's policy committees. Once the three parties reached an agreement, it would be difficult for individual LDP members to act as veto players to oppose the decision.

The Koizumi government needed to win passage of two pieces of legislation in order to move ahead with the antiterrorism plan. One bill would revise the Self-Defense Force Law to authorize SDF action to defend U.S. bases in Japan against unexpected terrorist attacks. The existing law authorized SDF action only when a situation was already in progress and could not be handled by the police. A second law would authorize rear-echelon support for U.S. forces in the Indian Ocean area, including provision of supplies and medical services, transportation of personnel, search and rescue activities, and humanitarian assistance to displaced persons. The 1999 Regional Crisis Law limited the area of such support to Japan's territory or the sea and airspace surrounding it. The new law would allow support in foreign territory with permission from the relevant foreign government.[64] More concretely, it would expand legitimate activity areas to territories and seas between the Indian Ocean and Japan.

On September 25 the three coalition parties agreed on the outline of the new law. The following day the government explained the legislation to representatives of the opposition parties. Just one day later the outline was finally reported to LDP members at the party's General Council. The members of LDP policy subcommittees, who had traditionally served as important veto players, were the last group to learn officially about the new legislation, at a September 28 joint meeting of the cabinet, defense, and foreign affairs subcommittees.

During this whole policy process, the task force in the Cabinet Secretariat played a central role. Meanwhile, the MOFA was suffering from a power struggle between its officials and Foreign Minister Makiko Tanaka. The Koizumi administration also questioned the competence of Tanaka to handle Diet deliberations without making mistakes. As a result, the Cabinet Secretariat took charge of the legislation, as allowed under the new Cabinet Law. CCS Yasuo Fukuda answered questions in the Diet, symbolizing the secretariat's leadership of the legislation.[65] The antiterrorism legislation passed in the Diet after just three weeks of deliberations. It was a smooth passage for such major, history-making legislation.

Based on the legislation, SDF vessels were dispatched to the Indian Ocean to provide refueling activities to vessels of the multinational forces. The SDF activities continued until 2009 and were highly appreciated by the international community, as Japan showed its willingness to contribute to international security beyond its checkbook diplomacy in the first Gulf War.

After the legislation was passed, Prime Minister Koizumi tried to take advantage of the momentum created to also pass the contingency legislation, which would provide a framework for dealing with an emergency in case of a military attack on Japan. The proposed bills clarified the government's decision-making process, strengthened the authority of the prime minister, facilitated action by the Self-Defense Forces, and allowed for limitations on personal rights in times of national emergency. This was the first attempt since the end of World War II for Japan's cabinet to pass new bills governing the nation's response to a military attack.

The Koizumi government followed the same strategy to enact legislation that would provide a permanent legal framework for allowing the SDF to use force in the event of an armed attack against Japan. Basically the same task force within the Cabinet Secretariat restarted its original task of drafting the contingency bills. Although the bills were suspended during the Diet sessions in 2002, in May 2003 during the ordinary session they passed the lower house after an agreement was reached between the ruling coalition and the Democratic Party. A combined 90 percent of the members who attended voted for one of the most controversial pieces of legislation in Japan's postwar history.

The same strategy was also adopted for the Iraq Special Measures Law (Law Concerning the Special Measures on the Humanitarian and Reconstruction Assistance Activities in Iraq). The task force in the Cabinet Secretariat drafted the new laws that would enable the dispatch of the Self-Defense Forces to Iraq for active contribution to humanitarian and reconstruction activities there. The legislation passed the Diet in July 2003, and the Japanese government dispatched the Self-Defense Forces to Iraq in February 2004.

Koizumi and North Korea

Another foreign policy development by Prime Minister Koizumi was his visit to Pyongyang in September 2002. In January of that year, the North Korean attitude toward Japan drastically changed. The State of the Union address by President George W. Bush identified North Korea as part of "the axis of evil." In the same speech Bush condemned Pyongyang by saying, "Some of these regimes have been pretty quiet since September the 11th. But we know their true nature. North Korea is a regime arming with missiles and weapons of mass destruction, while starving its citizens."[66] After taking the Bush administration expressed its strong stance against Pyongyang, the Kim Chong Il regime approached the Japanese government seeking normalization of relations with

Japan, which would make it difficult for the United States to attack North Korea. The normalization would be accompanied by economic aid to Pyongyang. The MOFA's Asian and Oceanian Affairs Bureau chief, Hitoshi Tanaka, saw a good opportunity. He stated, "As America took a hard policy toward North Korea, it looked toward at us. It was an opportunity for us."[67]

After contacting the North Korean negotiator, Tanaka consulted with Deputy CCS Furukawa. Furukawa encouraged him by saying it was a "great moral cause" to solve the abduction issue, normalize diplomatic relations, and contribute to peace in the peninsula.[68] Then Tanaka asked Prime Minister Koizumi if he would be willing to visit Pyongyang. Koizumi's answer was, "Let's make peace in the Korean Peninsula. In order to do so, we need to normalize Japan–North Korea relations by comprehensively solving the nuclear and abduction issues." Tanaka testified that Koizumi's belief in this never changed throughout his tenure.[69]

The minimum necessary condition set by the Japanese government was that North Korea provide information about Japanese abductees and make apology. But the Kim regime did not provide such information before the prime minister's visit to Pyongyang. As the bilateral negotiations hit a deadlock, Prime Minister Koizumi made a political decision, saying, "I am going to North Korea in order to make grand-scale peace. Even without receiving the information prior to the visit, I will go."[70]

Based on the prime minister's determination, Tanaka continued to negotiate with his North Korean counterpart. After a series of negotiations, Tanaka was convinced that Kim Chong Il would admit to having abducted Japanese nationals and offer an apology, and that North Koreans would provide information about the abductees and promise to return the Japanese who were still alive.

With this conviction, Koizumi became the first Japanese prime minister to visit North Korea, on September 17, 2002. As promised, the North Koreans provided information on the current status of the abductees before the summit meeting. But the information was shocking to the Japanese delegates: eight of the abductees had already died, and only five survived. As the Japanese delegates were smothered in depression, Prime Minister Koizumi stated his will: "It is neither our task to react or to involve ourselves in the issue emotionally. For our nation, it is important to get those still alive back home. For those whom they claim to be dead, we will demand thorough information."[71] At the morning session of the summit meeting, Koizumi brought up the abduction issue. Kim, however, did not admit or apologize for the abduction.

During the lunch break, the Japanese delegates got together in the waiting room. Deputy CCS Shinzō Abe voiced his opinion, knowing their conversation was wiretapped, that if the North Koreans did not admit or apologize for the abductions, the delegates should go back without signing a joint statement. Abe's statement changed the North Korean attitude. In the afternoon meeting, Kim admitted that the abduction was conducted by "part of North Korea's special organizations" and offered an apology to Koizumi. After receiving this statement, Japan signed the Pyongyang Declaration, which announced the commencement of normalization talks and included assurances from Japan of wide-ranging economic assistance in return for North Korea's "appropriate measures" on the abduction issue and a resolution of "security problems including nuclear and missile issues."

At the same time, Koizumi demanded the return of the five known surviving abductees. On October 15 the five arrived in Japan to reunite with their families and relatives after twenty-four years of abduction. The Japanese public reacted with overwhelming fury at the revelation of the kidnappings.

Although the North Koreans offered only a temporary visit, the abductees wanted to stay in Japan. Abe proposed that the prime minister not return the Japanese nationals to North Korea. On October 24, despite strong opposition from MOFA, Koizumi decided to allow the five to remain in Japan. Further, Tokyo demanded that North Korea allow other family members to join the returnees. Pyongyang denounced the Japanese government for betraying its trust and warned that it would postpone the bilateral security talks.

Some skeptics saw Koizumi's visit to Pyongyang as an attempt to recover his popularity, which had plunged after his sacking of popular foreign minister Makiko Tanaka in January 2002. If so, he succeeded. According to an *Asahi Shimbun* poll announced immediately after the Pyongyang meeting (September 19), 81 percent of those polled appreciated the meeting, and the Koizumi cabinet's approval rating rose from 51 to 61 percent.

In another *Asahi Shimbun* poll, dated November 5, 78 percent of respondents supported the Koizumi government's call for North Korea to abolish its nuclear program and return the abductees' family members. The poll also showed that as many as 95 percent expressed their concern about North Korea's nuclear program. Later in December, North Korea declared that it had resumed operation of its nuclear reprocessing facilities and expelled the International Atomic Energy Agency's inspectors. North Korea's brinkmanship posed a significant security threat to Japan and strengthened public support for the prime minister.

When North Korea launched seven missiles on July 5, 2006, it raised Japanese security concerns to an even higher level. At the end of May, the Koizumi government had been informed by American intelligence agencies about North Korean preparations for missile tests. CCS Shinzō Abe swiftly instructed Assistant CCS Hiroyasu Andō to prepare action plans to handle matters if North Korea tested missiles.

On June 15 Abe visited the American ambassador to Japan, Thomas Schieffer, and asked him to come to the Kantei when a planned missile test was suspected in order to exchange views and to demonstrate strong security cooperation between Japan and the United States. Abe and Schieffer also agreed to form a joint project team of experts in intelligence, defense, and foreign affairs. On that day the first meeting of the project team was held. By the end of June, the project team came up with plans for sanctions against North Korea. The plan included nine items: (1) a strong protest to the North Korean government; (2) disallowing the *Mangyong Bong*, a North Korean cargo and passenger vessel, to anchor at a Japanese port; (3) disallowing the entry of North Korean officials; (4) disallowing the reentry of officials of North Korean organizations in Japan; (5) disallowing Japanese official visits to North Korea; (6) disallowing the landing of charter flights between Japan and North Korea; (7) stricter export controls related to North Korea; (8) stricter execution of the laws on illegal activities by North Koreans; and (9) preparation for other measures.[72]

Meanwhile, MOFA, under the leadership of Minister Tarō Asō, began talking with foreign governments. Asō met with the American ambassador to ask for U.S. cooperation to immediately hold a United Nations Security Council meeting after an expected missile test, and to jointly send a strong message to Pyongyang. MOFA also contacted the French government, which then held the chairmanship of the Security Council, for a smooth operation of the Council.[73]

Abe asked two of his deputies as well as Foreign Minister Asō and Defense Minister Fukushirō Nukaga not to leave the Tokyo metropolitan area in case the suspected missile test took place. Thanks to this arrangement, Abe and the four officials gathered within an hour after the first news of the missile test came in at 4:00 a.m. Abe held the first press conference at 6:18 a.m. and met with Ambassador Schieffer half an hour later to announce their cooperation regarding the incident. At 7:24 a.m. the Koizumi cabinet held a Security Council meeting to authorize the nine-item plan that the joint team had prepared. This plan was immediately implemented. For example, the *Mangyong*

Bong was scheduled to anchor at a Niigata port on that day but was kept out of the port.[74]

Foreign Minister Asō instructed the Japanese representative to the United Nations in New York to promptly submit the prepared draft of a resolution to the Security Council. Asō then had a telephone conversation with Secretary of State Condoleezza Rice and confirmed that the United States and Japan would request a strong condemnation by the UN Security Council. After this conversation he talked with the Korean and Chinese foreign ministers to tell them that Japan and the United States were unified on this issue. Asō also called the foreign ministers of Russia, France, and Great Britain to ask for cooperation.[75]

Japanese diplomatic officials at the Representative Office had prepared a resolution that referred to article 7 of the UN Charter, which would authorize member states to implement strong sanctions against North Korea. They had lobbied officials of the other Security Council member states and received agreement from seven other nations, including the United States, to cosponsor the resolution. Therefore it was not too difficult to get the required two-thirds majority at the council, which had fifteen members. But China, with veto power, was initially not supportive of the proposal. Instead, Chinese officials proposed a chairman's statement with no legally binding power. Both Japan and the United States strongly opposed this plan.

China then asked for time to negotiate with North Korea, which the Security Council granted. Beijing sent Vice Foreign Minister Wu Dawei, but in vain. China eventually compromised and agreed to support the resolution on the condition that explicit reference to article 7 was removed. As a result, on July 15 the first resolution submitted by Japan to the UN Security Council was unanimously approved.

In the three case studies of foreign policy described above, the Kantei played a central role. For the antiterrorism legislation, the task force in the Cabinet Secretariat, instead of MOFA, drafted an important piece of national security legislation to be approved by the cabinet within a short period of four weeks. On the abduction issue, Prime Minister Koizumi and then Deputy CCS Abe made a series of political decisions beyond the scenario prepared by MOFA officials. In response to the North Korean missile test, Abe, by then CCS, in cooperation with Foreign Minister Asō, led a top-down style of decision making to successfully pass the first Japan-sponsored resolution at the UN Security Council. These cases under the Koizumi administration demonstrated a major shift from MOFA-led policy making to top-down decision making by the Kantei.

ACHIEVEMENTS AND FAILURES UNDER ABE

In the LDP presidential race to succeed Koizumi, Chief Cabinet Secretary Shinzō Abe won the election with wide support from across the LDP factions. When he formed his cabinet, Abe chose his friends and allies as cabinet ministers to reward them for their support. The first Abe cabinet at the outset received as high as a 63 percent approval rating, according to an *Asahi Shimbun* survey.[76]

Prime Minister Abe wanted to strengthen the Kantei in order to promote top-down decision making, as Koizumi did. The key position of CCS was given to Yasuhisa Shiozaki, a former Bank of Japan official known for his economic policy expertise. When Abe served as LDP secretary general, Shiozaki worked for him on the party reform. Abe was quite impressed with Shiozaki's administrative skills and asked him to assist his cabinet as CCS.[77] Abe removed Administrative Deputy CCS Masahiro Futahashi and asked his longtime friend Junzō Matoba, a former MOF official who retired as vice minister of the Land Agency in 1990, to assume the top position in the entire bureaucracy.[78] But as sixteen years had passed since Matoba had left the government, his ties with key bureaucratic officials were very limited.

To strengthen his support team, Abe appointed LDP Diet members to five positions as special advisers, the maximum number allowed by the revised Cabinet Law: Yuriko Koike (in charge of national security); Takumi Nemoto (economic and fiscal policy); Kyōko Nakayama (abduction); Eriko Yamatani (education); and Hiroshige Sekō (public relations). These advisers held office in the Kantei, and their appointments were regarded as Abe's determination as prime minister to take on policy initiatives.

In terms of fiscal policy making, Abe appointed Hiroko Ōta, as minister of economic and fiscal policy, to head CEFP meetings. Abe aimed to continue Koizumi's policy to pursue fiscal reform without a tax increase. He believed that economic growth should come first, and that Japan's fiscal balance would improve with a higher growth rate without a tax increase. This position led Abe to clash head on with Ministry of Finance officials, who wanted to raise the consumption tax and began acting as veto players against the prime minister.

Abe also appointed Masaaki Honma as chairman of the Government Tax Commission. Honma had been one of the most active supporters of the Koizumi reforms at the CEFP and aimed to support Abe's growth-first policy by opposing a tax increase and lowering the effective rate of corporate income taxes. Upon assuming the chairmanship, Honma moved the Secretariat of the

Tax Commission from the MOF to the Cabinet Office. This upset the MOF because the ministry would not be able to control the agenda of tax reform as it had been doing. In December, however, when a magazine article reported that Honma was using a government apartment to house his mistress, he was forced to resign from the chairmanship. Some experts suspected that MOF officials who were offended by Honma's actions and his stance against tax increases had intentionally leaked the information to the media.[79] This was the first sign of the scandals that would lead to Abe's declining power in the domestic policy arena.

During his first month in office, Abe's popularity dropped by 10 percent. Compared with the outspoken Koizumi, Abe's standpoint was seen as ambiguous by 55 percent of respondents. This was largely due to Abe's decision to allow eleven of the party rebels to come back to the LDP after being expelled by Koizumi for voting against the postal reform.[80] Abe had to face declining popular support from the beginning of his term. This development allowed the veto players within the LDP to fight against the prime minister's policy initiatives.

At the CEFP Abe and Ōta confronted the LDP construction zoku by announcing their intention to use road-related taxes for broader purposes. Road-related taxes, about 3.5 trillion yen a year, were used only for road construction to meet the demands of LDP politicians for more roads in their home districts. Many critics pointed out that these taxes were being used for wasteful and unnecessary road construction projects and that the funds should instead go into the general revenue. At the November 30 CEFP meeting, Abe announced that he would like to shift the road-related taxes to the general revenue. After a fierce battle between the Kantei and LDP zoku members, a political compromise was reached. The government would put only the surplus road tax revenue into the general expenditures after the funds for necessary road construction projects had been spent. The failure to move all the money into the general account was a major setback for Abe's plan to cut the fiscal deficit. CCS Shiozaki and Deputy CCS Matoba did not have enough administrative skill or political resources to mobilize Abe's top-down policy initiative. The Abe cabinet, with its declining popularity, could not fully take advantage of the CEFP to push forward his fiscal policy making reforms against the other veto players.

Another issue that Abe and Ōta picked up at the CEFP was civil service system reform, which even Koizumi had avoided during his tenure. In December 2006 private-sector members of the CEFP introduced a policy paper calling for the termination of *amakudari*, the institutional practice by which senior bureaucrats were placed in high-profile positions in the private and public sectors.[81] This practice was increasingly viewed as a drag on the private sector and the state that prevented structural reform. The paper was keenly criticized by the ministers of the MOF and the Ministry of Economy, Trade, and Industry.[82] Even at the Kantei, Deputy CCS Matoba saw the paper as antibureaucrat and was so upset that he boycotted the CEFP meeting. In addition, Administrative Reform Minister Genichirō Sata was not actively supportive of the bureaucratic reform. Abe and Ōta were surrounded by these veto players within his cabinet.[83]

The situation changed after Minister Sata resigned because of a political funds scandal and Yoshimi Watanabe, a leader of bureaucratic reform within the LDP, succeeded him. Newly appointed ministers are usually not prepared for their first press conference and tend to rely on prepared memos from the bureaucrats. Watanabe, however, without such a memo, talked passionately about his determination to pursue bureaucratic reform.[84] The bureaucrats strongly reacted to this appointment. Deputy CCS Matoba even threatened Watanabe: "The *amakudari* issue was over at the CEFP last year. If you pick it up again, there will be a coup."[85]

Prime Minister Abe, however, was supportive of Watanabe's reform effort. In March 2007 an independent lower house member submitted a question to the cabinet, asking whether the government forced private companies to accept retired bureaucrats. Watanabe prepared an answer that there were cases seen as forceful from the perspective of the people. This answer was first presented at the administrative vice-ministerial meeting and rejected. Abe decided to bring it to the cabinet meeting against the decision of the subcabinet meeting. This was the first incident in the over 120-year history of the subcabinet meeting in which one of its decisions was repealed by the cabinet.[86]

Watanabe prepared the bureaucratic reform legislation that would prohibit the custom of *amakudari* and establish instead a government-run placement center. This bill was enacted at the end of June 2007. However, for this law to be effective, the National Public Service Law needed to be revised. During the short tenure of the Abe cabinet, the bureaucratic reform was not completed, but it was later brought back under the Fukuda and Asō cabinets.

At the CEFP another important goal was to form Basic Policies, like those used by the Koizumi administration, to organize and pursue reform goals. But the power balance between the CEFP and the LDP had changed after Koizumi's October 2005 cabinet reshuffle. Kaoru Yosano, known as a pro-MOF member, took over as minister in charge of the CEFP, and the CEFP soon came under strong control of bureaucrats. To continue Koizumi's reform policy with regard to government financial institutions, Takenaka approached LDP secretary general Hidenao Nakagawa, who supported major restructuring of those institutions. While Yosano's CEFP presented arguments to preserve the current financial institutions, the LDP submitted a drastic reform plan. Koizumi fully supported the LDP plan to pursue, and the CEFP was no longer a control tower of economic policy in the last eleven months of the Koizumi cabinet.

When Ōta became the minister in charge of CEFP under the Abe cabinet, therefore, the council was already under strong bureaucratic control, and its power balance with the LDP was weakened. While Koizumi largely ignored the traditional preapproval process by the LDP, Ōta had to offer many compromises in the negotiations with the LDP in the process of forming the 2007 Basic Policy.[87] As a result, the Abe cabinet could not effectively utilize the CEFP in the area of domestic reform.

Although Abe tried to strengthen the Kantei, his attempt was unsuccessful. Many in the government pointed out that the appointment of five special advisers did not work well. Under the Koizumi government the CEFP played a pivotal role in domestic reform policies, while the prime minister's special assistants were former senior officials who coordinated with the bureaucracy over the policies made by the CEFP. On the other hand, Abe appointed Diet members to all five adviser positions, and they competed to independently pursue their own policies. They created unnecessary confusion and turf battles between the CEFP and cabinet ministers.[88] These developments under the Abe administration showed that institutions were only the necessary condition to exercise strong leadership. Taking advantage of them requires the prime minister's political will to fight against the other veto players, public support, and appropriate appointments in key positions for reform.

In strong contrast, Abe made several outstanding achievements in the area of foreign policy by moving quickly to improve relations with China and South Korea. During Koizumi's leadership, the prime minister's visit to Yasukuni Shrine offended Chinese and South Korean political leaders. Prime Minister Abe promised that, unlike Koizumi, he would not publicly visit the shrine in his official capacity of prime minister, though he refused to say whether he would visit it in private. In response, Chinese and South Korean leaders welcomed Abe's visit to Beijing and Seoul in October 2006, which significantly improved Japan's bilateral relationships with the two countries.

Abe also pushed forward three major pieces of national security legislation. First, he successfully enacted legislation to upgrade the Defense "Agency" to a "Ministry." Under the Koizumi government, the role of the SDF expanded to contribute to improving the international security environment. As the Defense Agency had been located under the Cabinet Office, the agency's budget requests and all its legislative actions needed to go through that office. Turning the agency into a ministry would remove such bureaucratic complications and would greatly improve the morale of its officials. The bill was coupled with a revision of the Self-Defense Forces Law, which elevated deployments outside of Japan to participate in UN peacekeeping operations or to provide logistical support for U.S. forces to one of the SDF's primary activities. The legislation passed the Diet in December 2006 with the support of not only the ruling parties but also the DPJ and the People's New Party (PNP, or Kokumin Shintō).

Second, Abe moved to establish procedures for a national referendum to amend the constitution. Although the constitution requires a national referendum for revision, there had been no law to govern the procedures. Legislation to set up these procedures had long been regarded as the first step toward revising the war-renouncing constitution and had been strongly opposed by the Socialist Party. The government party legislation was originally submitted in May 2006 under the Koizumi administration, but deliberations on the bill were not conducted until that fall under the Abe administration. The largest opposition party, the DPJ, submitted its own version of the legislation. The main difference was that the governing parties' version limited the referendum to constitutional revision while the DPJ broadened the range to include other important laws. The ruling parties' proposal passed the Diet on May 14, 2007.

Third, the Abe administration introduced a bill to facilitate changes regarding U.S. forces in Japan. The law would give subsidies to local governments that cooperate with these changes. Japan and the United States agreed to specific changes regarding U.S. forces, including reducing the number of marines stationed in Okinawa, moving the U.S. Army 1st Corps Headquarters from the state of Washington to Zama, Kanagawa prefecture, and further integrating Japanese and U.S. military capabilities. The legislation was enacted on May 23, 2007.

These legislative proposals were initiated and delivered with strong leadership from Prime Minister Abe. But these bills were not introduced by the Cabinet Secretariat as in the top-down decision-making style of the Koizumi administration. The Defense Agency itself proposed that it be turned into a ministry. The referendum bill was proposed by LDP and Kōmeitō legislators. The MOFA and the Defense Ministry prepared the facilitation of U.S. bases. The only national security–related bill introduced by the Cabinet Secretariat was one to establish a National Security Council. This bill, however, was not even discussed in the Diet during Abe's tenure and eventually died under the Fukuda administration. Despite his achievements in the foreign policy area, Abe did not take advantage of the Kantei's strengthened institutions.

On the political front, the Abe administration was attacked by the DPJ in the Diet for the missing pension records. In February 2007 DPJ lower house member Akira Nagatsuma pointed out in a budget committee meeting that there were a great number of cases of missing pensions.[89] Officials of the Ministry of Welfare and Labor told Abe that this was not going to be a big issue as the data actually existed.[90] As Abe promoted administrative reform, and the Social Insurance Agency, which handled pension records, became one of the targets owing to the inefficiency of its employees. In May the news was widely circulated that there existed fifty million cases of missing pension records. The media attacked the Abe administration for its inadequate response to the earlier question by Nagatsuma. Many LDP members believed that it was an intentional leak by the Social Insurance Agency officials. They labeled it "suicidal terrorism" to stop administrative reform drive by the Abe administration.[91] The massive media coverage on this issue further eroded public support for the Abe cabinet.

In addition, a series of scandals and controversial remarks involving cabinet members provoked public outrage. One month after Administrative Reform Minister Sata stepped down, Health and Labor Minister Hakuo Yanagisawa, in his public speech on the declining birth rate, referred to women as "childbearing machines."[92] Agricultural Minister Toshiharu Matsuoka was accused of misusing political funds. After continuing media coverage and accusations in the Diet committee hearing in May 2007, Matsuoka became Japan's first cabinet member in active service to commit suicide. One month later Defense Minister Fumio Kyūma resigned after his statement that the atomic bombings of Hiroshima and Nagasaki in 1945 "could not be helped" in order to prevent the Soviet Union from occupying parts of Japan. Norihiko Akagi, who succeeded Matsuoka as agriculture minister, was also accused by the media of misusing political funds.[93] This series of misbehaviors by cabinet ministers were a huge blow to the Abe government. According to an *Asahi Shimbun* survey in early July, the approval rate of the Abe cabinet plummeted to 28 percent.[94]

DEVELOPMENTS UNDER FUKUDA AND ASŌ

As a result, in the July 2007 upper house elections, the LDP lost and the DPJ became the largest party in the house. While Abe did stay in power even after this defeat, he suddenly announced his resignation on September 12 on health grounds. Former CCS Yasuo Fukuda defeated LDP secretary general Tarō Asō in the LDP presidential election to become prime minister. The approval rating for the Fukuda cabinet at the outset was 53 percent in an *Asahi Shimbun* poll, a significant recovery from the end of the Abe cabinet.[95]

Fukuda reappointed most of the cabinet members to their same positions as under the Abe administration. Among the few exceptions were Foreign Minister Nobutaka Machimura, who was appointed to the important post of CCS, and Education Minister Bunmei Ibuki, who took the powerful position of LDP secretary general.[96] In addition, Fukuda reappointed former administrative deputy CCS Futahashi to his old position. Abe had made a mistake by appointing his friends to important positions, including CCS and deputy CCS, but Fukuda appointed competent officials to these key positions.

With the loss of the majority in the upper house, the Fukuda cabinet had to face the powerful partisan veto players, who could reject most of the legislative bills sent up. While reform efforts by the Koizumi and Abe administrations were pursued against the opposition of the ministries and their patron zoku members, Fukuda could not afford to fight with these veto players. To conduct domestic reform, Fukuda formed the joint conference of the government and the ruling parties on social security and tax reform.

The CEFP was no longer in a pivotal position on domestic reform. Ōta was reappointed as minister in charge of the council, and other members were reappointed as well. They were asked to form policy for economic growth. In the 2008 Basic Policies, Ōta and her CEFP came up with four pillars of economic policies: (1) a 2.2 million job increase; (2) sector-specific productivity improvement; (3) globalization policies; and (4) further promotion of Japan's strength. Although the cabinet approved the Basic Policies in June 2008, Fukuda's resignation in September made it impossible for them to be reflected in the government budget.[97] The Fukuda cabinet constituted another example showing that without the prime minister's political will to fight against the other veto players and without public support, the national leader could not display strong leadership in a substantial reform.

However, the Fukuda cabinet did have a major achievement in bureaucratic reform. Yoshimi Watanabe was reappointed as administrative reform minister, and he came up with a plan to establish the Cabinet Human Resource Office and the Center for Personnel Interchanges Between the Government and Private Entities. The former would centralize the appointive authority of high government officials under the cabinet, and the latter would handle the placement of government officials in the private sector. The Center for Personnel Interchanges would prohibit *amakudari*, under which the government forced private companies to hire ex-bureaucrats with salaries and retirement fees far above the market standard. Instead, the newly created center would offer career search services to bureaucrats based on market needs. Because of bureaucratic opposition, CCS Machimura tried to block some of Watanabe's reform plan. At first Fukuda was not interested in bureaucratic reform, but later he became very supportive of Watanabe's effort.[98] In June 2008 the Basic Law on Reform of the National Public Service System passed the Diet, setting a framework to establish the new institutions.

On the national security policy front, the legislation to continue the SDF mission in the Indian Ocean for antiterrorism activities became a major issue in the fall 2007 Diet session. Abe's sudden resignation made it logistically impossible to extend the existing Antiterrorism Special Measures Law before its expiration on November 1. The Fukuda administration introduced new legislation that would dispatch the maritime SDF only for refueling operations to support maritime inspections in the Indian Ocean.

DPJ president Ichirō Ozawa publicly announced his opposition to the legislation. He proposed an alternative idea to promote Japan's participation in the International Security Assistance Force (ISAF) on Afghanistan soil, an operation that had been authorized by the United Nations. However, Ozawa's idea was not widely accepted by other DPJ members, as ground activities by the ISAF would be riskier than maritime operations. In November Ozawa met with Prime Minister Fukuda and agreed to form a coalition government with the LDP, although this idea did not reach fruition. This second initiative by Ozawa also met with strong opposition within the DPJ, and Ozawa publicly announced his resignation as DPJ president. Although he was persuaded to keep the presidency, this turmoil confused the DPJ's Diet operation regarding the antiterrorism legislation.

In December 2007 the ruling parties decided to extend the Diet session in order to pass the legislation with a two-thirds majority in the lower house, which would override the rejection by the upper house under article 59 of the constitution. On January 11, 2008, the legislation was enacted to authorize the government to restart maritime operations in the Indian Ocean.

Overriding the legislative action was politically risky, and the Fukuda administration had to utilize this measure with special caution. In January 2008, for example, LDP secretary general Bunmei Ibuki tried to use this tactic when he introduced a proposal that would extend the controversial temporary gasoline tax. However, this attempt met strong public resentment and Ibuki had to withdraw the proposal, leading to the expiration of the tax at the end of March. On April 30 the Fukuda cabinet passed the legislation to revive the gasoline tax with a two-thirds majority in the lower house.

This incident, however, exemplified the vulnerability of the Fukuda cabinet, with its unstable power base. After the passage, Fukuda's job approval rating plummeted to 20 percent, which was considered a politically dangerous level.[99] As his public support stayed at the low level of 20–25 percent between May and August,[100] Fukuda announced his resignation on September 9, hoping that his successor would be able to dissolve the lower house under a better political environment after the subsequent election.

When Tarō Asō took the prime ministership, his cabinet initially received support from 48 percent of the public.[101] Asō, however, did not immediately dissolve the lower house as Fukuda had hoped. On September 15 Lehman Brothers filed for bankruptcy protection; the largest bankruptcy filing in the history, by a company with assets over 600 billion dollars, gravely affected global financial markets. In the aftermath of the Lehman shock, the prime minister declared that he would postpone the general election in order to achieve economic recovery.

Asō appointed Kaoru Yosano back to the post of minister in charge of the CEFP. Yosano had no intention of taking advantage of the CEFP to promote domestic reform plans.[102] For example, he stated in an upper house budget committee meeting that the CEFP should not make policy decisions; rather, final decisions should be made by Diet members.

Asō shared Yosano's view. The two felt that the Japanese economy had been hit hard by the Lehman shock as well as the deregulation pursued by Koizumi and Takenaka. They preferred the bureaucracy-led economic policy, which would protect the traditional supporters of the LDP. Asō had no interest in pursuing drastic reform against the other veto players in the government and the LDP. As a result, the prime minister delivered two economic stimulus packages: one of five trillion yen for FY2008 and one of fifteen trillion yen for FY2009.

Asō's probureaucracy attitude also showed in his effort to reverse the bureaucracy reform. The establishment of the Center for Personnel Interchanges had been designed to stop the custom of *amakudari*. When the center was established under the Asō cabinet, its internal regulation set the lower limit of business contracts of private corporations with the government at 100 million yen, with exceptions for personnel with a high degree of expertise.[103] This effectively allowed all bureaucrats to float into positions with their career background.

The Basic Law enacted under the Fukuda cabinet had prohibited the government from arranging for former bureaucrats to move from one private entity to another. Asō, however, issued a government ordinance establishing loopholes that would revive the bureaucratic custom. Watanabe, upset at this situation, wrote an open letter to Asō asking whether the prime minister was going to allow the old custom, but Asō ignored the letter. In protest, Watanabe left the LDP to form a new party, the Your Party.

On the national security front, Asō successfully passed the legislation to extend the SDF's refueling activities in the Indian Ocean, and he enacted antipiracy legislation to dispatch SDF ships to protect foreign vessels from pirate attacks off Somalia. However, public support for his cabinet steadily declined.

When Asō finally decided to dissolve the lower house in July 2009, his support rate was as low as 17 percent.[104] In the August 30 general election, the DPJ recorded a historic victory, capturing 308 seats in the 480-member lower house to bounce the LDP out of power. The next chapter examines how the electoral system change of 1994 led to this power shift.

4 ELECTORAL CHANGES AND THEIR IMPACT

I N THE PREVIOUS CHAPTER we saw how institutional changes affected the decision-making process and strengthened the prime ministerial leadership under the Koizumi government. As described, the 1994 electoral system change shifted the power balance within the LDP, contributing to the establishment of the Koizumi administration. The electoral modifications also brought structural changes outside of the government, which eventually created a power shift that led to the DPJ government in September 2009. This chapter explores how the electoral changes affected Japan's political system.

DIRECT IMPACT OF THE INSTITUTIONAL CHANGES

The LDP greatly benefited from the malapportionment under the old multi-member-district election system, which overrepresented rural districts. As the LDP offered agricultural subsidies and public works to these areas where a high percentage of voters engaged in primary industries and the construction business, the longtime ruling party enjoyed overwhelming popularity in rural Japan. Although there was a massive population shift during Japan's high economic growth period, the LDP was hesitant to change the boundaries of the old districts. Under the old electoral system, in four different suits the Supreme Court ruled the malapportionment status unconstitutional as the maximum disparity was greater than 1:3.[1] The LDP government constantly came up with temporary solutions by making minor adjustments to decrease the disparity.

According to a study by Taku Sugawara, the LDP had enjoyed an average bonus of 17.2 seats owing to malapportionment in the eight general elections between 1972 and 1993. The LDP's bonus seats decreased to an average of 3.3 seats in the first four elections under the SMD system[2] (see table 4.1). These bonus seats created significant changes under the old electoral system. In the 1983 general election, for example, the LDP captured 250 seats, including 22 bonus seats, in the 512-seat lower house. The LDP was able to form a majority government by making a coalition with the New Liberal Club. Without the bonus seats, the LDP might not have been able to form a majority and could have lost control of the government.

After the new electoral laws were introduced in 1994, new boundaries were drawn to create three hundred SMDs. One of the laws specifically restricted the maximum disparity to no greater than 1:2.[3] However, the same law also

TABLE 4.1 The LDP's bonus seats in the lower house

YEAR	ELECTORAL SYSTEM	TOTAL SEATS	LDP SEATS	ADJUSTED LDP SEATS*	BONUS SEATS
1972	MMD	491	271	251.1	+19.9
1976	MMD	511	249	234.1	+14.9
1979	MMD	511	248	230.3	+17.7
1980	MMD	511	284	268.3	+15.7
1983	MMD	511	250	228.1	+21.9
1986	MMD	512	300	281.7	+18.3
1990	MMD	512	275	263.9	+11.1
1993	MMD	511	223	204.8	+18.2
1996	SMD	300	169	164.0	+5.0
2000	SMD	300	177	171.1	+5.9
2003	SMD	300	168	162.8	+5.2
2005	SMD	300	219	222.0	−3.0

Source: Sugawara Taku (2009), note 3.
*Adjusted LDP seats were calculated in the following manner. If a five-seat districts had a population size that would deserve 5.5 seats, two seats captured by the LDP would be counted as 2.2 seats ($5.5 \times (2/5) = 2.2$). This adjustment was made for all districts in order to calculate the total adjusted LDP seats.

created a disparity from the beginning by allocating one seat to each prefecture in addition to the seats allocated purely in proportion to population. As a result, the disparity in the first general election under the new SMD system in 1996 was a ratio of 1:2.3. The court ruled in 1999 that the disparity was constitutional as the election was conducted during a transitional period.

Although the LDP's bonus seats decreased with the electoral reform, the ruling party was able to increase lower house seats in the first election under the new SMD system in 1996. The LDP received only 38.6 percent of total votes in SMDs and 32.7 percent in proportional representation districts. But with these numbers of votes, the LDP was still able to capture 239 seats in the 500 lower house seats (47.8 percent), enabling the party to form a single-party minority government.

To compete with the LDP under the SMD system, the Japan Renewal Party, the Kōmeitō, the Japan New Party, the Democratic Socialist Party, and a couple of smaller groups that had broken away from the LDP merged to form the New Frontier Party (NFP) in December 1994. The NFP received nearly an equal numbers of votes (30 percent) in PR districts, garnering 60 seats. But in SMDs the NFP won only 96 seats (32 percent), with 30 percent of votes. In the three hundred SMDs, nearly one thousand non-LDP candidates were put forth, and anti-LDP votes were split among the opposition parties.[4] As a result, the LDP won 169 seats in these SMDs (56.3 percent).

The Democratic Party of Japan faced an election just two weeks after its inauguration. The DPJ maintained the same number of lower seats (52) as its preelection number. The Socialist Party lost its traditional supporters' votes by forming the coalition government with the LDP and decreased its seat numbers from 30 to 15. The Communist Party captured those votes and increased its seats from 15 to 26.

In 1997 another series of electoral system reforms was brought about. For many years there had been a gap in voter turnouts between urban and rural areas. Voters in rural areas had benefited greatly from the pork-barrel politics of the LDP and displayed their appreciation with high voter turnouts. On the other hand, in urban areas voters' interest in politics was not as high as in the countryside and naturally resulted in low voter turnouts. This significantly benefited the LDP.

After the 1996 general election recorded the lowest voter turnout, 59.7 percent, reforms were introduced in an attempt to increase the number of voters. First, voting hours were extended by two hours until 8 p.m. Second, parents were allowed to bring their small children to the balloting stations. Third, the conditions for absentee voting were relaxed. Voters were allowed to vote in hospitals and outside their residential areas or by mail. In 2003 absentee voting was also allowed in residential areas for an extended period of one week prior to the election date. These institutional changes significantly increased voter turnouts in urban areas in the 2005 and 2009 general elections, helped along by the amount of attention paid by the media, which further motivated the public to vote.

This tendency was clearly illustrated by Sugawara's study, which divides the three hundred SMDs into ten categories based on his rural-urban scale, which considers the ratio of the population engaged in primary industries and the construction business.[5] In the 1993 election, voter turnout is illustrated as a steep, upward-sloping curve that is low in urban areas and high in rural areas. In the 1996–2000 elections, the curves are also upward sloping, though they are not as steep as in 1993. However, in 2005 and 2009, the voter turnout curves are much flatter, narrowing the gap between urban and rural areas (see fig. 4.1).

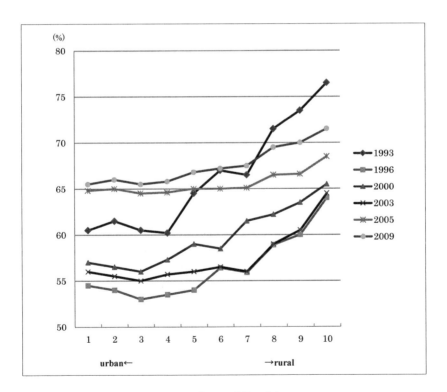

FIGURE 4.1. Voter Turnouts in Urban and Rural Areas

Source: Sugawara Taku, *Seron no Kyokukai: Naze Jimintō wa Taihai Shitanoka* (Tokyo: Kōbunsha Shinsho, 2009); see note 5.

The high voter turnout benefited the LDP in the 2005 election under Koizumi and helped the DPJ to take over the government in 2009.

Malapportionment remained a problem in the 2000s. Although the maximum disparity was greater than 1:2 in the 2000 and 2005 general elections, the Supreme Court decided the current status was constitutional for a transitional period. This led to a major civilian movement calling for a more equal vote weight. The Keizai Dōyūkai (Japan Association of Corporate Executives), one of the four major business organizations in Japan, was one of the groups in the movement. Finally, in March 2011 the Supreme Court ruled that the disparity in the 2009 general election with a maximum ratio of 1:2.3 was unconstitutional because more than ten years of the transitional period had passed without more of a balance being reached. The court called for a necessary legislative measure to be taken up in the Diet before the next general election.

CHANGES IN THE LDP

Changes and Continuity of Kōenkai

With the 1994 electoral reform, LDP incumbents had to align their kōenkai to new boundaries under the SMDs. The LDP established a branch and assigned one candidate in each of the three hundred SMDs. In some areas a party had a surplus of candidates. For example, the old Gunma third district had three powerful incumbents, Yasuo Fukuda, Yasuhiro Nakasone, and Keizō Obuchi, and was divided into only two new SMDs. LDP president Ryūtarō Hashimoto assigned Fukuda and Obuchi to the new two districts and requested that Nakasone run in the PR district on the condition that he would be at the top of the party list. In ten districts the LDP introduced the Costa Rica system, in which LDP candidates had to take a turn running in the SMD while the other rotated in the PR election.[6] Even in some areas with the right number of incumbents, district assignment was complicated as individual candidates insisted on running in the districts of their greatest strength.

Coordination problems remained after the district allocation was established as well. LDP candidates lost their traditional supporters outside their new districts and had to attract organizational voters in the new area. The LDP encouraged its candidates to establish alliances and cooperation agreements with other candidates to exchange supporters. According to a survey by *Yomiuri Shimbun*, 83 LDP candidates in the SMDs exchanged the list of their kōenkai members, joint election campaigns were conducted in 49

SMDs, a joint election office was established in 13 SMDs, and the introduction of kōenkai members was carried out in 66 SMDs. In total, some kind of electoral cooperation was accomplished in 215 SMDs out of the 300 SMDs.[7]

In the rest of the SMDs, no electoral cooperation was conducted, for several reasons. In some districts LDP candidates did not have close personal relationships with other candidates or even had relationships based on hate with former competitors. In several districts the LDP local office supported candidates from other political parties.

Electoral cooperation, of course, varied in terms of success levels. Ray Christensen found a bandwagon effect after examining case studies: "The likely winner in a district was better able to attract wavering potential supporters, and the candidate that seemed headed toward defeat suffered from defections. Though some support organizations might be committed to a specific candidate for ideological reasons, others support candidates for the access that they provide to the government."[8]

Such a bandwagon effect was also seen in the cooperation level of the LDP prefectural headquarters toward the SMD candidates. With the electoral system change, the prefectural headquarters played more important roles in almost half (46.7 percent) of the SMDs than they had in previous elections. Among the reasons for their more active roles, respondents observed that the opposition parties had strong candidates, that the prefectural headquarters were responsible for selection of the LDP candidate, and that the headquarters sought control over the candidates. In 15 percent of the SMDs, the headquarters had very little impact on whether an LDP candidate was too strong or too weak, often because there was a major conflict within the headquarters.[9] Overall the electoral change made many LDP prefectural headquarters more actively involved in the election campaign.

Many new LDP candidates had to form their kōenkai from scratch as they had nothing to offer other candidates in return. Fortunate candidates, however, could get electoral cooperation from incumbent Diet members. For example, Park Cheol Hee describes the case of Katsuei Hirasawa, who was assigned to run for his first election in the Tokyo 17th district. His district had formerly been part of the old Tokyo 10th district, where two LDP incumbents ran. The two Diet members split traditional LDP support organizations in the districts. With a strong recommendation from senior LDP politician Masaharu Gotōda, Hirasawa was able to get full electoral support from these Diet members. They introduced Hirasawa to their organizational supporters and even sent their assistants to help his election campaign.[10]

Some scholars argued that kōenkai were a product of the old electoral system, which forced competition among LDP members, and predicted that SMDs would eventually make kōenkai "unnecessary and even irrelevant."[11] After one and a half decades, however, kōenkai have survived. As Bradley M. Richardson and Dennis Patterson describe, virtually all Diet members "mobilized votes through their local organizations and social networks."[12] As mentioned in chapter 1, the 2008 handbook sold at the LDP headquarters encourages LDP candidates to form kōenkai, and kōenkai remain the core of their election campaign to expand their network of supporters.[13]

Christensen argues that kōenkai remain important because of Japan's strict regulations over election campaigns. Under the public office election law, candidates and campaign workers are not allowed to make door-to-door visits. The law includes strict regulations on the type of posters and direct mailings, the number of campaign offices and cars, and the amount of expenditures on campaign workers. Many candidates evade these restrictions by conducting most of their personal contacts with voters through kōenkai in the precampaign period, which do not count as formal campaign activities.[14]

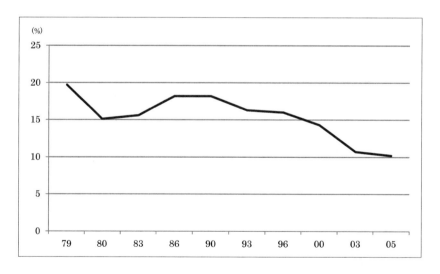

FIGURE 4.2. Voters' Affiliation Rate with Kōenkai

Source: Akarui Senkyo Suishin Kyōkai, *Dai-kai Shūgiin Sōsenkyo no Jittai: Chōsa Kekka no Gaiyō*, March 2006, 54. Unfortunately, the question on kōenkai affiliation was not asked in the 2009 survey by the same organization.

While kōenkai remain an important part of the election strategy of Diet members and candidates, their strength has declined significantly. The affiliation rate of voters with kōenkai decreased from 18 percent in late 1980s to 10 percent in 2005 (see fig. 4.2). A 2010 study by Ko Maeda examined the electoral performance in the 2009 general election of junior LDP incumbents with a less developed personal support base and veteran LDP incumbents with more developed kōenkai but found no statistical difference between them.[15] Kōenkai did not significantly insulate LDP candidates from the lower popularity of the LDP government.

Many candidates under the SMD system found the need to reach voters outside their core supporters. To directly contact voters, many DPJ politicians in urban areas began standing in populous areas to give short speeches on their political views. This became a popular election tactic among both DPJ and LDP candidates.

Weakening Factions

The problems caused by LDP factions were the primary reason for the 1994 electoral system and political finance reform. The old multimember-district system of the lower house, with three to five seats in a district, encouraged multiple candidates from the LDP. The competition among candidates from different LDP factions was much fiercer than with the opposition parties because the LDP candidates shared a similar support base. They had to rely not on the party organization but on their faction for financial and other campaign support. The old electoral system, therefore, was considered a cause of political corruption since LDP factions had to actively seek financial resources in order to compete. The new electoral system, with single-member districts, was introduced to weaken some functions of the LDP factions and eliminate factional competition in the general election.

The original purpose of LDP factions was to make their leader prime minister. Faction leaders maintained their factions despite the high cost of supporting members in order to become prime minister someday. The largest LDP faction, led by Kakuei Tanaka and later by Noboru Takeshita, had boasted of unity and had been decisive in the selection of the prime minister since the mid-1970s. When Takeshita's successor, Keizō Obuchi, ran for LDP presidency in 1998, however, another senior member of the faction, Seiroku Kajiyama, also declared his candidacy. Kajiyama had strong concerns about Japan's economy after the bubble burst, and he called for a drastic plan to deal with nonperforming loans in the financial sector. Kajiyama left the faction to run against Obuchi. Although Obuchi won the LDP presidential election with 225 votes, Kajiyama fought well, receiving 102 votes with no backing from any factions but relying only on his policy appeal. This symbolized the weakening of factional control over the presidential election and the people's high expectation for policy initiatives in economic reform.[16]

In September 1999 Obuchi had to run for reelection as LDP president. This time Kōichi Katō, leader of the Katō faction, challenged him. Katō was highly critical of Obuchi's fiscal expansion policy, which increased the government deficit. In the LDP presidential election, Obuchi won with 350 votes, but Katō was able to get 113 votes, reportedly including 35 from members of the Obuchi faction. This further illustrated the weakening unity of factions in the selection of the LDP president.

Former prime minister Ryūtarō Hashimoto took over the largest LDP faction after Obuchi's death in May 2000. When Prime Minister Yoshirō Mori resigned in April 2001, Hashimoto and three other LDP members—Junichirō Koizumi, Tarō Asō, and Shizuka Kamei—stood for the presidential election. Hashimoto, however, did not receive solid support from his own faction. When he declared his candidacy at the faction meeting, twenty members boycotted the meeting.[17] Younger members of the faction openly stated that they might vote against him.

For the 2001 presidential election, the LDP changed the electoral rule to triple the votes of local chapters from 47 to 141, in addition to 346 votes of LDP Diet members. Koizumi, who was quite popular among the public for his reform plans, captured nearly 90 percent of local votes and won a landslide victory with 298 votes out of 487. Hashimoto, who represented the largest LDP faction with 101 Diet members, won only 155 votes. Koizumi became the first LDP president and prime minister to be selected outside the traditional factional power balance.

After Koizumi became prime minister, he constantly attempted to eliminate factional influence. Koizumi totally ignored factional requests when he formed his cabinet and handpicked cabinet members. The allocation of cabinet posts was one of the most important functions of LDP factions. Koizumi effectively nullified this function. When Koizumi received an unprecedented level of initial public support with an over 80 percent approval rating, the biggest reason was his rejection of factional influence.

Under the Koizumi administration the LDP formed the Committee on Examination and Promotion of Party Reform (Tō Kaikaku Kenshō Suishin

Iinkai), headed by LDP secretary general Shinzō Abe. The first reform the committee promoted was to hold open recruitment for LDP candidates. In the April 2004 supplementary election for a lower house seat in the Saitama 8th district, the LDP opened up applications for candidacy to the public. As the subelection was held because the incumbent LDP lower house member was arrested for the violation of the public office election law, no faction wanted to send its candidate to run in such a hard election. To fill the vacancy, eighty-one people applied to become an LDP candidate. As a result, a thirty-seven-year-old lawyer Masahiko Shibayama was selected and won the election against all odds.[18]

When Prime Minister Koizumi dissolved the lower house on August 8, 2005, the LDP needed to find thirty-seven new candidates to run against the rebels who opposed Koizumi's postal reform. Koizumi's top political aid, Isao Iijima, and LDP secretary general Tsutomu Takebe handpicked high-profile competing candidates or "assassins" to run in their district.[19] But it was not enough. The committee decided to run an advertisement in national newspapers to recruit candidates. The advertisement was published on August 13, and within four days 868 people applied for lower house candidacy. The committee selected 26 applicants to run for the lower house.[20] This selection process was highly centralized by the LDP headquarters and not influenced by the LDP factions. This event significantly weakened the function of LDP factions to recruit new members.

While Prime Minister Koizumi freehandedly formed his first cabinet independent of factional influence, the selection of subcabinet members—senior vice ministers (*fuku daijin*) and parliamentary secretaries (*seimukan*)—followed the LDP's tradition of considering factional balance.[21] The committee tried to change this practice. When Koizumi formed his second cabinet in November 2003, the committee asked LDP Diet members to submit a self-assessment form with their top three desired posts and the reasons for their desire. A committee member who promoted this system, Hiroshige Sekō, explained the intention of the new system: "There was no way that faction leaders could know the aptitude, expertise, and detailed career aspirations of all the faction members. Thus it was appropriate to ask them to assess themselves."[22] The assessment forms were bound into a booklet and distributed to the chief cabinet secretary and cabinet ministers. Based on the self-assessment, the cabinet appointed subcabinet members. This practice was followed by the Abe cabinet as well. In addition to cabinet ministers, the selection of subcabinet members in the Abe administration was decided outside factional influences.

In addition to the LDP factions' declining influence in the selection of the party leader, the recruitment of new members, and the allocation of posts, their function as finance provider to their members weakened as well. The 1994 political reform under the Hosokawa cabinet drastically changed Japan's political funding system. While the new system provided government funds to political parties, it strengthened regulations on political funds by requiring more transparency and prohibiting corporate donations to political organizations other than recognized political parties after 1999. Although a loophole allowed individual lower house members to collect financial contributions through LDP branches in their districts, it became much more difficult for LDP factions to raise funds.

The amount of political funds that LDP factions collected drastically decreased after the 1994 reform, as shown in figure 4.3. Before 1994 some factions collected more than 2 billion yen a year. In 2002, however, the most successful faction collected only around 400 million yen.

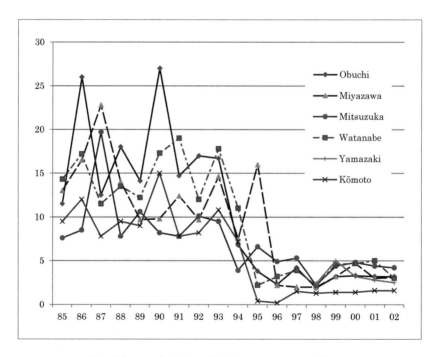

FIGURE 4.3. Fund Raising by Major LDP Factions (100 million yen)

Source: Takenaka Harutaka. *Shushō Shihai*, 155 (originally from Yomiuri Shimbun).

The names of the factions are as of June 1994.

Government funds became a major source of revenue for political parties and individual politicians. Under the 1994 Political Party Grant Law, the government had provided over 30 billion yen annually to political parties. In 2001, for example, the LDP received 14.5 billion yen from the government, which was nearly 69 percent of the party's total revenue. In the LDP the president and the secretary general hold the authority to allocate funds. This financial structure within the party changed the power balance between party leadership and the factions.

Weakening PARC

The new electoral system also weakened the LDP's influence over policy making. As we saw in chapter 1, policy making under the 1955 system was highly decentralized within the LDP as the Policy Affairs Research Council's subcommittees played a very influential role. Each LDP Diet member chose a couple of specific policy areas and belonged to related PARC subcommittees in order to accumulate policy expertise and influence government policies. Under the old multimember-district system, it was possible for LDP Diet members in the same district to divide their areas of policy expertise among themselves so that they could deal with different requests from their constituency. By becoming influential political players in specific policy areas, LDP Diet members solidified organizational support from specific interest groups. This was crucial under the old electoral system because they could win a seat by gaining less than 20 percent of votes cast.

Under the new SMD system, only one LDP lower house member represented each district, and the member had to deal with all kinds of cases. As a result, LDP lower house members were expected to be generalists rather than experts in a specific policy area. An agricultural expert in the LDP also needed to study commerce, construction, and transportation. Prime Minister Ryūtarō Hashimoto lamented, "This electoral system is horrible. . . . It does not allow policy specialists to grow."[23]

Until 1993 the PARC subcommittees required membership registration, and the published list of their membership was a best-selling item at the shop in the LDP headquarters. When the LDP became an opposition party under the non-LDP government led by Morihiro Hosokawa in 1993, the activities of the LDP's PARC significantly slowed down. Even after the LDP regained control of the government, the PARC did not fully recover the influence it used to enjoy.

Since 1994, except for a short period in 1998, the LDP has had to form coalition governments with other parties. Policy coordination among the government parties is required and is often more important than building consensus within the LDP. The PARC lost its dominant power in policy making. Under the coalition government with the Socialists and Sakigake, for example, government project teams with representatives from the three parties were formed to make policy decisions. In the political process of major national security legislation under the Koizumi government, the prime minister first sought agreement from the coalition partners and largely ignored consultation with the LDP policy subcommittees.[24] In domestic policy making, including postal reform, Prime Minister Koizumi constantly pursued his policy against objections from the PARC subcommittees. Koizumi set a precedent that the prime minister could ignore policy consultation with the PARC.

The influence of the PARC declined significantly through the 1990s and under the Koizumi government. According to the data from Michio Muramatsu's survey, 43.6 percent of bureaucrats in 1986 perceived zoku members in the PARC as the greatest influence on their ministry's policy formation and implementation, compared with 31.9 percent who saw the prime minister as the biggest influence. Over a sixteen-year period, zoku influence declined. In 2002 only 27.2 percent perceived zoku members as the greatest influence, and 56.9 percent regarded the prime minister as the most influential.[25] The power balance between the national leader and the LDP policy committee significantly changed in the eyes of bureaucrats during the 1990s.

After 1993, the PARC never recovered the influence it had enjoyed in the 1980s. Registration for membership in LDP policy subcommittees was terminated unless LDP members were appointed as chairmen or vice chairmen.[26] LDP Diet members now could join any subcommittee any time. The PARC subcommittees no longer served as a forum to make policy experts, but only as an information channel.

THE RISE OF THE DPJ

Opposing the LDP

As the new political institution changed many elements in the LDP, the Democratic Party of Japan also saw significant changes. The DPJ was established in September 1996 under the leadership of former Sakigake member Yukio Hatoyama, one day after the lower house was dissolved. When the Sakigake was a part of the coalition government with the LDP, Hatoyama was dissatisfied that his party had to compromise with the LDP against its policy principles. He decided to form a new party that would aim at building a more "citizen-centered" society. In his view, the conventional political parties existed to further the interests of their members and supporting groups and were not serving the people of Japan. In such a traditional framework, Hatoyama felt it would be difficult to bring about fundamental reform of the government system.

Hatoyama and his younger brother, Diet member Kunio Hatoyama, initiated the establishment of the DPJ to try to resolve the unfavorable situation. Another Sakigake member, Naoto Kan, who became popular among the public for uncovering the scandal in the Ministry of Health and Welfare over blood products infected with the HIV virus, joined the DPJ, helping to create wider public support for the new party. Kan became coleader of the DPJ to help Hatoyama prepare for the election.

On September 28, 1996, the DPJ held an inaugural meeting with 52 Diet members. Within two weeks an election was called for, and the newly established party announced the candidacy of 161 members for the general election. In the election anti-LDP votes were split among the DPJ and other opposition parties, including the NFP, the Socialist Party, and the Communist Party. The DPJ ended up receiving 6 million out of the 56.5 million popular votes in the new SMDs and 8.8 million votes in the eleven PR districts, which elected 52 DPJ members to the lower house. Considering its short history, this result could be seen as a success. But the DPJ failed to create the popular boom the party was hoping to see because its total number of lower house seats did not increase in the election.

The situation changed in December 1997 when the largest opposition party, the NFP, suddenly broke up. Its leader, Ichirō Ozawa, and his followers formed a new party, the Liberal Party. The rest of the NFP members formed five different groups.[27] DPJ leaders Kan and Hatoyama swiftly approached the former NFP groups, except Ozawa's Liberal Party and former Kōmeitō members. As a result, in April 1998 many of them joined to form the new DPJ, becoming the largest opposition to the LDP.

The DPJ gained organizational support from the Rengō (Japan Trade Union Confederation). Before the Rengō was established in 1989 by a merger of the two national groups of labor unions, the Sōhyō had supported the Socialist Party while the Dōmei had backed the Democratic Socialist Party (DSP). Even after the merger, the Rengō's political support continued to be split between the Socialists and the DSP (later the NFP, into which the DSP merged). The

Rengō's support for the Socialist Party, however, declined with the political changes of 1993. As many former Socialist members joined the DPJ, former Sōhyō groups within the Rengō shifted to support the DPJ.[28] After the NFP broke up in 1997, the entire Rengō organization supported the DPJ.

The first national-level election that the new DPJ faced was the upper house election in July 1998. A week before the election, most of the media predicted that the LDP would win. However, Prime Minister Ryūtarō Hashimoto revised his position on tax cuts during the election campaign. As a result, the LDP lost 17 seats, leaving it 23 seats short of a majority in the 252-seat upper house. This historic loss forced Hashimoto to resign. On the other hand, the DPJ increased from the preelection level of 18 to 27 seats. In the PR districts, the DPJ got 12.2 million votes while the LDP captured 14.1 million.

Becoming a More Viable Party

In May 2000 Prime Minister Yoshirō Mori stated before the Association of Shintō Shrines that Japan is a "divine nation centering on the emperor." As the statement's sentiment was compared to the nationalist fervor before and during World War II, the approval rate of the Mori cabinet dropped from 41 percent to 19 percent.[29] The opposition parties took advantage of Mori's statement to attack the government before the coming general election and submitted a no-confidence resolution against the cabinet in the lower house on June 2. That day, Prime Minister Mori dissolved the lower house before voting took place on the resolution. During the election campaign, Mori made another misstep after newspaper surveys showed that some 50 percent of the electorate remained undecided, by saying that these voters "should sleep in" on election day.

In the June 2000 general election, the LDP reduced its seat count from 271 to 233, and many of its key political figures, including current and former cabinet ministers, lost their seats, particularly in metropolitan areas. The DPJ increased its representation by more than 30 to 127 seats.

After the election, however, the DPJ had difficulty dealing with Junichirō Koizumi, who replaced the unpopular Mori. As indicated in the previous chapter, Koizumi promoted structural reform of the Japanese economy and government against the traditional LDP position and publicly stated he was willing to destroy the LDP if necessary. As Koizumi's reform efforts were in line with DPJ's policy objectives, many DPJ members welcomed him. When Koizumi made his first policy speech on May 7, 2001, DPJ Diet members applauded his determination to carry out reform while the LDP side remained silent.[30] Responding to a question on structural reform efforts in the National Basic Policy Committee, Koizumi publicly stated his commitment to drastically reforming seven special corporations. DPJ president Yukio Hatoyama praised Koizumi by saying, "Thank you for your statement. I highly appreciate it. . . . If the government party becomes the obstacle for you, we will support your reform if it is good for the people."[31] In the reform process, Koizumi often threatened antireform LDP and Kōmeitō members by hinting that he might seek to form a coalition with the DPJ.

The DPJ had an ambivalent position. After a series of discussions, the party reached the conclusion that it would "compete with the LDP but support Koizumi's reform efforts."[32] In the first national-level election that Koizumi faced, the July 2001 upper house election, the popular prime minister brought 64 seats to the LDP out of the 121 contested seats. In the unfavorable atmosphere, the DPJ put up a good fight by capturing 26 seats, a slight increase from its previous 24.

For a year after the upper house election, the DPJ did not have a good chance to recover popular support. After the 9-11 incident in 2001, deliberations in the Diet were concentrated on the antiterrorism legislation and the basic plan to send the SDF to the Indian Ocean as Japan's contribution to the war against terrorism. Although the DPJ opposed the original legislation, it decided to support the government's basic plan for the SDF dispatch. However, twenty-eight DPJ Diet members voted against the dispatch plan in opposition to the party's decision.[33] This development shed light on the DPJ's lack of consensus on national security policies.

A year later, in September 2002, the DPJ held a presidential election under the new rule in which party supporters could vote if they paid a fee of two thousand yen. This new rule was seen as beneficial to Naoto Kan, who had nationwide popularity. But Hatoyama was reelected DPJ president with support from former DSP members. In return, he appointed a former DSP member, Kansei Nakano, to the post of secretary general. In the following month, the DPJ under the leadership of Hatoyama and Nakano lost six out of seven supplementary elections for upper and lower house seats, reflecting the low public support rate for the DPJ.[34] Hatoyama tried to recover by seeking an alliance with the Liberal Party, but other DPJ members rejected this scheme and Hatoyama resigned.

In December 2002 Kan became DPJ president, but the party's public support remained at a low level. Kan took a gamble in imitating Hatoyama's strategy by pursuing a merger with Ozawa's Liberal Party, which also suffered from low public support. To improve their chances in the coming general

election, the DPJ and the Liberal Party agreed on the merger of the two parties in July 2003. This strategy worked well in the November 2003 general
election. The DPJ increased by 40 seats to 177 seats in the lower house. In PR
districts the DPJ for the first time gained the most votes, with 22.1 million (37.9
percent) compared with the LDP's 20.7 million votes (35.0 percent).

During his tenure as DPJ leader, Kan was eager to demonstrate to the public
that the DPJ was a viable opposition party capable of running the government.
He sought to display the party's solid understanding of and policy for national
security affairs when the Koizumi government submitted emergency bills to
the Diet in April 2003. Kan wanted to show the same ability to enact legislation
as his party did in 1998. Then the DPJ came up with financial reform legislation and successfully enacted its proposal, demonstrating policy-making ability
in economic matters. This time Kan's theme was defense affairs. If he could
tackle such a hard issue, then he could show his party's ability to govern. Kan
appointed a well-known defense expert, Seiji Maehara, to head a project team
on emergency legislation. Maehara produced a legislative proposal and submitted it to the Diet. As a result, the DPJ held a conference with the government parties and reached an agreement mostly based on the DPJ proposal.[35]
The proposal was enacted on June 6 with support of 202 of the 235 members
in the upper house.

However, this display of legislative capability did not win over the public
on the DPJ's ability to lead the country. After the November 2003 election in
which the DPJ did win significantly, the *Yomiuri Shimbun* conducted an opinion poll to ask the reasons for the DPJ's victory. Only 8 percent of respondents
chose the DPJ's capability to run the government, while 30 percent answered
that they did not want the LDP to win, and 27 percent responded that their
anti-LDP votes were cast for DPJ candidates.[36] The DPJ was not yet seen as a
viable opposition party.

After the election a series of scandals hit the DPJ. In the following month,
two DPJ Diet members were indicted for violating electoral laws in the general election, leading to their resignation as lower house members.[37] In January 2004 another DPJ lower house member was found to have made a false
statement about his academic background, which led to his resignation.[38] In
March a veteran DPJ lower house member, Kanju Satō, was arrested for swin-
dling his secretary's salary. These scandals made DPJ president Kan defensive
vis-à-vis the government parties. In April the DPJ lost all three supplementary
elections for lower house seats.

When it was found that several LDP cabinet ministers, including CCS Yasuo Fukuda, had not paid their pension fees, Kan harshly attacked them. The DPJ leader wanted to impress the public by showing his pension payment record, but soon it was revealed that Kan as well had a two-month unpaid pension period. After Fukuda took responsibility for his unpaid pension period and resigned as chief cabinet secretary, Kan was cornered by public pressure and resigned as DPJ president.

Katsuya Okada took over DPJ's leadership in May 2004. The pension problem continued to spread in the political community. It was found that Prime Minister Koizumi had a construction company pay his pension fee for four years although he was not working for it. When Okada asked questions on Koizumi's improper pension payment, the prime minister stated, "Life differs, companies differ, and employees differ," drawing on a phrase from a Japanese *enka* song.[39] Many people who heard Koizumi's statement felt ridiculed, and this drastically changed the political mood as the July 11 upper house election approached.[40]

The upper house election resulted in a DPJ victory. The DPJ received 21.1 million votes in PR districts, 4.3 million more than the LDP's 16.8 million votes. It also added twelve seats to its power in upper house by winning fifty-five seats (including six DPJ-supported independents), compared with the LDP's forty-nine seats. With this victory, Okada was reelected as DPJ president without any contest in September 2004.

The 2005 Postal Reform Election

In the 2005 ordinary Diet session, legislative attention was focused on postal reform, with especially fierce battles between the pro- and antireform groups within the LDP. In July the postal reform bill passed the lower house, but thirty-seven LDP lower house members did not support it. The bill was expected to be rejected in the upper house, as many LDP members stated they would vote against it.

DPJ president Okada expected that Koizumi would withdraw the bill prior to the voting, as "the rejection of the bill would usually mean a no-confidence vote against the Koizumi Cabinet."[41] Okada and other DPJ leaders also began to discuss the possibility of a general election. There were some concerns: it would be a general election against the popular prime minister; the election issue would be Koizumi's favorite topic—postal reform; and the DPJ had selected candidates in the most SMDs, but many were not well prepared. Despite these disadvantages, DPJ leaders concluded that it would be a good chance for a power shift. They calculated that the fights between the pro-reform and antireform candidates would split the votes of LDP supporters and should immensely benefit DPJ candidates.[42]

After the bill was rejected in the upper house, with twenty-two LDP members voting against it, Prime Minister Koizumi dissolved the lower house and called for voters' support, sending new LDP candidates, the so-called assassins, against the thirty-seven rebels in the lower house. As the public and the media focused on the battles between the assassins and the rebels, DPJ candidates were largely neglected during the election campaign.

Within the LDP the campaign strategy team was formed under the leadership of LDP upper house member Hiroshige Sekō. Before becoming a Diet member, Sekō served as director of public relations at Japan's giant telecommunications corporation, Nippon Telegraph and Telephone (NTT). Sekō and his team conducted public opinion surveys on whether the LDP should concentrate on the single issue of postal reform.

On the other hand, DPJ president Okada wanted to broaden the range of issues to create another "manifesto election," as in the 2003 general election. By broadening the election issues, the DPJ could avoid fighting on the stage where Koizumi had the advantage.[43] There also were some opinions in the media against focusing solely on postal reform issues. But after closely watching the results of their public opinion surveys, Sekō and his team decided to make it a single-issue election campaign.[44]

Prime Minister Koizumi asked voters whether they supported the privatization of the postal service. The DPJ's policy on postal reform was to downsize postal savings now and to privatize in the near future. The public was ambivalent about this. Koizumi attacked the DPJ's plan by calling the largest opposition party a protector of civil servants.

The LDP's communications strategy was correct. The result of the election was a landslide victory for the party, which won in 219 out of the 300 SMDs, in addition to 77 seats in PR districts. In contrast, the DPJ got only 52 SMD seats and 61 PR seats. There were 83 new LDP candidates who won by riding on Koizumi's coattails. They were labeled the "Koizumi Children" in the media.

The DPJ analyzed the reasons for this huge defeat. First, it was not prepared for a sudden dissolution of the lower house. The DPJ had a delayed start in forming its election headquarters. Its media strategy was not well planned and rather ad hoc. Second, the DPJ failed to set its own election issue. The LDP and Koizumi led the election campaign by taking advantage of media attention on the intraparty battles over postal privatization. Third, the DPJ failed to offer voters an alternative plan on postal reform. Its plan was to kill the government proposal; it did not submit its own legislative proposal. This offered Koizumi a chance to label the DPJ as antireformist. Fourth, the DPJ misread the voters' expectations for change. Voters wanted drastic reform and sympathized with Koizumi's fight against the traditional vested interests within the LDP. The DPJ was stuck with a seemingly passive attitude toward postal reform. Fifth, the DPJ had too much confidence from the last two elections. The DPJ dreamed that it could again capture the independent voters who had supported the party in the 2003 lower house and 2004 upper house elections.[45]

Taking responsibility for the defeat, Okada resigned as DPJ president. But Okada expressed his optimism for the next general election:

> The LDP had winners in most of the 300 SMDs. It will not be easy for those [LDP] legislators who were elected in the exciting election to be reelected. Even if many of them may be weak candidates in the next election, it would be difficult [for the LDP] to replace them as they are incumbents. The DPJ had many losers, and therefore we have room for new candidates. This [2005] general election revealed the high risks of the SMD system, as well as its great possibilities. I think that the next general election will be a great chance to realize the governmental power shift.[46]

To succeed Okada, two candidates ran for DPJ presidency: former president Naoto Kan and well-known young defense expert Seiji Maehara. To refresh the party image, DPJ Diet members elected Maehara. Maehara appointed Yukio Hatoyama as secretary general but also placed many young friends in leadership positions within the party.[47]

Maehara was concerned with the DPJ's overreliance on labor unions. As DPJ leader he declared that there should be a clear line between the DPJ and the largest labor union, the Rengō. When Maehara met with Rengō leader Tsuyoshi Takagi, he stated that the DPJ would not always follow the Rengō's policy requests and that the DPJ would not overly rely on electoral assistance from the labor union.[48] This upset many labor leaders, and the DPJ's relations with the labor unions soured.

In February 2006 DPJ lower house member Hisayasu Nagata alleged in a Diet session that a senior LDP member had accepted funds and bribes from former Livedoor CEO Takafumi Horie. Nagata's allegation was based on an e-mail from Horie. Later it was revealed that the e-mail Nagata was using was fake. In reaction, Nagata resigned from his lower house post. In the DPJ Maehara was highly criticized for not sharing information outside of his closed circuit of friends and for a lack of crisis management capability. Taking responsibility for allowing Nagata to take such action, Maehara resigned as DPJ president.

Ozawa's Electoral Strategy

After the fiasco caused by Maehara's inexperience, DPJ members wanted to have an experienced leader. As a result, Ichirō Ozawa became Maehara's successor in April 2006. As there were many anti-Ozawa members within the DPJ, Ozawa publicly declared that he would change things. Ozawa reappointed Hatoyama as secretary general and installed Kan as acting president. Thus he formed a "troika system" or a co-leadership style within the DPJ. Ozawa declared about the division of labor among the three leaders: "I will focus on elections, Mr. Kan will be in charge of debate in the Diet, and Mr. Hatoyama will be responsible for everything else."[49] According to DPJ deputy president Hirotaka Akamatsu, Ozawa clearly stated that Kan and Hatoyama could freely act as party leaders in their areas of responsibility, "But I wanted full authority over election, from the selection of candidates, the allocation of funds, and where I go and what I do."[50]

The first test for Ozawa's leadership was a supplementary election for a lower house seat in the Chiba prefecture's 7th district, scheduled on April 23, 2006. The candidate from the LDP was an elite bureaucrat from the Ministry of Economy, Trade, and Industry who had served as a lieutenant governor of Saitama prefecture. The DPJ candidate was a former bar hostess, Kazumi Ōta. Many experts predicted the LDP's victory. Ozawa orchestrated an election campaign against all odds.

To support Ōta, Ozawa needed the backing of key institutions for the DPJ in general, and for Ōta as a candidate. The first thing he tried to do was to restore the DPJ's relations with labor unions, which had been troubled under the leadership of Maehara. Ozawa contacted Rengō president Takagi and secretary general Nobuaki Koga and asked for their cooperation in the election. Ozawa visited the office of a small, leftist labor union in the Chiba 7th district.

Instead of asking the union leaders for election assistance, Ozawa just told them that they should make a DPJ government together. These leaders of the leftist unions were so impressed that they became fans of Ozawa.[51]

Ozawa's election campaign was called as an "upstream strategy," which he learned from his political mentor, Kakuei Tanaka. Tanaka taught him that candidates should start campaigning in low-population density areas by themselves and not rely on organizational votes. They needed to woo all kinds of voters. It was easy to speak in front of supportive groups, but if candidates chose the easy way, independent voters would not pay any attention. Candidates needed to choose the harder way and start by attracting independent voters. Ozawa told Ōta that she should follow this strategy.[52]

Ozawa then launched speech tours for himself and Ōta starting in the district's rural areas. The first region Ozawa visited was Sekiyadomachi, with a population of thirty thousand.[53] A couple hundred people came to see him. During the second visit, Ozawa and Ōta rode bicycles together in Nagareyama City. Ozawa chose the most popular spots for many candidates—high-traffic railroad stations—as the last spots for a visit.[54]

Ozawa requested that all DPJ Diet members visit the electoral district during the election campaign. He also asked them to submit a list of friends and relatives in Chiba prefecture and to visit offices and organizations where they had some affiliation. For example, Ozawa asked a DPJ member with a legal background to visit the local lawyers association, which had traditionally supported the LDP. He told the member, "If you visit with your lawyer's pin on, they would listen to their colleague."[55] Ozawa used whatever resources available to the DPJ and its members.

The result was Ōta's surprising victory. This victory established Ozawa's reputation as a great campaign strategist. Many DPJ members wanted Ozawa's leadership in running the next upper house election campaign in July 2007.[56]

Ozawa thus focused his activities on the upper house election. His emphasis was the twenty-nine prefectures with SMD, which were considered as key districts to win the election. The upper house members in the SMDs were singlehandedly responsible for bringing pork to their districts, such as public works and government subsidies. Therefore members of the government party traditionally had advantages. Because of the fiscal reconstruction of the central government under the Koizumi cabinet, however, it was more difficult for LDP members to bring pork to their constituencies. This situation gave the DPJ a chance to win in the SMDs. In February 2007 Ozawa began unofficial campaign tours with the labor leaders to visit those SMD prefectures.

In the tours, Ozawa met with local dignitaries and visited shopping districts during the daytime. In the late afternoon he exchanged opinions with local labor leaders for a couple of hours, and after that he went out for more discussions with them over dinner. A DPJ officer testified that Ozawa always reserved a small room at a small local pub, in which he and labor leaders could enjoy a relaxed, cozy feeling. He established personal relations with the local labor leaders by pouring drinks for them, and vice versa.[57] Ozawa's building of bonds with them strengthened the organizational support from the Rengō for DPJ candidates.

This was crucial to many new DPJ candidates. Local branches of labor unions sent people to campaign for DPJ candidates. Except for labor unions, the DPJ had no systematic organizational support. According to a former director of the DPJ secretariat, "Without assistance from the labor unions, it would be difficult for [DPJ candidates] even to put up posters."[58] The union help made it possible for DPJ candidates to run election campaigns with limited financial resources.

In addition to connecting with labor leaders, Ozawa visited agricultural co-ops and small business groups all over the nation. Although they were traditional supporters of the LDP, they did not refuse Ozawa's visit. Ozawa took advantage of his rich political career to expand the support base for the DPJ.[59]

Ozawa ordered DPJ candidates to apply the upstream strategy and instructed new candidates to give a short speech at fifty different locations per day in their constituency. One candidate testified that he closely followed Ozawa's instruction: "It was important for me to show myself to the voters. By giving a long speech, it was impossible to make to fifty different locations. Every few minutes, every four or five hundred meters, I stopped and told my name and one policy goal."[60] Many candidates followed Ozawa's instruction to conduct grassroots campaigning.

At the same time, Ozawa promoted electoral cooperation with other opposition parties. He successfully secured electoral cooperation with the Socialist Party in the districts where no Socialist candidate would run. In two SMDs (Yamagata and Toyama), the Socialist Party even withdrew its existing candidates. Ozawa also reached an agreement with the People's New Party (PNP). The DPJ and PNP jointly supported candidates in Toyama and Shimane SMDs.

Ozawa's focused efforts in SMDs and electoral cooperation with the PNP and the Socialist Party worked effectively. In eighteen of the twenty-nine SMDs, the DPJ candidates won, in addition to one PNP candidate and five independents that the DPJ recommended.[61] As the LDP won in only six SMDs, the results in the SMDs made for a big difference between the DPJ and the LDP, as Ozawa had expected. The DPJ won 60 seats out of the 121 contested seats, including 40 PR seats. Given its 49 other uncontested seats, the DPJ became the largest political party in the upper house with 109 seats.

LDP president Shinzō Abe declared that he would remain in the premier post despite the big defeat in the upper house. Abe tried to recover his public support by reshuffling the cabinet. However, his approval rate never recovered. In September Abe announced his resignation as national leader.

In contrast, Ozawa's leadership within the DPJ seemed significantly empowered with the election victories. That was sustained for several months. In November Ozawa met with Abe's successor, Prime Minister Yasuo Fukuda, and agreed to form a coalition government with the LDP. But the idea of forming the grand coalition created such strong opposition within the DPJ that Ozawa at once publicly announced his resignation as DPJ president. Although Ozawa was persuaded to keep the presidency, this turmoil put a dent in his leadership within the DPJ.

Prime Minister Fukuda was very disappointed. While Fukuda persuaded LDP leaders to form the coalition with the DPJ, Ozawa did not have any prior consultation with other party leaders. Fukuda recalls, "[The proposal] was discussed with a necessary precondition that Mr. Ichirō Ozawa would unify the DPJ. Mr. Ozawa thought that he could do it. Especially after the landslide victory in the upper house election, he had significant confidence."[62]

In March 2009 Ozawa's secretary was arrested for receiving a bribe from a construction company. After receiving public criticism over the scandal, Ozawa resigned as DPJ leader on May 11 in order to maximize DPJ's chance to win in the general election. In his resignation speech at the DPJ executive meeting, he stated, "If all the DPJ members unify themselves in the coming general election, the voters will understand us and the power shift will be achieved. If my resignation solidifies the party unity, I am happy to resign."[63] The subsequent DPJ leadership election was contested between two former DPJ presidents, Yukio Hatoyama and Katsuya Okada. Hatoyama, who received support from Ozawa's group, won. To prepare for the next general election, which could take place anytime between then and September, Hatoyama appointed Ozawa to the post of the acting president in charge of elections.

Ozawa declared that it was "his mission to make the DPJ government" as acting president.[64] To win the general election, the DPJ needed to win more than 150 seats in the three hundred SMDs. Ozawa identified fifty SMDs as priority districts and put the highest priority on running the election campaign and distributing funds in these districts. Ozawa began visiting these electoral districts all over the nation.[65]

Ozawa also sent fifteen of his personal secretaries to assist new candidates nationwide. These secretaries were experienced in election campaigns and helped the candidates to form kōenkai, hold meetings with voters, pay house visits, and establish supporting organizations.[66]

In addition, Ozawa negotiated electoral cooperation with the Socialist Party and the PNP. An agreement was reached among the three parties to cooperate in thirty-two SMDs. The DPJ received electoral support from the two opposition parties for DPJ candidates in nineteen SMDs, in return for DPJ support for eight Socialists, four PNP members, and one independent in thirteen SMDs. This cooperation was beneficial to the DPJ and the Socialists. All nineteen DPJ candidates were elected. Two of the eight SDP candidates and the one independent won election in the SMDs.

Ozawa's electoral strategy and the electoral cooperation with the other opposition parties worked well again. The DPJ won 221 seats in the SMDs in addition to 87 seats in the PR districts. The total of 308 seats was the largest number one political party had won in a lower house election under the current constitution. The LDP, on the other hand, saw its seats reduced from 303 to 119, lowering its share to around 25 percent in the lower house. The DPJ finally achieved its longtime goal of becoming the government party, and it did so with historic numbers.

ELECTION ANALYSIS

The LDP's Declining Tendency

The power shift from the LDP to the DPJ did not take place overnight. From its inception in 1996, the DPJ constantly increased its support base. In the first general election that year, it received only 10.6 percent of votes cast in the PR districts, compared with 38.6 percent for the LDP. While it won 52 lower house seats, it failed to create a popular boom. Within four years, however, the DPJ increased its share of votes in the 2000 general election to 25.2 percent, only 3 percent less than the LDP's captured votes in the PR districts. The DPJ increased its representation to 127 seats during the LDP administration under the leadership of unpopular prime minister Yoshirō Mori.

The power shift could have come earlier in the 2000s, but Koizumi came to power, drastically transforming the political environment. Koizumi promised to change Japan by changing the LDP. His political determination for structural reform regained popularity for the LDP government. In the 2001 upper house election, the LDP reversed its declining tendency to increase its share of votes in the PR districts to 38.6 percent. The DPJ received only 16.4 percent.

The Koizumi boom did not last long, however. In the 2003 general election, the DPJ captured the most votes in the PR districts with 37.9 percent, compared with the LDP's 35.6 percent. But the LDP did well in the SMDs, with 168 seats, largely because of electoral cooperation with its coalition partner, the Kōmeitō, so the coalition parties captured a secure majority in the lower house. In the 2004 upper house election, the DPJ won 55 of the 121 contested seats to become the party with the most seats, compared with the LDP's 49.

The 2005 general election was another exception in the declining tendency of the LDP. Koizumi captured media and public attention by running assassins—new LDP party contestants—against the postal rebels who were removed from the party because of their opposition to Koizumi's postal reform. The LDP received 42.8 percent of PR votes; in contrast, the DPJ received only 33.9 percent. But the 2001 upper house and the 2005 lower house elections were exceptions. The LDP's share of PR votes declined from 1996 to 2010, as shown in figure 4.4. In five recent elections, the LDP surpassed the DPJ only once, in the 2005 general election. The declining tendency of the LDP is more clearly illustrated in figure 4.5, which shows the LDP's lead over the DPJ in share of captured votes in the PR districts.

The rise of the DPJ did not totally rely on the decline of the LDP. As shown in a *Yomiuri Shimbun* poll on political party support, the DPJ was also able to capture votes of independents who had been frustrated by LDP rule. Between the 1970s and the 1980s, the percentage of the people who identified themselves as independents was relatively stable, between 20 and 30 percent. As Aiji Tanaka points out, the Socialist Party absorbed the anti-LDP voters during the two decades, as support rates for the LDP and the Socialists were almost a mirror image of each other. After 1993, however, the number of Socialist supporters kept declining, and more and more anti-LDP voters began identifying themselves as independents (see fig. 4.6).[67] The

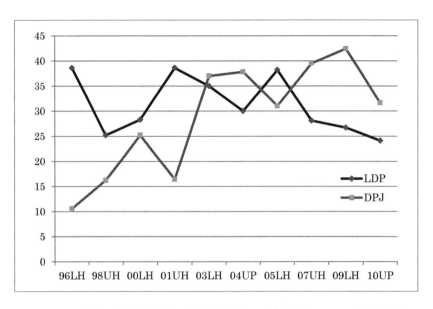

FIGURE 4.4. Votes by the LDP and DPJ in Proportional Representation Districts

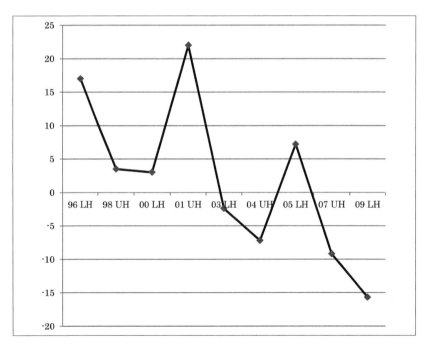

FIGURE 4.5. The LDP Lead over the DPJ in Proportional Representation Districts, 1996–2009

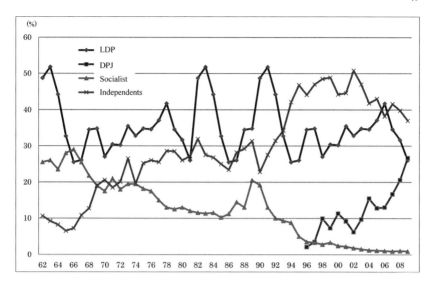

FIGURE 4.6. LDP Supporters, DPJ Supporters, and Independents, 1990–2009
Source: Yomiuri Shinbun Opinion Poll, cited from Tanaka Aijii, "Jimintō Suitai no Kōzō," 8.

numbers of independents began to decrease after 2003, and many of them became DPJ supporters. In short, the DPJ seems to have successfully absorbed former Socialist supporters and independents while the people were increasingly giving up on the LDP, leading eventually to the DPJ becoming the ruling party in 2009.

Toward a Two-Party System

With the decline of the LDP and the rise of the DPJ, Japan's party system has shifted toward a two-party system, which many reformers had hoped to establish with the new electoral system. After the NFP breakup in 1997, the DPJ became the largest opposition party. In the 2004 upper house election, the DPJ won more seats than the LDP. As a result of the 2007 election, the DPJ became the largest political party in the upper house. These developments established the DPJ as a viable alternative to the LDP.

Japan's shift toward a two-party system can be confirmed by examining the effective number of political parties. The most commonly used measure to calculate this figure is the Laakso-Taagepera (LT) index.[68] The LT index can be measured at the level of votes or seats. Here the LT index is calculated at the share of seats in the lower house as

$$LT = \frac{1}{\Sigma S_i^2},$$

with s being the share of the seats in the lower house of party i. The result of the calculation is presented in table 4.2.

The LT index for overall lower house seats (SMD and PR seats combined) was almost 3.0 in 1996 and 2000. But it dropped to 2.59 in 2003 and to 2.27 in 2005. Finally, in 2009 it became 2.10. In the PR system the index figure is naturally higher as it allows smaller parties to have a better chance to win seats. The index also showed a declining tendency. In 1996 it was 3.84. Largely because of the NFP breakup, the effective party number in the 2000 PR districts increased to 4.72. However, it dropped to nearly 3.0 in the following three elections. In the SMDs the LT index was already close to 2.0 in 1996 as political parties competed for a single seat. As the LDP in 2005 and the DPJ in 2009 won overwhelming majorities with almost 300 seats, the index figure was significantly below 2.0 (1.77 and 1.70, respectively).

Studies on the level of votes in each SMD also confirmed the tendency toward a two-party system. The average LT index of the 300 SMDs showed constant decline in the first four elections after the electoral reform (2.93 in 1996, 2.75 in 2000, 2.40 in 2003, 2.39 in 2005, and 2.26 in 2009).[69] The electoral institutional changes drastically moved Japan toward a two-party system.

The shift toward a two-party system was accelerated by the electoral strategy of the two parties as well. After forming a coalition government in

TABLE 4.2 Effective number of parties in the lower house

	OVERALL	SMDS	PR DISTRICTS
1996	2.93	2.36	3.84
2000	3.17	2.37	4.72
2003	2.59	2.29	3.03
2005	2.27	1.77	3.15
2009	2.10	1.70	2.91

1999, the LDP and the Kōmeitō had developed electoral cooperation. Winning seats in SMDs would be very difficult for a small political party without electoral cooperation with other parties. Electoral cooperation with the LDP enabled the Kōmeitō to win seven SMD seats in 2000, nine in 2003, and eight in 2005. (In the 2009 general election, the party could not win any SMD seats.)

The Kōmeitō also received votes in PR districts from LDP supporters. Many LDP candidates asked their supporters to vote for themselves in SMDs and for the Kōmeitō in PR districts. According to opinion polls, an increasing number of LDP supporters voted for the Kōmeitō. In the lower house elections, 14.3 percent of the Kōmeitō's votes came from LDP supporters in 2000, and the LDP supporters' share increased to 17.3 percent in 2003, 27.7 percent in 2005, and 17.6 percent in 2009.[70]

In return, the LDP received electoral support from the Kōmeitō for most of the SMDs. According to a study by Ikuo Kabashima, the LDP gained an additional thirty-four to forty-four SMD seats with electoral support from Kōmeitō supporters in the 2000 general election. The bonus seats from Kōmeitō support even increased to fifty-three to seventy-seven seats in the 2003 general election.[71] The government power shift could have occurred earlier without the Kōmeitō's electoral assistance to the LDP.

On the other hand, the DPJ under Ichirō Ozawa actively promoted electoral cooperation with the PNP and the Socialist Party to avoid the split of anti-LDP votes in the 2007 upper house election and the 2009 general election. The DPJ's tactics to avoid competition among the opposition parties in the SMDs naturally reduced the effective number of parties.

What further benefited the DPJ was the withdrawal of Communist candidates in many SMDs. The Japan Communist Party traditionally nominated candidates in every lower house district. The party continued this tradition even after the 1994 electoral reform, which increased the number of districts from 130 to 300. Although the party won two SMD seats in the 1996 general election, it had not won any SMD seats since the 2000 general election. SMD candidates who get less than 10 percent of the total valid votes in their district cannot get a refund of their 3-million-yen deposit. In the 2005 general election, the JCP lost 669 million yen as 223 of the 275 JCP candidates in the SMDs failed to get the required number of votes.[72] In the 2009 election, the JCP carefully picked 152 SMDs where its candidates had a chance to win more than 10 percent of cast votes and did not nominate candidates in the remaining 148 SMDs.

Among these 148 SMDs, the DPJ had candidates in 132 districts. According to a *Yomiuri Shimbun* survey, about 70 percent of JCP supporters cast their votes for DPJ candidates. As the JCP received an average of 14,000 votes in the SMDs in the 2005 general election, nearly 10,000 votes were suspected to have been cast for DPJ candidates. These votes from JCP supporters especially made a difference in the closely contested districts.[73]

On the other hand, the establishment of a new party, the Your Party (Minnanotō), pulled votes from the LDP candidates. As described in chapter 3, the Your Party was formed as former minister of administrative reform Yoshimi Watanabe, who had strongly disagreed with the Asō cabinet over bureaucratic reform, left the LDP. After Prime Minister Asō dissolved the lower house in August 2009, Watanabe formed a new party that aimed to make the government more democratic and less controlled by bureaucrats. The Your Party fielded thirteen candidates in the 2009 general elections, and five of them were elected.

A survey by Taku Sugawara explored the electoral performances of the LDP and the DPJ in eleven PR districts in the 2009 general election—the Your Party nominated its candidates in seven of the districts. The survey found that the DPJ votes did not make a statistical difference between the districts with and without Your Party candidates. In contrast, the LDP received 12.8 percent fewer votes in the PR districts with Your Party candidates than in the 2005 general election, and 6.2 percent fewer in the districts without such candidates.[74] In short, the emergence of the Your Party significantly decreased the LDP votes, while the withdrawal of the JCP candidates benefited the DPJ.

Voting Behavior and Swing Votes

One of the goals that electoral reformers pursued was more party-centered elections. Under the old multimember-districts system, LDP candidates competed to expand their kōenkai to increase personal supporters. The LDP as a party did not put so much effort into enlarging its membership. The past lower house elections under the old electoral system tended to be more candidate centered.

With the introduction of SMDs, the situation changed. According to surveys conducted by the Association for Promoting Fair Elections (Akarui Senkyo Suishin Kyōkai), 49.1 percent of voters cast their votes by attaching greater importance to candidates, while 40.6 percent gave greater importance to political

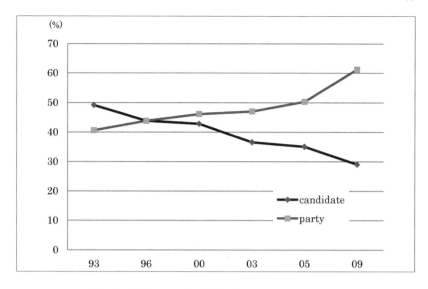

FIGURE 4.7. Choice of Party or Candidate?

parties in the 1993 general election (see fig. 4.7). The ratio of voters who put a higher priority on individual candidates than on the party constantly decreased under the SMD system. In the 2009 general election, as many as 61.2 percent of respondents voted for a party, compared with 29.0 percent for individual candidates.[75] The general election became more party centered, as reformers had hoped.

Ko Maeda conducted a systematic study to analyze whether the new electoral system has changed the focus of electoral competition from candidates to parties. To examine the extent to which the SMD vote results of LDP candidates were determined by the party's popularity, he compared the LDP's vote share in the PR tier (typically the more party-centered choice) with that of the SMD tier (typically the more candidate-centered choice) in the four general elections between 1996 and 2005. Maeda found that the election became increasingly party centered as the PR-SMD correlation coefficient increased from 0.458 in 2000 to 0.605 in 2003, and to 0.747 in 2005.[76]

As the general election became more party centered, the influence of swing voters became important. In the 2005 general election, voter turnouts increased by 7.7 percent (to 67.5 percent) from the 2003 general election, and the total number of votes increased by more than 8.3 million votes. As the LDP's votes increased by 6.4 million votes, the ruling party absorbed an

overwhelming majority of new voters. In the 2009 general election, voter turnout further increased by 1.8 percent, and the total number of votes increased
by 2.5 million votes. This means that 10.8 million more voters participated in
2009 than in 2003. The DPJ increased its votes in SMDs by 11.7 million votes
between 2003 and 2009, and in the 2009 election it absorbed the most new
voters in addition to the supporters of other parties.[77]

The electoral change from 2005 to 2009 constituted a national swing. Floating votes went to the LDP in 2005 and shifted to the DPJ in 2009 in a vast
majority of districts.[78] According to a survey, only 41.1 percent of those who
voted for LDP candidates in 2005 cast their ballots for LDP candidates in
2009. The same ratio of former LDP supporters turned their ballots to DPJ
candidates in 2009.[79]

The obvious factor behind the vote swing was the declining popularity of
the LDP government and the increasing expectations for the DPJ. In a *Yomiuri Shimbun* opinion poll, nearly 80 percent of respondents were disappointed
by the LDP, compared with 40 percent by the DPJ. The same poll showed
that more than 70 percent had some expectations for the DPJ, compared with
less than 50 percent for the LDP. Another study illustrates that more than 70
percent of those who turned their votes from the LDP in 2005 to the DPJ in
2009 considered the DPJ viable as government party.[80] With increasingly
lower expectations for the LDP and higher expectations for the DPJ, the vote
swing across the nation altered the makeup of the government in 2009. According to an *Asahi Shimbun* opinion poll, 81 percent of respondents observed
that the DPJ's landslide victory was because voters wanted to see an alternative government.[81] The electoral system with SMDs made it easier for Japanese
voters to express their frustration in the government and their desire for a new
government.

Vocal Minority vs. Silent Majority

In 1994, as a result of the Hosokawa government's political reform effort, a
new single-member electoral system was introduced. The malapportionment
under the old electoral system, which overrepresented rural areas, had contributed to the LDP's long reign. The ruling party extended its pork-barrel
politics for the rural constituencies through public works and agricultural
subsidies. The LDP maintained its government party status as a guardian of
vested interests. Hosokawa's electoral reform significantly, although not entirely,
corrected the rural overrepresentation. As the SMD system gives advantage to
a larger political party, however, the LDP was able to win a majority of SMDs

in the first four general elections until the public recognized the DPJ as a viable political party.

Targeting special interest groups was an effective electoral strategy under the old multimember-district system. In five-member districts, candidates could win a seat with around 10 percent of the total votes cast. LDP candidates tried to build a solid personal supporting base through their kōenkai and to establish ties with agricultural cooperatives, construction companies, and other groups that could provide them with organized votes. By catering to these groups, LDP incumbents secured their reelection.

Multiple representation by LDP incumbents accelerated the competition among them and their factions for votes. As the LDP party headquarters or prefectural branches could not focus their support on individual LDP candidates, factions competed to provide assistance to their members. To provide political funds to their members, factions actively sought to raise funds from interest groups in return for political pork. This led to corruption and contributed to the creation of a political system in which individual LDP members and the LDP as a whole served the interests of a vocal minority. In his 1955 book *Profiles in Courage*, John F. Kennedy warned of the danger of politicians serving the vocal minority of their constituents over the silent majority: "Some of them may have been representing the actual sentiments of the silent majority of their constituents in opposition to the screams of a vocal minority; but most of them were not."[82]

The 1994 political and electoral changes transformed the political environment. Overrepresentation of rural areas was drastically improved. The LDP had to nominate more candidates in urban areas and less in rural areas. LDP lower house members needed to reorganize their kōenkai to align them with new electoral boundaries. The revised political funding law made it more difficult for LDP factions to raise political funds, and individual LDP members became more reliant on political funds allocated by the LDP headquarters. Factions also significantly lost their influence in the selection of the party leader, the allocation of posts, and the recruitment of new candidates. LDP incumbents no longer had the luxury to concentrate on specific policy areas as specialists, but they had to be more versatile and cover diverse policy areas as they had to handle all kinds of requests from their constituencies as the sole political representative. LDP politicians now needed to serve outside of the traditional, vocal interest groups.

The 1997 electoral rule change stimulated public interest in the political process and brought more voters to the ballot, especially in urban areas. The newly participating voters served as swing votes to alter the government, and general elections became more party centered. The swing of votes created a landslide victory for the Koizumi cabinet in 2005 and for the DPJ in 2009. Many candidates, in both the LDP and the DPJ, realized that it was no longer an effective electoral strategy to appeal solely to vocal minorities; rather, they needed to court the silent majority, which created the national swings in 2005 and 2009.

5 | HATOYAMA'S ANTIBUREAUCRATIC
STANCE

A s DPJ PRESIDENT, I sincerely would like to express gratitude to the people. . . . Forty days during this summer, I believe that many voters seriously thought about the future. If that is true, the victor of this election and this power shift must be you, the people," stated Yukio Hatoyama in his victory declaration speech on election day on August 30, 2009, which saw his party unseat the longtime ruling LDP. In the speech, Hatoyama proclaimed that there were three meanings to the shift. First, it meant the alteration of the government. The LDP's long dominance was the result of the lack of viability of the past opposition parties. Japan needed to have a healthy party system in which viable political parties compete in policy ideas. Second, it meant generational change. Many young DPJ candidates defeated older LDP members, reflecting voters' desire to see fresh politicians who could change politics. The third change was a shift in sovereignty. The people wanted to end the bureaucracy-controlled government and to establish a true people-centered government.[1] Hatoyama promised voters that the DPJ government would be one led by political leaders, not by bureaucrats.

INSTITUTIONAL CHANGES BY THE DPJ

On September 16 Hatoyama was elected as prime minister in the Diet. At 10 p.m. he held his first cabinet meeting. The new national leader announced "The Basic Policy," in which he outlined three principles to promote political initiative and introduced a series of institutional changes to implement them.

The first principle was political leadership within the bureaucracy. The document stated that "the operation of the national government must be shifted from bureaucratic initiative or reliance on bureaucrats to political initiative or people's initiative."[2] To achieve this goal, the document asserted the establishment of a "three-political-appointees' conference" (*seimu sanyaku kaigi*) in each ministry in order to "plan and coordinate policies from a people's point of view."[3] In each conference the minister, senior vice minister, and parliamentary secretaries would make policy decisions.

On the other hand, the Hatoyama government abolished the administrative vice ministerial meeting. This bureaucratic subcabinet meeting was seen as a symbol of the government's bureaucratic supremacy as virtually all policy decisions needed to be approved by it before being submitted to the cabinet meeting. Hatoyama stated that his government would not "delegate governmental decisions to prior consultations solely by bureaucrats, such as vice ministers."[4]

On the same day the Hatoyama cabinet approved a document that provided guidelines for politico-bureaucratic relations with a clear division of roles between the two. In this document politicians are defined as "legislators who represent people" and have "responsibility to plan, coordinate, and decide administrative policies." Bureaucrats assist politicians by providing basic data and information and presenting policy options. The guidelines basically prohibited bureaucrats from making policy decisions or contacting other ministries for policy coordination. The document also limited contact between bureaucrats and politicians. It barred bureaucrats from contacting politicians other than their ministry officials and required them to keep records whenever other politicians contacted them.

In addition, it banned bureaucratic officials from holding press conferences. In the past administrative vice ministers regularly held press conferences for policy briefing. Under the DPJ government, political leaders within the ministry were allowed to give press conferences only in principle. Bureaucrats were allowed to speak only on technical matters and only after being requested to do so by the minister.[5] Both decision making and information control were handled by political leaders.

The second principle was the centralization of decision making in the hands of the cabinet. Under the LDP government, policy making was highly decentralized as prior consultation with the ruling party was required. As a result, the PARC subcommittees within the LDP long served as actual decision-making organs. Under the Hatoyama government, requests and suggestions from DPJ members would be delivered to the minister through political appointees. The Basic Policy clearly declared that "the decision of the government would be made by the cabinet, not by the party."[6]

To completely centralize policy making, DPJ secretary general Ichirō Ozawa abolished the DPJ's Policy Research Committee (PRC). As an opposition party, the DPJ formed the "Next Cabinet," modeled after British Shadow Cabinet. The members of the Next Cabinet also served as chairmen of the PRC subcommittee in their policy field. DPJ Diet members participated in PRC subcommittees to study and exchange their policy ideas. Ozawa circulated a memo declaring that all PRC functions would be shifted to the government. Instead of the PRC, the senior vice ministers of the government would hold the policy conference (*seisaku kaigi*), where all DPJ Diet members could join and express their views.[7] One DPJ Diet member wondered how this important decision was made and expressed his concern about how, in this setup, requests from constituents would be delivered to the government.[8]

The third principle was political leadership on policy coordination. Hatoyama stated in the Basic Policy that he and his chief cabinet secretary would organize British-style cabinet committees with related cabinet ministers to discuss and decide important policy matters. Under the LDP government, cabinet committees were very ceremonial. Policy decisions would have been made prior to the meetings, prepared by bureaucrats. Under the DPJ government, cabinet members would discuss the substance of policies and make political decisions at cabinet committee meetings. This direction was announced in the 2009 manifesto of the DPJ.

In addition to cabinet committees, the Hatoyama government introduced two new institutions—the National Strategy Office (NSO, Kokka Senryaku Shitsu) and the Government Revitalization Unit (GRU, Gyōsei Sasshin Kaigi). The NSO was established within the Cabinet Secretariat to replace the Council on Economic and Fiscal Policy. Hatoyama regarded the CEFP as the institution thorough which the LDP government promoted Japan's transformation to an excessively market-oriented economy and thought that its narrow focus on economic policy with market fundamentalism destroyed Japanese society.[9] The NSO was expected to provide an overarching vision for Japan as well as policy coordination among various ministries. Hatoyama appointed Naoto Kan as deputy prime minister in charge of the NSO. The NSO was first and foremost aimed at defeating the bureaucracy and controlling the government. Kan stated in his book that "the Hatoyama Cabinet established the NSO and appointed me to be in charge of it. This was a message sent to the bureaucracy that politicians would be responsible to make policies based on the principle of people's sovereignty."[10]

The GRU was established under the Cabinet Office "to completely review administration from the citizen's perspective" and to "scrutinize all budgets and programs and eliminate waste and abuses."[11] Hatoyama appointed Yoshito Sengoku to be in charge of the GRU. To deliver all the projects that the DPJ promised during the 2009 election campaign, the government would need 16.8 trillion yen. The GRU was expected to find funds by eradicating wasteful spending and by reworking the national government's 207-trillion-yen net expenditure, including special accounts.[12] The NSO and the GRU were considered "two wheels" of political initiative of the Hatoyama government.

A public opinion poll taken by the *Asahi Shimbun* immediately after the establishment of Hatoyama's cabinet showed a support rate of 71 percent, the second highest in history next only to the Koizumi cabinet, which had 78 percent support in April 2001. The biggest reason for the public's approval was the DPJ's policies, which drew support from 46 percent of respondents. The poll showed high expectations for the DPJ, as 49 percent of respondents believed that political control over the bureaucrats would be stronger, and 61 percent expected that the government change would enable the government to cut wasteful spending.[13]

POLICY MAKING UNDER THE NEW INSTITUTIONS

Budget Cutting by the GRU

The first policy issue the Hatoyama cabinet tackled was the review of the 2009 supplementary budget drawn up by the LDP government. Two days after the cabinet was established, Prime Minister Hatoyama called a meeting of the cabinet Committee on the Supplementary Budget. Its members were Hatoyama, Kan (in charge of the NSO), Sengoku (in charge of the GRU), Finance Minister Hirohisa Fujii, and Chief Cabinet Secretary Hirofumi Hirano.[14] Hatoyama appointed Sengoku to be in charge of cutting the 13.9-trillion-yen supplementary budget that the Asō cabinet had formed to deal with the post–Lehman shock economy. The goal was set to cut it by 3 trillion yen against the veto players in the spending ministries.

Fujii and the Ministry of Finance fully supported Sengoku's GRU with regard to the budget cut, and the MOF's budget examiners frequently visited the GRU office to provide advice and suggestions. On October 6 Sengoku held a press conference to announce that the supplementary budget was being cut by 2.5 trillion yen by freezing expenditures and getting refunds from local governments. Sengoku proudly stated, "Each minister tried and cooperated to freeze and return the already formed and executed budget items. This was very unusual; the first time."[15]

Still the 3-trillion-yen goal was not met. Sengoku requested members of the Hatoyama cabinet to make further cuts in expenditures. Seiji Maehara, minister for land, infrastructure, transport, and tourism, responded, "The meaning of the government change is to change how to spend tax money. We will shift from building-centered spending to people-centered spending." Maehara cut his ministry's supplementary budget by 887.5 billion yen, the largest amount among the ministries.[16] Several cabinet ministers did not want their ministry's budget cut, but Sengoku and Fujii persuaded them to agree to the budget. At the October 16 cabinet meeting, Sengoku proudly announced a budget cut of 2.93 trillion yen, which he considered as achieving the goal.[17]

The Hatoyama cabinet also needed to form the first budget for fiscal year (FY) 2010. On September 29 the prime minister called a meeting of the cabinet Committee on the Budget, whose members were the same as those for the supplementary budget. The five ministers agreed to abolish the budget guidelines made under the LDP government. The LDP's guidelines were to provide special measures amounting to 350 billion yen for the post-Lehman economic crisis while allowing a natural increase for social entitlement expenditures.[18] The submission deadline for the draft budget proposals from the ministries was October 15. The Hatoyama government declared that it would tackle an overall review of the whole budget for fiscal reconstruction to create funds for programs that the DPJ had promised during the general election campaign. The cabinet ministers were expected to review their ministry's budget from scratch and to make cuts.[19] These guidelines were approved by the subsequent cabinet meeting on the same day.

Although the Hatoyama cabinet demanded substantial reductions in expenditures, the initial draft budget proposals for FY2010 amounted to 95 trillion yen, the largest ever budget, with a 6.5-trillion-yen increase from the LDP's 2009 budget. The budget reductions by the cabinet ministers amounted to only 1.3 trillion yen. At the meeting of the cabinet Budget Committee, the members expressed their high expectations of Sengoku to again show his skill in budget cutting.[20] Again, the goal for budget cuts was set at 3 trillion yen.

The GRU was in charge of the budget cutting. This unit was officially chaired by Prime Minister Hatoyama, with Sengoku as vice chair. In addition, there were four cabinet ministers (Kan, Fujii, Hirano, and Minister of Internal Affairs and Communications Kazuhiro Haraguchi) and five private-sector members, including Kyocera CEO Kazuo Inamori and Kikkoman CEO Tomosaburō Mogi. Its secretariat was headed by Hideki Katō, a former MOF official who had promoted the budget cuts in local governments as president of a think tank called the Japan Initiative (Kōsō Nippon).

At its first meeting, on October 22, the GRU decided to conduct a series of program screenings (*jigyō shiwake*). Three working groups were formed: The first group would examine the budgets of the Ministries of Land, Infrastructure, Transportation, and Tourism (MLIT); Internal Affairs and Communications (MIC); Finance; and Environment. The second group would work on the Ministries of Health, Labor, and Welfare (MHLW); Foreign Affairs; and Economy, Trade and Industry (METI). The third group would deal with the Ministries of Education, Culture, Sports, Science, and Technology (MEXT); Agriculture, Forestry, and Fisheries (MAFF); and Defense (MOD).[21] Each working group would have DPJ Diet members and civilians examine the ministries' budget items.

Many of the budget items had been regarded as wasteful by the MOF in the budget examination process of the past years but had survived because of the strong pressure from veto players, including the spending ministries, LDP zoku members, and related interest groups. In the program screening it was emphasized that the working groups should look into these programs "from an outsiders' perspective" to judge "whether they were needed in the first place." Working group members were asked if the budget items were appropriate considering the size of the government budget deficit. The working groups were to hold discussions with the ministry officials in public hearings. It was important to open up discussions to show the public "what were the important points and priorities in the budget making" so that they could clear public suspicion, improve accountability of the ministries, and shift the budget-making power from the bureaucrats and zoku members to the people.[22]

There was no sanctuary in the program screening, as the working groups were asked to look into the special accounts. While the general account budget included most of the basic expenditures for current government operations, special accounts budgets were designed for special government programs or institutions, such as public enterprises, state pension funds, and public works projects financed with special taxes. The total amount of the special accounts reached more than 300 trillion yen. The MOF's budget examination on special accounts was not as detailed as that for the general accounts because the special account expenditures were financed by specific financial revenues. Under the Koizumi cabinet, Finance Minister Seijūrō Shiokawa once stated in a 2003 Diet committee meeting, "While people in the main building are fending off hunger with rice porridge, children in the outbuilding are feasting on sukiyaki," and he warned that deep cuts in the general-account budget would not restore fiscal health if extravagances financed by the special accounts continued.[23] But the Koizumi cabinet did not take action to reform such accounts. The DPJ government, with limited relations with the interest groups, would cut in the area that had been considered a sanctuary under the LDP government.

The GRU secretariat recruited fifty-nine staffers to prepare for the first series of public hearings on program screening.[24] The hearings were held in a gym located in Ichigaya, Tokyo, for nine days in November. The gym was packed with public observers, and the entire session was broadcast live on the Internet. The media also paid very close attention to the open debates between the defending bureaucrats and the screeners, who were on the offensive.

Under high public and media attention, the hearings examined 449 budget programs.[25] Behind the scenes, MOF bureaucrats assisted the DPJ members in cutting programs they had previously been unable to eliminate owing to the opposition of the veto players. After the nine days of hearings, the working groups had cut 690 billion yen of budget items and identified 1 trillion yen of endowment funds in the quasi-governmental organizations that could be used to finance the deficit. Although this did not reach the 3-trillion-yen goal, the program screening process helped the DPJ government to maintain a high level of public support. According to an *Asahi Shimbun* survey on November 5, the Hatoyama cabinet received a 62 percent approval rating, with 76 percent of respondents holding the screening program in high regard.[26]

Inactive National Strategy Office

While the GRU drew media and public attention, the activities of the National Strategy Office were very limited. The original plan was to establish a bureau at the Cabinet Secretariat that would coordinate all policy areas. Deputy Prime Minister Kan, who was in charge of the NSO, was expected to play a pivotal role in policy making under the Hatoyama cabinet. CCS Hirano would play a more limited policy-making role and instead would concentrate on political affairs, serving as liaison between the government and the ruling parties. However, Kan could not establish a bureau without new legislation, which was never introduced to the Diet. With an office status (equivalent to the division, or *ka*, in the bureaucratic hierarchy), the GRU's function was limited from the beginning.

Since 2006, when Ichirō Ozawa became DPJ president, the party had had a troika system in which three leaders—Ozawa, Hatoyama, and Kan—divided the roles and responsibilities as described in chapter 4. Under the Hatoyama government, Ozawa, as DPJ secretary general, would be in charge of all party affairs, and Kan was expected to be in charge of policy affairs. To fully control policy affairs, Kan sought to assume the chairmanship of the DPJ Policy Research Committee. With the backing of the committee members, he would be able to exercise his power within the government. However, Ozawa strongly demanded centralization of policy making in the cabinet and abolished the party's policy committees. Kan now had to run the new office without any support from the party.

In addition, the jurisdiction of the NSO became more and more limited. At first the NSO was assigned to deal with all policy areas, including foreign policy. On the second day of the Hatoyama government, however, Foreign Minister Katsuya Okada denied the NSO's involvement in foreign policy making unless the prime minister specifically assigned the task to the office.[27] The NSO then was to focus on domestic policies, such as the budget, taxation, and economic management in general. But Finance Minister Hirohisa Fujii publicly stated that the budget would be decided by the Ministry of Finance, and that the NSO should focus on national strategy, as its name suggested. The NSO was at least supposed to replace the Council for Economic and Fiscal Policy, which formed the outline of the budget under the LDP government, as described in chapter 3. But the NSO had no mandate, no authority, no budget, and a very limited staff.

On October 13 the first NSO staffer recruited from the private sector went to the office to find only four desks without any telephone lines or other staffers. As of the end of October, the NSO had only twelve staffers, compared with fifty-nine in the GRU. Many people had applied for positions, but the NSO had no budget to hire them. All staffers were seconded from the ministries and large corporations.[28] At the October 28 lower house floor meeting, LDP member Yasutoshi Nishimura criticized the inactivity of the office: "The NSO has not done anything. Although Deputy Prime Minister Kan attracted high attention when assuming [the ministership in charge of the NSO], you have no presence."[29] There had been high expectations for the NSO in the media and the public at the start of the DPJ government. With limited staff, however, as

Keisuke Tsumura, parliamentary secretary for the NSO, has testified, the NSO was kept busy drafting answers for the Diet meeting regarding the office's role and function and could not do anything more. Tsumura states, "[The NSO] was originally expected to coordinate all the policy matters. But soon we found that foreign policy was under the control of the MOFA, and budget under the MOF."[30]

To revitalize the function of the NSO, the cabinet Committee on the Budget announced in mid-November that the NSO would make "a draft of the basic policy of budget formation" and would be in charge of discussing "the major items of the DPJ's manifesto."[31] However, the NSO could not play this important role, which the CEFP had played under the Koizumi government, as the MOF already controlled the budget process.

One achievement of the NSO was the formation of "The New Growth Strategy Toward a Radiant Japan."[32] As the NSO's staffers were limited, Kan asked for staff support from the METI. They conducted a series of hearings with scholars and bureaucratic officials.[33] On December 30 the strategy was approved as a cabinet decision to outline policies to revitalize Japan's economic conditions in order to achieve a 3 percent economic growth rate (a nominal figure).

A week later, when Finance Minister Fujii resigned, Kan was appointed as his successor and left the NSO. GRU minister Yoshito Sengoku doubled up to also run the NSO. Sengoku had a very different political philosophy from Kan's and did not believe that economic growth was everything. For Sengoku it was more important to maximize the utility of the people.[34] The growth strategy formed by Kan was suspended as a result.

The NSO never functioned as expected. While the GRU received formal and informal support from the bureaucracy, especially the MOF, the NSO had very limited bureaucratic support to materialize policy initiatives. After the DPJ's defeat in the July 2010 upper house election, the ruling parties lost control of the chamber. The DPJ government gave up passing the legislation to legally authorize the NSO. As a result, the NSO was downgraded to a mere advisory organ to the prime minister with limited staff.

Political Leadership in Policy Making

Under the DPJ government, political appointees—the minister, the senior vice minister, and parliamentary secretaries—were expected to make all the important decisions of the ministry. As teamwork among appointees was very important, the appointments of the senior vice ministers and the parliamentary secretaries were made by the cabinet ministers. Under the LDP government, these subcabinet appointments were decided by the prime minister and the chief cabinet secretary, considering the factional balance. As discussed in chapter 4, under the later period of the Koizumi cabinet and during the Abe cabinet, subcabinet appointments were made after considering the preferences of individual LDP members. But the appointments were still made by the cabinet with factional balance in mind. Under the Hatoyama cabinet, however, the cabinet ministers could freely select their coworkers.

Health, Welfare, and Labor Minister Akira Nagatsuma writes in his book that, as his ministry covers so many policy areas, "it was impossible for one person to deal with [all the policy topics]. So, I needed deputy ministers and parliamentary secretaries that I could trust, and counting on good teamwork with them I would be able to exercise political leadership."[35] Under the LDP government, the minister seldom worked together with subcabinet members.[36] A former LDP cabinet minister recalled his experience: "A minister is like a single tree in the torrent." He can be easily swallowed in the flood of information provided by the bureaucracy.[37] Under the DPJ government, however, the ministers regularly held meetings with their subcabinet members, were briefed along with the bureaucrats, and collectively made policy decisions. These political appointees made policy decisions themselves rather than allowing bureaucratic officials to make them.

This totally changed the power balance between the political appointees and the bureaucrats. Under the LDP government the minister acted like the chairman of a corporation, mostly working on external affairs, while the administrative vice ministers were like corporate presidents, with real authority to control the entire bureaucracy. Under the DPJ government, Junya Ogawa, parliamentary secretary of the MIC, noted that "the minister is president, the senior vice minister is the senior managing director, and the parliamentary secretaries are executive directors. . . . The bureaucrats are merely assisting staff, and never part of the top executive." DPJ political appointees were careful not to be controlled by the bureaucrats. Ogawa stated, "Ninety-nine out of one hundred persons I meet in a day are bureaucrats. I need to be quite careful, otherwise I cannot control them."[38]

How these political appointees divided their responsibilities depended on the ministry. For example, in the MIC parliamentary secretaries often served as liaisons between the minister and bureaucrats. In the Cabinet Office, parliamentary secretaries supported the minister and the senior vice ministers. On the other hand, in the MOD the minister had overall responsibility and other political appointees divided their responsibility areas. The senior vice minister was in charge of the budget, one parliamentary secretary held responsibility over negotiations on the transformation of U.S. forces in Japan, and the other worked on reform of the ministry.[39]

In some of the ministries, the political appointees held exclusive meetings among themselves, not allowing any bureaucratic officials to attend. Some of them micromanaged administrative tasks and did not allow bureaucrats to make any decision. For example, the MEXT changed the internal rule to shift the decision-making authority for many ministerial tasks from the administrative vice minister to the senior vice minister. Official letters, which used to be sent under the name of the top bureaucrat, were now signed by the senior vice minister. The decision-making authority of the bureaucrats was drastically reduced.[40] As a result the lowered morale of the bureaucrats became a problem.[41]

Former deputy CCS Teijirō Furukawa was critical of the Hatoyama government's political initiative: "In the ministries, in principle, the political appointees—the minister, the senior vice minister, and the parliamentary secretaries—were totally in charge of [policy affairs]. The exclusion of policy experts caused huge confusion." He pointed out the reality of administrative operations: "Daily administrative work is unlimited. The three political appointees alone cannot handle all of it. Being politicians does not mean that they are experienced in the policy fields." Furukawa then described the ideal division of labor: "Politicians trust and use civil servants as policy experts and make their own decisions. In return, the civil servants respond to the trust."[42] The DPJ was losing this balance.

The abolition of the administrative vice ministerial meeting also affected the power structure within the government. This subcabinet meeting had 123 years of history since Japan's cabinet system was introduced. While the cabinet was the Japanese government's highest decision-making institution, decisions were not made in cabinet meetings under the LDP government. The agenda for a cabinet meeting was prepared at a subcabinet meeting, usually held the day before, and the agenda went to the cabinet meeting along with a proposed decision. Although the subcabinet meeting had no legal authority or basis for its existence, the cabinet seldom repealed decisions made at that meeting. Critics often described this subcabinet meeting as evidence of Japan's bureaucratic supremacy. Naoto Kan was a leading critic and included its abolition as a campaign promise in the November 2003 general election when he was DPJ president. As soon as the DPJ government was established, the subcabinet meeting was abolished.

The subcabinet meeting, however, had created important sources of power for the prime minister, the chief cabinet secretary, and especially the administrative deputy CCS who chaired the meeting. It had served as an important source of information from the government agencies. As all government policy issues had to be finalized at the subcabinet meeting, ministry officials usually had prior consultation with the CCS and the deputy CCS. When there were conflicts among different agencies, the CCS and the deputy CCS were expected to coordinate with the vice ministers and other high officials.

High-level policy coordination was conducted between the CCS and the administrative vice ministers, but before a policy issue was brought to the subcabinet meeting, consultations and negotiations took place among the deputy directors, directors, and bureau chiefs. Through the multilayered policy coordination, policy proposals were polished and materialized, to be presented to the subcabinet meeting in a finalized form. Under the Hatoyama cabinet DPJ political appointees, with very limited policy-making experience, handled most of the policy coordination among the ministries, destroying the bureaucratic networks.

Under the Koizumi government, according to former deputy CCS Teijirō Furukawa, the subcabinet meeting was often where the deputy CCS announced the intentions of the prime minister, and the first stage of the top-down decision-making process.[43] By announcing the national leader's intention at the meeting, the Kantei could make the entire government follow suit.

In addition, the subcabinet meeting was an important forum to share and exchange administrative information. Administrative vice-ministers learned what was going on in the other ministries, and they often discussed policy issues in front of the deputy CCS at the Kantei. Without the meeting, there was no opportunity for the top bureaucrats to share information or even meet with each other. As the political appointees totally controlled policy making, without bureaucratic involvement, vice ministers no longer knew the details of their ministry's policy to inform the Kantei.[44] After the abolition of the meeting, the Kantei lost this vital source of information, many opportunities for policy coordination, and the mechanism by which the prime minister could deliver his intentions and give orders to the entire government.

The position of the administrative deputy CCS had been considered the top post of Japan's entire bureaucracy and had served as the liaison between the prime minister and the bureaucracy. A couple of deputy CCSs were so powerful that the media portrayed them as shadow prime ministers under the LDP governments. The abolition of the subcabinet meeting, however, drastically diminished the power of the deputy CCS who served as its chair. Under the Hatoyama government, former MIC vice minister Kinya Takino assumed this position. As the policy decisions were made by political appointees in the ministries and policy coordination among different ministries was directly negotiated by the ministers and senior vice ministers, the deputy CCS had a very limited role in policy making. A Kantei staffer noted, "[Mr. Takino] is completely out of the loop. I wonder why he became the deputy CCS." The Office of the Assistant CCS was supposed to support the deputy CCS, but according to an *Asahi Shimbun* report, this office did not function at all under the Hatoyama cabinet.[45] The dysfunctional role of the deputy CCS and the office in the Kantei significantly weakened the power of the prime minister in policy making.

Centralization of Policy Making?

The DPJ abolished its policy committee in order to centralize policy making within the government. Under the LDP government, the ruling party required prior consultation before the government made a policy decision. As a result, the subcommittees of the LDP's Policy Affairs Research Council served as the first forum the government consulted on its policy proposals. Members of these subcommittees earned the label of zoku and served as the ultimate arbiters of political power on a specific policy area. They examined the government's policies and often amended them. They received petitions from their constituencies and delivered political pork to them. This decentralization of power weakened the influence of the cabinet and the prime minister in policy making.

After policy making was centralized within the DPJ government, the question for the DPJ was how to handle petitions from local governments and interest groups. Under the LDP government they lobbied to zoku members and the PARC through their representatives and national umbrella organizations. DPJ secretary general Ichirō Ozawa decided to centralize the petition system as well by making his office the sole window for petitions to the government. Under the DPJ government local governments and interest groups needed to file petitions through their representatives and DPJ prefectural headquarters. These petitions were gathered by the Office of the DPJ Secretary General to be ultimately delivered to the political appointees of the related ministry (see fig. 5.1).

In the Office of the Secretary General, Ozawa appointed fourteen deputy secretaries general to handle the petitions brought by local governments

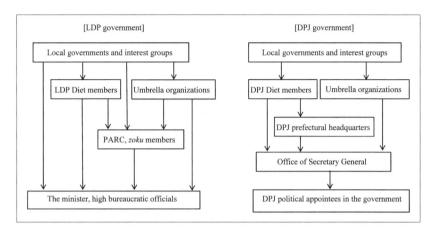

FIGURE 5.1. Petitions Under LDP and DPJ Governments

and deliver messages to the government officials. As more than four hundred DPJ Diet members brought petitions from their constituencies, this office absorbed vast amounts of political information from all over the nation. This significantly strengthened the political power of Secretary General Ozawa.[46]

This office became very powerful in budget formation process for FY2010. Prime Minister Hatoyama had difficulty forming the budget as the expected tax revenue fell to thirty-seven trillion yen and the initial budget proposal from the ministries amounted to ninety-five trillion yen. The DPJ government first tried to cut wasteful expenditures through the program screening, which trimmed only around two trillion yen of the government budget. On December 15, 2009, Prime Minister Hatoyama announced the basic guidelines of budget formation, which included the forty-four-trillion-yen ceiling of the government deficit bond in order to maintain market confidence (see table 5.1).[47]

On the following day Ozawa handed Hatoyama "the important requests for the FY2010 budget." In this list of requests, Ozawa proposed an income limit to receive the child allowance of thirteen thousand yen per child a month and the extension of the provisional tax on gasoline. These items could be interpreted as breaking the promises made in the DPJ's 2009 manifesto. These changes were considered necessary to meet the forty-four-trillion-yen ceiling of the deficit financing bond. Prime Minister Hatoyama basically swallowed most of Ozawa's requests, including the extension of the gasoline tax. The only item the prime minister rejected was the income limit to receive the child allowance as it was the highlighted policy in the 2009 DPJ manifesto. With

Table 5.1 Important requests for the FY 2010 budget

1. Child allowance of 13,000 yen per child with an income limit to receive

2. Free high school education

3. Individual income support for agriculture

4. Increased funds under local governments' independent control

5. Extension of the Special Law to support unpopulated areas

6. Establishment of forum between national and local governments

7. Construction of planned Shinkansen lines

8. Construction of planned highways

9. Increase in medical fees for patient treatment

10. Upgrading of pay of long-term-care workers

11. Repeal of the Services and Supports for Persons with Disability Act

12. Improvements in support measures for people with hepatitis

13. Maintenance of the provisional tax on gasoline

14. Elimination of highway tolls

15. Review of national programs and abolition of the financial burden for local governments

16. Review of the effectiveness of special taxation measures

17. Reduction in the budget for land improvement

18. Study of the environment tax

Source: Nihon Keizai Shimbun-sha, ed., *Seiken* [The ruling power] (Tokyo: Nihon Keizai Shimbun-sha, 2010), 214–17.

assistance from Ozawa, the Hatoyama government was able to form a budget within the proposed ceiling. This budget-making process was definitely not centralized in the hands of the cabinet as the party leadership showed strong political influence.

Hatoyama introduced institutional changes to strengthen political leadership vis-à-vis bureaucrats. In each ministry the top political appointees controlled decision making by excluding bureaucratic influence. Policy coordination among the ministries was shifted from the bureaucrats to the DPJ political appointees with limited experience. The DPJ abolished its policy councils in order to centralize policy making in the cabinet and established the centralized petition system in the Office of the Secretary General, which overrode the prime minister's decision on a major budget decision. With the new institutional arrangement set in place, Hatoyama had to handle the major national security issue of the relocation of the Futenma air base.

FUTENMA FIASCO: FOREIGN POLICY FAILURE

Hatoyama's Misperception

In the area of foreign relations, the DPJ in its 2009 manifesto promised to build a more equal alliance with the United States in order to establish a more autonomous foreign policy strategy, while making the greatest effort to develop closer relations with Asian neighbors to build an East Asian community.[48] Just before becoming prime minister, Hatoyama published an op-ed article in the *New York Times* titled "A New Path for Japan." In that piece Hatoyama expressed his doubts about the two institutions that the LDP government had regarded as the foundation of the Japanese government's direction and postwar economic success: market-based global capitalism and the U.S.-Japan alliance. He denounced the recent economic crisis that he said had resulted from American-style free-market economics. While he acknowledged the importance of the U.S.-Japan alliance, he insisted that East Asia "must be recognized as Japan's basic sphere of being." Then, he declared that "as a result of the failure of the Iraq war and the financial crisis, the era of U.S.-led globalism is coming to an end."[49] These statements were soon regarded as anti-Americanism. After becoming prime minister, Hatoyama tried to distance himself from these sentiments.

The first challenge Hatoyama had to face was the relocation of Futenma air base. In February 2009 the Japanese and U.S. governments signed an accord on the planned relocation of U.S. Marines from Okinawa to Guam. The necessary, fundamental condition for this relocation was to move U.S. Marine air base in Futenma to Henoko, Nago City, in northern Okinawa, which was agreed between the Japanese government and Nago City in April 2006. The following month the Japanese and U.S. governments signed a document titled "United States–Japan Roadmap for Realignment Implementation," which included the Henoko plan.[50] It took more than ten years to reach this agreement because many different interests and opinions of various political actors in

Okinawa prefecture, the U.S. government and military, the Japanese government, and the political parties were involved.

Okinawa prefecture alone was split into many groups with different interests. The leftists and the Okinawa media called for the relocation of the base outside of the prefecture. On the other hand, many landowners and local employees of the base, although not vocal, were hesitant to support a relocation. The local residents of Henoko wanted more financial compensation for damages and noise reduction from the future base. Construction companies and business leaders in Okinawa hoped to be involved in larger-scale construction work with massive land filling. Environmentalists opposed land filling to build an air base on the coast and were prepared to take physical action to halt any major development. The 2006 agreement was reached through a delicate balance among these different political and economic stances.[51]

In its 2009 manifesto the DPJ did not make any promises on the Futenma relocation issue. It simply mentioned "the direction of reexamining the realignment of the U.S. military forces in Japan and the role of U.S. military bases in Japan."[52] On July 19, 2009, just before the official campaign for the general election began, Hatoyama visited Okinawa and publicly stated that he would actively take actions to shift the relocation, "at least outside of the prefecture."[53] Hatoyama made this comment without prior consultation with his own party. One of the leading defense experts in the DPJ, Akihisa Nagashima, was caught by surprise and foresaw a future problem.[54]

This statement stemmed from Hatoyama's longtime belief that Okinawa's burden should be reduced. In 1996, for example, he published an article in a monthly magazine calling for a baseless alliance (*jōji chūryū naki anpo*).[55] Also, he was one of the main leaders within the DPJ to publish the party's "Okinawa Vision" in 2002. Following the 2008 prefectural assembly election, the DPJ updated the report and published the "Okinawa Vision 2008," in which the DPJ would seek to relocate the Futenma base outside of Okinawa prefecture, and eventually outside of the country.[56] Many Okinawans took Hatoyama's 2009 statement as a campaign promise.

According to a book written by journalists from the *Mainichi Shimbun*, Hatoyama was misinformed on the U.S. position on Futenma air base. In early August 2009 the DPJ sent two staffers to Washington at the request of the U.S. assistant secretary of state, Kurt Campbell, who wanted to learn DPJ's position on various foreign policy issues. They met with Japan experts in the U.S. government. Most of the questions the American officials asked were on the DPJ's policy toward Afghanistan. The DPJ had opposed the LDP government's dispatch of SDF vessels for refueling activities in the Indian Ocean to assist multinational naval vessels in fighting terrorism in Afghanistan, as doing so was not based on a clear request from the United Nations Security Council. In its manifesto the DPJ had expressed its policy of not extending the legislation to continue the SDF activities. In the discussions with U.S. officials, the two DPJ staffers received the impression that U.S. interest in the Futenma base was limited. When they came back to Japan from Washington, they reported to Hatoyama that the U.S. government would compromise on the relocation issue.[57] This encouraged Hatoyama to seek an alternative to the Henoko plan.

After the general election the DPJ, without a majority in the upper house, needed to form a coalition with the Socialist Party and the PNP. The three-party coalition would hold a majority in the upper house and a more than two-thirds majority in the lower house, which would be able to override the upper house's decision. Policy negotiations among the three parties began on September 2. On the night of September 8, Socialist leader Mizuho Fukushima made a phone call to Hatoyama and asked him to include the Okinawa base issue in the three-party agreement.[58] The following day the three parties came to a policy agreement that included the same language as in the DPJ's 2009 manifesto, simply mentioning the reexamination of U.S. military bases in Japan.[59] Although the agreement did not explicitly mention Futenma, Fukushima interpreted it as the first step toward the relocation of the air base outside of Okinawa.[60] The formation of this three-party coalition created partisan veto players within the government.

On September 16 the Hatoyama cabinet was formed. At the press conference held at the Kantei, the new foreign minister, Katsuya Okada, raised the Okinawa base issue as one of the three issues he would tackle in the first hundred days, along with climate change and assistance to Afghanistan and Pakistan.[61] Two days later Okada met with Assistant Secretary of State Campbell, who reasserted that the relocation of Futenma must be based on the 2006 agreement. Okada told Campbell that all four Okinawan lower house members elected in the last general election had promised the base would be relocated outside the prefecture, and that the DPJ had been opposed to the previous relocation plan made by the LDP government.[62] Therefore, he implied, the U.S. government needed to compromise and accept an alternative plan. Okada maintained his position that the DPJ government would conduct a thorough review and investigate other possibilities before making a final decision.

But the government officials in MOFA and MOD, who had experienced negotiations with Okinawa and the United States, recognized that the current plan was the only realistic option. Reflecting such sentiment, the new defense minister, Toshimi Kitazawa, stated on September 17 that it would be very difficult to "materialize the ideal," such as the relocation outside Okinawa or Japan.[63] Kitazawa told the author, "Unless there is a major change in international environment, I thought that we should not break the existing agreement."[64]

However, many other leading politicians did not share the view of the traditional bureaucratic veto players. Foreign Minister Okada quickly criticized Kitazawa's statement, saying that the defense minister should not make such a statement without prior consultation with the cabinet.[65] Kitazawa testified, "Mr. Okada is a very earnest man. He asked me to let him explore many opportunities."[66]

Four days later Okada met with Secretary of State Hilary Clinton in New York. In that meeting Okada told Clinton that "the Japanese government would consider concrete measures [for the Futenma relocation] in the days to come, and that he would hope to work in close cooperation with the U.S."[67] After the meeting Okada was asked by a Japanese journalist whether it would be possible to choose the current relocation plan after a thorough review. Okada's answer was "Of course. It should not take long as [the MOFA] has all the documents [from past negotiations]."[68] It was clear that Okada was not stuck with Hatoyama's statement but was willing to take a realistic option.

These mixed messages were delivered by the cabinet ministers during the first several days of the Hatoyama government. These statements confused the media and the public as to when and by whom the final decision would be made. On September 21 Hatoyama met with President Barack Obama. In the summit meeting, the two leaders did not get into the concrete issues surrounding the Futenma relocation.[69] When Hatoyama was asked by a Japanese journalist in Pittsburgh whether he had changed his stance on relocating the Futenma base outside Okinawa, he replied, "I have no intention to change my basic thinking." Hatoyama maintained that the primary interest of the United States was in securing continued Japanese assistance to Afghanistan, and he hinted that he could take time to reach the final decision on Futenma: "we need to figure out whether we should make the decision by the end of this year." The year-end deadline had been considered vital for a decision to implement the current relocation plan as the next mayoral election in Nago City would be held in January 2010. Based on Hatoyama's comment, on September 25 Okinawa's local newspaper, the *Ryukyu Shimpo*, published its digital edition with a large headline: "Futenma will be relocated outside the prefecture."[70]

Closed Window of Opportunity

On the same day, Defense Minister Kitazawa visited Okinawa to meet Governor Hirokazu Nakaima. Nakaima told Kitazawa that the Futenma relocation to outside Okinawa might be unrealistic, and that it would be beneficial for the Okinawan people to accept the existing plan. Kitazawa took the governor's comment seriously and promised to deliver it to the Hatoyama cabinet.[71] At a press conference at the end of his Okinawa visit, Kitazawa clearly stated his realistic position that it would be very difficult to choose a new option, and that any new option outside Okinawa would take many years.[72] Governor Nakaima and Defense Minister Kitazawa thus showed their support for pursuing the existing plan to relocate to Henoko.

Two weeks later Special Assistant to the Prime Minister Yoshikatsu Nakayama suggested on a television talk show that the prime minister might reach a decision that would conflict with the DPJ manifesto. When asked about Nakayama's statement, Hatoyama said, "I would not deny the possibility for change due to time factors."[73] Hatoyama's statement was interpreted as him leaning toward accepting the existing plan. The following day Hatoyama explained that the final decision should be made in consideration of three factors: the feelings of Okinawan people; the Japan-U.S. agreement; and the three-party-coalition agreement. This further confused the media on which direction the prime minister wanted to go on the Futenma issue. An American government official expressed his confusion to the author: "Different officials in Japan tell different opinions. We do not know who is responsible over the Futenma issue."[74]

A week later Land and Transport Minister Seiji Maehara, who was also in charge of Okinawa affairs, visited Okinawa. Maehara was known as an expert on national security issues and had been involved in the 1996 relocation agreement as a representative of Sakigake. In Okinawa Maehara expressed his doubt on the relocation to Henoko and his willingness to look for another option.[75]

Foreign Minister Okada echoed Maehara's call by suggesting the integration of Futenma into Kadena air base. This plan had been proposed by the Japanese government a couple of times in the 1990s, involving the integration of the 36th Marine Air Group into Kadena and the transfer of training operations for the marines to Iejima, a remote island in Okinawa. However, the plan was strongly opposed not only by U.S. forces but also by the cities surrounding the Kadena base—Okinawa City, Chatan, and Kadena—for noise and other environmental reasons.[76] At the October 23 press conference, Okada declared,

"The longer it takes, the longer the danger of Futenma remains. Considering that, I think that in fact the relocation outside the prefecture is not an option we can think of." Okada admitted that the Kadena integration plan was an option.[77]

When U.S. defense secretary Robert Gates visited Tokyo on October 21, Okada suggested the Kadena option. Gates said that reviewing was fine but emphasized the Henoko plan was the only possibility. Gates met with Defense Minister Kitazawa and Prime Minister Hatoyama and repeated the same message: "The Futenma relocation facility is the lynchpin of the realignment road map. Without the Futenma realignment, there will be no relocation to Guam. And without relocation to Guam, there will be no consolidation of forces and the return of land in Okinawa." At the same time, Gates hinted at the possibility of compromises by the United States: "With respect to some modest change in the runway of a few tens of meters or whatever, we regard that as a matter between the government of Okinawa and the people of Okinawa and the government here in Tokyo."[78]

This could have been a solution satisfactory to Okinawans. Okinawa prefecture and the City of Nago had requested moving the heliport further offshore for safety, noise, and construction benefit reasons. The U.S. government had refused any change in the original agreement. With the flexibility that Secretary Gates showed, the final agreement could have been made by the end of 2009. But Prime Minister Hatoyama did not take advantage of this opportunity.

At the October 27 press conference, Defense Minister Kitazawa presented a new interpretation of the existing Henoko plan, saying "the current agreement between Japan and the U.S. already includes an overseas relocation to Guam, as well as a domestic relocation outside Okinawa to Iwakuni air base (Yamaguchi prefecture). The primary step of the plan was indeed the relocation outside Okinawa—to the mainland and abroad—after which the remaining functions were decided to be moved to the coast of Henoko."[79] Kitazawa therefore argued that the current plan would meet Hatoyama's promise of relocating outside the prefecture and the nation, and he expressed his support for the Henoko plan. Hatoyama, however, flatly denied Kitazawa's interpretation. Hatoyama stated on November 7, "As the previous government did not have any doubt on the Japan-U.S. relations based on the dependence on the U.S., it did not explore new possibilities. But we would like to clearly express our own will on this issue . . . and to explore all the possibilities."[80] Hatoyama continued to express his will to pursue an alternative to the current plan.

On November 13 President Obama visited Tokyo to meet with Hatoyama. The two leaders agreed to establish a high-level working group to find a solution to the Futenma relocation issue. Hatoyama told Obama that he understood "the need to resolve the issue as soon as possible within the Working Group," and that he "would personally work proactively so that various discussions to be held would further reinforce and develop the Japan-U.S. alliance."[81] Obama pressured Hatoyama by expressing his desire to resolve this issue "expeditiously."[82] Hatoyama revealed in his e-mail magazine that there was an exchange between himself and Obama over the Futenma issue: Hatoyama said, "Please trust me," to which Obama replied, "Absolutely, I trust you."[83] From the context, Obama and other American government officials interpreted that Hatoyama was committed to an early solution based on the current plan.

On the following day, however, Hatoyama made statements that would blow up the trust the Americans had for him. During his visit to Singapore to attend the annual APEC meeting, Hatoyama told journalists that he did not promise to resolve the Futenma issue by the end of the year. He even said that "the president wants to think that the solution would be based on the current plan. But if that is the basis, we did not have to set a Working Group."[84] This statement created doubts among officials in Washington as to whether Hatoyama was serious about solving the issue.

The first meeting of the Working Group was held on November 17 in Tokyo. Attending were Foreign Minister Okada and Defense Minister Kitazawa from Japan, and Ambassador John Roos and Assistant Defense Secretary Wallace Gregson from the United States. They agreed to make a solution at an early stage. Prime Minister Hatoyama expressed that he would receive the decision made by the group as the most important one.[85] This statement was interpreted as Hatoyama's acceptance of the current plan.

On November 27 Hatoyama met with Okinawa governor Nakaima. As Nakaima had publicly stated that he would accept the Henoko plan if the base were shifted further offshore, the meeting was interpreted as a step toward an early solution on the current plan. On the same day the coalition partners of the DPJ began their actions. Socialist leader Mizuho Fukushima and PNP leader Shizuka Kamei met and agreed to set up a project team on Futenma under the direction of the coalition parties. After the meeting Fukushima and Kamei held a press conference to announce that the solution for the Futenma issue should not be made by the end of year. Fukushima contacted DPJ leaders to tell them that her party opposed an early solution.

After Socialist prime minister Murayama dropped the longtime ideological claim on the unconstitutionality of the SDF in 1994, the Socialist Party had seen a constant loss of Diet seats. To recover the traditional leftist supporters, Fukushima in February 2006 reinserted the unconstitutionality of the SDF in the party platform. In the Hatoyama coalition government, the Socialists wanted to strongly show their ideological stance against the U.S.-Japan alliance and thus acted as a strong partisan veto player.

According to the report by *Mainichi Shimbun* journalists, a Socialist member lobbied Ozawa to block the early solution on Futenma in order to avoid a breakup of the coalition. Until this time, Ozawa had stayed out of the policy-making circle on the Futenma issue as he promoted centralized policy making by the cabinet. But if the issue on the table could jeopardize the coalition government's stability, he could not remain silent. Without the support of the Socialist Party, it would be very difficult for the Hatoyama government to pass any legislation in the upper house. With Ozawa's agreement and aiming at keeping the three-party coalition government together, his close associate and the leader of the DPJ upper house members Azuma Koshiishi requested Defense Minister Kitazawa to postpone the decision for the sake of maintaining the coalition.[86]

Hatoyama now had to make a choice between maintaining the coalition government and good relations with the United States. As Ozawa preferred the former, Hatoyama had to follow him. On November 30, when Governor Nakaima requested that Hatoyama make a prompt decision on the current plan, the prime minister showed hesitation to move forward. On December 3 Hatoyama told Foreign Minister Okada and Defense Minister Kitazawa that he had given up on reaching a solution by the end of the year, and he asked them to continue negotiations with the United States.[87] In addition, Hatoyama asked the two ministers to continue to explore the possibilities for alternative plans to Henoko.[88]

According to classified data obtained by WikiLeaks, Maehara met with Ambassador Roos on December 9 and told him that "five DPJ cabinet members (Prime Minister Yukio Hatoyama, Chief Cabinet Secretary Hirofumi Hirano, Foreign Minister Katsuya Okada, Defense Minister Toshimi Kitazawa, and Maehara) met on the evening of December 8 and agreed that they could not accept moving forward with the Futenma Replacement Facility (FRF) because of opposition from the DPJ's coalition partner, the Social Democratic Party (SDP)." However, Maehara expressed, "if the U.S. does not agree to any alternative to the existing FRF plan, the DPJ would be prepared to go ahead with the current relocation plan and let the coalition break up if necessary after Golden Week (April 29 to May 5 in 2010)."[89] According to Maehara, the DPJ needed time to explore other possibilities before making the final decision, as DPJ leaders had publicly stated, but would be willing to take the current plan as the final decision if allowed this time.

On December 17 at a dinner at the conclusion of the U.N. climate-change summit in Copenhagen, Hatoyama informed Secretary of State Hilary Clinton that he would not make a decision about Futenma by the end of the year. According to Foreign Vice Minister Mitoji Yabunaka, Hatoyama also confirmed to Clinton that "the current Futenma Replacement Facility (FRF) plan would be the fallback if no other alternatives are found."[90] After the dinner Hatoyama told Japanese reporters that he had obtained "full understanding" from Clinton about Tokyo's need to delay the decision to explore other possibilities. Upset by Hatoyama's comment, Clinton met with the Japanese ambassador to the United States, Ichirō Fujisaki, and reasserted that the U.S. position had not changed.[91] The relationship of trust between Hatoyama and U.S. government officials thus was a big question mark.

During a December 15–18 visit by the author to U.S. government offices to discuss U.S.-Japan relations, one high official noted, "There are about fifty people in Washington who deal with Japan. Half of them want to pressure hard on Japan on the base issue, and the other half are against American strong pressure."[92] During this week, an interagency meeting on Japan was held at the White House. Japan handlers in the government confirmed the view that Futenma was just one of many important issues between the two countries, and that Washington would wait until the DPJ government finally agreed to the current plan.

On December 25 Hatoyama publicly announced that the decision on Futenma would be made by the end of May, including the examination of new locations.[93] Hatoyama revealed in an interview the reasons for the May 2010 deadline:

> With the expectation to settle the issue by the end of 2009, I could not postpone this for a whole year; the maximum would have been half a year. The budget bill would tie us up until March, and there was the circumstance involving the Socialist Party. Having Futenma relocation as an election issue would have made it impossible to contest the upper house election.[94]

Ozawa and Okiishi, who handled DPJ policies in the upper house, held the same view.[95] The domestic political calculation was the dominant reason for the decision to delay.

Failed Hatoyama Plan

Three days later Chief Cabinet Secretary Hirofumi Hirano announced that the Kantei would set up a coalition-party committee to examine the Okinawa base issues, headed by himself. The Kantei finally showed its involvement in the base issue. Until the end of May, this committee was expected to serve as a forum where Socialist Party and PNP members could express their opinions on the Futenma issue. The issue was now on the shoulders of CCS Hirano.

In the mayoral election of Nago City, the DPJ's headquarters in Okinawa decided to support Susumu Inamine, a candidate who had publicly stated his strong opposition to the current replacement plan involving Henoko. DPJ secretary general Ozawa sent his deputy, Kōji Satō, to Okinawa. Satō met with corporate representatives of the local construction companies and told them not to vote for the incumbent mayor, Yoshikazu Shimabukuro, who was seen as a probase politician and was supported by the LDP.[96] The result of the election on January 24, 2010, was a victory of the antibase candidate Inamine. The DPJ as a political party effectively killed the possibility for Nago City to accept the current plan.

CCS Hirano was surprised by the election result, as the media had predicted a victory for Shimabukuro. The loss of the probase mayor made it more difficult for the Hatoyama cabinet to handle the Futenma issue. On the following day, at a regular press conference, Hirano stated that there was "no need to take the election result into consideration" in order to maintain the current replacement plan as an option. This statement, however, angered people in Nago. Nago City Council chair Hiroshi Ashitomi, for example, said, "It seemed that the Hatoyama administration is sensitive to the U.S. government's moods. If the government continues to ridicule Okinawans, I think the people's rage will burst with unexpected vigor."[97]

Meanwhile, cabinet ministers in the Hatoyama government explored alternatives to the Henoko plan. Earlier Foreign Minister Okada had suggested the Kadena integration plan, but he had given up on this by early December.[98] Defense Minister Kitazawa tried to revitalize the old plan with a land-based heliport inside Camp Schwab. PNP policy committee chairman Mikio Shimoji agreed with this plan and tried to bring it to the three-party committee. But this met with strong objections from the Socialist Party. CCS Hirano came up with a plan to build a man-made island off the White Beach Naval Base. But Hatoyama personally rejected Hirano's plan because it would destroy a beautiful beach.[99]

Hatoyama had his own plan. On March 31 he revealed at a Diet session that he had a "plan in mind." According to Hatoyama, "the plan is at least as effective as, and probably more effective than, the current plan, which means more acceptable" in consideration of a reduced burden to Okinawa and maintaining a deterrence capability.[100] One year later Hatoyama revealed his secret plan, which was a partial relocation of the Futenma facility to Tokunoshima in Kagoshima prefecture.[101]

The Tokunoshima plan was originally suggested by Hatoyama's close associate, Seishū Makino. Tokunoshima is an island 160 kilometers away from the Okinawa main island and has space for the relocation of the Futenma facility. Hatoyama secretly ordered Makino to approach the local leaders of the island. When Makino's visit in late January was scooped by the *Asahi Shimbun*, CCS Hirano stated that he had no knowledge of the plan. There was no policy coordination at the Kantei. After the scoop was out, citizens in Tokunoshima began an antibase campaign.

Hatoyama sought a meeting with President Obama during the 2010 nuclear summit in Washington to explain the current situation of the Futenma issue. But no official meeting was set. Instead, Hatoyama had an unofficial meeting during the working dinner on April 12. The *Washington Post* ran an article portraying Hatoyama as "the biggest loser" at the summit. According to the article, Hatoyama had impressed Washington with his unreliability on the Futenma issue and had become "increasingly loopy" in the opinion of some Obama administration officials.[102] On April 18 the *Yomiuri Shimbun* ran a front-page article with the headline, "Can you follow through? U.S. president expressed doubt to Prime Minister Hatoyama."[103] The prime minister denied such a remark was made but refused to reveal what Obama actually said.

On the same day Tokunoshima citizens held an antibase meeting attended by fifteen thousand people, thought the island has a population of just twenty-six thousand. Two days later Deputy CCS Kinya Takino made a phone call to local leaders on Tokunoshima to set up a meeting with CCS Hirano. But with no room for discussion, the leaders refused to meet Hirano. When asked about Takino's call at a press conference, Hirano told journalists that he had just learned of it from the media report. Prime Minister Hatoyama confirmed that he had had no prior knowledge.

As noted earlier, the position of the deputy chief cabinet secretary was regarded as the top position in Japan's entire bureaucracy, playing a pivotal role between the prime minister and the executive branch. When a deputy CCS acted, it used to mean that he was coordinating the policy interests of the entire government. The position had been called the shadow prime minister under the LDP government. As the vice ministerial meeting was abolished under the Hatoyama government, the authority of the deputy CCS had drastically weakened. The deputy CCS no longer represented the Japanese government. This incident symbolized the fall of the Kantei's power.

Hatoyama still had hopes for the Tokunoshima plan. On April 28 he met with the former Diet member from the island, Torao Tokuda, who had maintained strong influence, and asked for his cooperation. But Hatoyama could not gain his support.[104] The prime minister finally gave up his "plan in mind" and decided to go back to the Henoko plan.

Resignation with No Alternative

On May 4 Hatoyama visited Okinawa for the first time as prime minister and met with Governor Nakaima. The prime minister apologized to the governor, saying, "It is realistically very difficult to move all [the Futenma facilities] to outside the prefecture. We will have to ask Okinawa to bear the burden."[105] Asked later by a journalist for the reason for his change, Hatoyama replied that he had not thought the presence of marines in Okinawa would work as a direct deterrent against war when he made the "out of the prefecture" statement. But Hatoyama had changed his thinking: "As I learned further, I realized the role of the marines within the entire U.S. forces in Okinawa, and the cooperation of all the facilities constituted a deterrent. . . . If you say [my thinking] was shallow, you may be right."[106]

But the political situation in Okinawa had drastically changed. As the antibase candidate had won the mayoral election, Nago City refused the Henoko plan. Respecting the local government's will, Governor Nakaima no longer supported the current plan even with some modification.

On May 10 Prime Minister Hatoyama held a cabinet committee meeting with Foreign Minister Okada, Defense Minister Kitazawa, Minister for Okinawa Affairs Maehara, and CCS Hirano to finalize the government's proposal for the agreement with the United States. While it was decided that Henoko would be the replacement site, as in the existing plan, the government would explore the possibility of building a pile-supported, pier-type runway. The plan also included transferring some training off of Okinawa to Tokunoshima, studying U.S.-Japan shared use of bases to further lighten the impact on Okinawa, and discussing a "green approach" to the bases. In the final agreement at the foreign and defense ministers (2 plus 2) meeting on May 28, most of the Japanese proposals were included. Although the final agreement did not explicitly mention a pile-supported, pier-type runway, it supported environmentally sensitive construction of the replacement facility, which could be "completed without significant delay."[107]

On the same day the Hatoyama cabinet had to approve the joint statement. But Socialist leader Mizuho Fukushima, as a cabinet minister, refused to sign the document, which clearly specified the relocation site of Henoko. She was asked whether she would sign it or resign as a cabinet member, but she refused both.[108] As a result, Fukushima became the fifth cabinet minister in postwar history to be dismissed.[109] With Fukushima's dismissal, the Socialist Party announced that it would leave the coalition government. This time, with no possible alternative plan, the Hatoyama cabinet chose the alliance with the United States over maintaining the coalition with the Socialists.

The break-off of the Socialists made for a very difficult political situation for the Hatoyama government. The DPJ and PNP had barely more than a majority of the seats (122 out of 242) in the upper house, losing a majority in several standing committees. The three-party coalition with a two-thirds majority in the lower house could override decisions in the upper house even after an election loss in the forthcoming upper house election, which would enable the DPJ administration to run the government. Without the Socialists, the DPJ now had to win in the July election.

According to *Asahi Shimbun* polls, however, Hatoyama's job approval rate of 71 percent in September 2009 declined steadily throughout his tenure. In mid-May, after his decision to go back to the current plan on Futenma, it dipped as low as 21 percent. Sixty-one percent of respondents believed that Hatoyama's acceptance of the Henoko plan was a violation of his campaign promise.[110]

Many DPJ upper house members voiced that they could not run their election campaigns under the unpopular prime minister. On June 2 at the DPJ Diet members' meeting, Hatoyama announced his resignation. He cited breaking a campaign promise to move the Futenma base outside Okinawa as one of the two main reasons for his resignation. Another reason was his own financial scandal. Hatoyama revealed in the same speech that he had asked DPJ secretary general Ozawa, who had a similar financial problem, to resign with him.[111]

The scandal had erupted in December 2009, when it was revealed that Hatoyama had received 1.2 billion yen from his mother, a wealthy heiress, and improperly reported the revenue as political donations under the names of deceased people. Two of Hatoyama's secretaries were indicted for falsifying reports of Hatoyama's fund management body. Hatoyama himself was not indicted as the prosecutors could not find evidence to prove he was a party to the false accounting entries. This incident significantly hurt the clean image of the DPJ, which had accused LDP politicians of financial scandals, and lowered the popularity of the Hatoyama government. In April 2010 one of Hatoyama's secretaries was found guilty, and LDP Diet members added political pressure against Hatoyama in the Diet session.

Secretary General Ozawa, as DPJ president in May 2009, had stepped down from that post after the arrest of his personal secretary for accounting irregularities and illegal donations from a large construction company. In April 2010 a prosecution inquest panel concluded that it was highly likely that Ozawa was an accomplice in a scandal involving a controversial land purchase in Tokyo.

Within the DPJ, political pressure mounted against Hatoyama and Ozawa. With their financial scandals, it would be very difficult for DPJ candidates to campaign for the July upper house election. Thus Hatoyama and Ozawa both resigned on June 4, with Hatoyama finishing his tenure in just nine months.

The DPJ had criticized the LDP government for its old and corrupt political style. However, the two top leaders of the government and the party faced their own financial scandals. These scandals allowed the opposition parties to attack the Hatoyama government, eventually leading to the resignation of Hatoyama and Ozawa.

Hatoyama's failure in the Futenma issue was largely due to his institutional changes. His excessive emphasis on political initiative effectively eliminated the bureaucratic support. His cabinet members sought alternative plans, and there was no policy coordination among the ministries. They found no plan better than the existing agreement that the bureaucrats recommended following. With the abolition of the DPJ policy councils, there was no support from the party. Secretary General Ozawa, strengthened by the new arrangement of his office, displayed his political influence to make Hatoyama choose the partisan veto players within the coalition over the United States. The weakened Kantei did not take action on this issue until the later stage of policy making, although the issue required interagency policy coordination. Neither CCS Hirano nor Deputy CCS Takino could play an instrumental role. The Futenma case clearly proved that the successful exercise of political leadership in complicated policy matters requires effective control of the bureaucracy, not the elimination of its involvement.

6 KAN'S STRUGGLE IN THE GOVERNMENT AND THE DPJ

AFTER PRIME MINISTER HATOYAMA announced his resignation on June 2, 2010, public and media attention swiftly shifted to the question of who would be his successor. Ichirō Ozawa engaged in his last task as DPJ secretary general, setting up an election for a new party president. As this election was due to the midterm resignation of the party president, the leadership selection would be decided by votes of DPJ Diet members only.

On the same day that Hatoyama resigned, Deputy Prime Minister Naoto Kan met with him to inform him that he would run for the party leadership. Kan also tried to meet with Ozawa, but Ozawa refused to see him. As Kan publicly declared his candidacy, DPJ leaders who had distanced themselves from Ozawa, such as Transport Minister Seiji Maehara, Foreign Minister Katsuya Okada, and Deputy Finance Minister Yoshihiko Noda, announced their support for Kan. At a press conference Kan revealed that Ozawa refused a meeting with him, saying, "Secretary General [Ozawa] drew some suspicion of the people [due to his financial scandal]. He should stay quiet at least for a while for himself, for the DPJ as well as for Japan's politics."[1] This was Kan's declaration that his government would avoid Ozawa's political influence.

Within the DPJ, Ozawa led the biggest group with some 150 Diet members. His group sought to find its own candidate but failed to do so. A younger DPJ member, Shinji Tarutoko (age fifty), declared his candidacy to run against Kan. In the DPJ presidential election on June 4, Kan defeated Tarutoko by a vote of 291 to 129.

After Kan was elected prime minister in the Diet, he quickly appointed Yoshito Sengoku as chief cabinet secretary and Yukio Edano as DPJ secretary general. Sengoku and Edano were widely known as anti-Ozawa leaders within the DPJ. Their appointment to the number two positions in the government and the ruling party signaled the establishment of an anti-Ozawa cabinet. According to an *Asahi Shimbun* opinion poll conducted on June 8–9, the new Kan cabinet received 60 percent of public support, a significant recovery from the 17 percent that the Hatoyama cabinet had received in the previous month. Sixty percent of respondents also supported Kan's anti-Ozawa stance in the appointments.[2]

INSTITUTIONAL CHANGES UNDER KAN

Upon assuming the office, Prime Minister Kan, signaling a shift from his earlier sentiment, announced that his cabinet would abandon the antibureaucratic stance. Under the Hatoyama cabinet, Kan was a leading cabinet member who displayed an antibureaucratic stance. On October 31, 2009, for example, he spoke at the DPJ meeting in Tokyo, stating, "[Bureaucrats] do not use their brain. They just had good grades [in their school days], but are very stupid."[3]

At first Kan rejected the political tradition of relying on memos that bureaucrats prepared for his statements on official occasions. His attitude totally changed, however, when he served as finance minister. At an upper house Budget Committee meeting in January 2010, an LDP member, Yoshimasa Hayashi, asked Kan about the impact of the multiplier effect of the child allowance policy promoted by the DPJ. With his limited knowledge of economics, Kan could not answer the question by himself, and the Diet deliberations stopped several times. In the end, Kan had to read the memo prepared by MOF bureaucrats.[4] After that, Kan always relied on bureaucratic support for policy issues.

On June 8, 2010, after six days of political maneuvering, the Kan cabinet was officially formed. On the same day Prime Minister Kan issued the Basic Policy, which was approved by his cabinet. It stated, "The three political appointees and bureaucrats, with their respective roles and responsibilities, shall closely share information and communicate with each other, and together run the government under true political leadership."[5] Two days later Kan called a meeting of top bureaucrats of the ministries, stating, "This nation is supported both by bureaucrats and by politicians. A good combination of the two and a good division of labor between the two would strengthen Japan's politics and administration. I would like to ask cooperation and efforts in that sense."[6] Kan believed the Hatoyama government had too stringently excluded bureaucrats in decision making when it emphasized political leadership. The Kan government changed this and now began inviting active involvement of bureaucrats in policy making so as to more effectively run the government.

Six months later the Kan government moved even further to promote integration between political leaders and bureaucrats in the ministries. Chief Cabinet Secretary Sengoku made a speech in front of the administrative vice ministers, asking them to participate in the three political appointees meeting. Under the Hatoyama government, the political appointees meeting in some of the ministries excluded bureaucratic participants and made policy decisions without bureaucrats' input. This created a division between political leaders and bureaucrats and significantly lowered the morale of many bureaucrats. The participation of top bureaucrats in the meeting would promote information sharing within the ministries as well as more active involvement of bureaucrats in policy making.

In January 2011 Prime Minister Kan also made a speech in front of the administrative vice ministers to ask for cooperation among bureaucrats:

> There have been trials and errors in the relationship between politicians and bureaucrats. In each ministry, I would like you to discuss with the minister and senior vice minister and make an agreement on the kinds of cases that should be handled solely by politicians, and others that should require involvement of the vice minister and other high bureaucratic officials. I would hope to establish a good form of cooperative relations between them.[7]

In the same speech Kan also mentioned the current problem of policy coordination among the ministries. As previously described, Kan had been a leading critic of the administrative vice ministerial meeting, which was abolished under the Hatoyama government. Policy coordination was expected to be conducted among the cabinet and subcabinet members. But the limited number of political actors could not handle the vast amount of administrative operations that required policy coordination among the ministries. As a result, the lack of coordination delayed many administrative operations. Kan stated, "I understand that policy coordination among the ministries used to be conducted through the administrative vice-ministerial meeting. In addition to interagency coordination through political channels by the ministers or senior vice ministers, we need coordination at various levels, such as among administrative vice ministers or bureau chiefs."[8] Kan basically admitted that the old vice ministerial meeting was a necessary organization for policy coordination, although he was not ready to reestablish the meeting.

Kan also changed the centralized policy making under the Hatoyama cabinet, which had abolished the Policy Research Committee within the DPJ. Some DPJ Diet members had complained that they were not allowed to be involved in decision making, while DPJ members in the government were busy running the government. Former DPJ secretary general Ozawa set up the policy conference in each ministry so that DPJ members outside the government could participate in policy discussions. Even Ozawa admitted that the policy conferences had not functioned very well.[9] Kan revived the DPJ Policy Research Committee and appointed Kōichirō Genba as its chairman. To avoid the dual decision-making structure that had developed under the LDP government, Kan appointed Genba as a cabinet minister to simultaneously represent the cabinet and the ruling party and serve as a liaison between the two.

DPJ secretary general Yukio Edano decided basically to maintain the petition system that Ozawa had created. However, Edano felt that the old system had served as a strong personal power source for Ozawa. In an interview with the *Asahi Shimbun*, Edano stated, "An organization that needs to rely on one particular person is not good as an organization. As a ruling party, we need to establish an organization to serve as the center of the nation whoever is in charge."[10] Edano shared his office with DPJ Policy Research Committee chairman Genba and asked deputy secretary general Gōshi Hosono, to take on the responsibility of handling petitions from local governments and interest groups. Edano wanted to decentralize the power that Ozawa had as DPJ secretary general.

In September 2010, when Edano became the deputy secretary general, he further institutionalized the DPJ's petition system. In the Office of Secretary General, he established two committees: the Organizational Committee would handle petitions from local governments, and the Corporation and Group Committee would accept requests from interest groups and corporations. The two committees would categorize requests and petitions and deliver them to the political appointees in the ministries. This process was more systematic and involved more DPJ Diet members.

ELECTION LOSS AND OZAWA'S CHALLENGE

On June 11, 2010, Prime Minister Kan made his first policy speech. Kan declared that his cabinet was "determined to exert strong political leadership in order to bring about a 'strong economy,' 'robust public finances,' and 'a strong social security system' in an integral manner."[11] To reconstruct positive financial conditions, Kan mentioned the need for tax reform. When he had served as finance minister under the Hatoyama cabinet, MOF bureaucrats had convinced him of the need for a tax increase. Four months prior, he had publicly stated the need to raise the consumption tax. Since then, financial reconstruction with a tax increase had been Kan's policy goal. On June 17, the DPJ announced the "Manifesto 2010," which emphasized financial reconstruction, including future tax reform as well as possible cuts in the DPJ programs promised in the 2009 manifesto. At a press conference, Kan told reporters that the consumption tax might be raised to 10 percent, as the LDP had suggested as its platform for the July 2010 upper house election.

Election day for the upper house was set for July 11. Kan's public statement about a consumption tax increase to 10 percent became a problem because it had been made without prior consultation with other DPJ leaders. Former DPJ secretary general Ozawa visited locations all over the nation in an unofficial election campaign, publicly criticizing Kan's statement as well as the new manifesto. Ozawa mentioned that the 2009 manifesto had promised not to increase the consumption tax for at least four years, and that Kan's statement was violating the earlier campaign promise. Ozawa also pointed out that the DPJ had won the 2009 general election by promising programs such as the child allowance, and that the DPJ should not cut these programs simply because the government had no money.[12] The disagreement within the ruling party was apparent.

During the election campaign, Kan revealed the unpreparedness within the government on the tax increase issue. On June 30 he was making campaign stops throughout the Tohoku area. As an increase in consumption tax would hit low-income earners hardest, Kan suggested a tax refund for them. In Aomori City he mentioned that people with income under 2 or 3 million yen would receive tax refunds. In Akita City he mentioned income under 3 or 3.5 million yen. Then, in Yamagata City, the prime minister changed again, to income under 3 or 4 million yen. Taxes are usually the most sensitive political issue, especially during an election campaign. The national leader is expected to show his determination in order to appeal to voters to bear an increased tax burden. But Kan's uncertain statements disappointed voters.

The result of the election was disappointing loss for the DPJ, which lost 11 of the 55 seats that were up for reelection, keeping only 44 seats. As a result, the ruling coalition of the DPJ and the PNP was 13 seats short of a majority in the upper house, with 109 seats out of 242. On the other hand, the LDP increased from 38 seats to 51 seats. The Your Party (Minnanotō), a new party that was opposed to a tax increase, won 10 seats to increase its political presence. Without a majority in the upper house, the Kan government would face political difficulties in running the government, just as did the LDP governments had under the leadership of Prime Ministers Fukuda and Asō.

At a press conference after the election, Prime Minister Kan admitted that his statements on a tax increase were a main reason for the loss. He stated, "How I brought up the consumption tax gave an abrupt impression to the people. . . . I forced my colleagues to run a very difficult election campaign. I am very sorry about this."[13] Many in the DPJ were shocked about the election loss and tried to figure out how to face the political difficulty that resulted from the loss of the majority in the upper house.

On July 29 the DPJ held a general meeting of Diet members to review the election results. The DPJ had collected opinions from its members all over the nation. Kan's tax hike statement was at the top of the list of reasons for the loss.[14]

After receiving many critical comments from DPJ Diet members on his responsibility for the loss, Kan asked them to let him stay in his post. "While recognizing my responsibility, I would like to continue my efforts [as prime minister]," Kan continued, "In the forthcoming DPJ presidential election in September, I would like to be judged by DPJ members."[15] Kan's goal now was to be reelected as party leader, with the election just seven weeks away.

Many DPJ members in the groups led by Hatoyama and Ozawa were critical of Kan's way of running the government and hoped that Ozawa would run against Kan. Ozawa was at first hesitant to run for the party presidency, as he was involved in an ongoing legal case. In April 2010 the Committee for the Inquest of Prosecution had overruled a decision by the Tokyo District Public Prosecutor's Office not to charge Ozawa for misreporting over 400 million yen in political funds. The decisions made by the inquest committee had not been legally binding until the 2009 revision by DPJ-led legislation. After the revision, if the inquest committee were to make the same decision twice, that decision could override the prosecutor's decision. The second decision by the committee sometime in the fall could lead to Ozawa's indictment.

Anti-Ozawa members in the DPJ voiced their objections to Ozawa's candidacy. Foreign Minister Katsuya Okada, for example, stated in a press conference on August 20, "I have a sense of incongruity for a person who might be indicted to become the party president and the prime minister. . . . The people, who want Mr. Ozawa to run, should return to the origin of the party [which called for clean politics]."[16] Minister for GRU Renhō Murata said on the same day, "People wanted clean politics from the DPJ. People's wish to remove political corruption under [the LDP] government created last year's power shift."[17] These comments reflected the anti-Ozawa opinions within the DPJ.

One week later Ozawa finally decided to announce his candidacy for party leadership. On September 2 Kan and Ozawa held an open debate at the Japan National Press Club. Ozawa portrayed himself as a can-do reformer with rich experience and administrative skills, criticizing Kan for allowing bureaucratic control over the budget process. Ozawa declared that he would carry out campaign promises made by the DPJ during the 2009 general election. On the other hand, Kan portrayed Ozawa as representing the old-style politics and stated that he himself would pursue clean politics.[18]

The 2010 DPJ presidential election was a very open process. There were a total of 1,222 points cast by different categories of voters. Each of 411 DPJ Diet members had 2 points, accounting for about 70 percent of the total with 822 points. Some 2,400 DPJ local assembly members collectively cast 100 points, and more than 34,000 DPJ supporters had 300 points, corresponding to the 300 single-member districts for the lower house.

In the September 14 election, Ozawa and Kan split the votes of DPJ Diet members, with Ozawa receiving 400 points and Kan 412 points. Ozawa earned the votes of about 200 members of his own group and of the Hatoyama group but received no votes from outside of these groups. The general public, represented by the DPJ supporter vote, overwhelmingly supported Kan with 249 points, compared with Ozawa's 51 points. Kan also won more votes from the local assembly members, with 60 points, compared with Ozawa's 40 points. In total, Kan won the presidency with 721 points against Ozawa's 491. Ozawa's financial scandal and the public's hesitation to change national leaders again after just three months worked against Ozawa.

Kan's job approval rating in an *Asahi Shimbun* poll, which had sunk to 37 percent after the July upper house election, surged to 57 percent immediately following the DPJ presidential election. Seventy-two percent of the respondents welcomed Kan's reelection, while only 12 percent preferred to see an Ozawa victory.[19] Kan now had a public mandate to run the government.

HANDLING OF THE SENKAKU INCIDENT

On September 7, as Kan and Ozawa were putting their energy into the party leadership election, a diplomatic incident shook Japan-China relations. A Chinese fishing trawler invaded Japan's territorial waters off the Senkaku Islands in the East China Sea. Japanese coastal guard patrol boats intercepted it, but the Chinese vessel attempted to escape and intentionally collided with the patrol boats. The fishing boat was detained and its captain and fourteen other crew members were captured. The Kan government now had to choose whether Japan needed to respond firmly to the illegal and dangerous action displayed by the Chinese vessel or should pursue a diplomatic solution for the sake of Japan-China relations.

The Senkaku Islands are located north of the southwestern end of the Ryukyu Islands and northeast of Taiwan. They are claimed by Japan and are under its administrative control. In old Chinese journals from the fifteenth to the seventeenth centuries, these uninhabited islands were mentioned as landmarks en route to the Ryukyu Islands. These documents, however, did not justify Chinese territorial claims over the islands.[20] In 1744 the Qing dynasty under the leadership of the Qianlong emperor published 356 volumes of official geography books, titled *Daqing yitongzhi* (Unified, Great Qing). In volume 260, the northeastern end of the territory of Taiwan was identified as somewhere around the present Keelung.[21] Despite China's claim that the Senkaku Islands had been its territory from ancient times, no official documents prove that they were ever claimed or effectively controlled by China or Taiwan.

In 1885 Japan moved to claim the islands as its territory, effectively controlling them by building a factory to process bonito. In January 1895, three months before the peace treaty was concluded after the Sino-Japanese War, Japan officially claimed sovereignty over the islands and they became a part of Okinawa prefecture. After World War II the United States military government ruled Okinawa, which naturally included the Senkaku Islands. Taiwan was returned to China without including the Senkaku Islands, and the Nationalist government did not make any complaints or claims over the islands at that time. When Japan signed a peace treaty with the Nationalist government on Taiwan in 1951, there was no discussion over the Senkaku Islands. In short, China or Taiwan never had effective control and never made any territorial claim over the islands until 1971.

There are some documents in the People's Republic of China and on Taiwan that admit that the Senkaku Islands are part of Okinawa. For example, the *People's Daily* ran an article on Okinawan people who opposed American bases in 1953 that explicitly mentioned that Okinawa included the Senkaku Islands.[22] The *World Atlas*, published in China in 1960, drew a borderline between Taiwan and Yonakunijima, indicating that the Senkaku Islands fell into Japan's territory. Volume 1 of *World Maps*, published by Taiwan's National Defense Research Institute in 1965, and Taiwan's 1970 national geography textbook for junior high school students also clearly identified the islands as Japan's territory with Japanese names.[23] However, the situation changed in 1968, when the United Nations Economic Commission for Asia and the Far East announced after an investigation that there was a large-scale oil deposit (almost as big as that in Iraq) on the continental shelf of the East China Sea. Three years later both Taiwan and China officially claimed sovereignty over the Senkaku Islands. In December 1971 the PRC Ministry of Foreign Affairs declared that the islands had been Chinese territory since ancient times.

Despite this statement, the islands did not become an obstacle in the negotiations between Tokyo and Beijing on establishing diplomatic ties. Chinese premier Zhou Enlai revealed that he had no personal interests in the islands when he spoke with Kōmeitō leader Yoshikatsu Takeiri, a special envoy, by saying, "I had no interest in [the Senkaku Islands issue], but because of the oil issue [Chinese] historians made it an issue."[24] As a result, the two governments reached an agreement to normalize relations by announcing a joint statement in September 1972 with no mention of the Senkaku Islands. At the conclusion of the Japan-China Peace and Friendship Treaty in August 1978, Vice Premier Deng Xiaoping suggested putting the Senkaku Islands issue aside. This has been the historical pattern: while Japan exercised administrative control over the islands, China was willing to shelve the issue. But with the rising national power of China and the increasing importance of ocean resources in recent years, the Senkaku Islands have become an area of tensions between the two countries.

Foreign Minister Katsuya Okada, who was in Berlin at the time of the trawler incident, stated that the Chinese trawler had been in Japan's territorial waters and therefore needed to be handled in accordance with domestic law. The Japan Coast Guard was under the command of Minister of Land, Infrastructure, and Transport Seiji Maehara, who had been critical of China's aggressive policy. Maehara pushed for a firm Japanese response. Chief Cabinet Secretary Yoshito Sengoku agreed with Okada and Maehara, and the Japanese government decided to officially arrest the captain of the fishing boat and charge him with obstruction of the execution of official duties. Sengoku said at a press conference on the morning of September 8, "There exists no issue of territorial sovereignty to be resolved concerning the Senkaku Islands. In consideration of the degree of the violation, we will handle the incident strictly under our jurisdiction and in accordance with domestic law."[25]

The Chinese authority saw this event as Japan's departure from its past low-key practice and reacted strongly. In the past Chinese citizens who attempted to land on the Senkaku Islands had been promptly expelled rather than being handled through Japan's legal process. The Chinese embassy immediately filed a complaint with the Ministry of Foreign Affairs. The same day China's assistant foreign minister, Hu Zhengyue, summoned Ambassador Uichirō Niwa and demanded an immediate release of the boat captain. On September 10 Foreign Minister Yang Jiechi did the same. The following day the Chinese government postponed negotiations with Japan on the joint development of a gas plant in the East China Sea.

On September 12 State Councilor Dai Bingguo summoned Ambassador Niwa in the middle of night to ask for "a clever, political decision." As Dai's status was next to that of the premier, this incident revealed the seriousness of the situation. The following day, at a press conference, CCS Sengoku announced the release of the fourteen crew members but the continued detention of the boat captain and expressed his hope for a positive response from China.

After the DPJ party leadership election on September 14, Kan reshuffled his cabinet. Three days later Foreign Minister Okada became DPJ secretary general and was replaced as foreign minister by previous transport minister Maehara. That same day it was learned that the Chinese government had transported new equipment to the gas field. Maehara announced at a press conference that Japan would take "necessary measures" against any drilling conducted at the gas field.[26]

On September 19 the Ishigaki Court announced that the detention of the boat captain would be extended. This meant that the Japanese court was preparing to bring the captain to trial. In protest to this decision, the Chinese government suspended cabinet-level exchanges with Japan and withdrew an invitation to one thousand Japanese students and children to attend the Shanghai Expo. On September 21 Chinese premier Wen Jiabao spoke at a meeting with representatives of Chinese Americans in New York, saying that the islands were Chinese territory and that the arrest of the captain was illegal. He said, "If Japan clings to its mistake, China will take further actions and the Japanese side shall bear all the consequences that arise."[27] Tokyo proposed high-level talks on the issue, but Beijing rejected the proposal. On the same day it was revealed that the Chinese government had ordered the suspension of exports of rare earth materials to Japanese companies.

Former U.S. deputy secretary of state Richard Armitage analyzed the incident and stated in his September 15 speech in Tokyo, "My view is what China senses is a distracted United States who has a chilled relationship with Tokyo. So they are testing what they can get away with."[28] He was referring to the turmoil over the Futenma relocation issue, discussed in chapter 5, after which the United States and Japan did not enjoy good relations. On September 23, however, at a meeting with Foreign Minister Maehara in New York, Secretary of State Hilary Clinton assured Japan that the United States had a commitment to it under article 5 of the U.S.-Japan Security Treaty to support Japanese sovereignty over the Senkaku Islands.[29]

Also on September 23, the Chinese news agency reported that Chinese authorities had arrested four employees of a Japanese construction firm, Fujita Corp., for entering a military zone without authorization in Shijiazhuang, Hebei province. Tokyo took the arrests as being related to the Senkaku Islands incident and suddenly caved in to Chinese pressure. On September 24 the Naha District Public Prosecutor's Office announced that it would release the Chinese captain, taking into account "the future of Japan's relationship with China." It was quite unusual for a prosecutor's office to reach a decision giving diplomatic considerations. The Kan government stated that there was no political intervention, and that the decision was made solely by the local prosecutor's office. Later, however, Special Assistant to the Prime Minister Kenichi Matsumoto revealed in an interview that Prime Minister Kan had made the decision to release the captain.[30]

Japanese government officials expected that the release of the captain would calm down the Chinese government, and that the Japanese businessmen would be also released. Instead, the Chinese Foreign Ministry expressed a strong protest and demanded that Japan offer "its apology and compensation for this incident."[31] On September 29 former DPJ deputy secretary general Gōshi Hosono visited Beijing as a private messenger and met with State Councilor Dai. The following day Chinese authorities released three of the four Fujita employees, and Dai contacted CCS Sengoku to finally establish high-level communication between the two countries. After their discussion, the fourth employee was released on October 9. Tensions between the two countries finally passed their peak.

Domestically, however, strong criticism arose against the Kan government for bowing to Chinese pressure and running away from its obligation to explain things clearly to the public. Many saw the government's poor handling of the issue as proof of a lack of strategic thinking on how to deal with diplomatic crises and a lack of a foreign policy strategy. The DPJ government's principle of avoiding bureaucratic control was seriously questioned.

Under the LDP government the administrative deputy CCS would have called a meeting of high officials of the related ministries and agencies and quickly formed the government policy. But the Kan cabinet never held a meeting at the Kantei on this issue, either at the cabinet level or at the high bureaucratic level.[32] Former deputy CCS Teijirō Furukawa pointed out that it was also very strange for the prosecutor in Naha to include diplomatic considerations in the judgment, and for government officials to place all the responsibility in the hands of the prosecutor's office.

Furukawa argues that the strange process and decisions were caused by the DPJ's attitude regarding bureaucratic influence:

> On the issue of diplomacy and national security, there are many delicate factors. You cannot understand Japan's past diplomacy, the relations with the United States and China, or the Senkaku issues by just reading papers. That's why there are experts in the MOFA and the Ministry of Defense. Politicians have different roles, and it is natural for them not to have an accumulation of [knowledge and experience] on a specific matter. That is why they need to utilize the group of experts with good judgment.[33]

CCS Sengoku admitted that there was misjudgment on the part of the Japanese government in not expecting a strong reaction from China. At the September 29 press conference, Sengoku revealed his miscalculation that the release of fourteen crew members would ease tensions with China, stating that he should have known better about China's level of understanding of Japan's judiciary system.[34] The Senkaku Islands incident illustrated the DPJ government's inability to deal with a diplomatic crisis, and its antibureaucratic approach worked negatively during the incident because it could not take advantage of the knowledge and experience of experts within the government.

The handling of the video clips of the incident recorded by the Coast Guard officials was also criticized. The Kan government decided to withhold the video from the public based on diplomatic considerations. The opposition parties, however, demanded the disclosure in return for Diet deliberations on the FY2010 supplementary budget. Thus on November 1 some thirty Diet members on the Budget Committee were allowed to see the 6.5-minute-long video, which clearly showed that the Chinese trawler intentionally hit the coast guard vessels. The Diet members then requested that the video be released to the public. Four days later, six files, totaling over forty-four minutes of video footage, were uploaded to a YouTube site by a coast guard official. While the Kan government was highly criticized for Transport Minister Sumio Mabuchi's loose control of information, people around the world now learned about the dangerous action of the Chinese fishing boat intentionally colliding with the Japanese vessels.

MOF-Led Budget Process

While the Kan government displayed poor crisis management skills in the Senkaku incident without substantial assistance from the bureaucracy, it relied heavily on MOF bureaucrats in the process of the FY2011 budget making. After Kan had difficulty answering questions by himself in the Diet as finance minister, he began to call upon MOF bureaucrats. When he mentioned the need for a tax increase before the upper house election, many observers saw a strong influence of austerity-minded MOF officials in his statement. In July 2010 Kan officially announced that the National Strategy Office would not be involved in the budget-making process and effectively reestablished an MOF-led budget process.

The FY2011 budget was the first budget that the DPJ government made from scratch. On June 22, 2010, the Kan government approved the Midterm Fiscal Frame as a cabinet decision, which required keeping the issuance of deficit financing bonds to around 44 trillion yen and the basic expenditure (excluding debt-servicing cost) to 71 trillion yen for FY2011.[35] On July 27 the Kan government announced the budget guidelines. In the budget process for FY2010, the Hatoyama cabinet had abolished the guidelines that had set a budget ceiling for the ministries under the LDP government. However, the ministries' budget requests increased beyond the Hatoyama cabinet's expectation and were out of control. The Kan administration decided to rejuvenate the old budget-forming process as requested by MOF officials.

The guidelines required a 10 percent cut in basic expenditures for all ministries. In return, the ministries could submit program proposals to Japan, the budgets for which could be allocated from the special budget if approved.[36] During the DPJ presidential election campaign, Ichirō Ozawa criticized Kan, saying that this ceiling approach was the same as that under the LDP government, and that there was no political leadership in the process. Kan's response was "just wait for the final result."[37]

Draft budget proposals for FY2011 were submitted by the ministries by September 1. According to the proposals, the total expenditure would be 93.8 trillion yen, which included basic expenditures of 69.7 trillion yen. The total special budget request amounted to 2.9 trillion yen.[38]

Before the cabinet approved these budget proposals, the Government Revitalization Unit again conducted a program screening. Under the Hatoyama administration, the GRU had drawn public and media attention when it screened government programs in public hearings. As most of the programs had been formed under the LDP government, it was a relatively an easy task for the GRU. In the fall of 2010, the GRU had to screen the programs that the Kan cabinet had formed.

In the public hearings the GRU program screeners had to debate with the DPJ political appointees who were defending the programs they had formed. Although the GRU working groups screened 160 government programs, the screening resulted in a cut of 350 billion yen, about half the reduction amount in the previous year.[39] The program screening to improve the government's fiscal condition no longer seemed to be an attractive process.

On December 24 the Kan cabinet approved a government budget plan. The budget included the general account of 92.4 trillion yen, the biggest budget in history. However, it met with Kan's goal to keep basic expenditures under 71 trillion yen and issue debt-financing bonds of around 44 trillion yen. This was not achieved because of political leadership of the Kan government, but by the numeric manipulation of MOF officials. The MOF officials gathered 7.2 trillion yen of the surplus and endowments from the special accounts. To finance the natural increase in social entitlements, the MOF officials reduced the initial budget for public investment and local allocation tax, which would be compensated for in the following supplementary budget.[40]

The biggest political issue in the FY2011 budget formation was how to deal with the child allowance. The DPJ's 2009 manifesto had promised that 13,000 yen per child would be given out each month in FY2010, and the amount would be doubled in 2011 and afterwards. As it was the DPJ's most important campaign promise, the Hatoyama government provided the promised amount in 2010. However, the GRU could not cut enough expenditures to finance the full amount of the child allowance. As a result, the Kan government decided to keep the 13,000 yen amount. The MOF's influence over the Kan administration on budget making was so strong that Prime Minister Kan had to continue his stance in favor of fiscal reconstruction.

DEFENSE GUIDELINES AND TPP

In the field of national security, the most important achievement of the Kan government was probably the new National Defense Program Guidelines. The previous defense guidelines had been issued in 2004 under the Koizumi government. The 2004 document revised the basic defense policy to confront security challenges in the post–cold war international environment, such as regional conflicts, failed states, the proliferation of weapons of mass destruction, terrorism, and piracy. In 2009 the LDP government decided to revise the guidelines to meet the changes in the area surrounding Japan—North Korea's continued nuclear and ballistic missile development programs and its brinkmanship diplomacy, China's advancement in its naval and air forces, missiles, outer space, maritime, and cyber capability as well as assertiveness in expansion in the East and South China Seas; and Russia's modernization of forces in the Far East. The Hatoyama government at first tried to revise the defense guidelines in accordance with the original deadline of December 2009 but then decided to postpone this work for another year.

Prime Minister Hatoyama formed a private advisory group, the Council on Security and Defense Capabilities in the New Era, headed by Keihan Electric Railway's chief executive, Shigetaka Satō. The council published policy recommendations in August 2010. Its report was very ambitious, as it considered necessary revisions for Japan's national security without taking into account the political environment, which might not allow them to be adopted.[41]

The most important conceptual change was a shift from the Basic Defense Force (Kibanteki Bōeiryoku) to a Dynamic Defense Force (Dōteki Bōeiryoku). The Basic Defense Force concept had long served as a theoretical base to allocate defense forces across the main islands in order to avoid the creation of a power vacuum in the region and to deter an outright invasion. As this concept was created in 1976 in the midst of the cold war, Japan had allocated a large number of heavy weapons and infantry to northern Japan against a possible Soviet invasion. The new Dynamic Defense Force concept would maximize the efficiency and effectiveness of Japan's defense forces by concentrating resources on what are truly necessary functions. The report also suggested revising Japan's current interpretation on collective self-defense and the Three

Principles on Arms Exports,[42] and the five principles for Japanese peace cooperation activities.

Based on this report, Ministry of Defense officials prepared a draft of the new defense guidelines. The report met pressure for revision from three different groups. The first group was the DPJ's Research Council on Foreign Policy and National Security, which formed the DPJ's own proposal. The proposal explicitly recommended the establishment of a National Security Office in the Cabinet Secretariat with twenty or so politicians and staffers, enhancement of the defense posture in the southwestern region, revision of the five principles for peacekeeping operations (PKO) activities, and establishment of new rules for arms exports.[43] One of the council's leading members, Motohiro Ōno, described the process as "revolutionary." "The traditional defense guidelines dealt only with the policy matters under the MOD. But we included PKO under the jurisdiction of the MOFA as well as arms export under the METI."[44]

The second group was a private advisory group for CCS Sengoku, headed by Tokyo University professor Shinichi Kitaoka. To maintain political leadership in the process of formulating the new guidelines, Sengoku held cabinet committee meetings with Defense Minister Toshimi Kitazawa, Foreign Minister Seiji Maehara, and Finance Minister Yoshihiko Noda. To counter MOD and MOFA opinions, Sengoku asked his advisory group to come up with recommendations. The group suggested emphasizing the importance of human security as a goal for the SDF. Kitaoka, as well as two representatives from the DPJ's Research Council on Foreign Policy and National Security, Akihisa Nagashima and Shūji Kira, joined the cabinet committee meetings, which were held more than twenty times. Nagashima described the committee meetings: "We had a very heated discussion with no bureaucrat's involvement. The policy-making process was true political leadership."[45]

The third influential group, the Socialist Party, was strongly opposed to any change in the Three Principles on Arms Exports. The Japanese business community wanted their revision to allow international joint developments in order for the domestic defense industry to survive. Socialist leader Mizuho Fukushima, however, argued that any revision would be a step for Japan to become a "merchant of death." When Prime Minister Kan met Fukushima, she said, "Do not include the revision of the Three Principles on Arms Exports in the new defense guidelines or you will enrage me. If [such a revision were] included, the Socialist Party would have to keep a distance from your government."[46]

On December 17 the new defense guidelines were approved by the Security Council and the cabinet. The government adopted the new concept of the Dynamic Defense Force, called for the establishment of a National Security Council and the enforcement of the defense posture in the southwest region and listed safeguarding human security as a major objective of Japan's security policy. On the other hand, the revision of the Three Principles on Arms Exports was not clearly stated in the final draft owing to opposition from the Socialist Party. But it stated that Japan would study "measures in response to changes in the international environment regarding defense equipment."[47]

Many in the government and the DPJ were satisfied to show the DPJ government's ability to formulate substantially original defense guidelines under strong political leadership. The Socialist Party was happy to be able to block arms exports, which disappointed the business community and the MOD. Defense Minister Kitazawa announced in his statement on the guidelines that the MOD would study the possibility of participation in international joint development and production of defense equipment.[48] It was quite unusual for the defense minister to make a statement on such an occasion. Kitazawa told the author, "Many journalists reported that the revision of the arms embargo was excluded in the report. But they were wrong. It provided the launch pad for the revision."[49] As Kitazawa explained, the Noda cabinet in December 2011 announced its policy to ease the arms embargo and allow international joint development and production projects of armaments.

While the announcement of the new defense guidelines was an achievement in the national security arena, Prime Minister Kan tried to achieve another foreign policy objective. In his second policy speech, on October 1, 2010, Kan stated, "We will look into participating in such negotiations as those for the Trans-Pacific Partnership (TPP) agreement and will aim to build an Asia-Pacific Free Trade Area. With a view toward making the East Asian Community a reality, I want to open our country to the outside world and move forward with concrete steps of negotiations to the extent possible."[50] With this statement, Kan identified Japan's participation in the TPP negotiation as his major policy goal.

The TPP is a multilateral free trade agreement that aims to further liberalize the economies of the Asia-Pacific region. It was originally signed by Brunei, Chile, New Zealand, and Singapore in 2005 and aimed at reducing all trade tariffs to zero by 2015. The agreement covers all the main pillars of free trade, including trade in goods and service, rules of origin, trade remedies, sanitary and phytosanitary measures, technical barriers to trade, intellectual property, government procurement, and competition policy.[51] In addition to the original four countries, the United States announced that it would begin negotiations to join the TPP in September 2008. Later Australia, Malaysia, Peru, and Vietnam joined the negotiations. With its comprehensiveness and membership, the TPP had the objective of shaping a high-standard, broad-based regional pact in the Asia-Pacific.

Kan made his statement without building a consensus within the DPJ. DPJ upper house member Akira Gunji, who had served as deputy agricultural minister under the Hatoyama administration, for example, questioned in a Diet session when and where the participation in the TPP had been discussed and complained that Kan's statement was "abrupt."[52]

Prime Minister Kan established an advisory council, the Council on the Realization of the New Growth Strategy, based on the cabinet decision on September 7. At its second meeting, on October 8, the council discussed participation in the TPP negotiation. Members from the private sector, such as Nippon Keidanren chairman Hiromasa Yonekura and Tokyo University professor Motoshige Itō, stressed the importance of joining the TPP for the future of Japan's economy. Almost all members were supportive of Japan's participation; the only exception was Agricultural Minister Michihiko Kano, who expressed concerns about the damage to the agricultural sector. At the end of the meeting, Kan declared an intention to formulate Japan's basic policy on the comprehensive economic partnership by the November 2010 APEC meeting in Yokohama.[53]

Against Kan's initiative on the TPP, DPJ members, especially those who represented rural agricultural areas, began taking action. On October 21 anti-TPP DPJ members held a meeting that attracted 110 Diet members. As many of them were members of the groups led by Ichirō Ozawa and Yukio Hatoyama, it looked like an anti-Kan group meeting.[54] The same day the council held its third meeting, inviting Mamoru Motegi, chairman of the National Association of Agricultural Co-operatives, to attend. Motegi enthusiastically claimed that the TPP, which does not allow exceptional protections, would totally destroy Japan's agricultural sector.[55]

On October 27 the Cabinet Secretariat disclosed the economic impact of Japan's participation in the TPP, as calculated by three agencies. The Cabinet Office's estimate suggested that it would increase Japan's GDP by 0.48–0.65 percent. On the other hand, the Ministry of Agriculture, Forestry, and Fisheries stated that the total elimination of tariffs on nineteen agricultural products would decrease the GDP by 1.6 percent. On the contrary, the METI calculated that the GDP would decrease by 1.53 percent if Japan did not participate in the TPP.[56] The difference of opinion within the government became quite apparent through these calculations, illustrating the lack of policy coordination by the Kantei.

On November 4 the DPJ Policy Research Council formed its policy toward the TPP. After the confrontation between pro-TPP and anti-TPP groups, a compromise was reached. The PRC's policy recommendation was to postpone a conclusion and to hold conferences to gather information and decide whether to participate in the organization. Based on this recommendation, the cabinet Committee on Comprehensive Economic Partnership created the Basic Policy, which stated that "it is necessary to act through gathering further information, and Japan, while moving expeditiously to improve its domestic environment, will commence consultations with TPP member countries." This was an ambivalent decision. The pro-TPP members were satisfied with the commencement of consultations with TPP member countries. At the same time, this would allow the anti-TPP members to block future participation. With this decision, Japan participated as an observer in the TPP discussions on November 13–14, 2010, held on the sideline of the APEC summit in Yokohama.

TROUBLES WITHIN THE GOVERNMENT AND THE PARTY

From November 2010 the DPJ government faced serious challenges. On November 14 Justice Minister Minoru Yanagida made a slip of tongue at a private meeting: "There are two statements for the justice minister to remember [when answering in the Diet]: 'I would like to refrain from giving an answer on a specific incident.' When I do not know what to answer, I just state this. Also, 'we are operating appropriately based on laws and evidence.' I do not remember how many times I used these phrases."[57] LDP Diet members strongly criticized his comments as an insult to the Diet. Yanagida apologized and withdrew his statement. But the opposition party demanded his resignation. On November 22 Yanagida resigned and CCS Sengoku simultaneously assumed the position of justice minister.

But Sengoku also found himself in trouble over his own slip of the tongue. At the November 18 Budget Committee meeting in the upper house, he described the Self-Defense Forces as an "instrument of violence."[58] Opposition party members strongly protested the chief cabinet secretary's choice of a left-wing expression. Sengoku later rephrased his description of the SDF to an "organization that uses force." The opposition parties passed resolutions in the upper house to censure Sengoku as well as Transport Minister Sumio Mabuchi, who was responsible the leakage of the video clip on the Senkaku Incident, and demanded their resignation. On January 14, 2011, Prime Minister Kan reshuffled his cabinet to remove Sengoku and Mabuchi.

Another shock hit the DPJ on January 31. Ichirō Ozawa was indicted for violating campaign finance laws based on the second decision by the Committee for the Inquest of Prosecution three months earlier. Ozawa asserted that he would prove his innocence in court. However, according to a poll conducted by the *Yomiuri Shimbun* on February 1–2, 51 percent of respondents felt it was appropriate for Ozawa to resign as Diet member, and 20 percent recommended that he leave the DPJ while staying on as a Diet member. Only 17 percent said he did not need to resign or leave the party. The job approval rate for the Kan cabinet dropped from 34 percent in mid-January to 27 percent, and 79 percent accused Kan of lacking leadership on this matter.[59]

On February 10 Prime Minister Kan met with Ozawa and asked him to leave the party. But Ozawa refused to do so voluntarily. Five days later the DPJ held its Standing Officers Council and decided to suspend the party privileges accorded to Ozawa. In protest, sixteen members of the Ozawa's group submitted their resignation as caucus (*kaiha*) members in the lower house without leaving the DPJ. This was a tricky action. All the political parties must form *kaiha* to register their members and officers with the speaker of the relevant house. Usually the parties and their *kaiha* are the same, but theoretically it was possible for Diet members to belong to the party but not to the *kaiha*. Without these sixteen votes, the ruling coalition no longer had a two-thirds majority in the lower house.

On March 1, when the lower house voted on the FY2011 budget, the sixteen members boycotted the voting. Although the Kan government was able to enact the budget, which required only a simple majority of the lower house, it had to postpone the voting on the budget-related bills that required a majority of both houses or a two-thirds majority in the lower house. The DPJ held a meeting in which it was decided to penalize the leader of the sixteen lower house members by suspending his party privileges for six months.

Another blow to the DPJ was the revelation that Foreign Minister Maehara had received a political contribution from a foreign resident at the upper house Budget Committee meeting on March 4.[60] The Political Fund Control Law prohibits politicians from accepting funds from foreign nationals. Two days later Maehara admitted he had received contributions of 250,000 yen during a period of five years from a South Korean resident in Kyoto, in violation of the law. Maehara announced his resignation in order not to create "a vacuum" in Diet deliberations on the budget and in diplomacy.[61]

Maehara was not the only cabinet member who received money from a foreign national. On March 11 the *Asahi Shimbun* carried an article stating that Prime Minister Kan himself had received 1.04 million yen from a South Korean resident.[62] Asked about it at the upper house Settlement Committee meeting on the same day, Kan admitted he received the funds but stated that he did not know the benefactor was a foreign national.[63] As Maehara had resigned as foreign minister for the same reason, the opposition parties demanded Kan's resignation in return for passage of the budget bill. With the budget bill held as hostage, Kan was in a position to be forced to resign or to call for a general election. But a massive earthquake changed the political situation entirely.

THE IMPACT OF THE GREAT EAST JAPAN EARTHQUAKE

Focusing on the Nuclear Accident

Japan was hit by a 9.0 magnitude earthquake just off the Tohoku coastline at 2:46 p.m. on March 11, 2011. The most powerful earthquake ever recorded in Japan shook apart homes and other buildings. Then a devastating tsunami slammed into northeastern Japan, sweeping away almost twenty thousand people. This also damaged the nuclear reactors at the Fukushima Daiichi Plant, creating fears of a meltdown.

The Kan government's initial reaction was quick. Four minutes after the earthquake, Prime Minister Kan established a liaison office at the cabinet's Situation Center to gather information.[64] At the same time Deputy CCS Kinya Takino and Deputy CCS for Crisis Management Tetsurō Itō called an Emergency Gathering Team meeting with eight bureau-chief-level officials of the different government agencies who were in charge of natural disasters.[65] This team assessed the severity of the situation and confirmed the emergency procedures at 3:08 p.m. Six minutes later Kan identified the situation as an "extremely unusual or devastating disaster" under the Disaster Countermeasure Basic Act and established a cabinet-level committee, the Emergency Disaster Response Headquarters, with himself in charge.[66] At 3:27 pm, Kan instructed Defense Minister Kitazawa to mobilize the SDF for "maximum activities."[67] At 7:03 p.m., following developments at the Fukushima nuclear plant, a "nuclear emergency" was declared based on the Act on Special Measures Concerning Nuclear Emergency Preparedness, and Kan established another cabinet-level committee, the Nuclear Emergency Response Headquarters, with the secretariat staffed by the Nuclear and Industry Safety Agency (NISA), an external bureau of the METI.[68] Necessary institutions for crisis management were set up in a timely manner as outlined by the government manual for crisis management, which had been developed under the LDP government.[69]

That evening Kan held a meeting with leaders of the opposition parties at the Kantei. He told them that he would like to put all energy into countermeasures for the disaster. Although the opposition parties had demanded Kan's resignation or a general election, the earthquake created a situation that made neither of the two options realistically possible. They agreed to stop the political fight and promised to cooperate on smooth passage of necessary legislation.[70]

The Kan government faced four challenges simultaneously. First, it needed to save and rescue earthquake victims widely spread in northeastern Japan and to engage in reconstruction of the area. Second, it had to control the large-scale damage of the nuclear power plant. Third, it was necessary to recover the distribution, transportation, and electric supply grids and to deal with the fear of the spread of radioactivity. Fourth, it had to recover Japan's economy, which was damaged by the postearthquake reduction of production, transportation, and consumption, as well as by the appreciation of yen and a drop in stock prices.[71] The Kan cabinet heavily focused on dealing with the nuclear accident.

Prime Minister Kan, who majored in applied physics at college and claimed to be an expert on nuclear policy, showed extremely strong interest in and concern over the damaged nuclear power plant run by Tokyo Electric Power Company (TEPCO). NISA director general Nobuaki Terasaka was present at the Kantei and was supposed to plan how to deal with the accident. However, being a METI official who happened to be in that position on the ministry's job rotation schedule with no science background, he could not make any proposals. When the Nuclear Safety Commission's chairman Haruki Madarame arrived at the Kantei at 9 p.m., he was surprised to find that the NISA had not provided any suggestions to the prime minister.[72]

The most serious and imminent problem was the outage involving the plant's electric power system, which operated the emergency cooling system. As a result, the temperature and pressures inside the pressure vessels of the nuclear reactors rose sharply. To bring the reactor under control, pressure-release vents needed to be opened. Madarame suggested venting the pressure vessel to Kan. At first TEPCO was hesitant because venting would release radioactive isotopes into the air and would cast doubt on the safety of the nuclear power industry.

TEPCO waited for emergency power vehicles to arrive to supply electricity for the cooling process. Although forty such vehicles arrived at the plant, the electricity was not recovered. No explanation was given to the Kantei. CCS Edano testified, "At that point, we began developing distrust of TEPCO officials."[73] Later they learned that the vehicles' voltage and connectors were not compatible with the plant's system.

At around midnight the head of the Fukushima plant decided to vent. However, the manual operation in the blackout situation with the high radiation levels at the reactor was very difficult. At 3:05 a.m. METI minister Banri Kaieda held a press conference with a TEPCO official to announce the venting of the Unit 1 vessel. Seven minutes later CCS Edano held a press conference to announce that it was necessary to open the vents, and venting would release radioactivity in the air.[74] But the plant operators could not open the valves for almost four hours. Edano recalled later, "We kept telling TEPCO to do it quickly, asking how come it wasn't happening."[75] No clear answer was given, and distrust grew. Finally, at 6:50 a.m., Minister Kaieda used his legal authority to force TEPCO to open the vent.[76] "To let TEPCO vent the vessel and put water into it to cool down was my mission of the moment," Kaieda testified.[77]

Prime Minister Kan arrived at the Fukushima nuclear plant at 7:11 a.m., just twenty-one minutes after Kaieda's order. Kan asked TEPCO officials why the venting was not happening. When the company vice president tried to explain, Kan said, "I did not come to hear such an excuse." The plant's director finally pledged to the prime minister to take action by even forming a "suicide corps."[78] Relieved by this statement, Kan left the plant at 8:04 a.m. One hour later TEPCO finally began the venting operation, opening the vents at 10:17 a.m. At 2:30 p.m. vapor came out of Unit 1 and the pressure level fell. At 3:36 pm, however, the hydrogen outside the Unit 1 reactor combined with oxygen and exploded the building, blasting contaminated smoke and debris into the air.[79]

Kan's visit to the nuclear plant was criticized. LDP upper house member Yukari Satō, for example, argued that the visit had delayed TEPCO's action to vent the nuclear reactor as the company began the operation only after Kan left the plant.[80] LDP lower house member Yasutoshi Nishimura also criticized Kan, saying that the chief commander of the government should not have visited the nuclear power plant, which had the possibility of exploding.[81] Still, Kan's excessive focus on the nuclear plant continued after his visit.

The Kan government was careful about the dissemination of information on the nuclear accident in order not to cause panic among the public. CCS Edano, who acted as chief government spokesman, declared a nuclear emergency at the March 11 (7:44 p.m.) press conference but said, "Let me repeat that there is no radiation leak, nor will there be a leak."[82] He was wrong, as TEPCO had already detected radiation at the plant perimeter at 5:30 p.m. In the meantime, an evacuation zone was established initially at a radius of 3 kilometers from the plant. Soon the zone was extended to 10 kilometers, and then to 20 kilometers. The Nuclear and Industrial Safety Agency came up with a report at 10 p.m. March 11, pointing out the possibility of meltdown of nuclear fuel rods in the No. 2 reactor.[83] The following day at the 2 p.m. press conference, NISA spokesman Kōichirō Nakamura mentioned the possibility of meltdown. Nakamura was removed from his position for making the public feel uneasy.

Information going out to the public about the nuclear plant accident was further complicated because the Kantei, TEPCO, and NISA all held separate press conferences. TEPCO gathered information on its Fukushima plant and sent it to the Kantei and NISA. Based on TEPCO's information, CCS Edano first held a press conference at the Kantei, and later the spokesman of the agency held another one with more technical details. After the March 12 explosion of the nuclear reactor, the Kantei and NISA began to consult with each other to decide what information would be open to the public. As a result, public announcements became more cautious and less informative, and the consultation process became more time and energy consuming.[84]

On March 15 Prime Minister Kan announced the establishment of the Joint Headquarters for the Fukushima Daiichi Nuclear Power Station Accident at the TEPCO building and asked METI minister Kaieda and Special Assistant to the Prime Minister Gōshi Hosono to work at the headquarters. The new joint headquarters for both the government and TEPCO would enable coordinated action and direct access to information for the development of timely announcements. Kan appointed former transport minister Sumio Mabuchi as his special assistant regarding the nuclear plant. In addition, he handpicked six new special advisers to the cabinet after the earthquake, bringing the total number to fifteen.[85] Kan explained these appointments in an interview with a weekly magazine: "We did not receive all the necessary information. Often, we could not judge whether what we received was primary information or hearsay, or whether it was facts or estimation. . . . So, in addition to the received information, I asked various experts for second opinions and made judgments based on those."[86] These appointments as well as the establishment of the headquarters reflected Kan's distrust of TEPCO and the bureaucracy, including NISA and the METI.

Difficulty of Policy Coordination

The initial reaction of the Kan government was heavily focused on the nuclear accident. The prime minister and the chief cabinet secretary were expected to handle a wide range of issues after the earthquake, including providing assistance to the victims; reconstructing the damaged areas; recovering the distribution, transportation, and electrical supply system; dealing with the fear of the spread of radioactivity; and tackling with Japan's economic damages. CCS Edano held thirty-seven press conferences during the first two weeks after the earthquake. Among them, nineteen were dedicated exclusively to the nuclear accident, and in an additional eight conferences it was a major topic.[87] Edano looked like a spokesman for the nuclear accident alone.

Because of the Kan government's heavy focus on the nuclear accident, the other issues did not receive enough political attention and care. Iwate prefecture governor Takuya Tasso complained, "As most of the Kantei became a part of TEPCO, it could not look at the whole picture of the Great East Japan Earthquake disaster. It should never have happened."[88] Although all the ministries and agencies tried to do their best for the rescue and reconstruction of the damaged areas, political decisions were needed to set priorities given limited human and physical resources, and to flexibly interpret laws for smooth operations. For example, private truck companies volunteered to transport relief supplies, but they were not guaranteed gasoline for the return trips. Many vehicles had difficulty getting entry permits to use highways that were closed to private cars. As Kan and Edano were busy dealing with the nuclear situation, Deputy CCSs Takino and Itō could not finalize decisions by themselves on these issues. It was not governmental initiative but private-sector efforts that set up a distribution network in the damaged areas. On March 15 Keidanren chairman Hiromasa Yonekura established hotlines with the governors of the damaged prefectures and negotiated with the Ministry of Defense to use the SDF for a distribution network.[89]

The lack of political leadership caused many issues that required policy coordination among different ministries to remain stuck. The abolition of the administrative vice ministerial meeting was one of the major reasons for poor policy coordination. Under the Koizumi government, the subcabinet meeting had served as the first stage of the top-down decision-making process initiated by the prime minister. Deputy CCS Teijirō Furukawa often announced Prime Minister Koizumi's intention at the meeting and informed the entire bureaucracy about policy directions. With the abolition of the subcabinet meeting, the Kantei lost an important forum for policy initiative and coordination with the national leader.

In order for the Kantei to improve its policy coordination capabilities, on March 17 Prime Minister Kan appointed Yoshito Sengoku, who had been removed from the CCS position two months earlier, as deputy CCS in charge of victim support. Kan established the Team in Charge of Assisting the Lives of Disaster Victims, statutorily headed by Minister of Disaster Management Ryū Matsumoto, but its de facto leader was Sengoku. Sengoku called a meeting with the top bureaucrats of the METI, MIC, MILT, and National Police Agency to improve the distribution situation. At the meeting he asked them which would be more effective: to gather the top officials of only the related ministries or of all the ministries. The top police official answered that if the representatives of the ministries gathered, it would be much easier to get cooperation from the entire bureaucracy in a timely manner. Sengoku thus decided to assemble the Liaison Meetings among Ministries and Agencies, attended by the top bureaucrats of all the ministries and agencies.[90] This was in fact a revival of the administrative vice ministerial meeting that the Hatoyama government had abolished.

With this liaison meeting, Sengoku began interagency policy coordination for disaster relief. The meeting provided opportunities for the top bureaucrats to exchange information and coordinate their actions. But the interagency coordination was needed at various working levels. Under the traditional bottom-up policy-making process, bureaucratic officers at the deputy director level began interagency negotiations, then at the director level as well as the bureau chief level. The Hatoyama government identified the interagency policy coordination as the jurisdiction of political leaders and prohibited bureaucrats from contacting officials of other ministries or politicians. The network for interagency coordination within the government was therefore basically destroyed. Iwate prefecture governor Tasso testified, "Our prefecture received relief assistance in a timely manner from individual ministries. But some assistance, which requires interagency policy coordination, took a long time."[91]

The position of deputy CCS for crisis management was established by Prime Minister Hashimoto's administrative reform efforts for such occasions as the

Great East Japan Earthquake. Then-deputy CCS Teijirō Furukawa requested the establishment of this post so that he could continue his routine work while the other deputy CCS would be totally in charge of crisis management. Itō, the deputy CCS for crisis management, gathered the Emergency Gathering Team in order to confirm the predetermined emergency policy immediately after the earthquake took place. His team met several times after major aftershocks but was never in charge of policy making or policy implementation.

When the U.S. government offered technical and logistical support for the nuclear plant accident, it would have been Itō's role to organize a Japanese task force to coordinate with U.S. forces in Japan. But Itō did not take such action. Former parliamentary secretary of defense Akihisa Nagashima was asked by Special Advisor to the Prime Minister Gōshi Hosono to coordinate between the Japanese and American governments. Nagashima proposed forming a bilateral committee for nuclear plant countermeasures, which Kan approved.[92] The committee received American technical advice and assistance, which significantly improved the situation at the nuclear plant.

Nagashima reflected that the crisis management team headed by Itō did not function at all, and he called the situation a "management crisis of crisis management." He noted that the Kantei had an institution, but the institution did not function as "all the ministries acted in nonemergency mode."[93] The chaotic situation was created by the complicated division of authority of the different ministries and the lack of communication among them. The lack of experience with interagency coordination during the eighteen months under the DPJ government caused the crisis of the crisis management system.

No-Confidence Motion Against Kan

On March 28 former DPJ leader Ichirō Ozawa made his first public appearance since the earthquake and met with his political disciple, Governor Tasso. Ozawa openly criticized the Kan government's response to the disaster. He told reporters that experts had for some time pointed out the possibility of a nuclear meltdown at the Fukushima Daiichi Plant, but that NISA, the cabinet, and TEPCO had all avoided the problem.[94]

Ozawa was not the only one who was critical of the government. According to a *Kyodo News* poll conducted on March 26–27, 58.2 percent of respondents disapproved of the government's response to the nuclear crisis, and 63.7 percent felt that Kan had not demonstrated leadership in handling the crisis.[95] *Kyodo News* also conducted a poll asking all forty-seven prefectural governors for their opinion, and all but the Fukushima governor responded. Thirty governors disapproved of the governmental actions regarding the nuclear crisis, and only two approved.[96]

Public frustration was expressed in the local elections held on April 10, which elected twelve governors and five mayors as well as local assemblies in forty-one prefectures and fifteen cities. The DPJ suffered a serious setback, reflecting broad disenchantment among voters regarding the Kan government's inability to deal with the March 11 crises, and about the continued deterioration of the economy. One month after the quake and tsunami, some 150,000 people remained in cramped and cold shelters.

Two days after the elections, NISA raised the severity of the nuclear crisis from 5 on an international scale to the highest level of 7, the same as the 1986 Chernobyl disaster. It was widely suspected that the government waited until after the local elections to minimize the announcement's political impact. On that day Kan held a press conference to express his determination for Japan's recovery, stating, "I pledge here and now in front of the entire nation to continue to give my all to Japan in order to overcome the earthquake and subsequent nuclear incidents and rebuild our country in such a way as to make it even better than before." But no journalist paid any attention to his comment. Most questions focused on the timing of the announcement to raise the nuclear crisis scale. One reporter even asked Kan if the prime minister would resign, taking responsibility for the loss in the local elections.[97]

On the same day Ozawa met with former prime minister Yukio Hatoyama, and they shared their disgust toward Kan for not appropriately informing the public of the crisis situation. Ozawa began the anti-Kan movement. The following day he attended a meeting of his followers among DPJ lawmakers at which he distributed his opinion paper. The paper stated, "If politicians cannot prepare themselves to take full responsibility in the end, for what purpose did they achieve the change of the government. The Kan government received a warning from voters who punished the party in Sunday's local elections."[98]

LDP president Sadakazu Tanigaki echoed Ozawa's claim. He held a press conference on April 14 in which he called for Kan's resignation. Tanigaki stated, "The slow response of the government toward the earthquake and nuclear crisis dropped Japan's credibility in the international community. In the local elections, Japanese people expressed that the Kan government should not be in charge of recovery. The time has come when the prime minister needs to consider his resignation."[99] The LDP leadership began preparations to submit a vote of no-confidence against Prime Minister Kan by the end of the current Diet session, scheduled for June 22.

On June 1 the LDP, the Kōmeitō, and the Sunrise Party of Japan (Tachiagare Nippon) submitted a no-confidence motion against the prime minister. The DPJ was sharply split between the pro-Kan group and Ozawa's followers. Five Ozawa-loyal senior vice ministers and parliamentary secretaries in the cabinet submitted their resignations to vote in favor of the LDP-led motion.[100] Some 70 members among Ozawa's followers as well as the members of Hatoyama's group expressed their support for the motion. Kan said that he would dissolve the lower house if the motion passed that house. Ozawa threatened that he and his followers would leave the DPJ and form a new party. The following morning Hatoyama met with Kan to urge party unity and avoid a possible breakup. Kan and Hatoyama wrote a memorandum:

1. We will not destroy the DPJ
2. We will prevent the LDP from returning to power.
3. We will be responsible for the reconstruction from the earthquake and the rescue of the victims by (1) the enactment of the Basic Act on Great East Japan Earthquake Reconstruction; (2) deciding on a schedule for early compilation of a second supplementary budget.

According to Hatoyama, Kan also verbally promised that he would resign after the third condition was fulfilled.

At around noon on the same day, in a meeting with DPJ lower house members, Kan stated, "I would like to pass on my responsibility to a younger generation once we reach a certain stage in tackling the disaster and I have fulfilled my role [for the postearthquake recovery]." After this meeting, Ozawa told his followers that they did not have to vote for the no-confidence motion as Kan promised to resign soon. As a result, that afternoon the no-confidence motion was rejected in the lower house.

After the Diet voting, Kan held a press conference. Reporters repeatedly asked when the prime minister would resign and what exactly a "certain stage" meant. Kan, however, did not specify when he would resign but stated that the cold shutdown of the nuclear reactors would bring the situation "under a certain level of control."[101] As the cold shutdown could take until January 2012, this statement was interpreted as Kan's intention to stay in power for another six months.

This statement upset Hatoyama. The former prime minister had thought that Kan would resign within a month. In a televised interview, Hatoyama called his successor a "swindler."[102] According to Japan's Diet custom, a no-confidence motion can be submitted only once in a single session. Legislatively, the political parties no longer had the means to remove the prime minister. Hatoyama stated that he might call for a DPJ general meeting to submit a motion to remove him as a party president.

KAN'S DENUCLEARIZATION PLAN AND RESIGNATION

Three days after the June 24 enactment of the Basic Act on Great East Japan Earthquake Reconstruction, Prime Minister Kan in a press conference made it public that he would resign after the passage of three pieces of legislation: (1) the supplementary budget bill for FY2011 to finance the reconstruction costs; (2) the bill on Special Measures for Government Bonds to issue deficit-financing bonds; and (3) the bill to promote renewable energy in order to reduce Japan's dependence on nuclear energy.[103]

While the first two bills were considered essential for postquake reconstruction, the renewable energy bill was politically controversial. Kan obviously wanted to establish his name as the prime minister who began the policy toward a nuclear-free Japan. The bill would require electric power companies to purchase renewable energy from private corporations and households at a higher price than the cost generated by nonrenewable resources. It would inevitably raise the price of electricity for households and industrial consumers.

Kan's challenge created confusion within the DPJ as well as in the main opposition LDP. The renewable energy bill had already been approved by the cabinet and submitted to the Diet on March 11, just before the earthquake struck. Many lawmakers were against Kan's initiative in promoting renewable energy, and when it was originally submitted the bill had no chance of passing the Diet. But in a nuclear crisis atmosphere the prime minister would remain in office if the bill was not enacted. An increasing number of politicians became amenable to Kan's Diet strategy to pass the bill in order to ensure the prime minister's resignation.

Kan created further confusion on July 6 when he suddenly ordered stress tests for all of Japan's halted nuclear plants as a condition for resuming operations. The tests would examine whether the reactors were capable of withstanding a natural disaster or terrorist attacks. Initially Kan gave the authority to METI minister Banri Kaieda to acquire the approval from local governments to resume operations of some nuclear reactors. Before the July 6 order, Japan was facing the threat of a power shortage over the peak summer months and the resumption of the nuclear reactors was needed. While many local governments hesitated to resume operations, Kaieda got approval from Mayor Hideo Kishimoto of Genkai City, Saga, to restart the plant there. On July 4 Kaieda officially instructed Kishimoto to restart the Genkai nuclear power plant. Then, two days later, the prime minister made his stress-test order, thus preventing the restart. This totally upset Kaieda, who expressed his intention to resign as METI minister in the near future.

Kan's next action created even more confusion. He abruptly introduced a new energy policy at a press conference, stating that Japan should phase out its reliance on nuclear power (which was the source of 24 percent of Japan's electric power).[104] Many critics in the political and business community did not necessarily disagree with his idea but were upset by Kan's unilateral action and lack of specifics for such a drastic plan. Two days later, at an informal session after a cabinet meeting, cabinet ministers criticized the prime minister for making the denuclearization statement without any prior consultation. Kan told his cabinet members that it was not a government policy but his "personal opinion."[105] At the July 21 Diet meeting, when Kaieda was asked about Kan's denuclearization statement, he expressed his disgust by describing it as "lighter than a feather."[106]

The opposition LDP formed the Special Committee on Comprehensive Energy Policy to discuss Kan's initiative on the promotion of renewable energy. By August 9 the committee had decided to support the basic concept to purchase renewable energy. But Kan's proposal had a few problems that needed revising. First, in the Kan plan the purchase price would be decided by the METI minister, without a transparent decision-making system. Second, the rising electricity cost might drive domestic manufacturing industries out of the country. Third, as the environment of renewal energy technology is changing rapidly, the new system should be flexible to adjust to future developments.

On August 12 a political compromise was made between the ruling DPJ and the opposition LDP. Based on the LDP proposal, the price for green energy would be decided by a parliament-appointed panel twice a year. It also included provisions that extra electricity costs for energy-intensive industries would be trimmed by 80 percent. In addition, the new law would have a mandatory review of the scheme built in after three years. Based on the agreement, the revised legislation passed the lower house on August 23. Kan had accomplished his political goal, which could be the first step toward Japan's denuclearization.

As the most controversial condition for his resignation was reached, Kan officially announced that he would resign as prime minister on August 26. With a sense of achievement over the renewable energy promotion as well as relief from heavy political responsibility, Kan announced his resignation with a broad smile on his face. The DPJ quickly set a date for the DPJ presidential election. The following day the campaign started, and the election was set for August 29. In it Finance Minister Yoshihiko Noda was chosen to be the new prime minister. The fourteen-month-old Kan government closed its history, becoming the fifth consecutive short-lived cabinet in the post-Koizumi period.

INSTITUTIONS AND POLITICAL

LEADERSHIP

Decentralization Under the LDP

Although Japan has a political framework similar to that of many parliamentary democracies, it has developed a set of unique traditions, which created different types of veto players. While the constitution's framers emphasized legislative supremacy over the executive, the postwar purge of many political leaders and the American decision to occupy Japan with the existing bureaucracy in place made the bureaucracy the cornerstone of policy making. In addition, the narrow interpretation of collective responsibility of the cabinet led to a requirement for unanimous consent for cabinet decisions. This unanimous consent rule, along with bureaucratic supremacy, limited the prime minister's power in decision making in postwar Japan and gave veto power to individual cabinet members and the bureaucrats behind them.

Under this bureaucratic supremacy, the lack of strong leadership allowed sectionalism to develop. Each section of the bureaucracy had its own interests and client industry to protect. Career bureaucrats spent their entire careers in a single ministry and became strong veto players to resist policy changes that negatively affect their clients. LDP zoku members, who developed their policy expertise to become important veto players, often allied with related ministries to protect their client industries. In return for such protection, the client industries provided them with electoral and financial assistance. The sectionalism of these veto players has been an issue facing successive prime ministers.

The old multimember-district electoral system also indirectly weakened the power of the prime minister. Multiple candidates for the lower house seats made it very difficult for the LDP headquarters or its prefectural branches to focus on a single candidate in each district. As a result, central party control over election campaigns was weak, leading to the development of kōenkai and the candidates' reliance on inner-party factions.

While the LDP's grassroots organizations were a collection of kōenkai of individual Diet members and candidates, its headquarters became a loose co-alition of five to eight major factions. The original goal of LDP factions was to put their leader in the premiership. To become and remain prime minister, a faction leader needed to keep the loyalty of at least a majority of the party supporting him while maintaining overall party harmony. Therefore he was politically forced to form a cabinet with members from factions not his own and over whom he had little control. Often the cabinet members were still highly loyal to their faction leader and not always in sync with the prime minister. Diverse loyalties weakened the cabinet's unity and thus its control over individual ministries. LDP governments had veto players within their cabinets.

As LDP factions and kōenkai became institutionalized, it became very costly for individual LDP Diet members to maintain their kōenkai and for factions leaders to maintain their factions. The faction leaders competed to raise political funds to distribute to faction members. Individual members also raised funds by themselves to conduct kōenkai activities. As a result, many LDP Diet members were into money politics, which became the focus of criticism in the 1980s. In the late 1980s the Recruit scandal involving many LDP political leaders triggered serious attempts at political and institutional reform.

INSTITUTIONAL CHANGE AND KOIZUMI'S POLITICAL LEADERSHIP

The piecemeal institutional changes of the 1990s had created a new political environment that weakened the power of the veto players within the ruling party and the government and encouraged top-down leadership by the prime minister. The 1994 electoral reform, for example, created a significant shift in the power balance within the LDP. In the old system, constituents brought casework and requests to the more senior, politically powerful politicians in their district if there were LDP representatives. Since the reform, young LDP members in the single-seat electoral districts receive virtually all requests from their constituents, giving them a stronger political base and putting them on more equal political footing with the party elders.

As a result, the new power that younger Diet members found themselves holding encouraged them to act independently of the LDP factions and helped

Junichirō Koizumi come to power in 2001. For the April 2001 LDP presidential race, the younger members demanded a more open election process, which led to Koizumi's landslide victory that year. Because factional support had little to do with his victory, Koizumi was able to reject factional influence in choosing his cabinet and to be more independent in his decision making.

In addition to the LDP presidential elections, institutional changes brought further structural changes related to LDP factions. The SMD system and the new political fund law lowered individual members' political and financial dependence on their faction in the election. Factions no longer played the pivotal roles of recruiting LDP candidates and distributing cabinet, subcabinet, party, and Diet positions, as the process was more centralized in the LDP headquarters and the cabinet. Today, while LDP factions still exist, their power has been significantly weakened.

Under the SMD system, the lower house members solely representing a district are expected to handle all kinds of casework. The legislators no longer enjoy the division of responsibility developed under the old multimember districts and have been forced to become policy generalists rather than specialists. The membership of the LDP's policy subcommittees was opened to all LDP Diet members. This weakened the political influence of the PARC policy subcommittees as veto players.

In addition, the 1999 and 2001 government reforms shifted power away from the ruling party and toward the prime minister. Koizumi exploited the shift in his bold action to almost ignore the inner-party consensus-building process on the antiterrorism legislation and the postal reform. The abolition of bureaucratic assistance in the Diet created a spotlight effect for Koizumi to make his case to the public on policy issues in his own words. It also gave the prime minister stronger legitimacy to form a more competent cabinet: he could choose those with special skills and stronger loyalty to the national leader, and not just on a factional basis. In addition, the 2001 administrative reform provided Koizumi with clear legitimacy to take stronger policy initiatives and empowered the Cabinet Secretariat to carry out his policy objectives. Koizumi also took advantage of the newly created Council of Economic and Fiscal Policy to promote domestic policy reform. These changes also helped Koizumi's more visible leadership style, which was welcomed by the public and the media and contributed to his popularity. The public saw Koizumi as a new kind of leader and strongly supported his leadership style. With Koizumi receiving such high popular support, the bureaucratic and intraparty veto players had to follow his leadership.

These changes alone, however, did not guarantee the success of a more centralized, top-down leadership, as demonstrated by the post-Koizumi leaders' subsequent failures. The Abe cabinet could not fully take advantage of the institutional changes to push forward Abe's domestic reforms. Abe tried to promote the growth-first policy without a tax increase through the CEFP, but his initiative was blocked by MOF officials who wanted to raise the consumption tax for fiscal reconstruction. Abe also tried to cut the road construction budget but met with strong opposition from LDP construction zoku members. On civil service reform, even Abe's administrative deputy CCS acted against his policy initiative. Without administrative support at the Kantei, Abe could not achieve domestic reform.

After the defeat in the 2007 election, the Fukuda administration had to face the new political situation with the upper house dominated by the opposition parties. With the strong partisan veto players in the upper house, Fukuda had to pass major pieces of legislation such as the antiterrorism law and the revival of the gasoline tax by using the two-thirds majority in the lower house to override the upper house's decision. This exhausted Fukuda's political resources. Similarly, the unstable political environment also troubled Prime Minister Asō throughout his term. He successfully delivered economic stimulus packages and important pieces of national security legislation only with the strong support from the bureaucracy. In return, Asō reversed the civil service reform scheme to please the bureaucrats. The post-Koizumi LDP leaders could not take advantage of the political institutions to push forward their policy initiatives against the other veto players.

Failure of the DPJ's Institutional Changes

In the 2009 general election campaign, the DPJ portrayed the governments under the LDP as "the bureaucracy-controlled government" and promised to establish a "people-centered government" by political leadership. To promote his political initiative for reform, Hatoyama introduced two new institutions. However, these institutions did not meet his expectations. The Government Revitalization Unit drew much public and media attention when it tried to cut wasteful government programs, contributing to the increased public approval rating of the Hatoyama cabinet. But it could never find enough funding to finance the new government programs that the DPJ promised during the 2009 election campaign to carry out. The National Strategic Office was created to serve as the pivotal organization to plan and implement important government policies. However, with no budget and no legal authority, the office was dysfunctional.

Prime Minister Hatoyama also announced the Basic Policy to introduce new rules to set a division of labor and responsibility between politicians and bureaucrats. Under the Hatoyama government, only the political leaders within the ministries were allowed to make policy decisions. Hatoyama prohibited bureaucrats from contacting other ministry officials and Diet members. During the one year of the Hatoyama administration, bureaucratic initiative through traditional log-rolling and policy coordination among the ministries were forbidden. As policy making by political leaders could not cover all the necessary administrative actions, many government operations became dysfunctional. These changes significantly lowered the morale of bureaucrats.

In addition, the DPJ government tried to introduce the centralized policy-making process by abolishing policy committees in the party. This kept many DPJ members from participating in the policy-making process, causing frustration within the party. Meanwhile, the Office of the Secretary General grew very powerful, as it handled all the petitions from all over the nation. Secretary General Ozawa was able to reverse governmental decisions, citing requests from constituencies.

The Futenma base issue became a good example of failed political leadership and fed an antibureaucratic stance. During the election campaign, Hatoyama promised the Okinawan people that he would relocate Futenma outside the prefecture, without knowing the feasibility of his scheme. The prime minister did not show clear vision on how to relocate the base throughout his tenure. Different cabinet ministers sought their own alternative plans but found that they were not feasible or not acceptable to Americans and Okinawans. When Hatoyama realized the infeasibility of his own plan, there were no alternative plans to the Henoko plan. Taking responsibility, Hatoyama resigned as prime minister.

Hatoyama's successor, Naoto Kan, had once been a leading critic of bureaucratic control of the government. But he changed his view when he became prime minister. On the first day of his government, Kan issued his basic policy, which encouraged bureaucrats to actively participate in policy making. Kan also changed Hatoyama's policy on centralizing decision making in the cabinet, reestablished the DPJ Policy Research Council, and appointed a cabinet minister as chair in order to maintain the principle of centralized decision making.

Despite institutional adjustments, the Kan government could not take advantage of the expertise of the bureaucrats. For example, Kan's Kantei did not form an effective task force of high bureaucratic officials in the case of the Senkaku Islands incident. The worst example was the Kan government's response to the Great East Japan Earthquake. Prime Minister Kan and CCS Edano heavily focused on the nuclear accident in Fukushima, leaving the relief work, cleanup, and recovery efforts from the quake and tsunami destruction largely untouched. While each ministry tried hard to respond to the needs of the damaged areas in Tohoku, many administrative operations that required interagency coordination were left undone with little political leadership being extended. The poor response of the Kan government led to anti-Kan activities within the DPJ and invited the opposition parties to submit a no-confidence motion against the cabinet. This eventually led to the prime minister's resignation at the end August 2011.

NODA'S "NO-SIDE" APPROACH

Yoshihiko Noda became the third DPJ prime minister on August 30, 2011. He brought changes to two political trends. The first change was the reversal of the confrontational approach. Prime Minister Koizumi started the confrontational trend by emphasizing his reformer image and willingness to destroy the LDP. He picked fights with the largest faction, led by Hashimoto and his successors, and labeled LDP members who opposed his policy initiative as anti-reformists. By openly showing the fight, Koizumi attracted public support to promote his reform. Under the LDP governments of Abe, Fukuda, and Asō, the opposition DPJ conducted a confrontational approach in the Diet by taking advantage of the LDP's minority status in the upper house, forcing the three prime ministers out of office.

Under the DPJ government, Prime Minister Hatoyama wanted to establish political leadership by avoiding bureaucratic influence in decision making. Hatoyama, however, ended up being criticized for being under strong political influence of DPJ secretary general Ichirō Ozawa. Prime Minister Kan tried to gain popular support by getting rid of Ozawa's influence. As a result, Kan was in a constant political battle with the pro-Ozawa group throughout his tenure.

A main battle in the August 2011 DPJ presidential race was competition between the pro-Ozawa and the anti-Ozawa candidates. In addition to Noda, former foreign minister Seiji Maehara ran from the anti-Ozawa camp. From the pro-Ozawa camp, METI minister Banri Kaieda declared his candidacy. Two relatively neutral candidates, Agriculture Minister Michihiko Kano and former transport minister Sumio Mabuchi, joined the race. As the campaign period was only three days, there was hardly any policy debate. Political maneuvering among intraparty groups defined the result of the election.

As the DPJ presidential election was a by-election due to Kan's resignation in the midst of his two-year term, it was conducted with the votes of only 398 DPJ Diet members. In the initial voting, Kaieda finished first with 143 votes from the Ozawa and Hatoyama groups, and Noda came in second with 102 votes. In the runoff, however, Noda picked up most of the votes of the Maehara and Kano groups and received 215 votes, defeating Kaieda, who earned 177 votes. In his victory speech, Noda expressed his wish to end the infighting between the pro-Ozawa and the anti-Ozawa groups by using a rugby term for game over: "Let this be the no-side moment." After a game is over, ruggers take no side and become friends. Noda's nonconfrontational approach was well received by the public; an *Asahi Shimbun* poll showed 53 percent public approval at the beginning of the Noda cabinet.

Based on his spirit of "no-side," Noda appointed Azuma Koshiishi, a close aide to Ozawa, to the powerful position of DPJ secretary general. Noda showed his emphasis on party harmony by forming a cabinet with a careful balance of inner-party groups. In addition, he abandoned centralized policy making by the cabinet, which the Hatoyama cabinet introduced. As many nongovernment DPJ members had been excluded from the policy-making process, this policy was unpopular among many DPJ members. Noda established subcommittees under the DPJ's Policy Research Council that were open to all DPJ Diet members to discuss policies and budget proposals. Noda even declared that the government would seek preapproval from the ruling party for all government decisions. Prime Minister Noda followed the traditions of the old LDP governments more than most recent LDP prime ministers had.

The second change was to terminate the antibureaucratic stance. Hatoyama had abolished the administrative vice ministerial meeting, which served as an important source of policy information as well as a forum for policy coordination. Before issues reached the meeting, interagency negotiations and coordination were conducted at different levels, among vice-ministers, bureau chiefs, and lower working officers. With the abolition of the meeting as well as the prohibition of bureaucratic log-rolling, the horizontal policy networks within the Japanese government were totally destroyed. While Prime Minister Kan tried to include bureaucrats in the policy process, he was unwilling to reestablish the vice ministerial meeting that he had long criticized as the symbol of bureaucratic supremacy. Despite his words about accommodating bureaucrats, Kan did not take advantage of bureaucratic expertise in the Senkaku Islands case. In response to the Fukushima nuclear accident, the prime minister showed a strong suspicion toward bureaucratic advice and constantly sought second opinions from his personal advisers.

On the other hand, Noda, immediately after he assumed office, declared no-side with regard to bureaucrats by announcing the establishment of the liaison conference among ministries and agencies (*fuchō renraku kaigi*), effectively revitalizing the old subcabinet meeting. While it began serving as an important forum for administrative information exchanges among ministries as well as between the Kantei and the bureaucracy, the multilayered interagency policy network, which was destroyed by Hatoyama, would need time to be reestablished.

CHICKEN GAME OVER TAX HIKE

The reestablishment of the subcabinet meeting symbolized Noda's probureaucracy attitude. Noda, who served as finance minister in the Kan cabinet, was convinced by MOF officials of the need for fiscal reconstruction. In his first policy speech, on September 13, he announced the need for a tax hike to finance reconstruction after the earthquake. Noda also stressed the importance of the midterm fiscal reform package to raise the consumption tax to finance social security for Japan's increasingly aging society, and he asked all political parties to participate in the policy discussions.[1]

Three days later the Government Tax System Research Committee announced the time-limited tax reform plan to raise 11.2 trillion yen in the coming ten years to finance the reconstruction costs. The committee proposed three options: (1) increase only corporate and individual income taxes; (2) increase income taxes as well as some indirect taxes; or (3) increase the consumption tax. Noda quickly instructed the committee to exclude the option of a consumption tax hike in order to avoid a conflict with former DPJ president Ozawa, who had led an anti–consumption tax increase campaign against the Kan cabinet. On September 28 the Noda cabinet approved a tax reform package that would raise the corporate tax for three years and the individual income tax and the cigarette tax for ten years.

The LDP strongly opposed the cigarette tax increase. The cigarette price had been raised by 100 yen per pack just one year earlier. An additional tax increase would hit the purse of low-income smokers. Without a majority in the upper house, the DPJ had to compromise and announced the exclusion of the cigarette tax on November 10. Instead, the cabinet came up with a plan to extend the individual income tax hike for twenty-five years. As a result, the reconstruction tax reform package passed the Diet on November 30 with the support from the DPJ, the PNP, the LDP, and the Kōmeitō.[2]

Having secured the funds for reconstruction, Noda then moved on to the next step: the midterm fiscal reconstruction plan. On December 5 he established the Government-Ruling Party Headquarters for Social Security Reform, headed by himself. The prime minister announced that the group would come up with a proposal to be enacted by June 2012, and he asked the government and the ruling parties to discuss the details of social security and taxation reform plans. Within the DPJ, the focus was on a consumption tax increase. As the DPJ had lost the 2010 upper house election after Prime Minister Kan publicly announced his intention to increase the consumption tax, there was strong opposition from lower house members who would have to run in the next general election.

On December 29 Prime Minister Noda attended a joint meeting of DPJ's Tax System Research Committee and the Fundamental Tax and Social Security Reform Research Committee in which he stated, "If we run away from this task now, what will happen to this country?" which effectively served to override the opposition. The joint meeting finally approved the plan to raise the consumption tax rate from 5 to 8 percent in April 2014 and to 10 percent in October 2015. On January 6, 2012, the Noda cabinet adopted a draft plan for social security and tax reform that included this tax hike.[3]

Ozawa again publicly criticized Noda's tax hike initiative. Ozawa saw Noda becoming a puppet of the bureaucratic veto players at the MOF like Kan had done, and as violating the DPJ's campaign promise not to increase taxes. Many of Ozawa's followers had run in the 2009 general election under a no-tax-hike promise and would have very little chance at being reelected if a DPJ-sponsored tax hike were to take effect. In a major interview article that appeared in the *Asahi Shimbun* on February 24, Ozawa hinted that he and his followers in the DPJ might break off from the party.[4] On the following day Prime Minister Noda held a secret meeting with LDP president Sadakazu Tanigaki, who had been a longtime proponent of a consumption tax increase. This meeting was regarded as Noda's attempt to achieve political cooperation with the LDP in order to bypass Ozawa and push forward the tax hike. In early March it was reported that Deputy Prime Minister Katsuya Okada approached the LDP to form a grand coalition to pass the tax legislation. Thus a game of chicken between Noda and Ozawa was under way. While Ozawa showed his willingness to break off from the party over the tax issue, Noda hinted that he was willing to cut off Ozawa's group and cooperate with the LDP.

The conflict between Noda and Ozawa was highlighted when the Noda cabinet approved the consumption tax bill on March 30. Four subcabinet members of the Ozawa group resigned in protest. In addition, twenty-nine Ozawa followers resigned from their party posts. One month later the Tokyo District Court found Ozawa not guilty of conspiracy to falsify political fund reports. DPJ secretary general Koshiishi requested the party reinstate Ozawa's party membership, which had been suspended because of the indictment. On May 8 the DPJ Standing Officer's Council granted Ozawa's party privileges. Ozawa now had greater freedom to fight against the tax hike.

In the hope of keeping the ruling party together, DPJ secretary general Koshiishi arranged a meeting between Noda and Ozawa on May 30. Noda asked Ozawa for his cooperation in enacting the tax legislation. Ozawa told the prime minister that he could not give his support as it would be a major tax hike of close to thirteen trillion yen. The gap between the two was not filled, but they agreed to meet again. At the second meeting, on June 3, Ozawa remained opposed to the tax hike, and Noda told Ozawa that he would enter negotiations with the opposition LDP instead.

In the negotiations the LDP demanded that Noda renounce the party manifesto and completely rework the Latter-Stage Elderly Health Care System. A compromise was reached on June 15. While Noda could keep an appearance of his commitment to the manifesto, he agreed to create a national conference on social security reform to review the health care program. Although the LDP wanted a promise of an early dissolution of the lower house, Noda did not offer anything up on this matter. With the agreement to review health care, the consumption tax bill passed the lower house on June 26. However, fifty-seven DPJ members voted against the legislation and sixteen avoided voting.

A week later Ozawa and forty-eight other Diet members (thirty-six lower house, twelve upper house) submitted letters of resignation to the DPJ. They formed a new party, People's Lives First (Kokumin no Seikatsu ga Daiichi). The party's top priority goals were to abandon a planned tax hike and to abolish nuclear power plants. Noda thought that Ozawa's break from the DPJ would improve his public approval rate. On the contrary, according to an *Asahi Shimbun* poll (July 7–8), Noda's approval rate sank to 25 percent. The result of the chicken game was that Ozawa could not stop the vote on the tax hike and Noda lost forty-nine Diet members while failing to receive public support.

The stage for the tax legislation moved to the upper house when its special committee began deliberation on July 13. On August 1, when Noda met with a labor leader, he mentioned his hope to form a budget for the next fiscal year. This could mean that he would remain in office until the next spring, upsetting LDP president Tanigaki. In a press conference Tanigaki stated "Honestly speaking, I have a feeling that [Prime Minister Noda] wants to pick a fight with me." Now Noda had to face another game of chicken, this time with the LDP.

The LDP told Noda that it would submit a motion of no-confidence against his cabinet unless the prime minister specified the timing of lower house dissolution. However, there was strong opposition to the early dissolution within the DPJ because at least a half of its lower house members would lose their seats in the election. Once Noda mentioned a concrete date for dissolution, he would have to face a fierce intraparty battle. Noda's response to the LDP was that he would call an election "in the near future." LDP president Tanigaki rejected this, and Noda asked for a meeting with him. The meeting was held on the night of August 8. The two party leaders agreed to pass the tax legislation as Noda promised to dissolve the lower house "sometime soon." As a result, the legislation to raise the consumption tax passed the upper house on August 10.

Politics Over the General Election

By the end of August 2012, LDP and Kōmeitō members were frustrated at seeing no sign that Noda would immediately dissolve the lower house. The two parties decided to submit a censure motion against the prime minister in the upper house. However, the seven other opposition parties had already submitted one, and they demanded that their motion should be voted on first. LDP president Tanigaki decided to vote for their motion, which criticized the three-party cooperation among the DPJ, LDP, and Kōmeitō on tax hikes and other policies.

The Kōmeitō did not vote for the motion, which could have meant self-denial of past policies, causing senior LDP leaders to criticize Tanigaki's decision and express their disapproval of his reelection as LDP president. Thus Tanigaki chose not to run in the LDP presidential election on September 26.

Former prime minister Shinzō Abe, former PARC chairman Shigeru Ishiba, LDP secretary general Nobuteru Ishihara, former CCS Nobutaka Machimura, and PARC deputy chairman Yoshimasa Hayashi all declared their candidacy for party leadership. In the first round of voting, these candidates fought for the 300 votes from LDP local branches and 198 votes from LDP Diet members. Ishiba led the first round, with 165 local and 33 Diet votes, but was defeated by Abe in the two-man runoff vote, which counted only Diet votes. Abe was to be the new face to fight against Prime Minister Noda, who had been reelected as DPJ president just five days earlier.

After new party leadership was elected in the two major parties, media and public attention swiftly shifted to the timing for the general election. On October 29 Noda made a policy speech during the extraordinary session of the Diet, which began that day. In the following question-and-answer session, Abe demanded an election by year's end. Noda simply responded that he would make his decision when the conditions were met. Two days later he presented those conditions, which included legislation to allow the government to issue deficit-financing bonds, establishment of a national council to revise the social security system, and electoral reform of the lower house.

This raised tensions within the DPJ, as many of its members were desperate to postpone the election, fearing a disastrous defeat. Meanwhile the Noda government approached the LDP and the Kōmeitō to request cooperation on the issuance of bonds to finance administrative operations. On November 13 the two parties agreed with the government, fulfilling the first condition for the general election. The same day the DPJ held a Standing Officers Council meeting, during which many members expressed their opposition to an early election, and Secretary General Okiishi was asked to express "the party consensus" to Noda.

In the Diet meeting the following day, however, Noda told Abe that he would be willing to dissolve the lower house on November 16 if the LDP agreed to the lower house electoral reform, which would correct the malapportionment and reduce the 180 proportional representation seats. At first Abe was surprised by Noda's offer, but then he acceded to the request. After consulting the LDP leadership, Abe agreed to establish a national council for social security reform and to pass the legislation to correct the malapportionment situation, and he suggested that the LDP would cooperate with the DPJ on the PR seat reduction in the next Diet session. Noda accepted Abe's response and dissolved the lower house on November 16, after the enactment of legislation on bond issuance and electoral reform.

In the December 16 general election, twelve parties fought for 480 lower house seats. In addition to the ten existing parties (DPJ, PNP, LDP, Kōmeitō, Your Party, Social Democratic Party, Communist Party, New Party Daichi, Renaissance Party, and New Party Nippon), two newly created parties entered the race—the Japan Restoration Party (JRP) and the Japan Future Party (JFP). The JRP was first led by popular Osaka City mayor Tōru Hashimoto, who drew public attention through mass media and Twitter. He strongly advocated decentralizing government authority. Tokyo governor Shintarō Ishihara joined the JRP to lead the election campaign under the flag of government decentralization. Shiga prefecture governor Yukiko Kada established the JFP under the flag of denuclearization. Ichirō Ozawa and his followers joined the JFP, which was later renamed as the People's Life Party.

The LDP won a landslide victory in the general election, capturing 294 lower house seats. With 31 seats won by the Kōmeitō, the new coalition government would have more than a two-thirds majority of the 480-seat house, which implied the ability to override rejection by the upper house. The DPJ experienced a disastrous defeat, securing only 57 seats. It lost 173 seats, including 7 seats held by incumbent cabinet ministers. A major contrast was found in the results of the two newly formed parties: the JRP picked up 54 seats, but the JFP only 9 seats. The newly elected prime minister, Shinzō Abe, would still have to face a split Diet without a majority in the upper house, but the two-thirds majority in the lower house would give him leverage to conduct smoother Diet operations than the DPJ governments had faced after the 2010 upper house election.

POLITICAL LEADERSHIP AND BUREAUCRATIC SUPPORT

The DPJ prime ministers did not take advantages of the institutional changes brought by Hashimoto's administrative reform. In fact, Hatoyama introduced additional institutional changes in order to establish political leadership but created more confusion than concrete results. Instead of establishing strong political leadership, Hatoyama's initiative created a weak bureaucracy. Kan tried to reverse excessive bureaucratic exclusion, but his distrust of bureaucrats came back over the responses to the earthquake. Seeing the failure of his two predecessors, Noda established a better relationship with the bureaucrats. But many experts observed that the prime minister was controlled by the bureaucrats, like many past LDP prime ministers.

The stories in this book tell us that centralized policy making is effective only when a motivated and talented leader can take advantage of institutional changes to control and cooperate with the bureaucracy. Without effective bureaucratic support, the prime minister cannot achieve major policy changes via top-down decision making.

Under the traditional LDP governments, with some exceptions, policy making in the government and the ruling party was highly decentralized. The LDP prime ministers relied heavily on the bureaucracy and zoku members in policy making. The leaders met strong opposition from the institutional and intraparty veto players when they introduced drastic, controversial policies. As a result, many reform policies ended up with political compromises. The situation of the LDP governments before Koizumi is portrayed in the upper left box of figure 7.1, which shows weak prime ministerial leadership and effective bureaucratic support.

Koizumi took advantage of institutional changes to carry out drastic reform plans using the top-down decision-making style. With his high popular support, he forced the veto players in the government and the ruling party to follow his direction. The Koizumi government is depicted in the upper right box of the figure as strong leadership and effective bureaucratic support. However, the post-Koizumi LDP leaders failed to take advantage of the new institutional arrangements and the situation reverted to that of the pre-Koizumi era.

Hatoyama introduced a new institutional arrangement in an attempt to establish political leadership. As illustrated in the Okinawa base issue, he did not show strong political leadership and failed to utilize bureaucratic support. The

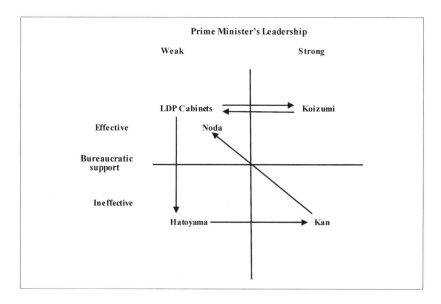

FIGURE 7.1. Leadership and Bureaucratic Support

Hatoyama administration can be categorized as one of weak leadership and ineffective bureaucratic support, as noted in the lower left box of figure 7.1.

Kan tried to show strong political leadership in the Senkaku Islands incident and the responses to the earthquake. But without effective bureaucratic support, he failed to deliver efficient responses in these crises. His confrontational approach with Ozawa's group eventually forced him out of office. The Kan government is illustrated in the lower right box as strong leadership and ineffective bureaucratic support. Noda learned the lessons from the two previous DPJ leaders and decided to adopt a nonconfrontational approach and effectively utilize bureaucratic support. As a result, he ended up being an old-style leader with decentralized decision making, like pre-Koizumi LDP prime ministers.

To successfully exercise political leadership, a Japanese prime minister needs to balance between centralized institutions and bureaucratic support. By doing so, the prime minister can beat institutional, partisan, and intraparty veto players and deliver drastic reform policies.

EPILOGUE

DEVELOPMENTS UNDER THE ABE CABINET

A S A RESULT OF THE LDP's landslide victory in the general election, Shinzō Abe again became the prime minister on December 26, 2012. Abe formed his cabinet, which he named a "crisis-busting cabinet." In his first cabinet in 2006, he appointed many of his close associates to cabinet and sub-cabinet positions. As a result, a series of scandals and controversial remarks by cabinet members provoked public outrage and weakened his cabinet. This time, Abe appointed competent LDP members to the key cabinet positions, including former prime minister Tarō Asō as both deputy prime minister and finance minister, Yoshihide Suga as chief cabinet secretary (CCS), and Akira Amari as economic minister.

In his policy speech on January 22, 2013, Abe outlined the policies that the LDP members nurtured over their three years as an opposition party in the areas of both domestic and foreign policy.

Among domestic policies, Abe's highest priority was economic revival. Abe reinstated the Council Economic and Fiscal Policy (CEFP), which the DPJ governments had abolished, as a control tower for a broad range of economic policies. In addition, he established the Headquarters for Japan's Economic Revitalization to specifically oversee the economic revival. Abe's economic plan was soon labeled as "Abenomics" by the media. Abenomics consists of monetary easing policy, an expansive fiscal policy, and economic growth strategies to encourage private investment.

At the first CEFP meeting on January 9, Prime Minister Abe declared to set a 2 percent inflation target and pressured the Bank of Japan (BOJ) to drastically ease the monetary policy to overcome chronic deflation and the strong yen which troubled many export-oriented corporations. Although BOJ Governor Masaaki Shirakawa was hesitant to set a numerical target for inflation, the BOJ finally released a joint statement with the government to "pursue monetary easing and aim to achieve the inflation target at the earliest possible time."

Even after the announcement of the joint statement, Prime Minister Abe kept pressuring the BOJ. For example, at the February 18 Diet meeting, Abe mentioned the possibility to proceed with revising the BOJ law if the central bank failed to comply with the government's desire for more aggressive measures to fight against deflation. Under pressure from Abe, BOJ governor Shirakawa stepped down on March 19, almost three weeks before his five-year term was due to end.

The market reacted positively to Abe's economic initiatives. On March 8, the Nikkei Stock Average returned to the level of the fall 2008 pre-Lehman shock era as the yen weakened to over 95 yen per dollar, giving an advantage to many Japanese export-oriented industries.

The appointment of a new BOJ governor was very important to reconfirm the government's commitment to the inflation target. Abe's pick for this key position was former MOF vice minister and Asian Development Bank President Haruhiko Kuroda, who had been a vocal critic of Shirakawa's BOJ policies for reacting too slowly on anti-deflation measures. Kuroda met the qualifications suggested by Abe's cabinet members and opposition parties, including experience of managing a large organization, strong English skills to communicate with the global community, and sharing Abe's call for a bolder monetary stimulus.

However, delicate political maneuvering was needed to achieve Diet approval for this major appointment. In 2008 under the Fukuda cabinet, the main opposition DPJ effectively blocked the appointment of former MOF officials to BOJ governorship by arguing that they might erode central bank independence.

More controversial was Abe's choice for BOJ deputy governor, Gakushūin University Professor Kikuo Iwata, who was seen as too radical by some lawmakers. The parliamentary approval was seen as one of the biggest challenges in the current Diet session for Abe as the ruling coalition did not have a majority in the upper house.

The DPJ, which held the most seats in the upper house, opposed Iwata's appointment. However, in order to split the opposition block Abe strategically persuaded other opposition parties to support the Iwata appointment, including the Japan Restoration Party and Your Party. As a result, the appointment of

Kuroda and Iwata as well as the promotion of BOJ Executive Director Hiroshi Nakaso to another deputy governor position was approved by the upper house on March 15.

These appointments completed the lineup for promoting the Abenomics economic policies. During the Diet hearing, Kuroda expressed his determination, saying "I will take whatever steps possible to pull the nation out of deflation." The government and the central bank were expected to closely work together to end two decades of economic stagnation.

The most urgent economic policy issue the Abe cabinet had to tackle was the formation of the FY2012 supplementary budget. During the election campaign, Abe had indicated that he would move swiftly on a large supplementary budget. On the day he assumed office, Prime Minister Abe instructed his cabinet members to start drafting it. On January 15, 2013, just three weeks into his premiership, the Abe cabinet approved a 13.1 trillion yen supplementary budget plan, the second-biggest of its kind, close to the record high of 14.7 trillion yen set by the Asō cabinet in spring 2009.

Of the 13.1 trillion yen, 10 trillion yen would be used for "emergency economic measures." About half of that amount would be spent on public works projects, under names such as "reconstruction and disaster prevention," "establishment of safe living condition," and "revitalization of local communies." The amount of public works projects in the supplementary budget was comparable to that of an annual budget. The austerity-minded Ministry of Finance accepted this budget in return for the consumption tax hike scheduled for spring 2014. The big supplementary budget was expected to boost the Japanese economy.

On the foreign policy front, Abe declared to undertake "a drastic reshaping" in his policy speech. Above all, the highest priority was given to reinforcing the Japan-U.S. alliance. Abe vowed to devote his "greatest possible efforts to lighten Okinawa's burden, including through the relocation of Futenma Air Station."

On February 22, Abe visited Washington to meet with American President Barack Obama. At the meeting, Abe promised to implement the bilateral agreement to relocate the Futenma station without delay. In his February 28 policy speech, the prime minister said, "We must not allow Futenma Air Station to remain at its current location indefinitely. We will build up a relationship of trust while listening carefully to the voices of the people of Okinawa. And, we will move forward at an early time regarding the relocation of Futenma Air Station."

The Japanese government initiated formal procedures to relocate the station to the Henoko district of Nago City. The Defense Ministry asked the Nago Fishermen's Cooperative for its consent on land reclamation work to build a new airfield. On March 11, the cooperative made a decision to support needed landfill in return for financial compensation. After receiving this approval, the Japanese government filed an application for the landfill project with the Okinawa Prefectural Government. As all the documents were in order, Okinawa accepted the application and would make the decision to allow the landfill or not by the governor within several months. These quick actions demonstrated the strong political determination of the prime minister and displayed a stark contrast to the DPJ governments that did not make any progress over this issue over a couple of years.

Another foreign policy issue that the Abe cabinet quickly moved on was the participation in the TPP. During the general election campaign, the LDP stated a policy platform that the party would oppose participation in the TPP negotiations as long as the requirement for participation is tariff elimination without exemptions. This effectively put off a final decision, and left ample room for entry to the negotiation with the existing countries. During his Washington visit, Abe sought an American assurance to allow exemptions for sensitive trade commodities, such as rice.

After extensive discussions over the topic, the prime minister and the president released a joint statement which stated, "Recognizing that both countries have bilateral trade sensitivities, . . . the two Governments confirm that . . . it is not required to make a prior commitment to unilaterally eliminate all tariffs upon joining the TPP negotiations." With this joint statement, Prime Minister Abe held a press conference on March 15 and announced the decision to participate in the TPP negotiations.

Among the national policy issues, there were two agenda items that Abe failed to achieve during his first premiership, and that he was eager to push through during his second cabinet: the establishment of a Japanese version of the U.S.-style National Security Council (NSC) and the reinterpretation of the Constitution to allow Japan to exercise the right of collective self-defense.

In mid-January, a hostage crisis developed when al-Qaeda–linked terrorists took more than 800 people hostage at a gas facility near In Amenas, Algeria, which resulted in the death of ten Japanese nationals. To Abe, this incident reconfirmed the need for the establishment of an NSC, which would gather and analyze information to deal with crisis situations. On February 15, Abe held the first meeting of a government panel of experts to consider the creation of an NSC. Within a couple of months, the panel was expected to compile a re-port. Based on the report, the government was to submit legislation during the current ordinary Diet session.

To discuss Japan's right to collective self-defense, Prime Minister Abe held an inaugural meeting of the Advisory Panel on Reconstruction of the Legal Basis for Security on February 8. This panel was first established under Abe's first cabinet, but its report was never implemented due to his sudden resigna-tion. The panel was to produce a similar report to recommend the reinterpre-tation of the Constitution to enable Japan to exercise the right of collective self-defense.

The revision of the Constitution was another issue Abe pledged to advance. In April 2012, the LDP came up with the draft proposal of revisions. The draft called for a revision of the pacifist Article 9, strengthens the role of the Emperor, and negates public servants' right to strike, among other things. On January 30, 2013, Abe stated at the lower house meeting that his first goal was to change Article 96 which governs the amendment process. Currently, an amendment must be passed by a two-third majority in both houses of the Diet and must be supported by a majority in the public referendum. Abe's goal was first to lower the bar to require just a simple majority of the two houses for further amendments.

The issue of constitutional revision was complicated by a series of court decisions announced in March 2013. High and local courts in Japan responded to sixteen law suits to declare that the current lower house seat allocation was unconstitutional or in "a state of unconstitutionality." Hiroshima High Court and its Okayama branch even ruled that the December 2012 general election was invalid. Two years before the ruling, the Supreme Court had already de-cided that the 2009 lower house election was in a state of unconstitutionality as described in chapter 4. However, the legislative branch failed to take necessary measures before the 2012 general election as required by the Supreme Court. There was an argument that lawmakers who were elected in an invalid elec-tion should not revise the Constitution.

These foreign policy and national security issues Abe wished to tackle were major, and it would require substantial efforts by the national leader and elabo-rate staff support. In order to carry out his initiatives, Abe appointed a former foreign vice minister, Shōtarō Yachi, as a counselor at the Cabinet Secretariat. Yachi asked Abe to appoint his most trusted confidant Nobukatsu Kanehara to Assistant CCS. Yachi and Kanehara were seen by many as Abe's chief advisers to control the government's foreign policy at the kantei.

In addition to the foreign policy area, Abe intended to take advantage of the expertise held by the government's bureaucracy. He reinstated the administrative vice ministerial meeting, which the Hatoyama cabinet had abolished. The new subcabinet panel began their weekly meeting on December 28, 2012. Prime Minister Abe attended its first meeting and stated, "In order to tackle the crises our country faces, it is necessary to promote real political leadership based on mutual trust between political leaders and bureaucrats."

The subcabinet meeting was expected to reestablish important sources of power for the prime minister, the CCS, and especially the administrative deputy CCS who serves as its chairman. The panel was to help promote the prime minister's policy initiatives within the ministries. As all government policies would be reported at the subcabinet meeting, the bureaucratic leaders would have prior consultation with the CCS and the deputy CCS, and would frequently ask for their coordination when conflicts exist among different agencies. Under the subcabinet panel, a multilayered network of interagency policy coordination among bureau chiefs, directors, and their deputies to promote the cabinet's initiative would be reestablished.

Prime Minister Abe faced major challenges to achieve the above major policy goals, and at the time of writing it is unknown how many of them Abe would be able to push through. But his policy goals were clearly stated, and he seemed to have extensive bureaucratic support. Among the leadership styles introduced in chapter 7, Abe's performance in the first several months might place him in the same category as Koizumi with strong leadership and effective bureaucratic support. So far, Abe has successfully balanced between centralized institutions and bureaucratic support and would likely beat institutional, partisan, and intraparty veto players in order to achieve, at least, some of his policy goals.

APPENDIX 1

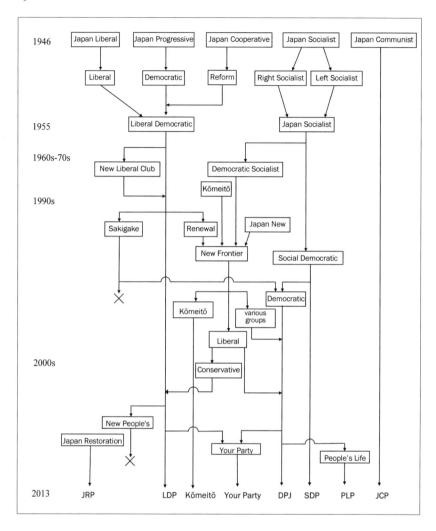

APPENDIX 1. Japan's Party System, 1946–2013

Note: The processes of fragmentation and mergers are simplified.

APPENDIX 2

Postwar Prime Ministers: Terms of Office

PRIME MINISTER	PARTY AFFILIATION	TERM OF OFFICE
Naruhiko Higashikuni	None	8/17/1945–10/9/1945
Kijūrō Shidehara	Progressive	10/9/1945–5/22/1946
Shigeru Yoshida	Liberal	5/22/1946–5/24/1947
Tetsu Katayama	Japan Socialist	5/24/1947–3/10/1948
Hitoshi Ashida	Democratic	3/10/1948–10/19/1948
Shigeru Yoshida	Democratic Liberal / Liberal	10/19/1948–12/10/1954
Ichirō Hatoyama	Liberal/Liberal Democratic	12/10/1954–12/23/1956
Tanzan Ishibashi	Liberal Democratic	12/23/1956–2/25/1957
Nobusuke Kishi	Liberal Democratic	2/25/1957–7/19/1960
Hayato Ikeda	Liberal Democratic	7/19/1960–11/9/1964
Eisaku Satō	Liberal Democratic	11/9/1964–7/7/1972
Kakuei Tanaka	Liberal Democratic	7/7/1972–12/9/1974
Takeo Miki	Liberal Democratic	12/9/1974–12/24/1976
Takeo Fukuda	Liberal Democratic	12/24/1976–12/7/1978
Masayoshi Ōhira	Liberal Democratic	12/7/1978–6/12/1980
Zenkō Suzuki	Liberal Democratic	7/17/1980–11/27/1982
Yasuhiro Nakasone	Liberal Democratic	11/27/1982–11/6/1987

PRIME MINISTER	PARTY AFFILIATION	TERM OF OFFICE
Noboru Takeshita	Liberal Democratic	11/6/1987–6/2/1989
Sōsuke Uno	Liberal Democratic	6/2/1989–8/8/1989
Toshiki Kaifu	Liberal Democratic	8/8/1989–11/5/1991
Kiichi Miyazawa	Liberal Democratic	11/5/1991–8/6/1993
Morihiro Hosokawa	Japan New	8/6/1993–4/28/1994
Tsutomu Hata	Renewal	4/28/1994–6/29/1994
Tomiichi Murayama	Japan Socialist	6/29/1994–1/11/1996
Ryūtarō Hashimoto	Liberal Democratic	1/11/1996–7/30/1998
Keizō Obuchi	Liberal Democratic	7/30/1998–4/5/2000
Yoshirō Mori	Liberal Democratic	4/5/2000–4/26/2001
Junichiō Koizumi	Liberal Democratic	4/26/2001–9/26/2006
Shinzō Abe	Liberal Democratic	9/26/2006–9/26/2007
Yasuo Fukuda	Liberal Democratic	9/26/2007–9/24/2008
Tarō Asō	Liberal Democratic	9/24/2008–9/16/2009
Yukio Hatoyama	Democratic Party of Japan	9/16/2009–6/8/2010
Naoto Kan	Democratic Party of Japan	6/8/2010–8/30/2011
Yoshihiko Noda	Democratic Party of Japan	8/30/2011–12/26/2012
Shinzō Abe	Liberal Democratic	12/26/2012–

NOTES

INTRODUCTION

1. Among typical studies using the political cultural approach are Chie Nakane, *Human Relations in Japan: Summary Translation of "Tate Shakai no Ningen Kankei"* (Tokyo: Ministry of Foreign Affairs, 1972); Bradley Richardson and Scott Flanagan, *Politics in Japan* (Boston: Little, Brown, 1984); and Gerald Curtis, *The Japanese Way of Politics* (New York: Columbia University Press, 1988).

2. Steven R. Reed stated, "It is safer to predict that nothing will ever change: Although you will be wrong sooner or later, you will always be in the majority. Japan has more than its share of scholars who are able to deny any changes. . . . It is extremely refreshing to see someone predicting change based on events that are likely to occur within our lifetimes." Steven R. Reed, book review on *Japan's Political Marketplace, American Journal of Sociology* 99, 6 (May 1994): 1656.

3. J. Mark Ramseyer and Frances McCall Rosenbluth, *Japan's Political Marketplace* (Cambridge: Harvard University Press, 1993), 3.

4. Ibid., 8–14. See also Masaru Kohno, *Japan's Postwar Party Politics* (Princeton: Princeton University Press, 1997).

5. Tatebayashi Masahiko, *Giin Kōdō no Seiji Keizaigaku: Jimintō Shihai no Seido Bunseki* [The logic of legislators' activities: Institutional analysis of LDP dominance in Japan] (Tokyo: Yūhikaku, 2004).

6. Frances McCall Rosenbluth and Michael F. Thies, *Japan Transformed: Political Change and Economic Restructuring* (Princeton: Princeton University Press, 2010).

7. Tsuji Kiyoaki, *Shinban Nihon Kanryōsei no Kenkyū* [New edition, Study on the Japanese bureaucratic system] (Tokyo: Tokyo Daigaku Shuppankai, 1969).

8. Chalmers Johnson, *MITI and the Japanese Miracle: The Growth of Industrial Policy, 1925–1975* (Stanford: Stanford University Press, 1982), 20–21.

9. T. J. Pempel and Keiichi Tsunekawa, "Corporatism Without Labor? The Japanese Anomaly," in *Trend Toward Corporatist Intermediation*, ed. Philippe C. Schumitter and Gerherd Lehmbruch, 231–69 (London: Sage, 1979).

10. Karel van Wolferen, *The Enigma of Japanese Power* (New York: Knopf, 1989).

11. Eugene J. Kaplan, *Japan: The Government-Business Relationship* (Washington, D.C.: Department of Commerce, 1972).

12. See Nakamura Akira, "Jiyūminshutō no Yottsu no Kao [The four faces of LDP]," in *Nihon no Seisaku Kettei: Jimintō, Yatō, Kanryō* [The policy-making in Japan: LDP, the opposition parties, and the bureaucracy], ed. Nakamura Akira and Takeshita Yuzuru, 3–63 (Tokyo: Azusa Shuppan, 1984); and Inoguchi Takashi and Iwai Tomoaki, *"Zoku Giin" no Kenkyū* [Study on "zoku members"] (Tokyo: Nihon Keizai Shimbun-sha, 1987).

13. Leonard J. Schoppa illustrates how sectional interests within the LDP effectively blocked a major policy effort of LDP leaders by using Nakasone's educational reform attempt as a case study. In this case study, the conservative education zoku members successfully blocked the prime minister's initiative by tying up with the conservative Education Ministry. In his conclusion, Schoppa argues that "the rise in *zoku* influence has made it particularly difficult for the party to achieve substantial policy *change*" and that "[The party] has suffered in its ability to achieve policy change that requires leadership from a broader, national perspective." Leonard J. Schoppa, "*Zoku* Power and LDP Power: A Case Study of the *Zoku* role in Education Policy," *Journal of Japanese Studies* 17, 1 (Winter 1991): 79–106.

14. van Wolferen, *The Enigma of Japanese Power*, 5.

15. George Tsebelis, *Veto Players: How Political Institutions Work* (Princeton: Princeton University Press, 2002), 19.

16. Ibid., 2.

17. Ellis S. Krauss and Robert J. Pekkanen, *The Rise and Fall of Japan's LDP: Political Party Organizations as Historical Institutions* (Ithaca: Cornell University Press, 2010).

18. Margarita Estévez-Abe, "Japan's Shift Toward a Westminster System: A Structural Analysis of the 2005 Lower House Election and Its Aftermath," *Asian Survey* 46, 4 (July/August 2006): 632–51.

19. Margarita Estévez-Abe, *Welfare and Capitalism in Post War Japan: Party, Bureaucracy, and Business* (New York: Cambridge University Press, 2008), 291–92.

1. Japanese Politics Under the LDP

1. Milo E. Rowell, "Report of Preliminary Studies and Recommendations of Japanese Constitution," December 6, 1945, General Headquarters, Supreme Commander for the Allied Powers. See also "Decision Amending SWNCC228: Reform of the Japanese Governmental System," January 7, 1946, State-War-Navy Coordinating Committee.

2. Three points were that (1) the emperor is the head of the state; (2) war as a sovereign right of the nation is abolished; and (3) the feudal system of Japan will cease. Government Section, Supreme Commander for the Allied Powers, *Political Reorientation of Japan* (Washington, D.C.: U.S. Government Printing Office, 1949), 102.

3. The seven subcommittees were (1) legislative, (2) executive, (3) judiciary, (4) civil rights, (5) local government, (6) finance, and (7) emperor, treaties, and enabling.

4. See Satō Tatsuo, *Nihonkoku Kenpō Tanjōki* [On the birth of the Japanese Constitution] (Tokyo: Chūkō Bunko, 1999, originally published in 1957 by the Printing Bureau, Ministry of Finance), 32.

5. Government Section, *Political Reorientation of Japan*, 104. This chapter is partly based on my previous study, *Leading Japan: The Role of the Prime Minister* (Westport, Conn.: Praeger, 2000), chap. 1.

6. Article 46 of the Government Section draft reads, "The Prime Minister introduces bills on behalf of the cabinet, reports to the Diet on general affairs of State and the status of foreign relations, exercises control and supervision over the several executive departments and agencies." http://www.ndl.go.jp/constitution/shiryo/03/076a_e/076a_etx.html (accessed July 13, 2010). On the role of the Cabinet Legal Bureau officials, see "Naikakuhō Kankei Kaidan Yōshi (Dai 3kai)" [The summary of conversation on the cabinet law no. 3], November 19, 1946, MOFA diplomatic record, A'-0091, 230–31.

7. Gotōda Masaharu, *Seiji Towa Nanika* [What is politics?] (Tokyo: Kōdansha, 1988), 90.

8. Ishihara Nobuo, *Shushō Kantei no Ketsudan* [The decisions of the prime minister's residence] (Tokyo: Chūō Kōronsha, 1997), 224.

9. The classic study on this view is Tsuji Kiyoaki, *Shinban Nihon Kanryōsei no Kenkyū* [New Edition, Study on the Japanese bureaucracy system] (Tokyo: Tokyo Daigaku Shuppan-kai, 1969).

10. Government Section, *Political Reorientation of Japan*, 128.

11. Ibid., 29.

12. John O. Haley, "Consensual Governance: A Study of Law, Culture, and the Political Economy of Postwar Japan," in *The Political Economy of Japan*, vol. 3, *Cultural and Social Dynamics*, ed. Shumpei Kumon and Henry Rosovsky (Stanford: Stanford University Press, 1992), 52.

13. T. J. Pempel, "Organizing for Efficiency: The Higher Civil Service in Japan," in *Bureaucrats and Policy Making: A Comparative Overview*, ed. Ezra N. Suleiman (New York: Holms and Meier, 1984), 96.

14. See Bradley M. Richardson and Scott C. Flanagan, *Politics in Japan* (Boston: Little, Brown, 1984), 344.

15. In early 1994 MITI minister Kumagai Hiroshi forced a bureau director to resign, and this became big news because political intervention in bureaucratic placement was extremely unusual.

16. The classic study in this area is by Kiyoaki Tsuji. Tsuji argues that the bureaucracy is the only national institute that maintained influence under the American Occupation authority. The bureaucracy, with support from the authorities, could exercise relatively strong power vis-à-vis the Diet and had established itself as pivotal in decision making. Kiyoaki, *Shinban Nihon Kanryōsei no Kenkyū*.

17. Ishihara Nobuo, *Kengen no Daiidō* [The major transfer of authority] (Tokyo: Kanki Shuppan, 2001), 82.

18. Ibid., 90.

19. Chalmers Johnson, *MITI and the Japanese Miracle* (Stanford: Stanford University Press, 1982.)

20. Government Section, *Political Reorientation of Japan*, 115.

21. Article 41 of the Government Section draft reads, "The Diet shall consist of one House of elected representatives with a membership of not less than 300 nor more than 500."

22. A statement by Minister on the Constitution Tokujirō Kanamori at the committee on Constitutional Revision, House of Representatives, 90th Imperial Diet, July 19, 1946. http://teikokugikai-i.ndl.go.jp/cgi-bin/TEIKOKU/swt_logout .cgi?SESSION=2595 (accessed July 14, 2010). See also Ray A. Moore and Donald L. Robinson, *Partners for Democracy: Crafting the New Japanese State Under MacArthur* (Oxford: Oxford University Press, 2002), 235.

23. For more details on the decision-making process, see Tanaka Yoshiaki, "Nihonkoku Kenpō Seitei Katei ni okeru Niinsei Shoan" [Bicameral proposals in the making of the Japanese Constitution], *Reference* (June 2004): 25–48.

24. Masumi Junnosuke, *Sengo Seiji 1945–55* [Postwar politics 1945–55] (Tokyo: Tokyo Daigaku Shuppankai, 1983), 1:132.

25. Government Section, *Political Reorientation of Japan*, 2:723.

26. The original number of lower house electoral districts was 117, which increased to 118 in 1953, 123 in 1964, 124 in 1970, and 130 in 1975. As an exception to the general rule of three to five seats in a district, the Amami district was created with only one seat in 1953. In 1986, to correct the inequality of seat distribution, two-seat constituencies were created in four districts, and a six-seat constituency in one district.

27. This section relies on my previous study, Tomohito Shinoda, "Japan," in *Party Politics and Democratic Development in East and Southeast Asia*, vol. 2, ed. Wolfgang Sachsenroder (Brookfield: Ashgate, 1998).

28. This term was introduced by political scientist Junnosuke Masumi. Masumi Junnosuke, "1955-nen no Seiji Taisei" [The political system of 1955], *Shisō* (June 1964).

29. The Japan Communist Party and a minor party each won a seat, and twelve seats were held by independents.

30. Maurice Duverger, *Political Parties: Their Organization and Activity in the Modern State* (New York: Wiley, 1963).

31. Steven Reed applies this law to the 1947 multimember system with three to five seats in a district and concludes, "Where *n* is the number of seats in the district . . . elections in simple plurality elections with multimember districts tend to produce competition among *n* + 1 candidates." Steven Reed, "Structure and Behavior: Extending Duverger's Law to the Japanese Case," *British Journal of Political Science* 20 (1990): 336.

32. Gerald Curtis, *The Japanese Way of Politics* (New York: Columbia University Press, 1988), 22.

33. J.A.A. Stockwin, "The Japan Socialist Party: Resurgence After Long Decline," in *The Japanese Party System*, 2d ed., ed. Ronald J. Hrebenar (Boulder: Westview Press, 1992), 87.

34. Masaru Kohno, *Japan's Postwar Party Politics* (Princeton: Princeton University Press, 1997), chap. 7.

35. Giovanni Sartori, *Parities and Party Systems: A Frame Work for Analysis* (Cambridge: Cambridge University Press, 1976).

36. Curtis, *The Japanese Way of Politics*, 36, 45–79.

37. Takashi Inoguchi, "The Political Economy of Conservative Resurgence Under Recession: Public Policies and Political Support in Japan, 1977–1983," in *Uncommon Democracies: The One-Party Dominant Regime*, ed. T. J. Pempel (Ithaca: Cornell University Press, 1990); and Kent E. Calder, *Crisis and Compensation: Public Policy and Political Stability in Japan, 1944–86* (Princeton: Princeton University Press, 1988). See also Ishikawa Masumi and Hirose Michisada, *Jimintō:*

Chōki Shihai no Kōzō [The LDP: The structure of long reign] (Tokyo: Iwanami Shoten, 1989); and Haruhiro Fukui and Shigeko N. Fukai, "Pork Barrel Politics, Networks and Local Economic Development in Contemporary Japan," *Asian Survey* 36, 3 (March 1996): 268–86.

38. Curtis, *The Japanese Way of Politics*, 45–79; Yasusuke Murakami, "The Age of New Middle Mass Politics: The Case of Japan," *Journal of Japanese Studies* 8, 1 (Winter 1982): 29–72. See also Ramseyer and Rosenbluth, *Japan's Political Market Place*; and Satō Seizaburō and Matsuzaki Tetsuhisa, *Jimintō Seiken* [The LDP administrations] (Tokyo: Chūō Kōron, 1986).

39. Ikuo Kabashima, "Supportive Participation with Economic Growth: The Case of Japan," *World Politics* 36, 3 (April 1984): 329–61. See also Kabashima Ikuo, *Seiji Sanka* [Political participation] (Tokyo: Tokyo Daigaku Shuppan-kai, 1988), chap. 7.

40. Raymond V. Christensen and Paul E. Johnson, "Toward a Context-Rich Analysis of Electoral Systems: The Japanese Example," *American Journal of Political Science* 39, 3 (August 1995): 596.

41. Gary W. Cox and Emerson Niou, "Seat Bonuses Under the Single Non-transferable Vote System: Evidence from Japan and Taiwan," *Comparative Politics* 26, 2 (January 1994): 231.

42. See Kohno, *Japan's Postwar Political Party Politics*, 130.

43. Christensen and Johnson, "Toward a Context-Rich Analysis of Electoral Systems," 596–97.

44. Sugawara Taku, "Chūsenkyokusei to Jimintō Seiken: 55nen Taiseika ni okeru Tanki Hiijōshiki Tōhyō no Keiryō Bunseki" [The medium electoral system and the LDP administration: Quantitative analysis on the impact of the single nontransferable vote under the 55 system], Ph.D. diss., University of Tokyo, 2007.

45. Ishikawa and Hirose, *Jimintō*, 73–78.

46. Miyake Ichirō, *Seitō Shiji no Bunseki* [Analysis on political party support] (Tokyo: Sōbunsha, 1985), 25.

47. Kobayashi Yoshiaki, *Gendai Nihon no Senkyo* [Contemporary Japanese elections] (Tokyo: Tokyo Daigaku Shuppan-kai, 1991), 13–14.

48. If the number of voters in a constituency was small, the district was over-represented. Therefore the correlation figure was negative if a party was benefiting from the malapportionment. If the figure was positive, a party was at a disadvantage from the unequal seat allocation. As the correlation figure for LDP increased to -.61 in the 1980s, the study shows that the LDP increasingly benefited from the malapportionment. Kawato Sadafumi, "Nihon no Senkyo Seido" [Japan's electoral

system], in *Gaisetsu Gendai Nihon no Seiji* [Introduction to contemporary Japanese politics], ed. Abe Hitoshi, Shindō Muneyuki, and Kawahito Tadashi (Tokyo: Tokyo Daigaku Shuppan-kai, 1990), 111–13.

49. On the rural orientation of the LDP, see Sugawara, "Chūsenkyokusei to Jimintō Seiken," chap. 5.

50. Miki told Toshiki Kaifu, who served as deputy chief cabinet secretary under the Miki cabinet, that he could not dissolved the lower house against the opposition of other cabinet members as he was "not a dictator." Kaifu Toshiki, *Seiji to Kane: Kaifu Toshiki Kaikoroku* [Politics and money: Memoir of Kaifu Toshiki] (Tokyo: Shinchō Shinsho, 2010), 65.

51. Takashi Inoguchi, "Political Surfing over Economic Waves: A Simple Model of the Japanese Political Economic System," paper presented at the 11th World Congress of the International Political Science Association, August 11–18, 1979. The following quantitative analysis studies support Inoguchi's thesis, Takatoshi Ito and Jin Hyuk Park, "Political Business Cycles in the Parliamentary System," *Economic Letters* 27 (1988): 233–38; and Thomas F. Cargill and Michael M. Hutchinson, "Political Business Cycles with Endogenous Election Timing: Evidence from Japan," *Review of Economics and Statistics* 73, 4 (November 1991): 733–39.

52. Masaru Kohno and Yoshitaka Nishizawa, "A Study of the Electoral Business Cycle in Japan: Elections and Government Spending on Public Construction," Comparative Politics 22, 2 (January 1990): 151–66.

53. Ichikawa Taichi, *"Seshū" Daigishi no Kenkyū* [Study on inherited Diet members] (Tokyo: Nihon Keizai Shimbunsha, 1990), 221.

54. Public Office Election Law, article 199, section 5.

55. Jiyūminshutō Senkyo Taisaku Honbu, ed., *Sōsenkyo Jissen no Tebiki* [Practical guide for general elections] (Tokyo: Jiyūminshutō, 2008).

56. Hirose Michisada, *Seiji to Kane* [Politics and money] (Tokyo: Iwanami Shinsho, 1989), 16–18.

57. Reed, "Structure and Behavior," 343.

58. Nathaniel Thayer, *How the Conservatives Rule Japan* (Princeton: Princeton University Press, 1969), 88.

59. Masumi Junnosuke, *Gendai Seiji: 1955 igo* [Contemporary politics: After 1955] (Tokyo: Tokyo Daigaku Shuppan, 1985), 385.

60. *Asahi Shimbun*, January 27, 1961.

61. Masumi, *Gendai Seiji*, 386.

62. Nonaka Naoto, *Jimintō Seiji no Owari* [The end of LDP politics] (Tokyo: Chikuma Shinsho, 2008), 116.

63. The original LDP party presidential election in January 1956 gave one vote each to 417 individual LDP Diet members (85 percent) and a total of 72 votes (15 percent) to representatives of the local branches.

64. Kawauchi Issei, *Ōhira Seiken 554 nichi* [The Ōhira administration: 554 days] (Tokyo: Gyōsei Mondai Kenkyūsho, 1982), 59.

65. *Asahi Nenkan 1978* (Tokyo: Asahi Shimbunsha, 1979), 235; and *Asahi Nenkan 1979*, 234. The 1.52 million includes some 170,000 party friends (*tōyū*) who were also eligible to vote in the primary.

66. Ellis S. Krauss and Robert J. Pekkanen challenge the conventional view of the direct impact of the old electoral system on the development of kōenkai, as such groups did not spring up immediately after the 1947 electoral reform. Rather, they emphasize the importance of historical sequences: the failure to subsume kōenkai into a party organization; the LDP merger; and the LDP presidential primary. Ellis S. Krauss and Robert J. Pekkanen, *The Rise and Fall of Japan's LDP: Political Party Organizations as Historical Institutions* (Ithaca: Cornell University Press, 2010), chap. 2.

67. Chie Nakane, *Human Relations in Japan: Summary Translation of "Tate Shakai no Ningen Kankei"* (Tokyo: Ministry of Foreign Affairs, 1972), 57–84.

68. Until 1993 Italy had an electoral system of proportional representation and multimember districts with preference voting. Between 1993 and 2005 the country shifted to a system with proportional representation and single-seat districts. After 2005 it reverted to a proportional representation system with a party list. See Dennis C. Beller and Frank P. Belloni, "Party and Faction: Modes of Political Competition," in *Faction Politics: Political Parties and Factionalism in Comparative Perspective*, ed. Frank P. Belloni and Dennis C. Beller, 432–35 (Santa Barbara: ABC Clio, 1978).

69. Ramseyer and Rosenbluth, *Japan's Political Marketplace*, 59.

70. Krauss and Pekkanen, *The Rise and Fall of Japan's LDP*, chap. 4.

71. Kohno, *Japan's Postwar Party Politics*, 101–4.

72. Thayer, *How the Conservatives Rule Japan*, chaps. 2 and 4. About the prewar history of political factions, see Robert Scalapino, *Democracy and the Party Movement in Prewar Japan* (Berkeley: University of California Press, 1953). Yamamoto Shichihei argues that Japan's modern political history is the history of political factions, which started with *hanbatsu* or factions based on the original feudal clan in the Meiji government based on the politician's clan origins. Yamamoto Shichihei, *Hanbatsu no Kenkyū* [Study on factions] (Tokyo: Bungei Shunjū, 1989).

73. There was a prearrangement between Ishibashi and Ishii that the third-place candidate would support the second-place winner. Shigeru Hori stated in

his memoir that as representative of the Ikeda group, he negotiated with Iwao Yamazaki, who represented the Ishii faction. Hori Shigeru, *Sengo Seiji no Oboegaki* [Memorandum of postwar politics] (Tokyo: Mainichi Shimbun, 1975), 104.

74. Satō and Matsuzaki, *Jimintō Seiken*, 240.

75. Watanabe Tsuneo, *Hanbatsu to Tatōka Jidai* [Factions and the multiparty era] (Tokyo: Sekka-sha, 1967), 142.

76. Sōsuke Uno (1989) and Toshiki Kaifu (1989–91) were chosen without being a faction leader in the wake of political scandals that made other possible candidates ineligible.

77. Arguments for this function of LDP factions, see Haruhiro Fukui, "Japan: Factionalism in a Dominant Party System," in *Faction Politics: Political Parties and Factionalism in Comparative Perspective*, ed. Frank P. Belloni and Dennis C. Beller (Santa Barbara: ABC-Clio, 1978), 65–66.

78. See Ishikawa Masumi, *Dēta Sengo Seijishi* [Data on postwar political history] (Tokyo: Iwanami Shoten, 1984), 210–12.

79. Watanabe, *Hanbatsu to Tatōka Jidai*, 150–57.

80. George R. Packard, *Protest in Tokyo: The Security Treaty Crisis of 1960* (Princeton: Princeton University Press, 1966), 64–81.

81. Yomiuri Shimbun Seiji-bu, ed., *Sōri Daijin* [The prime minister] (Tokyo: Yomiuri Shimbun-sha, 1971, rev. 1972), 89.

82. Even Suzuki himself recognizes that his explanation was poorly done. Suzuki Kenji, *Rekidai Sōri Sokkin no Kokuhaku* [The confessions of close associates of prime ministers] (Tokyo: Mainichi Shimbun-sha, 1991), 160.

83. Yuzuru Hatakeyama, assistant to Prime Minister Suzuki, revealed in a 2010 television program that MOFA officials explained that the word alliance did not connote a military component. *NHK Special No.3, Nichibei Ampo 50-nen: Domei e no Michi* [50 years of U.S.-Japan security relations: The road to alliance] (Tokyo: Nippon Hōsō Kyōkai, December 11, 2010).

84. The presidential term was extended to three years between 1972 and 1978 and from 2003 to the present.

85. Masumi, *Gendai Seiji*, 351.

86. Iseri Hirofumi, *Hanbatsu Saihensei* [The reorganization of factions] (Tokyo: Chūko Shinsho, 1983), 164–65.

87. Taketsugu Tsurutani, "The LDP in Transition? Mass Membership Participation in Party Leadership Selection," *Asian Survey* 20, 8 (August 1980): 850–56.

88. These included factions formerly led by Etsusaburō Shiina, Naka Funata, Mikio Mizuta, and Kōjiro Ishii.

89. Satō and Matsuzaki, *Jimintō Seiken*, 243.

90. Asahi Shimbun Seiji-bu, *Takeshita-ha Shihai* [Control by the Takeshita faction] (Tokyo: Asahi Shimbun-sha, 1992), 177–78.

91. After the second reelection of Satō as LDP president in 1978, the number of cabinet posts held by the mainstream factions became more proportional to their membership size. Satō and Matsuzaki, *Jimintō Seiken*, 66.

92. Kawato Sadafumi, "Jimintō ni okeru Yakushoku no Seidoka" [The institutionalization of rules governing promotion in the LDP], *Hōgaku* 59, 6 (1996): 34–46.

93. Prime Minister Toshiki Kaifu testifies, "It was a custom for faction leaders to send a letter to recommend personnel from their own factions. The letter usually had several names. There was a type of letter without priority, but some faction leaders indicated their priority with circles and double circles. Kaifu Toshiki, *Seiji to Kane: Kaifu Toshiki Kaikoroku* [Politics and money: The memoir of Kaifu Toshiki] (Tokyo: Shinchō Shinsho, 2010), 90–91.

94. Satō and Matsuzaki, *Jimintō Seiken*, 39–44.

95. Ishikawa and Hirose, *Jimintō*, 186–96.

96. Watanabe Tsuneo, *Tōshu to Seitō: Sono Rīdāshippu no Kenkyū* [Party leaders and political parties: Study on their leadership] (Tokyo: Kōbun-sha, 1961), 87–88.

97. Kishi Nobusuke, Yatsugi Kazuo and Itō Takashi, *Kishi Nobusuke no Kaisō* [Memories of Kishi Nobusuke] (Tokyo: Bungei Shunjū, 1981), 185.

98. Gotōda Masaharu, *Naikaku Kanbō Chōkan* [Chief cabinet secretary] (Tokyo: Kōdansha, 1989), 3.

99. Before the 1955 LDP inception, there were two cases: that of Rikizō Hirano under the Katayama cabinet in 1947 and Kōzen Hirokawa under the Yoshida cabinet in 1953. Under the LDP government, two cases occurred with Masayuki Fujio under the Nakasone cabinet in 1986 and Yoshinobu Shimamura under the Koizumi cabinet in 2005. Under the DPJ government, Mizuho Fukushima was dismissed by Prime Minister Yukio Hatoyama in May 2010.

100. Fujimoto Takao, *Fujimoto Takao no Daijin Hōkoku* [Report of Minister Fujimoto Takao] (Tokyo: Planet Shuppan, 1989), 74–82.

101. Tomiichi Murayama, interview by author, September 13, 1996.

102. The PARC had seventeen subcommittees between 1973 and 2001. Before 1973 it had fifteen; after 2001, twelve.

103. Letter from LDP General Council chairman Munenori Akagi to the chief cabinet secretary, 23 February 1962.

104. See Nakamura Akira, "Jiyūminshutō no Yottsu no Kao" [The four faces of LDP], in *Nihon no Seisaku Kettei: Jimintō, Yatō, Kanryō* [Policy making in Japan:

LDP, the opposition parties, and the bureaucracy], ed. Nakamura Akira and Takeshita Yuzuru (Tokyo: Azusa Shuppan, 1984), 3–63.

105. Ishihara, *Kengen no Daiidō*, 85.

106. Ibid.

107. Inoguchi Takashi and Iwai Tomoaki, *"Zoku Giin" no Kenkyū* [Study on "zoku members"] (Tokyo: Nihon Keizai Shimbun-sha, 1987), 103–4; and Tatebayashi Masahiko, *Giin Kōdō no Seiji Keizaigaku: Jimintō Shihai no Seido Bunseki* [The logic of legislators' activities: Institutional analysis of LDP dominance in Japan] (Tokyo: Yūhikaku, 2004), 69.

108. In 1986 there were 183 LDP Diet members on the Construction subcommittee, 178 on the Agriculture and Forestry subcommittee, and 154 on the Commerce and Industry subcommittee. Inoguchi and Iwai, *"Zoku Giin" no Kenkyū*," 133.

109. The three most unpopular subcommittees in 1986 were Judiciary (36 members), Environment (36), and Science and Technology (37). Ibid.

110. Tatebayashi, *Giin Kōdō no Seiji Keizaigaku*, chap. 3. Krauss and Pekkanen were interested in Tatebayashi's finding but found little evidence that LDP members intentionally chose their PARC assignments to seek different specialization from other LDP members in the same district. Krauss and Pekkanen, *The Rise and Fall of Japan's LDP*, 171–78.

111. Satō and Matsuzaki, *Jimintō Seiken*, 61–62.

112. Tazaki Shirō, *Takeshita-ha Shitō no Nanajū Nichi* [Seventy days of fierce battles of the Takeshita faction] (Tokyo: Bunshun Bunko, 2000), 170–73.

113. Iwai Tomoaki, *"Seiji Shikin" no Kenkyū* [Study on the "political fund"] (Tokyo: Nihon Keizai Shimbun, 1990), 66.

114. Ibid., 72–87.

115. The Shōwa Denkō scandal of 1948 was a case in which the president of Shōwa Denkō Company was arrested for passing bribes to government officials in an effort to receive government-financed loans. As Deputy Prime Minister Suehiro Nishio was involved in this scandal, this incident led to the fall of the cabinet led by Hitoshi Ashida. The shipbuilding scandal of 1954 involved many powerful politicians, including future prime ministers Hayato Ikeda and Eisaku Satō, who received bribes for enacting laws to provide low-interest loans to the shipbuilding industry. The so-called black-mist scandals of 1966 were a series of political corruption scandals involving many LDP political leaders, including Eisaku Satō. The media poetically referred to them as "black mist." In the 1976 Lockheed scandal, as noted previously, former prime minister Kakuei Tanaka was arrested for accepting a bribe to select Lockheed planes for a major Japanese airline.

2. The Politics of Institutional Reform

1. Asahi Journal Henshū-bu, *Rikurūtogēto no Kakushin* [The core of Recruit-gate] (Tokyo: Suzusawa Shoten, 1989); and Asahi Shimbun-sha Seronchōsa-shitu, *Takeshita Seiken no Hōkai: Rikurūto Jiken to Seiji Kaikaku* [The collapse of the Takeshita administration: The Recruit scandal and political reform] (Tokyo: Asahi Shimbun-sha, 1989).

2. *Kyodo News Service*, April 13–14, 1989.

3. Gotōda Masaharu, *Seiji towa Nanika* [What is politics] (Tokyo: Kōdansha, 1988), 177–80.

4. Liberal Democratic Party, *Seiji Kaikaku Taikō* [The outline of political reform], May 23, 1989, quoted in Iio Jun, "Takeshita, Uno, Kaifu Naikaku" [The Takeshita, Uno, Kaifu cabinets], in *Seiji Kaikaku 1800 nichi no Shinjitsu* [The truth about 1,800 days of political reform], ed. Sasaki Takeshi, 39–48 (Tokyo: Kōdansha, 1999).

5. *Nihon Keizai Shimbun*, June 26, 1989.

6. Kaifu Toshiki, *Seiji to Kane: Kaifu Toshiki Kaikoroku* [Politics and money: Memoir of Kaifu Toshiki] (Tokyo: Shinchō Shinsho, 2010), 134.

7. Ibid., 101.

8. The poll was conducted on September 6–7, 1989. Asahi Shimbun-sha Seronchōsa-shitu, *Naikaku Shijiritsu Seitō Shijiritsu* [The approval rate for cabinets and political parties] (Tokyo: Asahi Shimbun-sha, April 1996), 63.

9. Kaifu, *Seiji to Kane*, 135–36.

10. Hideo Otake, "Forces for Political Reform: The Liberal Democratic Party's Young Reformers and Ozawa Ichiro," *Journal of Japanese Studies* 22, 2 (Summer 1996): 279.

11. Prime Minister Toshiki Kaifu's policy speech on March 2, 1990. http://www.ioc.u-tokyo.ac.jp/~worldjpn/documents/texts/pm/19900302.SWJ.html (accessed March 1, 2011).

12. For the details of this legislative process, see Tomohito Shinoda, *Koizumi Diplomacy: Japan's Kantei Approach in Foreign and Defense Affairs* (Seattle: University of Washington Press, 2007), chap. 2.

13. Iio, "Takeshita, Uno, Kaifu Naikaku," 89.

14. For the details on Okonogi's decision and Kajiyama's involvement, see Hirano, *Ozawa Ichirō tono Nijūnen*, 46–49.

15. Kaifu testifies that he used the expression *jūdaina kesshin*, not *jūdaina ketsui*, which generally implies the prime minister's determination to dissolve the lower house. Kaifu, *Seiji to Kane*, 148.

16. Kaifu, *Seiji to Kane*, 150–54. See also Morita Minoru, *Seihen: Jimintō Sōsaisen Uramen Antō-shi* [Political upheaval: History of the behind-the-scene battles for the LDP presidency] (Tokyo: Tokuma Shoten, 1991), 143–70; and Nihon Keizai Shimbun-sha, ed., *Dokyumento Seiken Tanjō* [Documentary, the birth of an administration] (Tokyo: Nihon Keizai Shimbun-sha, 1991), 117–202.

17. Miyazawa Kiichi, *Shin Goken Sengen* [New declaration to protect the constitution] (Tokyo: Asahi Shimbun, 1995), 49.

18. *Shinkakuryō ni Kiku: Miyazawa Naikaku no Kadai* [Asking the new cabinet members about the policy agenda of the Miyazawa cabinet] (Tokyo: Nippon Hōsō Kyōkai, November 6, 1991). Quoted in Taniguchi Masaki, "Miyazawa Naikaku" [The Miyazawa cabinet], in Sasaki, *Seiji Kaikaku 1800 nichi no Shinjitsu*, 99.

19. Policy speech of Prime Minister Kiichi Miyazawa, January 24, 1991. http://www.ioc.u-tokyo.ac.jp/~worldjpn/documents/texts/pm/19920124.SWJ.html (accessed March 7, 2011).

20. Iokibe Makoto, Itō Motoshige, and Yakushiji Katsuyuki, eds., *Ozawa Ichirō: Seiken Dasshuron* [Ozawa Ichirō: Argument for taking over the government] (Tokyo: Asahi Shimbun-sha, 2006), 83–87; and Hironaka Yoshimichi, *Miyazawa Seiken 644 nichi* [The Miyazawa administration's 644 days] (Tokyo: Gyōsei, 1998), 205–10.

21. For Ozawa's story, see Hirano, *Ozawa Ichirō tono Nijūnen*, 60–63. For Kajiyama's, see Nonaka Hiromu, *Watashi wa Tatakau* [I fight] (Tokyo: Bungei Shunjū, 1996), 81–87.

22. Ozawa Ichirō, *Kataru* [Talk] (Tokyo: Bungei Shunjū, 1996), 76–80.

23. Ozawa claims that political reform was the main reason to form this group. Iokibe, Itō, and Yakushiji, eds., *Ozawa Ichirō*, 93–95. On the other hand, a member of the anti-Ozawa group, Hiromu Nonaka, sees it as power struggle within the faction. Nonaka, *Watashi wa Tatakau*, 91–95.

24. Taniguchi, "Miyazawa Naikaku," 142.

25. The eight groups were the Japan Socialist Party, Renewal Party, Kōmeitō, Democratic Socialist Party, Japan New Party, Sakigake, and United Social Democratic Party.

26. Iwai Tomonobu, "Hosokawa Seiken" [The Hosokawa cabinet], in Sasaki, *Seiji Kaikaku 1800 nichi no Shinjitsu*, 164–66.

27. Hosokawa Morihiro, *Naishōroku: Hosokawa Sōri Daijin Nikki* [Self-review: The diary of Prime Minister Hosokawa] (Tokyo: Nikkei Shimbun Shuppan-sha, 2010), 30–33.

28. The poll was conducted on September 5–6, 1989. Asahi Shimbun-sha Seronchōsa-shitu, *Naikaku Shijiritsu Seitō Shijiritsu*, 70.

29. Policy speech by Prime Minister Morihiro Hosokawa, September 21, 1993. http://www.ioc.u-tokyo.ac.jp/~worldjpn/ (accessed March 7, 2011).

30. Iwai, "Hosokawa Seiken," 186.

31. Hosokawa, *Naishōroku*, 210.

32. Hirano, *Ozawa Ichirō tono Nijūnen*, 92–93.

33. Yoshirō Mori, interview by Sōichiro Tahara in Tahara Sōichiro, *Atama no nai Kujira* [A headless whale] (Tokyo: Asahi Shimbun-sha, 1997), 82–86. See also Iokibe Makoto, Itō Motoshige, and Yakushiji Katsuyuki, eds., *Mori Yoshirō: Jimintō to Seiken Kōtai* [Mori Yoshirō: The LDP and power shift] (Tokyo: Asahi Shimbun-sha, 2007), 152–57.

34. Suzuki Ryōichi, *Wakariyasui Seiji Shikin Kiseihō* [Political fund control law easy to understand] (Tokyo: Gyōsei, 1995), 30–32, 89–178.

35. Iwasaki Masahiro, "Seiji Shikin, Fuhai Bōshi" [Political fund and anticorruption] in *Seiji Kaikaku 1800 nichi no Shinjitsu*, ed. Sasaki, 488–93.

36. This section relies on my previous studies: Tomohito Shinoda, "Japan's Decision Making Under the Coalition Governments," *Asian Survey* 38, 7 (July 1998): 708–10; and *Leading Japan: The Role of the Prime Minister* (Westport, Conn.: Praeger, 1998), 28–32.

37. Michiyo Nakamoto, "Hosokawa Plan Has Pleased Few and Made Many Unhappy," *Financial Times*, February 4, 1994. See also Paul Blustein, "Japanese Leader Forced to Retreat on Taxes," *Washington Post*, February 5, 1994.

38. LDP secretary general Yoshirō Mori revealed that Shizuka Kamei was a messenger representing the LDP and held discussions with Murayama's close associate, Kōken Nosaka. Iokibe, Itō, and Yakushiji, eds., *Mori Yoshirō*, 163–72.

39. Tomiichi Murayama told the author in an interview on this policy shift that "since the 1980s the international environment drastically had changed. Within the Socialist Party it had been discussed that the party should be on the same stage to talk with the LDP in order to become a viable party. I personally did not think that the SDF with the existing size was unconstitutional. If the prime minister who was the highest commander of the SDF said that the forces were unconstitutional, he could not stay in office, and the three-party coalition would break up. As I became a prime minister from the Socialist Party, the party needed to change its traditional position." Tomiichi Murayama, interview by author, September 13, 1996.

40. Ibid.

41. Nihon Keizai Shimbunsha, ed., *Renritsu Seiken no Kenkyū* [Study on the coalition governments] (Tokyo: Nihon Keizai Shimbunsha, 1994), 71–76.

42. Sassa Atsuyuki, *Kiki Kanri Saishō Ron* [On leadership in crisis management] (Tokyo: Bungei Shunjū, 1995), 164–65; and Murayama Tomiichi, *Sōjanō:*

Murayama Tomiichi 'Shushō Taiken' no Subete wo Kataru [Murayama Tomiichi talks about everything in his premier experience] (Tokyo: Daisan Shobō, 1998), 90.

43. Ishihara Nobuo, *Kantei 2668 nichi: Seisaku Kettei no Butaiura* [2,668 days at the Prime Minister's Office: Behind the scenes of decision making] (Tokyo: NHK Shuppan, 1995), 214–15.

44. Igarashi Kōzō, *Kantei no Rasen Kaidan* [The spiral staircase of the prime minister's office] (Tokyo: Gyōsei, 1997), 47.

45. Murayama's response to the question by Toshihiro Nikai at the lower house floor meeting, January 20, 1995. http://kokkai.ndl.go.jp/cgi-bin/KENSAKU / (accessed March 10, 2011).

46. *Asahi Shimbun*, January 29, 1995.

47. Igarashi, *Kantei no Rasen Kaidan*, 93.

48. *Nihon Keizai Shimbun*, January 17, 2005.

49. Ibid., March 12, 1996.

50. According to a *Kyodo News* poll of September 28–29, 1996, for example, the approval rating for the Hashimoto cabinet rose to 52.3 percent from 47.0 percent on July 13–14.

51. They were Management and Coordination Agency (MCA) minister Kabun Mutō and former Diet member Kiyoshi Mizuno.

52. They were Yōtarō Iida of Mitsubishi Heavy Industry, who chaired the Administrative Reform Committee; Shōichirō Toyota of Toyota Motors, who chaired the Economic Policy Council; and Ken Moroi of Chichibu Onoda Co., who chaired the Council on Government Decentralization.

53. The five scholars were Akito Arima of Tokyo University, Kuniko Inoguchi of Sophia University, Hayao Kawai of the International Center for Japanese Culture, Kōji Satō of Kyoto University, Yūichi Shionoya of Hitotsubashi University, and Tokiyasu Fujita of Tohoku University. The two media representatives were Mikio Kawaguchi of NHK and Tsuneo Watanabe of *Yomiuri Shimbun*, and the labor representative was Jinnosuke Ashida of the Rengō.

54. A poll taken by Kyodo News Service on December 7–8, 1996.

55. One member explains this process: "None of the members had had experience in the bureaucracy. We did not know exactly where to start reform efforts. We needed to acquire basic knowledge about the problems of the administration by inviting experts." Ken Moroi, interview by author, October 22, 1998.

56. Mizuno Kiyoshi, "'Gyōkaku Kaigi: Kanryō tono Kōbō" [The Administrative Reform Council: Fights with bureaucrats], *Bungei Shunjū*, October 1997, 105–7.

57. *Nihon Keizai Shimbun*, June 20, 1997.

58. Hashimoto told the two scholars, "I will take care of all the political sides. Do not bend to political pressure, and provide a good proposal based on your conscience as a scholar." Fujita Tokiyasu, "Gyōkaku Kaigi Iin Zen Uchimaku wo Kataru" [An Administrative Reform Council member discloses all behind the scenes], *Bungei Shunjū* (February 1998): 389.

59. A poll taken by *Kyodo News Service* on July 12–13, 1997.

60. This section relies on the author's previous work, *Leading Japan*, chap. 7.

61. Although Hashimoto held several meetings between the government and the LDP on administrative reform between January and July 1997, the ruling party had very limited influence over the interim report.

62. The total postal savings amounted 225 trillion yen at the end of 1996.

63. A poll taken by *Asahi Shimbun* on September 7–8, 1997, *Asahi Shimbun*, September 10, 1997.

64. *Tokyo Shimbun*, September 17, 1997.

65. Fujita, "Gyōkaku Kaigi Iin," 390–91.

66. Ken Moroi, interview by author, October 22, 1998.

67. Instead of the privatization, the proposal suggested that (1) funds from the postal savings would not be used for Fiscal Loan and Investment Programs; (2) part of funds would finance the government deficit; (3) the interest rate on postal savings would be lower than that of private banks; and (4) the number of employees of post offices would be significantly reduced. *Nihon Keizai Shimbun*, September 28, 1997.

68. The reasons they raised were that intimate relations between politicians and specific industry were not desirable and that industry's and the ministry's interests were considered over national interests. The opinion poll was conducted on October 25–26, 1997, with 1952 samples. *Yomiuri Shimbun*, November 4, 1997.

69. *Nihon Keizai Shimbun*, October 19, 1997. Also Gyōsei Kaikaku Kaigi Jimu-kyoku, "Gyōsei Kaikaku Kaigi dai 32kai Giji Gaiyō," October 15, 1997.

70. The new Ministry of National Land and Transportation would be a merger of the Ministries of Construction and Transportation and the Agencies of National Land, Hokkaido Development, and Okinawa Development.

71. The other members included two scholars from the Administrative Reform Council, Kōji Satō and Tokiyasu Fujita, and six new members: former deputy chief cabinet secretary Nobuo Ishihara, Tadao Koike of *Mainichi Shimbun*, former Economic Planning Agency chief Sumiko Takahara, Teruhito Emoto of Rengō, Nobuo Yamaguchi of the Tokyo Chamber of Commerce, and Tetsurō Nishizaki.

72. This section relies on Shinoda, *Leading Japan*, 36–39.

73. The Flag-Anthem Law legally recognizes the Hinomaru as Japan's National Flag and *Kimigayo* as the national anthem. The Anti-Organizational Crime bills included legislation to allow law enforcement authorities to wiretap in investigations into organized crime.

74. The rate of enactment was 87 percent, slightly higher than the 83 percent in the previous year.

75. Toshihiro Nikai of the Liberal Party was appointed minister of transportation, and Kunihiro Tuzuki of the Kōmeitō became director general of the Management and Coordination Agency.

76. The nine members were Shizuka Kamei, Shin Sakurai, and Kimitaka Kuze of the LDP, Hirohisa Fujii, Toshio Suzuki, and Kuniji Toda of the Liberal Party, and Tsutomu Sakaguchi, Katsuyuki Higasa, and Otohiko Endō of the Kōmeitō. They were chairmen, deputy chairman, or vice chairman of the policy council of each party.

77. Nonaka Hiromu, *Rōhei wa Shinazu: Nonaka Hiromu Zenkaikoroku* [Old soldiers never die: The memoir of Nonaka Hiromu] (Tokyo: Bungei Shunjū, 2003), 148–49.

78. Hirano, *Waga Tomo Ozawa Ichirō*, 107.

3. INSTITUTIONAL CHANGES AND KOIZUMI'S LEADERSHIP

1. This section relies on the author's previous study, Tomohito Shinoda, *Koizumi Diplomacy: Japan's Kantei Approach in Foreign and Defense Affairs* (Seattle: University of Washington Press, 2007), 87–90.

2. Private communication with Tarō Kōno, December 8, 2000.

3. "Denwa Ippon no Koizumi-ryū," *Asahi Shimbun*, April 26, 2001.

4. Seventy-two percent of the respondents pointed out this reason. Poll taken by *Asahi Shimbun*, April 27–28, 2001; "Koizumi Naikaku, Shiji Saikō 78%," *Asahi Shimbun*, April 30, 2001.

5. This section relies on the author's previous study, *Koizumi Diplomacy*, chap. 3.

6. One of the Administrative Reform Council members told the author, "Strengthening the cabinet function was a much more important achievement for the council than reorganizing the ministries." Ken Moroi, interview by author, Tokyo, October 22, 1998.

7. Masaharu Gotōda, *Naikaku Kanbō Chōkan* [Chief cabinet secretary] (Tokyo: Kōdan-sha, 1989), 3.

8. Ibid., 4.

9. For example, the order of succession under the second Koizumi cabinet was (1) CCS Yasuo Fukuda, (2) Finance Minister Sadakazu Tanigaki, (3) Agriculture, Forestry, and Fisheries Minister Yoshiyuki Kamei, (4) Internal Affairs and Communications Minister Tarō Asō, and (5) Economy, Trade, and Industry Minister Ichirō Nakagawa.

10. For more details, see Shinoda, *Leading Japan*, 73.

11. Ishihara Nobuo, *Kan Kaku Arubeshi* [The way the bureaucrats should be] (Tokyo: Shōgakukan Bunko, 1998), 189.

12. This section relies on the author's previous study, Tomohito Shinoda, "Stronger Political Leadership and the Shift in Policy-making Boundaries in Japan," in *Decoding Boundaries in Contemporary Japan: The Koizumi Administration and Beyond*, ed. Glenn D. Hook, 101–19 (London: Routledge, 2011).

13. CEFP, "Keizai Zaisei Shimon Kaigi Unei Kisoku" [Operational Regulation of the Council of Economic and Fiscal Policy], January 6, 2001. http://www5.cao .go.jp/keizai-shimon/minutes/2001/0106/item3.pdf (accessed March 23, 2011).

14. CEFP, "Heisei 13 nendo Dai 4 kai Gijiroku," February 27, 2001. http:// www5.cao.go.jp/keizai-shimon/minutes/2001/0227/shimon-s.pdf. See also Takenaka Heizo, *Kōzō Kaikaku no Shinjitsu: Takenaka Heizō Daijin Nisshi* [Truth about structural reform: Diary of Minister Takenaka Heizō] (Tokyo: Nihon Keizai Shimbunsha, 2006), 249.

15. "Naikaku Sōri Daijin Danwa" [Statement of the prime minister], April 26, 2001. http://www.kantei.go.jp/jp/koizumispeech/2001/0426danwa.html (accessed March 23, 2011).

16. Policy speech by Prime Minister Junichirō Koizumi, May 7, 2001. http:// www.kantei.go.jp/jp/koizumispeech/2001/0507syosin.html (accessed March 23, 2011).

17. CEFP, "Heisei 13 nendo Dai 8 kai Gijiroku," May 18, 2001, 2. http://www5.cao .go.jp/keizai-shimon/minutes/2001/0518/minutes-s.pdf (accessed March 23, 2011).

18. Ibid., 10.

19. Takenaka, *Kōzō Kaikaku no Shinjitsu*, 251.

20. CEFP, "Heisei 13 nendo Dai 8 kai Gijiroku," May 18, 2001, 7.

21. Teijirō Furukawa, interview by author, October 30, 2003.

22. Iijima Isao, *Koizumi Kantei Hiroku* [Secret story of the Prime Minister's Office under Koizumi] (Tokyo: Nihon Keizai Shimbunsha, 2006), 62.

23. Shimizu Masato, *Kantei Shudō* [Initiative of the Prime Minister's Office] (Tokyo: Nihon Keizai Shimbunsha, 2005), 250.

24. CEFP, "Heisei 13 nendo Dai 13 kai Gijiroku," August 3, 2001, 14. http://www5.cao.go.jp/keizai-shimon/minutes/2001/0803/minutes-s.pdf (accessed March 23, 2011).

25. Iijima, *Koizumi Kantei Hiroku*, 67.

26. The seven areas are (1) environmental issues; (2) the aging population, (3) the development of local facilities, (4) urban revitalization, (5) science and technology, (6) human resource development, and (7) information and technology.

27. Iijima, *Koizumi Kantei Hiroku*, 67.

28. Takenaka, *Kōzō Kaikaku no Shinjitsu*, 262.

29. Ibid., 274.

30. "Kōzō Kaikaku to Keizai Zaisei no Chūki Tembō," December 25, 2001, 1. http://www5.cao.go.jp/keizai-shimon/minutes/2001/1225/item2.pdf (accessed March 23, 2011).

31. Cabinet Office, "Koko made Susunda Koizumi Kaikaku" [Koizumi reform advanced this far], June 8, 2006, 8. http://www5.cao.go.jp/keizai-shimon/explain/pamphlet/0608.pdf (accessed March 23, 2011).

32. Ministry of Finance, "Highlights of the Budget for FY2007," December 2006. http://www.mof.go.jp/english/budget/e20061224a.pdf (accessed March 23, 2011).

33. "Kōzō Kaikaku to Keizai Zaisei no Chūki Tembō," December 25, 2001, 1.

34. Teijirō Furukawa, interview by author, October 30, 2003.

35. Official of the Secretariat of the Headquarters for Administrative Reform, interview by author, October 20, 2003.

36. Teijirō Furukawa, interview by author, October 30, 2003.

37. For example, postal savings amounted 239 trillion yen by the end of FY2001, while the total of private banks' saving accounts was 490 trillion yen.

38. Iijima, *Koizumi Kantei Hiroku*, 211–14.

39. Ibid., 228.

40. CEFP, "Heisei 15 nendo Dai 20 kai Gijiroku," September 26, 2003, 2. http://www5.cao.go.jp/keizai-shimon/minutes/2003/0926/minutes_s.pdf (accessed March 29, 2011).

41. The five basic principles were (1) revitalization, (2) compatibility, (3) utility improvement, (4) resource utilization, and (5) employment consideration. Takenaka, *Kōzō Kaikaku no Shinjitsu*, 150–53.

42. Takenaka, *Kōzō Kaikaku no Shinjitsu*, 176.

43. Takahashi Yōichi, *Saraba Zaimushō* [Farewell to the Ministry of Finance] (Tokyo: Kōdan-sha, 2008), 110–14.

44. CEFP, "Min'eika Kihon Hōshin Kosshi" [Outline of the basic privatization policy], August 6, 2004. http://www5.cao.go.jp/keizai-shimon/minutes/2004/0806 /item2.pdf (accessed March 29, 2011).

45. *Nihon Keizai Shimbun*, August 7, 2004.

46. Takenaka, *Kōzō Kaikaku no Shinjitsu*, 168–69.

47. Iijima, *Koizumi Kantei Hiroku*, 246–47.

48. Ibid., 248–50.

49. Takenaka, *Kōzō Kaikaku no Shinjitsu*, 180.

50. Takahashi, *Saraba Zaimushō*, 110–14.

51. Ibid., 184.

52. Iijima, *Koizumi Kantei Hiroku*, 254–55.

53. Ibid., 260.

54. *Asahi Shimbun*, July 29, 2005, and *Nihon Keizai Shimbun*, July 31, 2005.

55. Iijima, *Koizumi Kantei Hiroku*, 271.

56. Ibid., 273.

57. For example, see an editorial of *Asahi Shimbun*, August 9, 2005.

58. Ibid.

59. Ibid., August 10 and 17, 2005.

60. Ibid., September 12, 2005.

61. This section relies on Shinoda, *Koizumi Diplomacy*, chaps. 4–6.

62. "U.S. Welcomes Japan's Anti-Terrorism Assistance Package," White House press release, September 20, 2001. http://www.globalsecurity.org/military/library /news/2001/09/mil-010920-usia12.htm (accessed March 25, 2011).

63. Teijirō Furukawa, interview by author, September 9, 2011.

64. This law was written by the MOFA's Treaty Division director, Hiroshi Ōe, in forty minutes. Yomiuri Shimbun Seiji-bu, ed., *Gaikō wo Kenka nishita Otoko: Koizumi Gaikō 2000-nichi no Shinjitsu* [The man who turned diplomacy into fight: The truth of the 2,000 days of Koizumi diplomacy] (Tokyo: Shinchō-sha, 2006), 135. The author confirmed this with Mr. Ōe himself.

65. The 1992 International Peace Cooperation Law was also drafted by the Cabinet Secretariat. But most of the questions were answered by MOFA officials.

66. George W. Bush, "State of the Union Address," January 29, 2002. http:// stateoftheunionaddress.org/2002-george-w-bush (accessed March 25, 2011).

67. Tanaka Hitoshi and Tahara Sōichirō, *Kokka to Gaikō* [The nation and diplomacy] (Tokyo: Kōdan-sha, 2005), 28.

68. Tanaka Hitoshi, *Gaikō no Chikara* [The power of diplomacy] (Tokyo: Nihon Keizai Shimbun Shuppan-sha, 2009), 116.

69. Tanaka and Tahara, *Kokka to Gaikō*, 28.

70. Ibid., 41.

71. Ibid., 53–54.

72. Abe Shinzō, "Tatakau Seijika Sengen: Kono Kuni no tameni Inochi wo Suteru" [Declaration to fight as a politician: Willing to stake my life for this country], *Bungei Shunjū* (September 2006): 96–97.

73. Asō Tarō, "Nihon Gaikō: Shiren to Tassei no Jūichi-nichikan" [Japan's diplomacy: 11 days of challenge and achievement], *Bungei Shunjū* (September 2006): 135.

74. Abe, "Tatakau Seijika Sengen," 98.

75. Asō, "Nihon Gaikō," 137–38.

76. *Asahi Shimbun*, September 28, 2006.

77. Kakizaki Meiji and Hisae Masahiko, *Kūhaku no Saishō: "Team Abe" ga otta Risō to Genjitsu* [Empty prime minister: Ideal that "Team Abe" pursued and reality] (Tokyo: Kōdan-sha, 2007), 30–33.

78. It has been reported that Futabashi was removed because Abe was upset with him when Futabashi failed to report to Prime Minister Koizumi and Abe about the 2004 suicide case of a Japanese diplomat at the Japanese Council General in Shanghai. Yomiuri Shimbun Seiji-bu, ed., *Shinkū Kokkai: Fukuda "Hyōryū Seiken" no Shinsō* [Empty Diet: Truth of Fukuda drifting government] (Tokyo: Shinchō-sha, 2008), 184.

79. For example, see Takahashi, *Saraba Zaimushō*, 240–44; and Shimizu Masato, *Keizai Zaisei Senki: Kantei shudō Koizumi kara Abe e* [Record of battles over economic and fiscal issues: The Kantei initiative from Koizumi to Abe] (Tokyo: Nihon Keizai Shimbun-sha, 2007), 377.

80. According to the same *Asahi Shimbun* poll, 47 percent of the respondents opposed the rebels' comeback, while 39 percent accepted it. *Asahi Shimbun*, November 14, 2006.

81. Itō Takatoshi, Niwa Uichirō, Mitarai Fujio, and Yashiro Naohiro, "Kōmuin Kaikaku ni tsuite," December 7, 2006. http://www5.cao.go.jp/keizai-shimon/minutes/2006/1207/item4.pdf (accessed April 1, 2011).

82. CEFP, "Heisei 18 nendo Dai 28 kai Gijiroku," December 7, 2006. http://www5.cao.go.jp/keizai-shimon/minutes/2006/1207/minutes_s.pdf (accessed April 1, 2011). For details, see Takahashi, *Saraba Zaimushō*, 216–34.

83. Ōta Hiroko, *Kaikaku Gyakusō: Seisaku Kettei ni Nani ga Okitanoka* [Setback of reform: What happened to decision making] (Tokyo: Nihon Keizai Shimbun-sha, 2010), 38–40.

84. Takahashi, *Saraba Zaimushō*, 234–38. Watanabe's press conference is available at Government Internet TV, http://nettv.gov-online.go.jp/prg/prg923.html (accessed April 1, 2011).

85. Watanabe Yoshimi, *Kōmuin Seido Kaikaku ga Nihon wo Kaeru* [Bureaucratic reform will change Japan] (Tokyo: Asuka Shinsha, 2009), 41.

86. Surprised by Abe's action, deputy CCS Matoba had to circulate a paper among the vice ministers to officially approve the answer. Ibid., 46–49; Takahashi, *Saraba Zaimushō*, 244–46; and Hasegawa Yukihiro, *Nihonkoku no Shōtai.* [What Japan really is] (Tokyo: Kōdan-sha, 2009), 84.

87. Ōta, *Kaikaku Gyakusō*, 56–58.

88. Ibid., 31–35; and Itō Tatsuya, *Sōri Kantei no Shinjitsu: Ozawa Minshutō tono Tatakai* [The truth about the Prime Minister's Office: Battle with Ozawa's DPJ] (Tokyo: PHP Kenkyūsho, 2010), 97.

89. See Akira Nagatsuma questions in the lower house budget committee meeting on February 14, 2007. http://kokkai.ndl.go.jp/cgi-bin/ (accessed April 6, 2011).

90. Takahashi, *Saraba Zaimushō*, 254.

91. Watanabe, *Kōmuin Seido Kaikaku ga Nihon wo Kaeru*, 49–51.

92. Hakuo Yanagisawa's speech to LDP Shimane prefectural assembly members, January 27, 2007.

93. Agriculture Minister Norihiko Akagi resigned on August 1, 2007, after the July 29 upper house election for taking responsibility for lowering the Abe cabinet's approval rating.

94. *Asahi Shimbun*, July 2, 2007.

95. Ibid., September 27, 2007.

96. Defense Minister Masahiko Kōmura succeeded Machimura as foreign minister, Shigeru Ishiba succeeded Kōmura as defense minister, and Kisaburō Tokai took over the education ministership from Bunmei Ibuki.

97. Ōta Hiroko, *Kaikaku Gyakusō*, 142–45.

98. Watanabe, *Kōmuin Seido Kaikaku ga Nihon wo Kaeru*, 57–66.

99. *Asahi Shimbun*, May 1, 2008.

100. Ibid., September 2, 2008.

101. Ibid., September 11–12, 2008.

102. Kaoru Yoshino's statement in the upper house budget committee meeting on March 6, 2009. http://kokkai.ndl.go.jp/cgi-bin/ (accessed April 4, 2011).

103. A decision by the director, Center for Personnel Interchanges between the Government and Private Entities, Cabinet Office, December 31, 2008. http://www.kanmin.go.jp/about/seido02.html (accessed April 4, 2011).

104. *Asahi Shimbun*, July 18–19, 2009.

4. ELECTORAL CHANGES AND THEIR IMPACT

1. The 1972 lower house election was ruled unconstitutional, with a maximum disparity of 1:4.99, in 1976; the 1980 election, with 1:3.94 (ruled in 1983); the 1983 election, with 1:4.40 (1985); and the 1990 election, with 1:3.18 (1993). The 1986 election, with a 1:2.92 maximum disparity, was ruled constitutional as it was less than 1:3.

2. Sugawara Taku, "Jimintō Seiji Jikai no Kōzō to Katei" [The structure and process of self-destruction of LDP politics], in *Henbō suru Nihon Seiji: 90nendai igo "Henkaku no Jidai" wo Yomitoku* [Changing Japanese politics: Understanding "the era of change" after the 90s], ed. Mikuriya Takashi (Tokyo: Keisō Shobō, 2009), 27–28.

3. Article 3, the Law to Establish the Council for Lower-House Districts Apportionment.

4. A total of 1,261 candidates ran in the SMDs, with 288 from the LDP. Together with the PR districts, the total number was 1,503 candidates.

5. In areas 1–10, the average ratio of the population engaged in primary industries and construction is 7.2 percent, 9.3 percent, 10.3 percent, 11.1 percent, 12.5 percent, 14.3 percent, 16.3 percent, 19.6 percent, 26.3 percent, and 38.8 percent, respectively. Sugawara Taku, "2009-nen Senkyo Bunseki (1)" [Analysis of the 2009 election] September 19, 2009. http://go2senkyo.com/senkyo_news/0909/0909190474/1.php (accessed April 19, 2011).

6. In the 1996 election the Costa Rica system was used in the following districts: Akita 3rd, Fukushima 3rd, Ibaragi 3rd, Gunma 1st, Chiba 6th, Chiba 11th, Chiba 12th, Niigata 6th, Gifu 4th, and Kagoshima 3rd.

7. This survey was based on the responses from forty-eight *Yomiuri Shimbun* journalists who were in charge of election reports in forty-six prefectures and two offices in Tokyo. Kataoka Masaki and Yamada Masahiro, "Yomiuri Senkyohan e no Ankēto Chōsa Bunseki" [Analysis of questionnaire to election journalists at Yomiuri], in *Seikai Saihen no Kenkyū: Shinsenkyo Seido niyoru Sōsenkyo* [Study on political reorganization: General election under the new electoral system], ed. Ōtake Hideo (Tokyo: Yūhikaku, 1997), 342–44.

8. Ray Christensen, "The Effect of Electoral Reforms on Campaign Practices in Japan: Putting New Wine in the old Bottles," *Asian Survey* 38, 10 (October 1998): 993.

9. The respondents at *Yomiuri Shimbun* stated that the LDP headquarters played more important roles in ninety SMDs, less important roles in thirty SMDs, and the same roles in seventy-seven SMDs. Kataoka and Yamada, "Yomiuri Senkyohan e no Ankēto Chōsa Bunseki," 343–44.

10. Hirasawa Katsuei, *Seijika wa Rakuna Shōbai Jyanai* [Being a politician is not an easy business] (Tokyo: Shūei-sha, 2007), 51–54; and Baku Choruhī [Park Cheol Hee], *Daigishi no Tsukurarekata: Shōsenkyoku no Senkyo Senryaku* [How lower house members are made: Electoral strategy in the single-member districts] (Tokyo: Bunshun Shinsho, 2000), 74–79.

11. Haruhiro Fukui and Shigeko N. Fukai, "Pork Barrel Politics, Networks and Local Economic Development in Contemporary Japan," *Asian Survey* 36, 3: 268–86. See also Ramseyer and Rosenbluth, *Japan's Political Marketplace*.

12. Bradley M. Richardson and Dennis Patterson, "Political Traditions and Political Change: The Significance of Postwar Japanese Politics for Political Science," *Annual Review of Political Science* 4 (June 2001): 97.

13. Jiyūminshutō Senkyo Taisaku Honbu, ed., *Sōsenkyo Jissen no Tebiki* [Practical guide for general elections] (Tokyo: Jiyūminshutō, 2008).

14. Christensen, "The Effect of Electoral Reforms," 989–92.

15. Ko Maeda, "Factors Behind the Historic Defeat of Japan's Liberal Democratic Party in 2009," *Asian Survey* 50, 5 (September/October 2010): 896–98.

16. Ōtake Hideo, *Nihongata Popyurizumu: Seiji e no Kitai to Genmetsu* [Japanese-style populism: Expectations and disappointments in politics] (Tokyo: Chūkō Shinsho, 2003), 35–37.

17. *Sankei Shimbun*, April 13, 2001. See also *Seiji Hakai: Koizumi Kaikaku towa Nanika* [Destroying politics: What is Koizumi reform], ed. Nihon Keizai Shimbun-sha Seijibu, 181–83 (Tokyo: Nihon Keizai Shimbun-sha, 2001).

18. Sekō Hiroshige, *Jimintō Kaizō Purojekuto 650-nichi* [650 days of the LDP reform project] (Tokyo: Shinchō-sha, 2006), 19–31.

19. Iijima Isao, *Koizumi Kantei Hiroku* [Secret story of the Prime Minister's Office under Koizumi] (Tokyo: Nihon Keizai Shimbun-sha, 2006), 275–78.

20. Sekō, *Jimintō Kaizō Purojekuto 650-nichi*, 110–18.

21. See Cheol Hee Park, "Factional Dynamics in Japan's LDP Since Political Reform: Continuity and Change," *Asian Survey* 41, 3 (May/June 2001): 459.

22. Sekō, *Jimintō Kaizō Purojekuto 650-nichi*, 49–50.

23. Tazaki Shirō, *Seijika Shikkaku: Naze Nihon no Seiji wa Dame Nanoka* [Disqualified politicians: Why Japanese politics is not good] (Tokyo: Bungei Shunjū Shinsho, 2009), 121–23.

24. See the case studies of the 2001 antiterrorism legislation, the 2003 emergency legislation, and the 2003 Iraq Reconstruction legislation. Shinoda, *Koizumi Diplomacy*, chaps. 4–6.

25. Itō Mitsutoshi, "Core Executive-ron to Kanryōsei" [Core executive theory and the bureaucracy], in *Core Executive to Kanbu Kōmuin Seido no Kenkyū*

[Study on the core executive and executive bureaucratic system], ed. Muramatsu Michio (Kizugawa: Kōtō Kokusai Mondai Kenkyūsho, 2007), 73–74.

26. Tatebayashi Masahiko, *Giin Kōdō no Seiji Keizaigaku: Jimintō Shihai no Seido Bunseki* [The logic of legislators' activities: Institutional analysis of LDP dominance in Japan] (Tokyo: Yūhikaku, 2004), 72.

27. The five groups were (1) Kokumin no Koe (Voice of the People), an anti-Ozawa group led by Michihiko Kano; (2) New Party Fraternity, with former DSP members; (3) New Party Peace, with former Kōmeitō members; (4) Reimei Club (Dawn Club), with upper house members; and (5) Reform Club, led by Tatsuo Ozawa.

28. Kume Ikuo, *Rōdō Seiji: Sengo Seiji no Naka no Rōdō Kumiai* [Labor politics: Labor union in the postwar politics] (Tokyo: Chūkō Shinsho, 2005), 38–41.

29. *Asahi Shimbun*, May 30, 2000.

30. DPJ policy chairman Katsuya Okada testifies that he found himself applauding Koizumi's speech. Okada Katsuya, "Koizumi Seiji tono 5nen" [Five years with Koizumi politics], August 18, 2006. http://www.katsuya.net/report/koizumiseiji/pdf /koizumiseiji_5.pdf (accessed April 22, 2011).

31. Hatoyama's statement in the National Basic Policy Committee of the lower house, November 21, 2001. http://www.hatoyamayukio.info/minutes/011121.html (accessed April 28, 2011).

32. Statement by the director of the DPJ secretariat, Atsuo Itō. Itō Atsuo, *Seitō Hōkai: Nagatachō no Ushinawareta Jūnen* [The collapse of the political parties: Lost ten years of Nagatachō] (Tokyo: Shinchō Shinsho, 2003), 167.

33. Higashi Yasuhiro, "Minshutō no Hataage" [The establishment of the DPJ], in *Minshutō Jūnenshi* [Ten-year history of DPJ], ed. Tachibana Tamiyoshi, 72–73 (Tokyo: Daiichi Shorin, 2008).

34. The DPJ received only 4.1 percent, compared with the LDP with 34.6 percent. Poll conducted by *Yomiuri Shimbun*, October 26–27, 2002.

35. For more details, see Shinoda, *Koizumi Diplomacy*, chap. 5.

36. *Yomiuri Shimbun*, November 18, 2003.

37. The two DPJ lower house members were Sayuri Kamata and Azuma Konno. The NTT labor union members who supported their election campaign hired an NTT-related marketing company to make phone calls to voters.

38. DPJ lower house member Junichirō Koga claimed that he had B.A. from Pepperdine University, even though he did not graduate.

39. Prime Minister Junichirō Koizumi was a devoted fan of Chiyoko Shimakura, whose song goes "Life differs, men differ, women differ [*Jinsei iroiro, otoko mo iroiro, onna mo iroiro*]." Junichirō Koizumi's statement at the lower house Committee on Audit and Oversight of Administration, June 2, 2004.

40. Okada, "Koizumi Seiji tono 5nen," 83; Higashi Yasuhiro, "Minshutō to Jiyūtō no Gappei" [The merger of the DPJ and the Liberal Party], in Minshutō Jūnenshi, 97; and Itō Atsuo, Minshutō: Yabō to Yagō no Mekanizumu [The DPJ: The mechanism of ambition and illicit liaison] (Tokyo: Shinchō Shinsho, 2008).

41. Okada, "Koizumi Seiji tono 5nen," 117.

42. Ibid., 117–18.

43. Ibid., 118.

44. Sekō Hiroshige, Jimintō Kaizō Purojekuto 650-nichi (Tokyo: Shinchō-sha, 2006), 94–108.

45. Democratic Party of Japan, "Fukai Hansei to Saisei eno Ketsui: Shin no Kaikaku no Hata wo Kakageru" [Deep remorse and determination for revival: Raising the flag of reform], November 8, 2005. http://www.dpj.or.jp/governance/taikai/images/BOX_UN0240.pdf (accessed May 6, 2011).

46. Okada, "Koizumi Seiji tono 5nen," 121.

47. For example, Maehara's friends from the Matsushita Institute of Government and Management, Yoshihiko Noda and Kōichiro Genba, became Diet policy chairman and deputy secretary general. Another friend from the University of Kyoto, Gōshi Hosono, was appointed director of executive office.

48. According to media reports, Maehara told Takagi, "If there were disagreements over policies, the political party and its supporting organizations would act case by case," and "DPJ's local branches cannot win election by just relying on labor unions. They should spread their supporting base beyond labor unions." Kyodo News Service, November 8, 2005. http://www.47news.jp/CN/200511/CN2005110801000705.html (accessed May 9, 2011).

49. See also Kawamoto Suguru, "2007-nen Saninsen deno Yakushin" [Remarkable progress in the 2007 upper house election], in Minshutō Jūnenshi, 128.

50. Cited in Shiota Ushio, Shinban Minshutō no Kenkyū [New edition, study on the DPJ] (Tokyo: Heibon-sha Shinsho, 2009), 230.

51. "Jimintō wo Furueagarasu Kore ga Ozawa Senkyo da," Daily Gendai (July 1, 2009).

52. Ozawa Ichirō, Ozawa Shugi [Ozawa-ism] (Tokyo: Shūeisha International, 2006), 19–23.

53. After the 2003 merger, Sekiyadomachi officially became part of Noda City.

54. "Jimintō wo Furueagarasu Kore ga Ozawa Senkyo da," originally published in Daily Gendai in July 2009. http://www.ozawa-ichiro.jp/massmedia/contents/appear/2009/ar20090723115326.html (accessed May 10, 2011).

55. Ibid.

56. Itō, *Minshutō*, 99.

57. "Jimintō wo Furueagarasu Kore ga Ozawa Senkyo da"; and testimony of Nobukaki Koga, cited in Shiota Ushio, *Shinban Minshutō no Kenkyū*, 140.

58. Itō, *Minshutō*, 194.

59. Kawamoto, "2007-nen Saninsen deno Yakushin," 128–29.

60. "Jimintō wo Furueagarasu Kore ga Ozawa Senkyo da."

61. Among the five independents, three later joined the DPJ, one joined the PNP, and one remained independent.

62. Fukuda Yasuo, "Hajimete Kataru Dairenritsu to Sōri no Shikaku" [First talk on the great coalition and the qualifications to become prime minister], *Bungei Shunjū*, June 2011, 171.

63. "Kyotō Icchi de Tatakaeba Kanarazu Kateru: Ozawa Daihyō ga Jōkan de Jinin no Shini wo Setsumei" [We will win if we fight with party unity: President Ozawa explains his true intention of resignation at the executive meeting], May 12, 2009. http://www.dpj.or.jp/news/?num=15908 (accessed May 16, 2011).

64. "Sōsenkyo Shōri de Minshutō Seiken wo Tsukurukoto ga Watashi no Shimei, Ozawa Daihyō Daikō" [It is my mission to make the DPJ government victorious in the general election], May 22, 2009. http://www.dpj.or.jp/news/?num=16010 (accessed May 16, 2011).

65. "50 no Jūten Senkyoku ni Shūchū Shien" [Concentrated assistance to the 50 priority districts], *Nikkan Gendai*, July 7, 2009.

66. "Zenkoku ni Chiru Densetsu no Hisho Gundan no Yakuwari" [The role of the legendary secretary group spread all over the nation], *Nikkan Gendai*, July 7, 2009.

67. Tanaka Aiji, "Jimintō Suitai no Kōzō: Tokuhyō Kōzō to Seisaku Tairitsujiku no Henka" [The structure of the LDP's decline: The structure of its captured votes and policy cleavages], in *2009-nen Naze Seiken Kōtai Dattanoka* [Why power shifted in 2009], ed. Tanaka Aiji et al., 8–10 (Tokyo: Keisō Shobō, 2009).

68. The index was outlined in Markku Laakso and Rein Taagepera, " 'Effective' Number of Parties: A Measure with Application to West Europe," *Comparative Political Studies* 12, 1 (1979): 3–27.

69. Steven R. Reed, "Duverger's Law Is Working in Japan," *Japanese Journal of Electoral Studies* 22 (2007): 96–106; and Rosenbluth and Thies, *Japan Transformed*, 186.

70. Sugawara Taku, "Jimintō Seiji Jikai no Kōzō to Katei," 32–33; and Akarui Senkyo Suishin Kyōkai, *Dai 44-kai Shūgiin Sōsenkyo no Jittai: Chōsa Kekka no Gaiyō* [The situation of the 44th lower house general election: Outline of survey

results] (March 2006), 58. The share of LDP supporters' votes in the upper house PR system was 8.1 percent in 2001, 18.1 percent in 2004, 16.8 percent in 2007, and 26.5 percent in 2010.

71. The smaller numbers are based on the assumption that 60 percent of Kōmeitō supporters cast votes for LDP candidates, and the bigger numbers assume 80 percent. Kabashima Ikuo, *Sengo Seiji no Kiseki: Jimintō System no Keisei to Henyō* [The track of postwar politics: The formation and changes of the LDP System] (Tokyo: Iwanami Shoten, 2004), 321–24 and 376–82.

72. Ko Maeda, "Re-examining the Contamination Effect of Japan's Mixed Electoral System Using the Treatment-Effects Model," *Electoral Studies* 27 (2008): 724.

73. Kohno Masaru, "Senkyo Kekka kara Mita Minshutō Asshō, Jimintō Taihai no Kōzu," in *2009-nen Naze Seiken Kōtai Dattanoka* [Why power shift in 2009], ed. Tanaka Aiji et al. (Tokyo: Keisō Shobō, 2009), 46–49.

74. Sugawara Taku, "2009-nen Sōsenkyo Bunseki (2): Minnanotō no Tokuhyō Kōzō ni Mieru Jimintō no Mirai" [Analysis on the 2009 general election (2): The future of the LDP as shown by the vote structure of the Your Party], September 29, 2009. http://go2senkyo.com/senkyo_news/0909/0909260820/1.php (accessed June 6, 2011).

75. Under the old multimember system, the answer to this question was mixed. In the 1970s more voters put priority on the party, and during most of the 1980s more voters put higher value on the candidate. Akarui Senkyo Suishin Kyōkai, *Dai 45-kai Shūgiin Sōsenkyo no Jittai*, 57.

76. Ko Maeda, "Has the Electoral-System Reform Made Japanese Elections Party-Centered?" in *Political Change in Japan: Electoral Behavior, Party Realignment and the Koizumi Reforms*, ed. Steven Reed, Kenneth Mori McElwain, and Kay Shimizu (Stanford: Walter H. Shorenstein Asia-Pacific Research Center, 2009), 47–66.

77. This was pointed out by Aiji Tanaka in "Jimintō Suitai no Kōzō," 10–11.

78. See Maeda, "Has the Electoral-System Reform Made Japanese Elections Party-Centered?" 889–92.

79. Akarui Senkyo Suishin Kyōkai, *Dai 45-kai Shūgiin Sōsenkyo no Jittai*, 53–55.

80. Yamada Masahiro, "2009-nen Sōsenkyo ni okeru Seiken Kōtai to Swing Voting" [The power shift and swing voting in the 2009 general election] *Senkyo Kenkyū* 26, 2 (2010): 10–11.

81. Opinion poll conducted by *Asahi Shimbun*, August 31–September 1, 2009.

82. John F. Kennedy, *Profiles in Courage* (New York: Harper, 1955), 220.

5. HATOYAMA'S ANTIBUREAUCRATIC STANCE

1. Hatoyama Yukio, "Kokumin no Saranaru Shōri ni Mukete" [Toward further victory of the people] August 30, 2009; Hirata Oriza, and Matsui Kōji, *Sōri no Genkō: Atarashii Seiji no Kotoba wo Mosakushita 266-nichi* [The manuscript of the prime minister: 266 days of exploring new political wording] (Tokyo: Iwanami Shoten, 2011), 122–25.

2. "The Basic Policy," cabinet decision, September 15, 2009, paragraph 3. http://www.kantei.go.jp/jp/kakugikettei/2009/0916kihonhousin.html (accessed June 10, 2011). The impact of institutional changes on the DPJ's policy making was examined in my previous work, "Japan's Failed Experiment: The DPJ and Institutional Changes for Political Leadership," *Asian Survey* 52:5 (September/October 2012).

3. "The Basic Policy," paragraph 4.

4. Ibid., paragraph 5.

5. "Sei to Kan no Arikata" [How politicians and bureaucrats should be], an agreement at the cabinet meeting, September 16, 2009. http://www.kantei.go.jp/jp/kakugikettei/2009/0916arikata.html (accessed June 14, 2011).

6. "The Basic Policy," paragraph 4.

7. "Seifu-Yotō Ichigenka ni Okeru Seisaku no Kettei ni tsuite" [Policy making in the unified system of the government and the ruling party], September 18, 2009. http://data.tezj.jp/2009-0918seisaku_ichigenka.pdf (accessed June 14, 2011).

8. Statement by lower house member Takashi Kii, September 21, 2009. http://takataka2007.blog111.fc2.com/blog-entry-433.html (accessed June 14, 2011).

9. Hatoyama Yukio,"Watashi no Seiji Tetsugaku" [My political philosophy], *Voice* (September 2009).

10. Kan Naoto, *Daijin Zōhoban* [The minister, revised edition] (Tokyo: Iwanami Shinsho, 2009), 227.

11. "2009 Change of Government: The Democratic Party of Japan's Platform for Government." http://www.dpj.or.jp/english/manifesto/manifesto2009.pdf (accessed June 14, 2011).

12. Ibid.

13. "Hatoyama Naikaku Shiji 71%" [71% support for the Hatoyama cabinet], *Asahi Shinbun*, September 18, 2009.

14. There were two observers, Deputy CCS Kōji Matsui and Senior Vice Minister Motohisa Furukawa from the Cabinet Office. "Hosei Yosan ni Kansuru Kakuryō Iinkai" [Cabinet committee meeting on supplementary budget], September 18, 2009. http://www.kantei.go.jp/jp/hatoyama/actions/200909/18kakuryou.html (accessed June 16, 2011).

15. Asahi Shimbun Seiken Shuzai Sentā, ed., *Minshutō Seiken 100-nichi no Shinsō* [The truth of 100 days under the DPJ government] (Tokyo: Asahi Shimbun-sha, 2010), 61.

16. Ibid., 62.

17. Yomiuri Shimbun Seiji-bu, *Minshutō Meisō to Uragiri no 300-nichi* [The DPJ, 300 days of drifting and betraying] (Tokyo: Shinchō-sha, 2010), 33–34.

18. "Heisei 22-nendo Yosan no Gaisan Yōkyū ni Atatte no Kihontekina Hōshin ni tsuite" [Basic guidelines for draft budget proposals for FY2010], cabinet understanding, July 1, 2009. http://www.mof.go.jp/budget/budget_workflow/budget/fy2010/h22gla.pdf (accessed June 16, 2011).

19. "Heisei 22-nendo Yosan Hensei no Hōshin ni tsuite" [Guidelines for budget formation for FY2010], cabinet decision, September 29, 2009. http://www.kantei.go.jp/jp/kakugikettei/2009/0929h22yosan.pdf (accessed June 16, 2011).

20. Shimizu Masato, "Seiken Kōtai no 600-nichi" [600 days after the government change], in *Zemināru Gendai Nihon Seiji* [Seminar on contemporary Japanese politics], ed. Sasaki Takeshi and Shimizu Masato (Tokyo: Nihon Keizai Shimbun-sha, 2011), 87.

21. "Kaku Working Group no Tantō Fushō ni tsuite" [Ministries allocated among the working groups]. http://www.cao.go.jp/sasshin/kaigi/honkaigi/d1/pdf/s6-2.pdf (accessed June 17, 2011).

22. "Jigyō Shiwake wo Fukumu Konkai no Saishutsu Minaoshi no Kangaekata" [Perspectives on budget review, including the program screening]. http://www.cao.go.jp/sasshin/kaigi/honkaigi/d1/pdf/s5–1.pdf (accessed June 17, 2011).

23. Finance Minister Seijūrō Shiokawa's statement at the lower house Committee on Financial Affairs, February 25, 2003.

24. Among the fifty-nine GRU staffers, twelve came from the private sector. Yomiuri Shimbun "Minshuism" Shuzaihan, *Haishin Seiken* [The betraying government] (Tokyo: Chūōkōronshin-sha, 2011), 39.

25. "Jigyō Shiwake no Taishō to naru Jigyō Soshiki Tō" [List of programs and organizations for program screening]. http://www.cao.go.jp/sasshin/oshirase/pdf/program-list.pdf (accessed June 17, 2011).

26. "Naikaku Shijiritsu 62%, Muda Sakugen Hyōka 76%, Seron Chōsa" [Cabinet approval 62%, high regard for wasteful spending cut 76%, public opinion], *Asahi.com*, November 15, 2009. http://www.asahi.com/seikenkotai2009/TKY200911150288.html (accessed June 17, 2011).

27. Foreign Minister Okada stated: "The National Strategy Division has not yet become a legally stipulated organization, and as such we must have a flexible view on it. In principle, my understanding is that the division will put much of its efforts

into matters related to the budget in the immediate term. In addition, the division will probably be in charge of specific matters assigned by Prime Minister Hatoyama, which, I assume, would include diplomatic matters. Currently no instructions on diplomatic matters have been issued to the division. That is my understanding." Press conference by Minister for Foreign Affairs Katsuya Okada, September 17, 2009. http://www.mofa.go.jp/announce/fm_press/2009/9/0917.html (accessed July 17, 2011).

28. Hayashi Yoshimasa and Tsumura Keisuke, *Kokkai Giin no Shigoto: Shokugyō toshite no Seiji* [The work of Diet members: Politics as profession] (Tokyo: Chūkō Shinsho, 2011), 226.

29. Lower house floor meeting, October 28, 2009. http://www.shugiin.go.jp/index.nsf/html/index_kaigiroku.htm (accessed June 17, 2011).

30. Hayashi and Tsumura, *Kokkai Giin no Shigoto*, 227.

31. "Yosan Hensei ni kansuru Kakuryō Iinkai ni okeru Gōi Jikō" [An agreement at the cabinet committee on budget], November 17, 2009. http://www.kantei.go.jp/jp/singi/kokkasenryaku/pdf/20091117goui.pdf (accessed July 20, 2011).

32. "The New Growth Strategy (Basic Policy Toward a Radiant Japan," December 30, 2009. http://www.kantei.go/jp/foreign/topics/2009/1230sinseichousenryaku_e.pdf (accessed July 20, 2011).

33. Hayashi and Tsumura, *Kokkai Giin no Shigoto*, 230–31.

34. Ibid., 233–34.

35. Nagatsuma Akira, *Manekarezaru Daijin: Sei to Kan no Shin Rūru* [Uninvited minister: New rule between politicians and bureaucrats] (Tokyo: Asahi Shinsho, 2011), 107.

36. Hara Eiji, *Kanryō no Retorikku: Kasumigaseki wa Naze Meisō Surunoka* [Bureaucratic rhetoric: Why the Kasumigaseki wanders astray] (Tokyo: Shinchō-sha, 2010), 40.

37. Nagatsuma, *Manekarezaru Daijin*, 107–08.

38. Statement by the MIC parliamentary secretary, Junya Ogawa, "Seimukan wa Kanryō no Jōshi" [Parliamentary secretary is a superior of the bureaucrats], *Asahi Shimbun*, December 24, 2009.

39. Statement by MOD parliamentary secretary Akihisa Nagashima. Ibid.

40. "Jikan Usureyuku Sonzaikan" [Vice minister with diminishing presence], *Asahi Shimbun*, January 15, 2010.

41. "Kasumigaseki tono Kyōsei wo Saguru" [To explore coexistence with the bureaucrats], *Asahi Shimbun*, March 16, 2010.

42. Teijirō Furukawa, interview by *Nihon Keizai Shimbun*, in Nihon Keizai Shimbun-sha, ed., *Seiken* [The ruling power] (Tokyo: Nihon Keizai Shimbun-sha, 2010), 495–97.

43. Teijirō Furukawa, interview by author, October 30, 2003.

44. Teijirō Furukawa, interview by *Nihon Keizai Shimbun*, 495–97.

45. "Kasumigaseki tono Kyōsei wo Saguru."

46. "Kanjichōshitsu Ozawa-shi no Shiro" [The Office of Secretary General, the castle of Mr. Ozawa], *Asahi Shimbun*, November 19, 2009.

47. "Yosan Hensei no Kihon Hōshin" [The basic guidelines of budget formation], December 15, 2009. http://www.kantei.go.jp/jp/kakugikettei/2009/1215yosan _kihonhoushin.pdf (accessed June 22, 2011).

48. This section largely relies on my work, "Searching for a Dream Plan: Two-Level Game Analysis of the Futenma Relocation Issue Under the Hatoyama Cabinet Policies," *Japanese Journal of Political Science* (forthcoming).

49. Yukio Hatoyama, "A New Path for Japan," *New York Times*, August 27, 2009.

50. "United States-Japan Roadmap for Realignment Implementation," May 1, 2006. http://www.mofa.go.jp/region/n-america/us/security/scc/doc0605.html (accessed July 6, 2011).

51. For the details of complicated conditions, see a book written by former vice minister of defense Takemasa Moriya, who was involved in the negotiation process with Okinawa and the United States. Moriya Takemasa, *"Futenma" Kōshō Hiroku* [Secret records of negotiation over "Futenma"] (Tokyo: Shinchō-sha, 2010).

52. "2009 Change of Government," 28.

53. Mainichi Shimbun Seiji-bu, ed., *Ryūkyū no Seijōki: "Futenma" wa Owaranai* [Stars and stripes in Okinawa: "Futenma" that never ends] (Tokyo: Kōdan-sha, 2010), 48.

54. Akihisa Nagashima, interview by author, August 4, 2011.

55. Hatoyama Yukio, "Minshutō, Watashi no Seiken Kōsō," *Chūō Kōron* (November 1996).

56. "Okinawa Vision 2008," July 8, 2008. http://www.dpj.or.jp/news/files /okinawa(2).pdf (accessed June 23, 2011).

57. The two DPJ staffers were Kiyoshi Sugawa of the DPJ Policy Committee and Satoshi Honjō, personal secretary of Okada. Mainichi Shimbun Seiji-bu, ed., *Ryūkyū no Seijōki*, 70–75.

58. Fukushima Mizuho, *Meisō Seiken tono Tatakai* [Fight against the stray government] (Tokyo: Asukī Shinsho, 2011), 36–37.

59. "Renritsu Seiken Juritsu ni Atatte no Seisaku Gōi" [Policy agreement to establish a coalition government], September 9, 2009. http://www.dpj.or.jp/news /files/20090909goui.pdf (accessed June 27, 2011).

60. Fukushima Mizuho, *Meisō Seiken tono Tatakai*, 38.

61. "Hatoyama Naikaku Kakuryō Kisha Kaiken Okada Katsuya Daijin" [Press conference of ministers of the Hatoyama cabinet, Minister Katsuya Okada], Seifu Internet Television, September 16, 2009. http://nettv.gov-online.go.jp/prg/prg2758 .html (accessed June 27, 2011).

62. "Okada Gaimu Daijin Kaiken Kiroku" [Record of conference by Foreign Minister Okada], September 18, 2009. http://www.mofa.go.jp/mofaj/press/kaiken /gaisho/g_0909.html#9-B.

63. "Daijin Rinji Kaiken Gaiyō" [Summary of an ad hoc conference by the minister], September 17, 2009. http://www.mod.go.jp/j/press/kisha/2009/09/17.html (accessed June 27, 2011).

64. Toshimi Kitazawa, interview by author, December 1, 2011.

65. "Okada Gaimu Daijin Kaiken Kiroku," September 18, 2009.

66. Toshimi Kitazawa, interview by author, December 1, 2011.

67. "Japan-U.S. Foreign Ministerial Meeting Summary," September 21, 2009. http://www.mofa.go.jp/region/n-america/us/meet0909.html (accessed June 27, 2011).

68. Mainichi Shimbun Seiji-bu, ed., *Ryūkyū no Seijōki*, 85.

69. Hatoyama stated in a press conference, "I thought I should avoid the detailed issue. I feel that we can reach a mutually beneficial solution by building trust through comprehensive review on national security issues." "Hatoyama Sōri no Kokuren Sōkai Oyobi G20 Pittsburg Summit Shusseki Naigai Kisha Kaiken" [Press conference by Prime Minister Hatoyama on his attendance at the U.N. General Assembly and G20 Pittsburgh Summit], September 25, 2009. http://kantei .go.jp/jp/hatoyama/statement/200909/26naigai.html (accessed June 27, 2011).

70. "Futenma wa Kengai Iten" [Futenma will be relocated outside the prefecture], *Ryukyu Shimpo*, extra digital edition, September 25, 2009. http://ryukyushimpo .jp/uploads/img4abc4b46536e8.pdf (accessed June 27, 2011).

71. "Daijin Rinji Kaiken Gaiyō" [Summary of ad hoc conference by the minister], September 25, 2009. http://www.mod.go.jp/j/press/kisha/2009/09/25a.html (accessed June 27, 2011).

72. "Daijin Rinji Kaiken Gaiyō" [Summary of ad hoc conference by the minister], September 26, 2009. http://www.mod.go.jp/j/press/kisha/2009/09/25a.html (accessed June 27, 2011).

73. Mainichi Shimbun Seiji-bu, ed., *Ryūkyū no Seijōki*, 97–98; Asahi Shimbun Seiken Shuzai Sentā, ed., *Minshutō Seiken 100-nichi no Shinsō*, 67–68.

74. U.S. government official, interview by author, October 22, 2009.

75. "Maehara Okinawa Tantō Daijin, Henoko Igai no Isetsuchi Sagashitai" [Minister of Okanawa Affairs Maehara wants to look for another relocation place

than Henoko], *Ryukyu Asahi Hoso*, October 3, 2009. http://www.qab.co.jp/news/2009100312306.html (accessed June 27, 2011).

76. Former vice defense Minister Moriya revealed the reasons for U.S. opposition: "The U.S. forces opposed the plan for three reasons: First, controlling low-speed helicopters and high-speed fighters simultaneously would be too much of a burden on the air traffic controllers. Second, the plan would make Kadena an airfield with sixty to seventy each of helicopters and the fighters conducting exercises even in peacetime, and in a contingency the number of aircraft could grow two- or threefold. Kadena could not handle this volume. Third, Kadena was considered too noisy even at that time. Aprons for P-3C antisubmarine patrol planes were moved and noise-blocking walls were built under the SACO agreement as noise-reducing measures. The U.S. side pointed out that such measures to reduce the burden of the citizens of Kadena would be naught." Moriya Takemasa, "Jimoto Riken ni Furimawasareru Futenma, Nichibei Dōmei" [Futenma and Japan-U.S. alliance dragged by local concession hunters], *Chūō Kōron* (January 2010), 109.

77. "Gaimu Daijin Kaiken Kiroku" [Conference record of the foreign minister], October 23, 2009. http://www.mofa.go.jp/mofaj/press/kaiken/gaisho/g_0910.html#5-B (accessed June 28, 2011).

78. "Japan-U.S. Defense Ministers Joint Press Conference," October 21, 2009. http://www.mod.go.jp/e/pressrele/2009/091021.html (accessed June 28, 2011).

79. "Press Conference by the Defense Minister," October 27, 2009. http://www.mod.go/jp/e/pressconf/2009/10/091027.html (accessed June 28, 2011).

80. "Kyōkona Nichibei Kankei wo Mezashite" [Toward strengthened Japan-U.S. relations], November 7, 2009. http://www.mmz.kantei.go.jp/jp/m-magazine/backnumber/2009/1107ub/index.html (accessed June 28, 2011).

81. "Joint Press Conference by Prime Minister Yukio Hatoyama of Japan and President Barack Obama of the United States of America," November 13, 2009. http://www.kantei.go.jp/foreign/hatoyama/statement/200911/13usa_kaiken_e.html (accessed June 28, 2009).

82. "Japan-U.S. Summit Meeting," November 13, 2009. http://www.mofa.go.jp/region/n-america/us/pv0911/summit.html (accessed June 28, 2011).

83. "Yuruginai Shinrai Kankei" [Firm trust relationship], November 19, 2009. http://www.mmz.kantei.go.jp/jp/m-magazine/backnumber/2009/1119eb/index.html (accessed June 28, 2009).

84. Mainichi Shimbun Seiji-bu, ed., *Ryūkyū no Seijōki*, 128; and Shimizu, "Seiken Kōtai no 600-nichi," 128.

85. "Jinsokuna Ketsuron de Icchi, Futenma Sagyō Grūpu Hatsukaigō" [Agreement on prompt solution at the first meeting of the Futenma Working Group],

Ryukyu Shimpo, November 18, 2009. http://ryukyushimpo.jp/news/storyid-152989
-storytopic-3.html (accessed June 28, 2011).

86. Mainichi Shimbun Seiji-bu, ed., *Ryūkyū no Seijōki*, 138–39.

87. "Taibei yori Renritsu Yūsen" [Higher priority on the coalition over relations with the U.S.], *Asahi Shimbun*, December 4, 2009.

88. Mainichi Shimbun Seiji-bu, ed., *Ryūkyū no Seijōki*, 156.

89. "[Wikileaks] Japan: Ambassador Roos's meeting with Maehara," December
10, 2009. http://tourkaba3.wordpress.com/2011/05/13/09tokyo2822/ (accessed June
29, 2009).

90. "[Wikileaks] Japan: Ambassador's December 21 Lunch Meeting with Vice
Minister Yabunaka," December 30, 2009. http:tourkaba3.wordpress.com/2011/05
/13/09tokyo2946/ (accessed June 29, 2009). Hatoyama later denied that he made
such a statement.

91. Japanese media reported that Clinton called in Fujisaki on the snowy day
when most of the government building was shut down. According to State Department spokesperson Phillip Crowley, the Japanese ambassador was not called
in but came to see Clinton. Daily Press Brief, Washington, D.C., December 22,
2009. http://www.state.gov/r/pa/prs/dpb/2009/dec/133952.htm#JAPAN (accessed
June 29, 2009).

92. High official of the U.S. government, interview by author, December 16, 2009.

93. "Hatoyama Naikaku Sōri Daijin Kisha Kaiken" [Press conference by Prime
Minister Hatoyama], December 25, 2009. http://www.kantei.go.jp/jp/hatoyama/
statement/200912/25kaiken.html (accessed June 29, 2009.

94. "Hatoyama Zenshushō Ichimon Ittō" [Q&A with former prime minister
Hatoyama]. *Ryukyu Shinpo*, February 13, 2011. Translation provided in Satoko
Norimatsu, "Hatoyama's Confession: The Myth of Deterrence and the Failure to
Move a Marine Base Outside Okinawa," *Asia-Pacific Journal* 9, 3 (February 28,
2011): http://www.japanfocus.org/-Norimatsu-Satoko/3495 (accessed June 30, 2011).

95. Shimizu Masato, "Seiken Kōtai no 600-nichi," 146.

96. Mainichi Shimbun Seiji-bu, ed., *Ryūkyū no Seijōki*, 169–73.

97. "Nago citizens are angered at Hirano remarks," *Akahata*, January 27, 2010,
translation provided by *Japan Press Weekly*. http://www.japan-press.co.jp/2010/2656
/USF8.html (accessed June 30, 2011).

98. On December 5 Okada stated in Nago City, "I have talked with the U.S.
government for two months. But the American stance that they cannot change
the bilaterally agreed plan remained. . . . If you keep refusing, Futenma will stay,
and the transfer of 8,000 marines will be canceled." Mainichi Shimbun Seiji-bu,
ed., *Ryūkyū no Seijōki*, 152–53.

99. Ibid., 178–90, 208–9.

100. Hatoyama's response to LDP president Teiichi Tanigaki, National Basic Policy Committee, March 31, 2010.

101. "Hatoyama Zenshushō Ichimon Ittō."

102. Al Kamen, "Among Leaders at Summit, Hu's First," *Washington Post*, April 14, 2010.

103. "Jitsugen Dekirunona, Bei Daitōryō Hatoyama Shushō ni Ginen," *Yomiuri Shimbun*, April 18, 2010.

104. "Hatoyama Zenshushō Ichimon Ittō."

105. "Shushō, Okinawa nimo Tokunoshima nimo Iten Kentō Tsutaeru" [The prime minister asks both Okinawa and Tokunoshima to consider relocation], *Yomiuri Shimbun*, May 4, 2009.

106. Hatoyama's comment to Japanese journalists, May 4, 2009. http://bastos .fc2web.com/page054.html (accessed June 30, 2011). Hatoyama later denied his own comments by saying the statement was just "pretext" in an interview with the *Ryukyu Shimpo* and was criticized for being irresponsible. He stated: "When Tokunoshima Island refused to host an alternative facility, we had no choice but to move it to Henoko, so I had to come up with a rationale to justify it. I didn't know the presence of marines in Okinawa would work directly as a deterrent against war, but without the marines, the U.S. military would not be able to function fully in terms of interoperability, and that would affect deterrence. As for the deterrent effect of the marines themselves, you all think they are not a deterrent, and that is also my understanding. If you say it was a pretext, then it was a pretext. But I thought I could still use the word 'deterrence' in a broader sense. "Hatoyama Zenshushō Ichimon Ittō."

107. "Joint Statement of the U.S.-Japan Security Consultative Committee," May 28, 2010. http://www.mofa.go.jp/region/n-america/us/security/scc/joint1005 .html (accessed July 1, 2011).

108. For Fukushima's determination, see Fukushima Mizuho, *Meisō Seiken tono Tatakai*, 69–76.

109. See chapter 1, note 105.

110. "Naikaku Shiji Sarani Gerakushi 21%" [Further declining cabinet approval to 21 %], *Asahi Shimbun*, May 17, 2010.

111. "Ryōin Giin Sōkai, Hatoyama Daihyō no Jinin wo Shōnin" [The DPJ Diet members' meeting approves the resignation of President Hatoyama], June 2, 2010. http://www.dpj.or.jp/article/18288/ (accessed July 1, 2011).

6. Kan's Struggle in the Government and the DPJ

1. Press conference by Deputy Prime Minister Naoto Kan, June 3, 2010. http://www.youtube.com/watch?v=DD3JyEHkrIE (accessed July 12, 2011).

2. "Kan Naikaku Shiji 60%" [Job approval for the Kan cabinet 60 percent], *Asahi Shimbun*, June 10, 2010.

3. "Kan Senryakushō, Kasumigaseki wa Ōbaka" [Minister for national strategy Kan, bureaucrats are very stupid], *Yomiuri Shimbun*, November 1, 2009.

4. Hayashi Yoshimasa and Tsumura Keisuke, *Kokkai Giin no Shigoto: Shokugyō toshite no Seiji* [The work of Diet members: Politics as profession] (Tokyo: Chūkō Shinsho, 2011), 202–5.

5. "Kihon Hōshin" [The Basic Policy], cabinet decision, June 8, 2010. http://www.kantei.go.jp/jp/kakugikettei/2010/08kihonhousin.pdf (accessed July 13, 2011).

6. "Jimujikan Tō eno Sōri Kunji" [Prime minister's speech to the administrative vice ministers], June 10, 2010. http://www.kantei.go.jp/jp/kan/actions/201006/10shiji_jikan.html (accessed July 13, 2011).

7. "Jimujikan Tō eno Sōri Kunji" [Prime minister's speech to the administrative vice ministers], January 21, 2011. http://www.kantei.go.jp/jp/kan/actions/201101/21kunji.html (accessed July 13, 2011).

8. Ibid.

9. Ozawa stated, "The operation of the policy conferences kept the senior vice ministers and the parliamentary secretaries very busy. But the conferences were ceremonial. I understand that everybody was not able to participate in policy discussions." Japan National Press Club, ed., "Minshutō Daihyōsen Rikkōhosha Tōronkai" [Debate by DPJ presidential candidates], September 2, 2010. http://www.jnpc.or.jp/files/opdf/472.pdf (accessed July 14, 2011).

10. "Nagatachō Tantō no Kanbō Chōkan" [Chief cabinet secretary in charge of Nagatachō], *Asahi Shimbun*, June 11, 2010.

11. "Policy Speech by Prime Minister Naoto Kan at the 174th Session of the Diet." http://www.kantei.go.jp/foreign/kan/statement/201006/11syosin_e.html (accessed July 13, 2011).

12. Shimizu, "Seiken Kōtai no 600-nichi," 177–78.

13. "Kan Daihyō Kisha Kaiken" [Press conference by President Kan], July 11, 2010. http://www.youtube.com/watch?v=y9EsCIEljMo&feature=related (accessed July 13, 2011).

14. DPJ secretary general Edano summarized the reasons for the election loss into the following eight factors: (1) public surprise based on the way in which debate over the consumption tax had been embarked on; (2) insufficient explanation of

the administration's achievements in the ten months since the change of government; (3) unclear positioning of the House of Councilors Manifesto, and voters' inability to understand the connection between it and the previous year's general election manifesto; (4) the way in which additional candidates had been fielded in multiple-seat districts; (5) insufficient communication about policies emphasizing the regions; (6) the party's organizational weakness in the regions; (7) the need to further strengthen measures for dealing with various organizations; (8) how the election campaign was fought as a ruling party. "General Meeting of DPJ Diet Members convened to discuss election review," July 29, 2010. http://www.dpj.or.jp/english/news/index.html?num=18661 (accessed July 14, 2011).

15. "General Meeting of DPJ Diet Members," July 29, 2010. http://www.dpj.or.jp/article/18636 (accessed July 14, 2011).

16. "Gaimu Daijin Kaiken Kiroku" [Record of conference by the foreign minister], August 20, 2010. http://www.mofa.go.jp/mofaj/press/kaiken/gaisho/g_1008.html#4-H (accessed July 14, 2011).

17. "Renhō Naikaku Tokumei Tantou Daijin Kisha Kaiken" [Press conference by CAO minister Renhō], August 20, 2010. http://www.cao.go.jp/minister/1006_renho/kaiken/2010/0820kaiken.html (accessed July 14, 2011).

18. Japan National Press Club, ed., "Minshutō Daihyōsen Rikkōhosha Tōronkai."

19. "Shushō Zokutō Yokatta 72%" [72% welcome the reelection of the prime minister], *Asahi Shimbun*, September 16, 2010.

20. Serita Kentarō, *Nihon no Ryōdo* [Japan's territory] (Tokyo: Chūkō Sōsho, 2002), 116–32.

21. This historical evidence was found by Masao Shimojō. Shimojō Masao, "Senkaku wa Chūgoku no mono? Kutsugaesu Shōko koko ni ari" [Is Senkaku China's? There exists evidence against it], *Wedge Infinity*, December 1, 2010. http://wedge.ismedia.jp/articles/-/1152 (accessed July 20, 2011).

22. "Struggle of the People of the Ryukyu Islands Against U.S. Occupation," *People's Daily*, January 8, 1953.

23. Maps are available at http://senkakuchizu.dousetsu.com/page014.html (accessed March 8, 2012).

24. "The Second Meeting Between Yoshikatsu Takeiri and Zhou Enlai," July 28, 1972, *Data Base World and Japan*, http://www.ioc.u-tokyo.ac.jp/~worldjpn/documents/texts/JPCH/19720728.O2J.html (accessed July 19, 2011).

25. Yomiuri Shimbun "Minshuism" Shuzaihan, *Haishin Seiken* [The betraying government] (Tokyo: Chūōkōronshin-sha, 2011), 232–33.

26. "Press Conference by Minister for Foreign Affairs Seiji Maehara," September 17, 2010. http://www.mofa.go.jp/announce/fm_press/2010/9/0917_03.html (accessed July 20, 2011).

27. "Chinese Premier Urges Japan to Release Chinese Skipper Immediately, Unconditionally," September 22, 2010. http://www.china-embassy.org/eng/zt/wen jiabaoun/t754931.htm (accessed July 20, 2011).

28. Masami Ito, "Beijing Testing Japan-U.S. Relationship, Armitage Warns." *Japan Times*, September 16, 2010.

29. "Nichibei Gaishō Kaidan" [Japan-U.S. Foreign Ministerial Meeting], September 23, 2010. http://www.mofa.go.jp/mofaj/area/usa/visit/1009_gk.html (accessed July 20, 2011).

30. According to Matsumoto, there was a major error in the videotape presented by the prosecutor's office, and Sengoku advised to Kan that it would be very difficult to win the trial. "Tēpu ni Kashi" [Problem with the tape], *Sankei Shimbun*, September 26, 2011. http://sankei.jp.msn.com/politics/news/110926/plc11092612200013-n1.htm (accessed April 2, 2012).

31. "Statement by the Ministry of Foreign Affairs of the People's Republic of China," September 25, 2010. http://www.fmprc.gov.cn/eng/zxxx/t755932.htm (accessed July 20, 2011).

32. Deputy CCS Motohisa Furukawa's answer at the lower house Judiciary Affairs Committee, October 22, 2010.

33. Nihon Keizai Shimbun-sha, ed., *Seiken*, 497–99.

34. Shimizu, "Seiken Kōtai no 600-nichi," 214.

35. "Zaisei Unei Senryaku" [Fiscal management strategy], cabinet decision, June 22, 2010. http://www.kantei.go.jp/jp/kakugikettei/2010/100622_zaiseiunei -kakugikettei.pdf (July 21, 2011).

36. "Heisei 23nendo Yosan no Gaisan Yōkyū Kumikae Kijun nit suite" [Budget reform guidelines for the FY2011 budget], cabinet decision, July 27, 2010. http://www .mof.go.jp/budget/budger_workflow/budget/fy2011/sy220727.pdf (accessed July 21, 2011).

37. National Press Club, ed., "Minshutō Daihyōsen Rikkōhosha Tōronkai," 6.

38. "Heisei 23nendo Ippan Kaikei Gaisan Yōkyūgaku Tō" [Draft budget proposal for the FY2011 general account], September 1, 2010. http://www.mof.go.jp /budget/budger_workflow/budget/fy2011/ (accessed July 21, 2011).

39. "Renhō Naikakufu Tokumei Tantō Daijin Kisha Kaiken Yōshi" [Summary of press conference by CAO minister Renhō], January 20, 2011. http://www.cao.go.jp /minister/1101_renho/kaiken/2011/0120kaiken.html (accessed July 21, 2011).

40. Shimizu, "Seiken Kōtai no 600-nichi," 32–33.

41. Yoshihide Soeya, member of the council, conversation with author, December 10, 2010.

42. The principles were first declared at the Diet in 1967 to ban arms exports to (1) communist bloc countries, (2) countries subject to a UN-led arms exports ban,

and (3) countries involved in or likely to be involved in international conflicts. In 1976 these principles were extended to other areas as well.

43. "'Bōei Taikō' no Minaoshi ni Kansuru Teigen" [Proposal for the revision of the defense guidelines], DPJ Research Council on Foreign Policy and National Security, November 30, 2010. http://www.dpj.or.jp/download/4129.pdf (accessed August 8, 2011).

44. Personal communication with Motohiro Ōno, November 25, 2011.

45. Akihisa Nagashima, interview by author, August 4, 2011.

46. Fukushima, *Meisō Seiken tono Tatakai*, 114–15.

47. "National Defense Program Guidelines for FY 2011 and beyond," December 17, 2010. http://www.mod.go.jp/e/d_act/d_policy/pdf/guidelinesFY2011.pdf (accessed July 22, 2011).

48. "Bōei Daijin Danwa" [Statement by the defense minister], December 17, 2010. http://www.mod.go.jp/j/approach/agenda/guideline/2011/daijin.pdf (accessed July 22, 2011).

49. Toshimi Kitazawa, interview by author, December 1, 2011.

50. "Policy Speech by Prime Minister Naoto Kan at the 176th Extraordinary Session of the Diet," October 1, 2010. http://www.kantei.go.jp/foreign/kan/statement /201010/01syosin_e.html (accessed July 27, 2011).

51. "Trans-Pacific Strategic Economic Partnership Agreement." http://www. mfat.govt.nz/downloads/trade-agreement/transpacific/main-agreement.pdf (accessed July 27, 2011).

52. Akira Gunji's question at the upper house floor meeting, October 7, 2010.

53. "Dai2kai Shinseichō Senryaku Jitsugen Kaigi Giji Yōshi" [Minutes of the third meeting of the Council on the Realization of the New Growth Strategy], October 8, 2010. http://www.npu.go.jp/policy/policy04/pdf/20101015/20101015_gijiy oshi.pdf (accessed July 27, 2011).

54. Shimizu Masato, "Seiken Kōtai no 600-nichi," 219.

55. "Dai3kai Shinseichō Senryaku Jitsugen Kaigi Giji Yōshi" [Minutes of the second meeting of the Council on the Realization of the New Growth Strategy], October 21, 2010. http://www.npu.go.jp/policy/policy04/pdf/20101027/20101027 _gijiyoshi.pdf (accessed July 27, 2011).

56. "EPA ni Kansuru Kakushu Shisan" [Estimates on EPA], October 27, 2010. http://www.npu.go.jp/policy/policy08/pdf/20101027/siryou2.pdf (accessed July 27, 2011).

57. "Yanagida Hōmudaijin Nukenuke to Hatsugen" [Justice Minister Yanagida's imprudent statement], November 16, 2010. http://www.youtube.com/watch? v=iiGuf5vNVb8 (accessed July 29, 2010).

58. Yoshito Sengoku's answer at the upper house Budget Committee meeting, November 18, 2010.

59. Yomiuri Shimbun "Minshuism" Shuzaihan, *Haishin Seiken*, 284.

60. Foreign Minister Seiji Maehara's answer to a question by Shōji Nishida, upper house Budget Committee meeting, March 4, 2011.

61. "Press Conference by Minister for Foreign Affairs Seiji Maehara," March 6, 2011. http://www.mofa.go.jp/announce/fm_press/2011/3/0306_01.html (accessed August 1, 2011).

62. "Kan Shushō ni Ihō Kenkin no Utagai" [Prime Minister Kan suspected for illegal contribution], *Asahi Shimbun*, March 11, 2011.

63. Prime Minister Naoto Kan's response to a question by Mitsunobu Fujitani, upper house Settlement Committee meeting, March 11, 2011.

64. "Oshirase" [Note], March 11, 2011. http://www.kantei.go.jp/saigai/pdf/20110311setti.pdf (accessed August 1, 2011).

65. In addition to the two deputy CCSs, the emergency team included the Cabinet Office's chief counselor for disaster measures; the Ministry of Land, Infrastructure, and Transport and Tourism's river bureau chief; the National Police Agency's security bureau chief; Japan Meteorological Agency's deputy director general; the Fire and Disaster Management Agency's deputy director general; the Japan Coast Guard's director general for guard and rescue; the Ministry of Health, Labor, and Welfare's chief technical counselor; and the Ministry of Defense's operational policy bureau chief. "Kinkyū Sanshū Chīmu" [The emergency team]. http://www.cas.go.jp/jp/gaiyou/jimu/pdf/kinkyu_team.pdf (accessed August 1, 2011).

66. "Disaster Countermeasure Basic Act," National Land Agency, June 1977. http://www.adrc.asia/documents/law/DisasterCountermeasuresBasicAct.pdf (accessed August 1, 2011).

67. "Sōri Shiji" [Instruction by the prime minister]. http://www.kantei.go.jp/saigai/pdf/siji.pdf (accessed August 1, 2011).

68. "Declaration of Nuclear Emergency," March 11, 2011. http://www.kantei.go.jp/foreign/incident/20110311Nuclear_Emergency.pdf (accessed August 2, 2011).

69. "Kinkyū Jitai ni Taisuru Seifu no Shodō Sochi ni Tsuite" [Initial actions of the government in emergency cases], cabinet decision, November 21, 2003.

70. "Daijishin de Seiji Kyūsen" [Political battle suspended by a great earthquake]. *Yomiuri Shimbun*, March 12, 2011.

71. These four points are raised by Masato Shimizu in "Seiken Kōtai no 600-nichi," 8.

72. Haruki Madarame, interview by the Independent Investigation Commission on the Fukushima Daiichi Nuclear Accident (hereafter, the Fukushima Commission), December 17, 2011.

73. Yukio Edano, interview by the Fukushima Commission, December 10, 2011.

74. "Kanbō Chōkan Kisha Happyō" [Press conference by the chief cabinet secretary], March 12, 2011, 3:12 a.m. http://www.kantei.go.jp/jp/tyoukanpress/201103/12 _a2.html (accessed August 9, 2011).

75. Eric Talmadge and Mari Yamaguchi, "First 24 Hours Shaped Japan Nuke Crisis," Associated Press, July 2, 2011. http://abcnews.go.com/Business/wireStory? id=13982317 (accessed August 9, 2011).

76. This was ordered under the authority given to the minister by the 1957 Act on the Regulation of Nuclear Source Material, Nuclear Fuel Material and Reactors.

77. Banri Kaieda, interview by the Fukushima Commission, October 1, 2011.

78. Fukushima Genpatsujiko Dokuritsu Kenshō Iinkai, *Chōsa Kenshō Hōkusho* [Research and investigation report] (Tokyo: Nippon Saiken Initiative Zaidan, 2012), 79.

79. Nuclear and Industrial Safety Agency, "Hoanin Puresu Happyō Shiryō no Shūsei ni Tsuite" [Revision of press material of the Nuclear and Industrial Safety Agency]. http://www.meti.go.jp/earthquake/nuclear/pdf/20110701–2nisa.pdf (accessed August 9, 2011).

80. Yukari Satō's question at the upper house Budget Committee meeting, March 28, 2011.

81. Yasutoshi Nishimura's question at the lower house Budget Committee meeting, May 16, 2011.

82. "Kanbō Chōkan Kisha Happyō" [Press conference by the chief cabinet secretary], March 11, 2011, 7:44 p.m. http://www.kantei.go.jp/jp/tyoukanpress/201103/11 _p3.html (accessed August 9, 2011).

83. Yasutoshi Nishimura's question at the lower house Budget Committee meeting, May 16, 2011.

84. Kotaki Mariko, "Genshiryoku Hoanin Micchaku Rupo, Dengon Gēmu no Sankasha ga Oosugiru" [Reportage on the Nuclear and Industry Safety Agency: Too many participants in the message game], *Nikkei Business On Line*, March 18, 2011. http://business.nikkeibp.co.jp/article/manage/20110317/219019/?rt=nocnt (accessed August 9, 2011).

85. The six newly appointed advisers included four nuclear specialists (Toshisō Kosako, Masanori Aritomi, Masaki Saitō, and Hiroshi Tasaka), one IT specialist (Yasushi Hibino), and one crisis management specialist (Noboru Yamaguchi).

86. Kan Naoto, "Sōri Kan Naoto 3.11-go wo Kataru" [Prime Minister Kan Naoto talks about post-3-11], *Shūkan Asahi*, August 19, 2011, 21.

87. This was the author's calculation based on the data between March 11 and 24 on the web page of the Prime Minister's Office. http://www.kantei.go.jp/saigai /report.html (accessed August 9, 2011).

88. Tsso Takuya, "All Japan no Shiten Mote" [Need to have the all Japan viewpoint], *Asahi Shinbun*, March 8, 2012.

89. Shimizu, "Seiken Kōtai no 600-nichi," 13–14.

90. Ibid., 14.

91. Takuya Tasso, interview by author, July 26, 2011.

92. The attendees of the meeting from Japan were Deputy CCS Tetsurō Fukuyama; the special advisor to the prime minister, Gōshi Hosono; Akihisa Nagashima; the deputy CCS for crisis management, Tetsurō Itō; assistant CCSs Chikao Kawai and Tetsuya Nishikawa; Director of Cabinet Intelligence Shinichi Vematsu; and representatives of TEPCO as well as the related ministries. Akihisa Nagashima, "Genbatsu Taiō ni Kansuru Nichibei Chōsei no Saikōchiku ni Tsuite no Teian" [Proposal to reconstruct U.S.-Japan coordination toward the countermeasures for the nuclear plant], March 20, 2011.

93. See also Nagashima Akihisa, "Genpatsu Taisho: Nichibei Kyōryoku no Butaiura" [Countermeasures for the nuclear plant: Behind the scenes of U.S.-Japan cooperation], *Voice*, (July 2011): 134–39.

94. "Ozawa-shi ga Iwate Iri, Kan Naikaku no Genpatsu Taiō Hihan" [Mr. Ozawa goes to Iwate, criticizes the Kan cabinet's response to the nuclear plant], *Asahi Shimbun*, March 28, 2011. http://www.asahi.com/politics/update/0328/TKY201103280189.html (accessed August 24, 2011).

95. "Genpatsu Taiō Hyōkasezu 58%" [58% disapprove of the response to the nuclear plant], *Kyodo News*, March 27, 2011. http://www.kyodonews.jp/feature/news04/2011/03/post-3131.html (accessed August 24, 2011).

96. The two prefectures that approved of the government's reaction were Yamanashi and Nagano. "Hansūchō ga Shushō Hyōkasezu" [More than a majority disapprove of the prime minister], *Kyodo News*, March 30, 2011. http://www.kyodonews.jp/feature/news04/chiji_q.html (accessed August 24, 2011).

97. "Press Conference by Prime Minister Naoto Kan," April 12, 2011. http://www.kantei.go.jp/foreign/kan/statement/201104/12kaiken_e.html (accessed August 24, 2011).

98. "Ozawa Blasts Kan over Disaster Management," *Jiji Press*, April 13, 2011.

99. "Tanigaki Sōsai Teirei Kisha Kaiken" [Regular press conference by President Tanigaki], April 13, 2011. http://www.youtube.com/watch?v=8N1Vo1CZ3Zo (accessed August 24, 2011).

100. The five subcabinet members were the senior vice minister of the Cabinet Office, Shōzō Azuma; the senior vice minister of land, infrastructure, and transportation, Wakio Mitsui; the senior vice minister of internal affairs and communications, Katsumasa Suzuki; the parliamentary secretary of the Environmental

Ministry, Takeshi Hidaka; and the parliamentary secretary of internal affairs and communications, Akira Uchiyama.

101. "Press Conference by Prime Minister Naoto Kan," June 2, 2011. http://www .kantei.go.jp/foreign/kan/statement/201106/02kaiken_e.html (accessed August 25, 2011).

102. The video clip is available at http://www.news24.jp/articles/2011/06/03/04183906 .html# (accessed August 25, 2011).

103. "Press Conference by Prime Minister Naoto Kan," June 27, 2011. http://www .kantei.go.jp/foreign/kan/statement/201106/27kaiken_e.html (accessed August 25, 2011).

104. "Press Conference by Prime Minister Naoto Kan," July 13, 2011. http:// www.kantei.go.jp/foreign/kan/statement/201107/13kaiken_e.html (accessed August 25, 2011).

105. "N-phaseout Merely Kan's Private View," *Yomiuri Shimbun*, July 16, 2011. http://www.yomiuri.co.jp/dy/national/T110715005591.htm (accessed August 25, 2011).

106. Banri Kaieda's answer at the upper house Budget Committee meeting, July 21, 2011.

7. INSTITUTIONS AND POLITICAL LEADERSHIP

1. "Policy Speech by Prime Minister Yoshihiko Noda to the 178th Session of the Diet," September 13, 2011. http://www.kantei.go.jp/foreign/noda/statement/2011 09/13syosin_e.html (accessed March 23, 2012).

2. The legislation was opposed by the Socialist Party, the JCP, and the Your Party.

3. "Shakai Hoshō Zei Ittai Kaikaku Soan ni tsuite" [On a draft plan of fundamental social security and tax reform], January 6, 2012. http://www.cas.go.jp/jp/ seisaku/syakaihosyou/pdf/240106houkoku.pdf (accessed March 23, 2012).

4. Interview with Ichirō Ozawa, *Asahi Shimbun*, February 24, 2012.

BIBLIOGRAPHY

ENGLISH LANGUAGE SOURCES

Aberbach, Joel D., Robert D. Putnam, and Bert A. Rockman. *Bureaucrats and Politicians in Western Democracies.* Cambridge: Harvard University Press, 1981.

Angel, Robert C. *Explaining Economic Policy Failure: Japan in the 1969–1971 International Monetary Crisis.* New York: Columbia University Press, 1991.

——. "Prime Ministerial Leadership in Japan: Recent Changes in Personal Style and Administrative Organization." *Pacific Affairs* 61 (Winter 1988/89): 583–602.

Baker, Andy, and Ethan Scheiner. "Adaptive Parties: Party Strategic Capacity Under Japanese SNTV." *Electoral Studies* 23 (2004): 251–78.

Belloni, Frank P., and Dennis C. Beller, eds. *Faction Politics: Political Parties and Factionalism in Comparative Perspective.* Santa Barbara: ABC Clio., 1978.

Blaker, Michael. *Japanese International Negotiating Style.* New York: Columbia University Press, 1977.

Brooks, William L. "The Politics of the Futenma Base Issue in Okinawa: Relocation Negotiation in 1995–1997, 2005–2006." *Asia-Pacific Policy Papers Series.* Washington, D.C.: Reischauer Center, 2010.

Budge, Ian, and Hans Keman. *Parties and Democracy: Coalition Formation and Government Functioning in Twenty States.* Oxford: Oxford University Press, 1990.

Burns, James MacGregor. *Leadership.* New York: Harper Colohan Books, 1978.

Calder, Kent E. *Crisis and Compensation: Public Policy and Political Stability in Japan, 1944–86.* Princeton: Princeton University Press, 1988.

——. *Embattled Garrisons: Comparative Base Politics and American Globalism.* Princeton: Princeton University Press, 2007.

——. "Japan in 1990: Limits to Change." *Asian Survey* 31, 1 (January 1991): 21–35.

———. "Kanryō vs. Shomin: Contrasting Dynamics of Conservative Leadership in Postwar Japan." In *Michigan Papers in Japanese Studies No. 1: Political Leadership in Contemporary Japan*, edited by Terry Edward MacDougall, 1–28. Ann Arbor: Center for Japanese Studies, University of Michigan, 1982.

Campbell, John Creighton. *Contemporary Japanese Budget Politics*. Berkeley: University of California Press, 1977.

Cargill, Thomas F., and Michael M. Hutchinson. "Political Business Cycles with Endogenous Election Timing: Evidence from Japan." *Review of Economics and Statistics* 73, 4 (November 1991): 733–39.

Carlile, Lonny E., and Mark C. Tilton, eds. *Is Japan Really Changing Its Ways? Regulatory Reform and the Japanese Economy*. Washington, D.C.: Brookings Institution, 1998.

Cheng, Peter P. "Japanese Interest Group Politics: An Institutional Framework." *Asian Survey* 30, 3 (March 1990): 251–65.

Christensen, Ray. "An Analysis of the 2005 Japanese General Election: Will Koizumi's Political Reforms Endure?" *Asian Survey* 46, 4 (July/August 2006): 497–516.

———. "The Effect of Electoral Reforms on Campaign Practices in Japan: Putting New Wine in the old Bottles." *Asian Survey* 38, 10 (October 1998): 986–1004.

———. "Redistricting in Japan: Lessons for the United States." *Japanese Journal of Political Science* 5,2 (Summer 2004): 259–85.

Christensen, Raymond V., and Paul E. Johnson. "Toward a Context-Rich Analysis of Electoral Systems: The Japanese Example." *American Journal of Political Science* 39, 3 (August 1995): 575–98.

Cook, Karen Schweers, and Margaret Levi, eds. *The Limitis of Rationality*. Chicago: University of Chicago Press, 1990.

Cowhey, Peter F. "Domestic Institutions and the Credibility of International Commitments: Japan and the United States." *International Organization* 47, 2 (Spring 1993): 299–326.

Cox, Gary W., and Emerson Niou. "Seat Bonuses Under the Single Nontransferable Vote System: Evidence from Japan and Taiwan." *Comparative Politics* 26, 2 (January 1994): 221–36.

Curtis, Gerald. "Big Business and Political Influence." In *Modern Japanese Organization and Decision-Making*, edited by Ezra Vogel, 33–70. Berkeley: University of California Press, 1975.

———. *The Japanese Way of Politics*. New York: Columbia University Press, 1988.

———, ed. *Japan's Foreign Policy After the Cold War: Coping with Change*. Armonk, N.Y.: M. E. Sharpe, 1993.

———. *The Logic of Japanese Politics*. New York: Columbia University Press, 1999.

Drifte, Reinhard. *Japan's Foreign Policy*. London: Routledge, 1990.

Duverger, Maurice. *Political Parties: Their Organization and Activity in the Modern State*. New York: Wiley, 1963.

Estévez-Abe, Margarita. "Japan's Shift Toward a Westminster System: A Structural Analysis of the 2005 Lower House Election and Its Aftermath." *Asian Survey* 46, 4 (July/August 2006): 632–51.

———. *Welfare and Capitalism in Post War Japan: Party, Bureaucracy, and Business*. New York: Cambridge University Press, 2008.

Fujimura, Naofumi. "Executive Leadership and Fiscal Discipline: Explaining Political Enterpreneruship in Cases of Japan." *Japanese Journal of Political Science* 10, 2 (Summer 2009): 175–90.

———. "The Power Relationship Between the Prime Minister and Ruling Party Legislators: The Postal Service Privatization Act of 2005 in Japan." *Japanese Journal of Political Science* 8, 2 (August 2007): 233–61.

Fukui, Haruhiro. "Japan: Factionalism in a Dominant Party System." In *Faction Politics: Political Parties and Factionalism in Comparative Perspective*, edited by. Frank P. Belloni and Dennis C. Beller, 43–72. Santa Barbara: ABC-Clio, 1978.

———. "The Liberal Democratic Party Revisited: Continuity and Change in the Party's Structure and Performance." *Journal of Japanese Studies* 10, 2 (Summer 1984): 385–435.

———. *Party in Power*. Berkeley: University of California Press, 1970.

———. "Policy Making in the Japanese Foreign Ministry," in *The Foreign Policy of Modern Japan*, edited by Robert Scalapino, 3–35. Berkeley: University of California Press, 1977.

———. "Studies in Policymaking: Review of the Literature." In *Policymaking in Contemporary Japan*, edited by T. J. Pempel, 22–59. Ithaca: Cornell University Press, 1977.

———. "Tanaka Goes to Peking." In *Policymaking in Contemporary Japan*, edited by T. J. Pempel, 60–102. Ithaca: Cornell University Press, 1977.

———. "Too Many Captains in Japan's Internationalization: Travails at the Foreign Ministry." *Journal of Japanese Studies* 13, 2 (Summer 1987): 359–81.

Fukui, Haruhiro, and Shigeko N. Fukai, "Pork Barrel Politics, Networks and Local Economic Development in Contemporary Japan." *Asian Survey* 36, 3: 268–86.

Gaunder, Alisa. *Political Reform in Japan: Leadership Looming Large*. London: Routledge, 2007.

———, ed. *The Routledge Handbook of Japanese Politics*. London: Routledge, 2011.

Gene, Park. "The Politics of Budgeting in Japan: How Much Do Institutions Matter? *Asian Survey* 50, 5 (September/October 2010): 965–89.

Government Section, Supreme Commander for the Allied Powers. *Political Reorientation of Japan.* Washington, D.C.: U.S. Government Printing Office, 1949.

Haley, John O. "Consensual Governance." In *The Political Economy of Japan*, vol. 3, *Cultural and Social Dynamics*, edited by Shumpei Kumon and Henry Rosovsky, 32–62. Stanford: Stanford University Press, 1992.

——. "Governance by Negotiation: A Reappraisal of Bureaucratic Power in Japan." *Journal of Japanese Studies* 13, 2 (Summer 1987): 343–57.

Hayao, Kenji. "The Japanese Prime Minister and Public Policy." Ph.D. dissertation, University of Michigan, 1990.

——. *The Japanese Prime Minister and Public Policy.* Pittsburgh: University of Pittsburgh Press, 1993.

Hayes, Louis D. *Introduction to Japanese Politics.* New York: Paragon House, 1992.

Higa, Mikio. "The Role of Bureaucracy in Contemporary Japanese Politics." Ph.D. dissertation, University of California, Berkeley, 1968.

Hook, Glenn D., ed. *Decoding Boundaries in Contemporary Japan: The Koizumi Administration and Beyond.* London: Routledge, 2011.

Hosoya, Chihiro, and Tomohito Shinoda, ed. *Redefining the Partnership: The United States and Japan in East Asia.* Lanham, Md.: University Press of America, 1998.

Hrebenar, Ronald J., ed. *The Japanese Party System.* 2d ed. Boulder: Westview Press, 1992.

Igarashi, Takeshi. "Peace-Making and Party Politics: The Formation of Domestic Foreign-Policy System in Postwar Japan." *Journal of Japanese Studies* 11, 2 (Summer 1985): 323–56.

Inoguchi, Takashi. "Japan's Response to the Gulf Crisis: An Analytic Overview." *Journal of Japanese Studies* 17, 2 (Summer 1991): 257–73.

——. "Political Surfing over Economic Waves: A Simple Model of the Japanese Political Economic System." Paper presented at the 11th World Congress of the International Political Science Association, August 11–18, 1979.

Inoguchi, Takashi, and Daniel Okimoto, ed. *The Political Economy of Japan*, vol. 2: *The Changing International Context.* Stanford: Stanford University Press, 1988.

Inoguchi, Takashi, G. John Ikenberry, and Yoichiro Sato, eds. *The U.S.-Japan Security Alliance: Regional Multilateralism.* New York: Palgrave Macmillan, 2011.

Ito, Takatoshi, and Jin Hyuk Park. "Political Business Cycles in the Parliamentary System." *Economic Letters* 27 (1988): 233–38.

Jain, Purnendra, and Takashi Inoguchi. *Japanese Politics Today: Beyond Karaoke Democracy*. New York: St. Martin Press, 1997.

Johnson, Chalmers. "Japan: Who Governs? An Essay on Official Bureaucracy." *Journal of Japanese Studies* 2, 1 (Autumn 1975): 1–28.

———. *MITI and the Japanese Miracle*. Stanford: Stanford University Press, 1982.

Jou, Willy. "Partisan Bias in Japan's Single-Member Districts." *Japanese Journal of Political Science* 10, 1 (March 2009): 1–20.

Kabashima, Ikuo. "Supportive Participation with Economic Growth: The Case of Japan." *World Politics* 36, 3 (April 1984): 329–61.

Kabashima, Ikuo, and Jeffrey Broadbent. "Preference Pluralism: Mass Media and Politics in Japan." *Journal of Japanese Studies* 12, 2 (Summer 1986): 309–38.

Kaplan, Eugene J. *Japan: The Government-Business Relationship*. Washington, D.C.: Department of Commerce, 1972.

Kato, Junko. *The Problem of Bureaucratic Rationality: Tax Politics in Japan*. Princeton: Princeton University Press, 1994.

Katzensten, Peter J. *Rethinking Japanese Security: Internal and External Dimensions*. London: Routledge, 2008.

Kawasaki, Tsuyoshi. *The Politics of Contemporary Japanese Budget Making: Its Structure and Historical Origins*. Working Paper Series No. 58. Toronto: Joint Centre for Asia Pacific Studies, 1993.

Kennedy, John F. *Profiles in Courage*. New York: Harper, 1955.

Kernell, Samuel, ed. *Parallel Politics: Economic Policymaking in Japan and the United States*. Washington, D.C.: Brookings Institution, 1991.

Koelble, Thomas A. "The New Institutionalism in Political Science and Sociology." *Comparative Politics* 27, 2 (January 1995): 231–43.

Kohno, Masaru. *Japan's Postwar Party Politics*. Princeton: Princeton University Press, 1997.

Kohno, Masaru, and Yoshitaka Nishizawa. "A Study of the Electoral Business Cycle in Japan: Elections and Government Spending on Public Construction." *Comparative Politics* 22, 2 (January 1990): 151–66.

Kosai, Yutaka. "The Politics of Economic Management." In *The Political Economy of Japan*, vol. 1, *The Domestic Transformation*, edited by Kozo Yamamura and Yasukichi Yasuba, 555–92. Stanford, California: Stanford University Press, 1987.

Krauss, Ellis S., and Benjamin Nyblade. "'Presidentialization' in Japan? The Prime Minister, Media and Elections in Japan." *British Journal of Political Science*, 35, 2 (April 2005): 357–68.

Krauss, Ellis S., and Robert J. Pekkanen. "Explaining Party Adaptation to Electoral Reform: The Discreet Charm of the LDP?" *Journal of Japanese Studies* 30, 1 (Winter 2004): 1–34.

———. *The Rise and Fall of Japan's LDP: Political Party Organizations as Historical Institutions.* Ithaca: Cornell University Press, 2010.

Kumon, Shumpei. "Japan Faces Its Future: The Political-Economics and Administrative Reform." *Journal of Japanese Studies* 10, 1 (Winter 1984): 143–65.

Kumon, Shumpei, and Henry Rosovsky, eds. *The Political Economy of Japan*, vol. 3, *Cultural and Social Dynamics.* Stanford: Stanford University Press, 1992.

Laakso, Markku, and Rein Taagepera. " 'Effective' Number of Parties: A Measure with Application to West Europe." *Comparative Political Studies* 12, 1 (1979): 3–27.

Lincoln, Edward. *Japan's Unequal Trade.* Washington, D.C.: Brookings Institution, 1990.

MacDougall, Terry Edward, ed. *Political Leadership in Contemporary Japan.* Michigan Papers in Japanese Studies, No. 1. Ann Arbor: Center for Japanese Studies, 1982.

Maeda, Ko. "Factors Behind the Historic Defeat of Japan's Liberal Democratic Party in 2009." *Asian Survey* 50, 5 (September/October 2010): 888–907.

———. "Re-examining the Contamination Effect of Japan's Mixed Electoral System Using the Treatment-Effects Model." *Electoral Studies* 27 (2008): 723–31.

Maki, John, ed. and trans. *Japan's Commission on the Constitution: The Final Report.* Seattle: University of Washington Press, 1980.

March, James G., and Johan P. Olsen. *Rediscovering Institutions: The Organizational Basis of Politics.* New York: Free Press, 1989.

McFarland, Andrew S. *Power and Leadership in Pluralist Systems.* Stanford: Stanford University Press, 1969.

McNelly, Theodore. *Politics and Government in Japan.* 3rd ed. Lanham, Md.: University Press of America, 1972.

Mény, Yves. *Government and Politics in Western Europe: Britain, France, Italy, Germany.* 2nd ed. Oxford: Oxford University Press, 1993.

Mishima, Ko. "Grading Japanese Prime Minister Koizumi's Revolution: How Far Has the LDP's Policymaking Changed?" *Asian Survey* 47, 5 (September/October 2007): 727–48.

Mochizuki, Mike Masato. "Managing and Influencing the Japanese Legislative Process: The Role of Parties and the National Diet." Ph.D. dissertation, Harvard University, 1981.

Moore, Ray A., and Donald L. Robinson. *Partners for Democracy: Crafting the New Japanese State Under MacArthur.* Oxford: Oxford University Press, 2002.

Murakami, Yasusuke. "The Age of New Middle Mass Politics: The Case of Japan." *Journal of Japanese Studies* 8, 1 (Winter 1982): 29–72.

Muramatsu, Michio. "In Search of National Identity: The Politics and Policies of the Nakasone Administration." *Journal of Japanese Studies* 13, 2 (Summer 1987): 271–306.

Muramatsu, Michio, and Ellis Krauss. "The Conservative Policy Line and the Development of Patterned Pluralism." In *The Political Economy of Japan*, vol. 1, *The Domestic Transformation*, edited by Kozo Yamamura and Yasukichi Yasuba, 516–54. Stanford: Stanford University Press, 1987.

Muramatsu, Michio, and Masaru Mabuchi. "Introducing a New Tax in Japan." In *Parallel Politics: Economic Policymaking in Japan and the United States*, edited by Samuel Kernell, 184–207. Washington, D.C.: Brookings Institution, 1991.

Nakane, Chie. *Human Relations in Japan: Summary Translation of "Tate Shakai no Ningen Kankei."* Tokyo: Ministry of Foreign Affairs, 1972.

Neary, Ian. "Serving the Japanese Prime Minister." In *Administering the Summit: Administration of the Core Executive in Developed Countries*, edited by B. Guy Peters, R.A.W. Rhodes, and Vincent Wright, 196–222. New York: St. Martin's Press, 2000.

Neward, Kathleen, ed. *The International Relations of Japan*. London: Macmillan, 1990.

Norimatsu, Satoko. "Hatoyama's Confession: The Myth of Deterrence and the Failure to Move a Marine Base Outside Okinawa." *Asia-Pacific Journal* 9, 3 (February 28, 2011). http://www.japanfocus.org/-Norimatsu-Satoko/3495.

North, Douglass C. *Institutions, Institutional Change and Economic Performance.* Cambridge: Cambridge University Press, 1990.

Oka, Takashi. *Policy Entrepreneurship and Elections in Japan*. London: Routledge, 2011.

Okazaki, Hisahiko. *A Grand Strategy for Japanese Defense.* Lanham, Md.: University Press of America, 1986.

O'Malley, Eoin, and Francesco Cavatorta. "Finding a Party and Losing Some Friends: Overcoming the Weaknesses of the Prime Ministerial Figure in Italy." *Contemporary Politics* 10, 3–4 (September–December 2004): 271–86.

Oros, Andrew L. *Normalizing Japan: Politics, Identity and the Evolution of Security Practice*. Stanford: Stanford University Press, 2008.

Orr, Robert M., Jr. *The Emergence of Japan's Foreign Aid Power.* New York: Columbia University Press, 1990.

Otake, Hideo. "Forces for Political Reform: The Liberal Democratic Party's Young Reformers and Ozawa Ichiro." *Journal of Japanese Studies* 22, 2 (Summer 1996): 269–94.

Ozawa, Ichiro. *Blueprint for a New Japan: The Rethinking of a Nation*. Tokyo: Kodansha International, 1994.

Packard, George R. *Protest in Tokyo: The Security Treaty Crisis of 1960*. Princeton: Princeton University Press, 1966.

Page, Glenn D., ed. *Political Leadership: Readings for an Emerging Field*. New York: Free Press, 1972.

Park, Cheol Hee. "Factional Dynamics in Japan's LDP Since Political Reform: Continuity and Change." *Asian Survey* 41, 3 (May/June 2001): 428–61.

Park, Yung H. *Bureaucrats and Ministers in Contemporary Japanese Government*. Berkeley: Institute of East Asian Studies, University of California, 1986.

Patrick, Hugh, and Henry Rovosvky. *Asia's New Giant*. Washington, D.C.: Brookings, 1976.

Patterson, Dennis, and Ko Maeda. "Prime Ministerial Popularity and the Changing Electoral Fortunes of Japan's Liberal Democratic Party." *Asian Survey* 47, 3 (May/June 2007): 415–33.

Pempel, T. J. "Between Pork and Productivity: The Collapse of the Liberal Democratic Party." *Journal of Japanese Studies* 36, 2 (Summer 2010): 227–54.

——. "The Bureaucratization of Policy making in Postwar Japan." *American Journal of Political Science* 18 (November 1987): 271–306.

——. "Organizing for Efficiency: The Higher Civil Service in Japan." In *Bureaucrats and Policy Making: A Comparative Overview*, edited by Ezra N. Suleiman, 72–106. New York: Holms and Meier, 1984.

——, ed. *Policymaking in Contemporary Japan*. Ithaca: Cornell University Press, 1977.

——. *Regime Shift: Comparative Dynamics of the Japanese Political Economy*. Ithaca: Cornell University Press, 1998.

——. "The Unbundling of 'Japan, Inc.': The Changing Dynamics of Japanese Policy Formation." *Journal of Japanese Studies* 13, 2 (Summer 1987): 271–306.

——, ed. *Uncommon Democracies: The One-Party Dominant Regime*. Ithaca: Cornell University Press, 1990.

Pempel, T. J., and Keiichi Tsunekawa. "Corporatism Without Labor? The Japanese Anomaly." In *Trend Toward Corporatist Intermediation*, edited by Philippe C. Schumitter and Gerherd Lehmbruch, 231–69. London: Sage, 1979.

Powell, Walter W., and Paul J. DiMaggio, eds. *The Insitutionalism in Organizational Anaysis*. Chicago: University of Chicago Press, 1991.

Pyle, Kenneth B. "In Pursuit of a Grand Design: Nakasone Between the Past and the Future." *Journal of Japanese Studies* 13, 2 (Summer 1987): 243–70.

———. *Japan Rising: The Resurgence of Japanese Power and Purpose*. New York: Century Foundation, 2007.

Ramseyer, J. Mark, and Frances McCall Rosenbluth. *Japan's Political Marketplace*. Cambridge: Harvard University Press, 1993.

Reed, Steven. "Duverger's Law Is Working in Japan." *Japanese Journal of Electoral Studies* 22 (2007): 96–106.

———. "Structure and Behavior: Extending Duverger's Law to the Japanese Case." *British Journal of Political Science* 20 (1990): 335–56.

Reed, Steven, Kenneth Mori McElwain, and Kay Shimizu, ed. *Political Change in Japan: Electoral Behavior, Party Realignment and the Koizumi Reforms*. Stanford: Walter H. Shorenstein Asia-Pacific Research Center, 2009.

Reed, Steven, and Ethan Scheiner. "Electoral Incentives and Policy Preferences: Mixed Motives behind Party Defections in Japan." *British Journal of Political Science* 33, 3 (July 2003): 469–90.

Richardson, Bradley M., and Scott C. Flanagan. *Politics in Japan*. Boston: Little, Brown, 1984.

Richardson, Bradley M., and Dennis Patterson. "Political Traditions and Political Change: The Significance of Postwar Japanese Politics for Political Science." *Annual Review of Political Science* 4 (June 2001): 93–115.

Rosenbluth, Frances McCall. *Financial Politics in Contemporary Japan*. Ithaca: Cornell University Press, 1989.

Rosenbluth, Frances McCall, and Michael F. Thies. *Japan Transformed: Political Change and Economic Restructuring*. Princeton: Princeton University Press, 2010.

Rowell, Milo E. "Report of Preliminary Studies and Recommendations of Japanese Constitution," December 6, 1945. General Headquarters, Supreme Commander for the Allied Powers.

Saito, Shiro. *Japan at the Summit: Japan's Role in the Western Alliance and Asian Pacific Cooperation*. London: Routledge, 1990.

Samuels, Richard. *Machiavelli's Children: Leaders and Their Legacies in Italy and Japan*. Ithaca: Cornell University Press, 2003.

———. *Securing Japan: Tokyo's Grand Strategy and the Future of East Asia*. Ithaca: Cornell University Press, 2007.

Sartori, Giovanni. *Parities and Party Systems: A Framework for Analysis*. Cambridge: Cambridge University Press, 1976.

Scalapino, Robert A. *Democracy and the Party Movement in Prewar Japan*. Berkeley: University of California Press, 1953.

———, ed. *The Foreign Policy of Modern Japan*. Berkeley: University of California Press, 1977.

Scalapino, Robert A., and Masumi Junnosuke. *Parties and Politics in Contemporary Japan*. Berkeley: University of California Press, 1962.

Schoppa, Leonard J. "Zoku Power and LDP Power: Case Study of the Zoku Role in Education Policy." *Journal of Japanese Studies* 17,1 (Winter 1991): 79–106.

Schlesinger, Jacob M. *Shadow Shoguns: The Rise and Fall of Japan's Postwar Political Machine*. New York: Simon & Schuster, 1997.

Schoff, James, L., ed. *Crisis Management in Japan and the United States: Creating Opportunities for Cooperation amid Dramatic Change*. Dulles, Md.: Brassey's, 2004.

Schwartz, Frank J. *Advice & Consent: The Politics of Consultation in Japan*. New York: Cambridge University Press, 1998.

Shibusawa, Masahide. *Japan and the Asia Pacific Region*. London: Croom Helm, 1984.

Shinoda, Tomohito. "Becoming More Realistic in the Post–Cold War: Japan's Changing Media and Public Opinion on National Security," *Japanese Journal of Political Science* 8, 2 (Fall 2007): 171–90.

——. "The Costs and Benefits of U.S.-Japan Alliance from the Japanese Perspective." In *The U.S.-Japan Security Alliance: Regional Multilateralism*, edited by John Ikenberry, Yoichiro Sato, and Takashi Inoguchi. New York: Palgrave Macmillan, 2011.

——(with Ian Holliday). "Governing from the Centre: Core Executive Capacity in Britain and Japan,", *Japanese Journal of Political Science* 3 (2002): 91–111.

——. "Japan." In *Party Politics and Democratic Development in East and Southeast Asia*, vol. 2, edited by Wolfgang Sachsenroder, 88–131. Brookfield: Ashgate, 1998.

——. "Japan's Decision Making Under the Coalition Governments." *Asian Survey* 38, 7 (July 1998): 703–23.

——. "Japan's Cabinet Secretariat and Its Emergence as Core Executive," *Asian Survey* 45, 5 (September/October 2005): 800–821.

——. "Japan's Failed Experiment: The DPJ and Institutional Changes for Political Leadership." *Asian Survey* 52, 5 (September/October 2012): 799–821.

——. "Japan's Parliamentary Confrontation on the Post-Cold War National Security Policies," *Japanese Journal of Political Science* 10, 3 (Fall 2009): 267–87.

——. "Japan's Political Changes and Their Impact on U.S.-Japan Relations." In *Redefining the Partnership: The United States and Japan in East Asia*, edited by Chihiro Hosoya and Tomohito Shinoda, 43–58. Lanham, Md.: University Press of America, 1998.

——. "Japan's Political Leadership: The Prime Minister's Power, Style and Conduct of Reform." In *Asian Economic and Political Issues*, vol. 2, edited by Frank Columbus, 1–31. New York: Nova, 1999.

——. "Japan's Top-Down Policy Process to Dispatch the SDF to Iraq," *Japanese Journal of Political Science* 7, 1 (April 2006): 71–91.

——. *Koizumi Diplomacy: Japan's Kantei Approach in Foreign and Defense Affairs.* Seattle: University of Washington Press, 2007.

——. "Koizumi's Top-Down Leadership in the Anti-Terrorism Legislation: The Impact of Institutional Changes," *SAIS Review* (Winter/Spring 2003): 19–34.

——. "LDP Factions: Their Power and Culture." *Bulletin*, Japan-American Society of Washington 25, 2 (February 1990): 4–7.

——. *Leading Japan: The Role of the Prime Minister.* Westport, Conn.: Praeger, 1998.

——. "Ozawa Ichiro as an Actor in Foreign Policy Making." *Japan Forum* 16, 1 (2004): 37–62.

——. "The Prime Ministerial Leadership." In *Handbook of Japanese Politics*, edited by Alisa Gaunter, 48–59. London: Routledge, 2011.

——. "Searching for a Dream Plan: Two-Level Game Analysis of the Futenma Relocation Issue Under the Hatoyama Cabinet." *Japanese Journal of Political Science* (forthcoming).

——. "Stronger Political Leadership and the Shift in Policy-making Boundaries in Japan." In *Decoding Boundaries in Contemporary Japan: The Koizumi Administration and Beyond*, edited by Glenn D. Hook, 101–19. London: Routledge, 2011.

——. "Truth Behind LDP's Loss." *Washington Japan Journal* 2 (Fall 1993): 26–28

Steinmo, Sven, Kathleen Thelen, and Frank Longstreth, eds. *Structuring Politics: Historical Institutionalism in Comparative Analysis.* Cambridge: Cambridge University Press, 1992.

Suleiman, Ezra N., ed. *Bureaucrats and Policy Making: A Comparative Overview.* New York: Holms and Meier, 1984.

Thayer, Nathaniel B. *How the Conservatives Rule Japan.* Princeton: Princeton University Press, 1969.

Tsebelis, George. *Veto Players: How Political Institutions Work.* Princeton: Princeton University Press, 2002.

Tsurutani, Taketsugu. "The LDP in Transition? Mass Membership Participation in Party Leadership Selection." *Asian Survey* 20, 8 (August 1980): 844–59.

Tsurutani, Taketsugu, and Jack B. Gabbert. *Chief Executives: National Political Leadership in the United States, Mexico, Great Britain, Germany, and Japan.* Pullman: Washington State University Press, 1992.

Van Wolferen, Karel G. *The Enigma of Japanese Power.* New York: Knopf, 1989.

——. "The Japan Problem." *Foreign Affairs* 65 (Winter 1987): 288–303.

Vogel, Ezra F., ed. *Modern Japanese Organization and Decision-Making.* Berkeley: University of California Press, 1975.

Yayama, Taro. "The Recruit Scandal: Learning from the Causes of Corruption." *Journal of Japanese Studies* 16, 1 (Winter 1990): 93–114.

Young, Jeffrey D. *Japan's Prime Minister: Selection Process, 1991 Candidates, and Implications for the United States.* CRS Report 91–695 F. Congressional Research Service, Library of Congress, September 24, 1991.

JAPANESE LANGUAGE SOURCES

Abe Hitoshi, Shindō Muneyuki, and Kawahito Tadashi. *Gaisetsu Gendai Nihon no Seiji* [Introduction to contemporary Japanese politics]. Tokyo: Tokyo Daigaku Shuppan-kai, 1990.

Abe Shinzō. "Tatakau Seijika Sengen: Kono Kuni no tameni Inochi wo Suteru" [Declaration to fight as a politician: Willing stake my life for this country]. *Bungei Shunjū*, September 2006.

———. *Utsukushii Kuni e* [To a beautiful country]. Tokyo: Bunshun Shinsho, 2006.

Abe Shinzō and Okazaki Hisahiko. *Kono Kuni wo Mamoru Ketsui* [Determined to protect this country]. Tokyo: Fusō-sha, 2004.

Akarui Senkyo Suishin Kyōkai. *Dai 22-kai Sangiin Tsūjō Senkyo no Jittai: Chōsa Kekka no Gaiyō* [The situation of the 22nd upper house election: Outline of survey results]. March 2011.

———. *Dai 44-kai Shūgiin Sōsenkyo no Jittai: Chōsa Kekka no Gaiyō* [The situation of the 44th lower house general election: Outline of survey results]. March 2006.

———. *Dai 45-kai Shūgiin Sōsenkyo no Jittai: Chōsa Kekka no Gaiyō* [The situation of the 44th lower house general election: Outline of survey results]. March 2010.

Arai Shunzō and Morita Hajime. *Bunjin Saisho Ōhira Masayoshi* [The intellectual prime minister Ōhira Masayoshi]. Tokyo: Shunjū-sha, 1982.

Araki Toshio, Hasuike Minoru, Kawato Sadafumi, and Aiuchi Toshikazu, eds. *Tōhyō Kōdō ni okeru Renzoku to Henka* [Continuity and changes in voting behavior]. Tokyo: Bokutakusha, 1983.

Asahi Journal Henshū-bu. *Rikurūtogēto no Kakushin* [The core of the Recruit-gate]. Tokyo: Suzusawa Shoten, 1989.

Asahi Shimbun Seiji-bu. *Takeshita-ha Shihai* [Control by the Takeshita faction]. Tokyo: Asahi Shimbun-sha, 1992.

Asahi Shimbun Seiken Shuzai Sentā, ed. *Minshutō Seiken 100-nichi no Shinsō* [The truth of 100 days under the DPJ government]. Tokyo: Asahi Shimbun-sha, 2010.

Asahi Shimbun-sha Seronchōsa-shitu. *Naikaku Shijiritsu Seitō Shijiritsu* [The approval rate for cabinets and political parties]. Tokyo: Asahi Shimbun-sha, April 1996.

——. *Takeshita Seiken no Hōkai: Rikurūto Jiken to Seiji Kaikaku* [The collapse of the Takeshita administration: The Recruit scandal and political reform]. Tokyo: Asahi Shimbun-sha, 1989.

Asano Masahiko. *Shimin Shakai ni okeru Seido Kaikaku: Senkyo Kōhosha Rikurūto* [System reform in civil society: Election candidate recruitment]. Tokyo: Keiō Daigaku Shuppankai, 2006.

Asō Tarō. "Nihon Gaikō: Shiren to Tassei no Jūichi-nichikan" [Japan's diplomacy: Eleven days of challenge and achievement]. *Bungei Shunjū*, September 2006.

Baku, Choruhī [Park Cheol Hee]. *Daigishi no Tsukurarekata: Shōsenkyoku no Senkyo Senryaku* [How lower house members are made: Electoral strategy in the single-member districts]. Tokyo: Bunshun Shinsho, 2000.

Doi Takako. "Watashi no Rirekisho" [My personal history]. *Nihon Keizai Shimbun*, September 1992.

Eda Kenji. *Dare no Sei de Kaikaku wo Ushinau noka.* [Whose fault is it to lose reform]. Tokyo: Shinchō-sha, 1999.

Eda Kenji and Nishino Tomohiko. *Kaikaku Seiken ga Kowareru Toki* [The time when the reform cabinet collapses]. Tokyo: Nikkei BP-sha, 2002.

Fujimoto Kazumi, ed. *Kokkai Kinō Ron: Kokkai no Shikumi to Un'ei* [Arguments for the functional diet: The mechanism and operation of the Diet]. Tokyo: Hōgaku Shoin, 1990.

Fujimoto Takao. *Fujimoto Takao no Daijin Hōkoku* [Report of Minister Fujimoto Takao]. Tokyo: Planet Shuppan, 1989.

Fukuda Hiroshi. *Seshū Seijika ga Naze Umarerunoka?* [Why are there hereditary politicians?]. Tokyo: Nikkei BP-sha, 2009.

Fukuda Takeo. Interview. "Waga Shushō Jidai" [My time as the prime minister]. *Chūō Kōron* (October 1980):291–95.

——. *Kaiko 90 nen* [Memoir of 90 years]. Tokyo: Iwanami Shoten, 1995.

——. "Watashi no Rirekisho" [My personal history]. *Nihon Keizai Shimbun*, January 1993.

Fukuda Yasuo. "Hajimete Kataru Dairenritsu to Sōri no Shikaku" [First talk on the great coalition and the qualifications to become prime minister]. *Bungei Shunjū*, June 2011.

Fukuoka Masayuki. *Nihon no Seiji Fūdo: Niigata Sanku ni Miru Nihon Seiji no Genkei* [Japan's political culture: The Niigata third district as Japan's political prototype]. Tokyo: Gakuyō Shobō, 1985.

Fukushima Genpatsujiko Dokuritsu Kenshō Iinkai. *Chōsa Kenshō Hōkokusho* [Research and investigation Report]. Tokyo: Nippon Saiken Initiative Zaidan, 2012.

Fukushima Mizuho. *Meisō Seiken tono Tatakai* [Fight against the stray government]. Tokyo: Asukī Shinsho, 2011.

Funabashi Yōichi. *Dōmei Hyōryu* [Floating Alliance]. Tokyo: Iwanami Shoten, 1997.

Furui Yoshimi. *Shushō no Shokumu Kengen* [The official authority of the prime minister]. Tokyo: Makino Shuppan, 1983.

Furukawa Teijirō. *Kasumigaseki Hanseiki* [Half my life in Kasumigaseki]. Saga: Saga Shimbun-sha, 2005.

Gotōda Masaharu. . *Jō to Ri* [Emotion and logics]. Tokyo: Kōdansha, 1998.

———. *Naikaku Kanbō Chōkan* [Chief cabinet secretary]. Tokyo: Kōdansha, 1989.

———. *Sasaeru Ugokasu* [To support and mobilize]. Tokyo: Nihon Keizai Shimbun-sha, 1991.

———. *Seiji Towa Nanika* [What is politics?]. Tokyo: Kōdansha, 1988.

———. *Sei to Kan* [Politics and bureaucracy]. Tokyo: Kōdansha, 1994.

Hanamura Nihachirō. *Seizaikai Paipu Yaku Hanseiki* [My life as a channel between the political and business worlds]. Tokyo: Tokyo Shinbun, 1990.

Hara Eiji. *Kanryō no Retorikku: Kasumigaseki wa Naze Meisō Surunoka* [Bureaucratic rhetoric: Why the Kasumigaseki wanders astray]. Tokyo: Shinchō-sha, 2010.

Hara Yoshihisa. *Kishi Nobusuke: Kensei no Seijika* [Kishi Nobusuke: The politician of power]. Tokyo: Iwanami Shinsho, 1995.

Hasegawa Yukihiro. *Kanryō tono Shitō 700-nichi* [700 days of desperate struggle with the bureaucrats]. Tokyo: Kōdan-sha, 2008.

———. *Kantei Haiboku* [The defeat of the Prime Minister's Office]. Tokyo: Kōdan-sha, 2010.

———. *Nihonkoku no Shōtai* [What Japan really is]. Tokyo: Kōdan-sha, 2009.

Hashimoto Ryūtarō. *Seiken Dakkairon* [To regain power]. Tokyo: Kodansha, 1994.

Hata Yasuko. *Shushō Kotei* [The prime minister's official residence]. Tokyo: Tokyo Shinbunsha, 1996.

Hatoyama Yukio. "Watashi no Seiji Tetsugaku" [My political philosophy]. *Voice* (September 2009).

Hayano Tōru. *Nihon Seiji no Kessan: Kakuei vs. Koizumi* [Japan's political settlement: Kakuei vs. Koizumi]. Tokyo: Kōdansha Gendai Shinsho, 2004.

———. *Renritsu Kōbō Monogatari* [The tale of battle under the coalition]. Tokyo: Asahi Shimbun-sha, 1999.

Hayashi Shigeru and Tsuji Kiyoaki, ed. *Nihon Naikaku Shiroku* [The history of the Japanese cabinet]. Tokyo: Dai-ichi Hōki, 1981.

Hayashi Yoshimasa and Tsumura Keisuke. *Kokkai Giin no Shigoto: Shokugyō toshite no Seiji* [The work of Diet members: Politics as profession]. Tokyo, Chūkō Shinsho, 2011.

Hirano Sadao. *Jiyutō no Chōsen* [Challenge of the Liberal Party]. Tokyo: President-sha, 1998.

———. *Kōmeitō Sōkagakkai to Nihon* [Kōmeitō Sōkagakkai to Nihon]. Tokyo: Kōdan-sha, 2005.

———. *Ozawa Ichirō tono Nijūnen* [Twenty Years with Ozawa Ichirō]. Tokyo: President-sha, 1996.

———. *Waga Tomo Ozawa Ichirō* [My friend Ozawa Ichirō]. Tokyo: Gentō-sha, 2009.

Hirasawa Katsuei. *Seijika wa Rakuna Shōbai Jyanai* [Being a politician is not an easy business]. Tokyo: Shūei-sha, 2007.

Hirata Oriza and Matsui Kōji. *Sōri no Genkō: Atarashii Seiji no Kotoba wo Mosakushita 266-nichi* [The manuscript of the prime minister: 266 days of exploring new political wording]. Tokyo: Iwanami Shoten, 2011.

Hironaka Yoshimichi. *Miyazawa Seiken 644 nichi* [The Miyazawa administration's 644 days]. Tokyo: Gyosei, 1998.

Hirose Michisada. "Gyōsei Kaikaku to Jimintō" [Administrative reform and the LDP]. *Sekai* (August 1981): 245–57.

———. *Hojokin to Seikentō* [Subsidies and the government party]. Tokyo: Asahi Shimbun-sha, 1981.

———. *Seiji to Kane* [Politics and money]. Tokyo: Iwanami Shinsho, 1989.

Hiwatari Nobuhiro and Saitō Jun. *Seitō Seiji no Konmei to Seiken Kōtai* [The chaos of party politics and the power shift]. Tokyo: Tokyo Daigaku Shuppankai, 2011.

Honzawa Jirō. *Jimintō Habatsu* [LDP factions]. Tokyo: Pīpuru-sha, 1990.

Hori Shigeru. *Sengo Seiji no Oboegaki* [Memorandum of postwar politics]. Tokyo: Mainichi Shimbun, 1975.

Horie Fukashi and Umemura Mitsuhiro, eds. *Tōhyō Kōdō to Seiji Ishiki* [Voting behavior and political consciousness]. Tokyo: Keiō Tsūshin, 1986.

Hoshi Hiroshi. *Jimintō to Sengo: Seikentō no Gojūnen* [LDP and postwar: 50 years of the ruling party]. Tokyo: Kōdansha Gendai Shinsho, 2005.

Hosokawa Morihiro. *Naishōroku: Hosokwa Sōri Daijin Nikki* [Self-review: The diary of Prime Minister Hosokawa]. Tokyo: Nikkei Shibun Shuppan-sha, 2010.

Hosokawa Morihiro and Iwakuni Tetsundo. *Hina no Ronri* [The logic of the local community]. Tokyo: Kōbunsha, 1991.

Hosoya Chihiro and Shinoda Tomohito. *Shin Jidai no Nichibei Kankei* [A new era of U.S.-Japan relations]. Tokyo: Yūhikaku, 1998.

Ichikawa Taichi. *"Seshū" Daigishi no Kenkyū* [Study on hereditary Diet members]. Tokyo: Nihon Keizai Shimbun-sha, 1990.

Igarashi Fumihiko. *Kore ga Minshutō da* [This is the DPJ]. Tokyo: Taiyō Kikaku Shuppan, 1996.

Igarashi Kōzō. *Kantei no Rasen Kaidan* [The spiral staircase of the Prime Minister's Office]. Tokyo: Gyōsei, 1997.

Iijima Isao. *Jitsuroku Koizumi Gaikō* [True record of Koizumi diplomacy]. Tokyo: Nihon Keizai Shimbun-sha, 2007.

———. *Kanryō* [The bureaucracy]. Tokyo: Seishi-sha, 2012.

———. *Koizumi Kantei Hiroku* [Secret story of the Prime Minister's Office under Koizumi]. Tokyo: Nihon Keizai Shimbun-sha, 2006.

Iio Jun. *Mineika no Seiji Katei: Rinchō-gata Kaikaku no Seika to Genkai* [Political process of privatization: The achievements and limitations of the Rinchō-style reform]. Tokyo: Tokyo Daigaku Shuppan-kai, 1993.

———. *Nihon no Tōchi Kōzō: Kanryō Naikakusei kara Giin Naikakusei e* [Japanese governing system: From bureaucratic cabinet system to parliamentary system]. Tokyo: Chūkō Shinsho, 2007.

Ikeda Hayato. *Kinkō Zaisei* [Balanced budget]. Tokyo: Jitsugyō no Nihon-sha, 1952.

Imai Ryōsuke. "Naze Jimintō wa Hitoriku de Zanpai Shitanoka" [Why did the LDP lose horribly in the singe-seat districts?]. *Chūō Kōron*, October 2007: 190–99.

Imai Takeru. *Giin Naikaku-sei* [Parliamentary system]. Tokyo: Burēn Shuppan, 1991.

Inoguchi Takashi. *Gendai Nihon Seiji Keizai no Kōzu* [The composition of contemporary Japanese political economy]. Tokyo: Tōyō Keizai Shinpō, 1983.

———. *Kokka to Shakai* [The nation and the society]. Tokyo: Tokyo Daigaku Shuppan-kai, 1988.

Inoguchi Takashi and Iwai Tomoaki. *"Zoku Giin" no Kenkyū* [Study on "Zoku members"]. Tokyo: Nihon Keizai Shimbun-sha, 1987.

Inose Naoki. *Dōro no Kenryoku: Dōro Kōdan Mineika no Kōbō 1000-nichi* [Power on the road: 1,000-days of battles over the privatization of the road public corporations]. Tokyo: Bungei Shunjū, 2003.

Iokibe Makoto, Itō Motoshige, and Yakushiji Katsuyuki, eds. *Mori Yoshirō: Jimintō to Seiken Kōtai* [Mori Yoshirō: The LDP and power shift]. Tokyo: Asahi Shimbun-sha, 2007.

———. *Ozawa Ichirō: Seiken Dasshuron* [Ozawa Ichirō: Argument for taking over the government]. Tokyo: Asahi Shimbun-sha, 2006.

Iseri Hirofumi. *Hanbatsu Saihensei* [The reorganization of factions]. Tokyo: Chuko Shinsho, 1983.

Ishida Hirohide. *Ishibashi Seiken 71 nichi* [71 days of the Ishibashi administration]. Tokyo: Gyōsei Mondai Kenkyū-sho, 1985.

Ishihara Nobuo. *Kan Kaku Arubeshi* [The way the bureaucrats should be]. Tokyo: Shōgakukan Bunko, 1998.

———. *Kantei 2668 nichi: Seisaku Kettei no Butaiura* [2,668 days at the prime minister's residence: Behind the scenes of decision making]. Tokyo: NHK Shuppan, 1995.

———. *Kengen no Daiidō* [The major transfer of authority]. Tokyo: Kanki Shuppan, 2001.

———. *Shushō Kantei no Ketsudan* [The decisions of the prime minister's residence]. Tokyo: Chūō Kōron-sha, 1997.

Ishikawa Masumi. *Dēta Sengo Seijishi* [Data on postwar political history]. Tokyo: Iwanami Shoten, 1984.

Ishikawa Masumi and Hirose Michisada. *Jimintō: Chōki Shihai no Kōzō* [The truth about the Prime Minister's Office: The structure of long reign]. Tokyo: Iwanami Shoten, 1989.

Isshiki Masaharu. *Nanika no Tame ni sengoku38 no Kokuhaku* [For something, confession of sengoku38]. Tokyo: Asahi Shinbun Shuppan, 2011.

Itō Atsuo. *Minshutō: Yabō to Yagō no Mekanizumu* [The DPJ: The mechanism of ambition and illicit liaison]. Tokyo: Shinchō Shinsho, 2008.

———. *Seiji no Sūji: Nihonichi Hara ga Tatsu Data Book* [Numbers in politics: The most irritating data book]. Tokyo: Shinchō Shinsho, 2005.

———. *Seitō Hōkai: Nagatachō no Ushinawareta Jūnen* [The collapse of the political parties: Lost ten years of Nagatachō]. Tokyo: Shinchō Shinsho, 2003.

Itō Masaya. *Ikeda Hayato Sono Sei to Shi* [Ikeda Hayato: His life and death]. Tokyo: Shiseidō, 1966.

Itō Nobuhiro. "Kokka Kōmuin Seido Kaikaku no Keii to Dōkō" [The history and transition of the national public servant system reform]. *Kokuritsu Kokkai Toshokan Issue Brief* 671, March 3, 2010.

Itō Tatsuya. *Sōri Kantei no Shinjitsu: Ozawa Minshutō tono Tatakai* [The truth of the Prime Minister's Office: Battle with Ozawa's DPJ]. Tokyo: PHP Kenkyūso, 2010.

Iwai Tomoaki. *Rippō Katei* [The legislative process]. Tokyo: Tokyo Daigaku Shuppan-kai, 1988.

——. *"Seiji Shikin" no Kenkyū* [Study on the "political fund"]. Tokyo: Nihon Keizai Shimbun, 1990.

Iwai Tomoaki and Inoguchi Takashi. "Zeisei-zoku no Seiji Rikigaku" [Political dynamics of tax *zoku*]. *Chūō Kōron* (March 1987): 96–106.

Jiyūminshutō, ed. *Ketsudan Anotoki Watashi wa Kōshita: Jimintō Sōri, Sōsai, Kanbō Chōkan ga Kataru* [Decision I made at that time: LDP prime ministers, presidents, and chief cabinet secretaries talk] (Tokyo: Chūō Kōron Jigyō Shuppan, 2006).

Jiyūminshutō Senkyo Taisaku Honbu, ed. *Sōsenkyo Jissen no Tebiki* [Practical guide for general elections]. Tokyo: Jiyūminshutō, 2008.

Kabashima Ikuo. *Seiji Sanka* [Political participation]. Tokyo: Tokyo Daigaku Shuppan-kai, 1988.

——. *Seiken Kōtai to Yūkensha no Taido Henyō* [Power shift and the changes of voters' behavior]. Tokyo: Bokutakusha, 1998.

——. *Sengo Seiji no Kiseki: Jimintō System no Keisei to Henyō* [The track of postwar politics: The formation and changes of the LDP System]. Tokyo Iwanami Shoten, 2004.

Kabashima Ikuo and Sugawara Taku. "Kōmei ga Dochira wo Erabuka de Seiken wa Kawaru" [Kōmei's choice will change the government]. *Chūō Kōron* (January 2004): 90–99.

Kabashima Ikuo and Yamada Masahiro. "Kōenkai to Nihon no Seiji" [*Kōenkai* and Japanese politics]. *Nenpō Seijigaku* (1994): 211–31.

Kaifu Toshiki. *Seiji to Kane: Kaifu Toshiki Kaikoroku* [Politics and money: Memoir of Kaifu Toshiki]. Tokyo: Shinchō Shinsho, 2010.

Kaizuka Keimei et al., , eds. *Zeisei Kaikaku no Chōryū* [The trend for tax reform]. Tokyo: Yūhikaku, 1990.

Kakizaki Meiji and Hisae Masahiko. *Kūhaku no Saishō: "Team Abe" ga otta Risō to Genjitsu* [Empty prime minister: Ideal that "Team Abe" pursued and reality]. Tokyo: Kōdan-sha, 2007.

Kan Naoto. *Daijin Zōhoban* [The minister, revised edition]. Tokyo: Iwanami Shinsho, 2009.

——. "Sōri Kan Naoto 3.11-go wo Kataru" [Prime Minister Kan Naoto talks about the post 3.11]. *Shūkan Asahi*, August 19, 2011:18–23.

Kanamori Hisao, ed. *Sengo Keizai no Kiseki: Sairon Keizai Hakusho* [Trace of postwar economy: Reexamining the Economic White Papers]. Tokyo: Chūō Keizai-sha, 1990.

Kanemaru Shin. *Tachiwaza Newaza* [Fighting in various ways]. Tokyo: Nihon Keizai Shimbun-sha, 1988.

Kataoka Hiromitsu. *Naikaku no Kinō to Hosa Kikō* [The function of the cabinet and the supporting organizations]. Tokyo: Seibun-dō, 1982.

Katō Junko. *Zeisei Kaikaku to Kanryōsei* [Tax reform and the bureaucracy]. Tokyo: Tokyo Daigaku Shuppankai, 1997.

Katō Shūjirō. *Nihon no Senkyo: Nani wo Kaereba Seiji ga Kawarunoka* [Japan's election: What do we need to change in order to change politics]. Tokyo: Chūkō Shinsho, 2003.

Kawaguchi Hiroyuki. *Kanryō Shihai no Kōzō* [The mechanism of bureaucratic control]. Tokyo: Kōdan-sha, 1987.

Kawakita Takao. *Ōkurasho: Kanryō Kikō no Chōten* [The Ministry of Finance: The top of the bureaucracy]. Tokyo: Kōdan-sha, 1989.

Kawato Sadafumi. "Jimintō ni okeru Yakushoku no Seidoka" [The institutionalization of rules governing promotion in the LDP]. *Hōgaku* 59, 6 (1996): 34–46.

———. *Senkyo Seido to Seitō Shisutemu* [Electoral system and political party system]. Tokyo: Bokutaku-sha, 1989.

Kawato Sadafumi, Yoshino Takashi, Hirano Hiroshi, and Katō Junko. *Gendai no Seitō to Senkyo* [Contemporary political parties and election]. Tokyo: Yūhikaku, 2011.

Kawauchi Issei. *Ōhira Seiken 554 nichi* [The Ōhira administration: 554 Days]. Tokyo: Gyōsei Mondai Kenkyū-sho, 1982.

Kishi Nobusuke. *Kishi Nobusuke Kaisō-roku* [Memoirs of Kishi Nobusuke]. Tokyo: Kōsaido, 1983.

Kishi Nobusuke, Yatsugi Kazuo, and Itō Takashi. *Kishi Nobusuke no Kaisō* [Memories of Kishi Nobusuke]. Tokyo: Bungei Shunjū, 1981.

Kishimoto Kōichi. *Gendai Seiji Kenkyū: "Nagata-chō" no Ayumi to Mekanizumu* [Study on contemporary politics: Development and mechanism of Nagata-chō]. Tokyo: Gyōken, 1988.

Kishiro Yasuyuki. *Jimintō Zeisei Chōsa-kai* [The LDP Tax System Research Council]. Tokyo: Tōyō Keizai Shinpō-sha, 1985.

Kitanishi Makoto and Yamada Hiroshi. *Gendai Nihon no Seiji* [Contemporary Japanese politics]. Tokyo: Hōritsu Bunka-sha, 1983.

Kitaoka Shinichi. "Nidai Seitōsei e no Ayumi wo Kangei suru" [I welcome the step toward a two-party system]. *Chūō Kōron* (January 2004): 78–88.

Kiyomiya Ryū. *Fukuda Seiken 714 nichi* [The Fukuda administration: 714 days]. Tokyo: Gyōsei Mondai Kenkyū-sho, 1984.

Kobayashi Yoshiaki. *Gendai Nihon no Senkyo* [Contemporary Japanese elections]. Tokyo: Tokyo Daigaku Shuppan-kai, 1991.

——. *Seido Kaikaku Ikō no Nihongata Minshushugi:Senkyo Kōdō ni okeru Ren- zoku to Henka* [Japanese-style democracy after the political reform: Continu- ity and change in electoral behavior]. Tokyo: Bokutaku-sha, 2008.

Koga Junichirō. *Seiji Kenkin: Jittai to Ronri* [Political contribution: Reality and logic]. Tokyo Iwanami Shinsho, 2004.

Koike Yuriko. *Joshi no Honkai* [Spirit of a woman]. Tokyo: Bunshun Shinsho, 2007.

Kōno Masaru. *Seido* [Institution]. Tokyo: Tokyo Daigaku Shuppan-kai, 2000.

Kōno Tarō. *Watashi ga Jimintō wo Tatenaosu* [I will put the LDP back again]. Tokyo: Yōsen-sah, 2010.

Kōsaka Masataka. *Saishō Yoshida Shigeru* [Prime Minister Yoshida Shigeru]. Tokyo: Chūō Kōron-sha, 1968.

Kubo Wataru. *Renritsu Seiken no Shinjitsu* [The truth about the coalition govern- ments]. Tokyo: Yomiuri Shinbunsha, 1998.

Kume Ikuo. *Rōdō Seiji: Sengo Seiji no Naka no Rōdō Kumiai* [Labor politics: Labor unions in postwar politics]. Tokyo: Chūkō Shinsho, 2005.

Kurihara Yūkō. *Ōhira Moto Sōri to Watashi* [Former Prime Minister Ōhira and me]. Tokyo: Kōsai-dō, 1990.

Kuriyama Takakazu. *Nichibei Dōmei: Hyoryu kara no Dakkyaku* [The Japan-U.S. Alliance: From Drift to Revitalization]. Tokyo: Nihon Keizai Shinbunsha, 1997.

Kusuda Minoru. *Shuseki Hishokan: Satō Sōri tono Jūnenkan* [Chief secretary: Ten years with Prime Minister Satō]. Tokyo: Bungei Shunjū, 1975.

——, ed. *Satō Seiken: 2797 nichi* [The Sato administration: 2,797 days]. Vols. 1 and 2. Tokyo: Gyōsei Mondai Kenkyū-sho, 1983.

Magosaki Ukeru. *Nihon no Kokkyō Mondai: Senkaku, Takeshima, Hoppō Ryōdo* [Japan's border issues: Senkaku, Takeshima, Northern territory]. Tokyo: Chi- kuma Shinsho, 2011.

Mainichi Shimbun Seiji-bu, ed. *Kenshō Kaifu Naikaku* [Inspecting the Kaifu cabinet]. Tokyo: Kadokawa Shoten, 1991.

——, ed. *Kenshō Shushō Kantei* [Inspecting the Prime Minister's Office]. Tokyo: Asahi Sonorama, 1988.

——. *Ryūkyū no Seijōki: "Futenma" wa Owaranai* [Stars and stripes in Okinawa: "Futenma" that never ends]. Tokyo: Kōdan-sha, 2010.

Maki Tarō. *Nakasone Seiken 1806 nichi* [The Nakasone administration: 1,806 days]. Vols. 1 and 2. Tokyo: Gyōsei Mondai Kenkyūsho, 1988.

——. *Nakasone to wa Nandattanoka* [What was Nakasone?]. Tokyo: Sōshi-sha, 1988.

Masumi Junnosuke. "1955nen no Seiji Taisei" [The political system of 1955]. *Shisō* (June 1964): 55–72.

———. *Gendai Seiji 1955 nen igo* [Contemporary politics after 1955]. Tokyo: Tokyo Daigaku Shuppan, 1985.

———. *Sengo Seiji 1945-55 nen* [Postwar politics 1945–55]. Tokyo: Tokyo Daigaku Shuppan, 1983.

Masuyama Mikitaka. *Gikai Seido to Nihon Seiji: Giji Uneino Keiryō Seijigaku* [Parliamentary system and Japanese politics: Quantitative study on the deliberations]. Tokyo: Bokutaku-sha, 2003.

Matsuoka Hideo. *Rengō Seiken ga Hōkai shita Hi: Shakaitō Katayama Naikaku kara no Kyōkun* [The day the coalition government collapsed: A lesson from the Katayama Socialist Cabinet]. Tokyo: Kyōiku Shiryō Shuppan-kai, 1990.

Matsushita Keiichi. *Seiji Gyōsei no Kangaekata* [How to think about politics and government]. Tokyo: Iwanami Shinsho, 1998.

Matsuzaki Tetsuhisa. *Jidai nitotte Soshite Watashitachi nitotte Nihon Shintō towa Nande Attanoka* [What the Japan New Party was about to the time and to us]. Tokyo: Free Press, 1995.

Miki Mutsuko. *Shin Nakuba Tatazu: Otto Miki Takeo to no Gojūnen* [No rising without his belief: Fifty years with my husband, Miki Takeo]. Tokyo: Kōdan-sha, 1989.

Mikuriya Takashi, ed. *Henbō suru Nihon Seiji: 90nendai igo "Henkaku no Jidai" wo Yomitoku* [Changing Japanese Politics: Understanding "the era of change" after the 90s]. Tokyo: Keisō Shobō, 2009.

Mikuriya Takashi and Makihara Izuru, eds. *Kikigaki Takemura Masayoshi Kaikoroku* [Oral biography of Takemura Masayoshi]. Tokyo: Iwanami Shoten, 2011.

Mikuriya Takashi and Nakamura Takahide, eds. *Kikigaki Miyazawa Kiichi Kaikoroku* [Oral biography: The memoir of Miyazawa Kiichi]. Tokyo: Iwanami Shoten, 2005.

Mineyama Akinori. *Kaitai Shinsho Zeisei Kaikakushi* [Explanations: History of tax reforms]. Tokyo, Keibun-sha, 1991.

Minkan Seiji Rinchō. *Nihon Henkaku no Bijon* [Grand vision of political reform]. Tokyo: Kōdan-sha, 1993.

Miyake Ichirō. *Nihon no Seiji to Senkyo* [Japanese politics and election]. Tokyo: Tokyo Daigaku Shuppankai, 1995.

———. *Seitō Shiji no Bunseki* [Analysis on political party support]. Tokyo: Sōbun-sha, 1985.

———. *Tōhyō Kōdō* [Voting behavior]. Tokyo: Tokyo Daigaku Shuppankai, 1989.

Miyake Ichirō, Nishizawa Yoshitaka, and Kohno Masaru. *55nen Taisei ka no Seiji to Keizai* [Politics and economy under the 55 system]. Tokyo: Bokutaku-sha, 2001.

Miyake Ichirō, Yamaguchi Sadamu, Muramatsu Michio, and Eiichi Shindō. *Nihon Seiji no Zahyō: Sengo Yonjūnen no Ayumi* [Charts of Japan's politics: Forty years of steps in the postwar]. Tokyo: Yūhikaku, 1985.

Miyamoto Ken'ichi, ed. *Hojokin no Seiji Keizai Gaku* [Political economy of subsidies]. Tokyo: Asahi Shimbun-sha, 1990.

Miyazawa Kiichi. *Sengo Seiji no Shōgen* [Testimony on postwar politics]. Tokyo: Yomiuri Shimbun-sha, 1991.

———. *Shin Goken Sengen* [New declaration to protect the Constitution]. Tokyo: Asahi Shinbun, 1995.

———. *Tokyo-Washington no Mitsudan* [The secret conversations between Tokyo and Washington]. Tokyo: Chuko Bunko, 1999.

Miyazawa Toshiyoshi. *Nihonkoku Kenpō* [The Japanese Constitution]. Tokyo: Nihon Hyōron-sha, 1955, rev. 1978.

Mori Kishio. *Shushō Kantei no Himitsu* [Secrets of the Prime Minister's Office]. Tokyo: Chōbunsha, 1981.

Morita Minoru. *Seihen: Jimintō Sōsaisen Uramen Antō-shi* [Political upheaval: History of the behind-the-scene battles for the LDP presidency]. Tokyo, Tokuma Shoten, 1991.

Moriya Takemasa. *"Futenma" Kōshō Hiroku* [Secret records of negotiation over "Futenma"]. Tokyo: Shinchō-sha, 2010.

Murakami Yasusuke. *Shin Chūkan Taishū no Jidai* [The era of new middle mass]. Tokyo: Chūō Kōron, 1983.

Murakawa Ichirō. *Jimintō no Seisaku Kettei Shisutemu* [The policy-making system of the LDP]. Tokyo: Kyōiku-sha, 1989.

———. *Nihon no Seisaku Kettei Katei* [Japanese policy-making process]. Tokyo: Gyōsei, 1985.

Muramatsu Michio, ed. *Core Executive to Kanbu Kōmuin Seido no Kenkyū* [Study on the core executive and the executive bureaucratic system]. Kizugawa: Kōtō Kokusai Mondai Kenkyūsho, 2007.

———. *Seikan Sukuramu-gata Rīdāshippu no Hōkai* [The breakdown of politico-bureaucratic scrimmage-style leadership]. Tokyo: Tōyō Keizai Shimpō-sha, 2010.

———. *Sengo Nihon no Kanryōsei* [Postwar Japan's bureaucratic system]. Tokyo: Tōyō Keizai Shinpō-sha, 1981.

Muramatsu Michio and Itō Mitsutoshi. *Chihō Giin no Kenkyū: "Nihonteki Seiji Fūdo" no Shuyakutachi* [Study on local politicians: Main actors of Japanese political culture]. Tokyo: Nihon Keizai Shimbun-sha, 1986.

Muramatsu Michio, Itō Mitsutoshi, and Tsujinaka Yutaka. *Nihon no Seiji* [Japan's politics]. Tokyo: Yūhikaku, 1992.

Murayama Tomiichi. *Murayama Tomiichi ga Kataru Tenmei no 561 nichi* [Destined 561 days told by Murayama Tomiichi]. Tokyo: K.K. Best Sellers, 1996.

——. *Sōjanō: Murayama Tomiichi 'Shusho Taiken' no Subete wo Kataru* [Murayama Tomiichi talks everything on his premier experience]. Tokyo: Daisan Shobo, 1998.

——. "Watashi no Rirekisho" [My personal history]. *Nihon Keizai Shinbun*, June 1996.

Nagai Yōnosuke. "Atsuryoku Dantai no Nihonteki Kōzō [Japanese structure of interest groups]." *Nenpō Seijigaku: Nihon no Atsuryoku Dantai*, 1960.

Nagamori Seiichi. *Habatsu* [Factions]. Tokyo: Chikuma Shinsho, 2002.

Nagatomi Yūichirō. *Kindai wo Koete: Ko Ōhira Sōri no Nokosareta mono* [Beyond the contemporary era: What the late prime minister Ōhira left for us]. Tokyo: Ōkura Zaimu Kyōkai, 1983.

Nagatsuma Akira. *Manekarezaru Daijin: Sei to Kan no Shin Rūru* [Uninvited minister: New rules between politicians and bureaucrats]. Tokyo: Asahi Shinsho, 2011.

Naikaku Sōri Daijin Kanbō, ed. *Takeshita Naikaku Sōri Daijin Enzetsu-shū* [Speeches of Prime Minister Takeshita Noboru]. Tokyo: Nihon Kōhō Kyōkai, 1990.

Nakagawa Hidenao. *Shushō Hosa* [Assistant to the prime minister]. Tokyo: PHP Kenkyusho, 1996.

Nakamura Akira and Takeshita Yuzuru, eds. *Nihon no Seisaku Katei: Jimintō, Yatō, Kanryō.* [Japanese policy process: The LDP, the opposition parties, and the bureaucrats]. Tokyo: Azusa Shuppan-sha, 1984.

Nakamura Keiichirō. *Miki Seiken 747 days* [The Miki administration's 747 days]. Tokyo: Gyōsei Mondai Kenkyū-sho, 1981.

——. *Sōri no Utsuwa* [Caliber for the prime minister]. Tokyo: Kobunsha, 1996.

Nakano Shirō. *Tanaka Seiken 886 nichi* [The Tanaka administration: 886 days]. Tokyo: Gyōsei Mondai Kenkyū-sho, 1982.

Nakasone Yasuhiro. "Kokumin Rinchō to Jiritsu Jijo no Gyōkaku" [Rinchō for the people and administrative reform for self-reliance]. *Jiyū Minshu* (June 1981):15–19.

——. *Seiji to Jinsei* [Politics and life]. Tokyo: Kōdansha, 1992.

——. *Tenchi Ujō* [The heaven and earth with emotion]. (Tokyo: Bungei Shunjū, 1996).

Namikawa Shino. *Gyōsei Kaikaku no Shikumi* [The mechanism of administrative reform]. Tokyo: Toyo Keizai Shinposha, 1997.

Nihon Gyōsei Gakkai, ed. *Naikakuseido no Kenkyū* [A study on the cabinet system]. Tokyo: Gyōsei, 1987.

——, ed. *Gyōsei Kaikaku no Suishin to Teikō* [The promotion of resistance against the administrative reforms]. *Annuals of the Japanese Society for Public Administration* 5 (1966).

Nihon Keizai Shimbun-sha, ed. *Dokyumento Seiken Tanjō* [Documentary, the birth of an administration]. Tokyo: Nihon Keizai Shimbun-sha, 1991.

——, ed. *Ōkurasho no Yūutsu* [Headache of the finance ministry]. Tokyo: Nihon Keizai Shimbun-sha, 1992.

——, ed. *"Renritsu Seiken" no Kenkyū* [Study of Coalition Governments]. Tokyo: Nihon Keizai Shimbun-sha, 1994.

——, ed. *Seifu to ha Nanika* [What is the government]. Tokyo: Nihon Keizai Shimbun-sha, 1981.

——, ed. *Seiken* [The ruling power]. Tokyo: Nihon Keizai Shimbun-sha, 2010.

Nihon Seiji Gakkai, ed. *Seiken Kōtaiki no Senkyoku Seiji* [Constituency politics during the power transition period]. Tokyo: Bokutakusha, 2011.

Noda Yoshihiko. *Minshu no Teki: Seiji Kōtai ni Taigi ari* [The enemy of democracy: Justice exists in power shift]. Tokyo: Shinchō Shinsho, 2011.

——. "Waga Seiken Kōsō: Imakoso 'Chūyō' no Seiji wo" [My government plan: Now we need "moderate" politics]. *Bungei Shunjū* (September 2011): 94–103.

Noji Tsuneyoshi and Kozuka Kaoru. *Ozawa Senkyo ni Manabu Hito wo Ugokasu Chikara* [Lessons from Ozawa's election on how to mobilize people]. Tokyo: Kanki Shuppan, 2009.

Nonaka Hiromu. *Rōhei wa Shinazu: Nonaka Hiromu Zenkaikoroku* [Old soldiers never die: The memoir of Nonaka Hiromu]. Tokyo: Bungei Shunjū, 2003.

——. *Watashi wa Tatakau* [I fight]. Tokyo: Bungei Shunjū, 1996.

Nonaka Naoto. *Jimintō Seiji no Owari* [The end of LDP politics]. Tokyo: Chikuma Shinsho, 2008.

Nosaka Kōken. *Seiken: Henkaku eno Michi* [The administration: Road toward change]. Tokyo: Suzusawa Shoten, 1996.

Nukaga Fukushirō. *Seiji wa Gēmu Dewanai: Senryakuteki Nihon Kaihō Keikaku* [Politics is not a game: Strategic scheme to open Japan]. Tokyo: Sankei Shimbun Shuppan, 2010.

Ōhinata Ichirō. *Kishi Seiken 1241 nichi* [The Kishi administration: 1,241 Days]. Tokyo: Gyōsei Mondai Kenkyū-sho, 1985.

Ōhira Masayoshi. *Watashi no Rirekisho* [My personal history]. Tokyo: Nihon Keizai Shimbun-sha, 1978.

Ōhira Masayoshi Kaisōroku Kankō-kai. *Ōhira Masayoshi Kaisō-roku: Tsuisō hen and Denki-hen* [Memoirs of Ōhira Masayoshi: Vol. 1., Reminiscence, and Vol. 2, Biography]. Tokyo: Ōhira Masayoshi Kaisōroku Kankō-kai, 1982.

Okada Naoyuki. *Seron no Seiji Shakaigaku* [Poltical social studies of public opinion]. Tokyo: Tokyo Daigaku Shuppankai, 2001.

Okano Kaoru, ed. *Naikaku Sōri Daijin* [The prime minister]. Tokyo: Gendai Hyōron-sha, 1985.

Okazawa Norio. *Seitō* [Political parties]. Tokyo: Tokyo Daigaku Shuppan-kai, 1988.

Ōkubo Shōzō. *Hadaka no Seikai* [Political world as naked]. Tokyo: Simul Shuppan-kai, 1975.

Ōsuga Mizuo. *Shushō Kantei Konjaku Monogatari* [The prime minister's residence: Past and present]. Tokyo: Asahi Sonorama, 1995.

Ōta Hiroko. *Kaikaku Gyakusō: Seisaku Kettei ni Nani ga Okitanoka* [Setback of reform: What happened to decision making]. Tokyo: Nihon Keizai Shimbun-sha, 2010.

———. *Keizai Zaisei Shimon Kaigi no Tatakai* [Battles at the Council of Economic and Fiscal Policy]. Tokyo: Tōyō Keizai Shimpō-sha, 2006.

Ōtake Hideo. *Gendai Nihon no Seiji Kenryoku Keizai Kenryoku* [Political and economic power in contemporary Japan]. Tokyo: San'ichi Shobō, 1979.

———. *Koizumi Junichirō Populism no Kenkyū: Sono Senryaku to Shuhō* [Study on Koizumi Junichirō's populism: His strategy and tactics]. Tokyo: Tōyō Keizai Shinpō-sha, 2006.

———. *Nihongata Popyurizumu: Seiji e no Kitai to Genmetsu* [Japanese-style populism: Expectations and disappointments in politics]. Tokyo: Chūkō Shinsho, 2003.

———. *Nihon Seiji no Tairitsujiku: 93-nen Ikō no Seikai Saihen no Naka de.* [Cleavage of Japanese politics: Under the political reorganization after 1993]. Tokyo: Chūkō Shinsho, 1999.

———. *Seikai Saihen no Kenkyū: Shinsenkyo Seido ni yoru Sōsenkyo* [Study on political reorganization: General election under the new electoral system]. Tokyo: Yūhikaku, 1997.

———. *Seisaku Katei* [The policy process]. Tokyo: Tokyo Daigaku Shuppankai, 1990.

———. *Sengo Seiji to Seijigaku* [Postwar politics and political science]. Tokyo: Tokyo Daigaku Shuppankai, 1995.

Ozato Sadatoshi. *Hiroku Nagatachō: Ushinawareta Jūnen wo Koete* [Secret story of Nagatachō: Beyond the lost decade]. Tokyo: Kōdan-sha, 2002.

Ozawa Ichirō. *Kataru* [Talk]. Tokyo: Bungei Shunjū, 1996.

———. *Nippon Kaizō Keikaku* [Japan reform plan]. Tokyo: Kōdan-sha, 1993.

———. *Ozawa Shugi* [Ozawa-ism]. Tokyo: Shūeisha International, 2006.

Saitō Jun. *Jimintō Chōki Seiken no Seiji Keizaigaku: Rieki Yūdō Seiji no Jiko Mujun* [The political economy of the LDP regime]. Tokyo: Keisō Shobō, 2010.

Sakurada Takeshi and Shikanai Nobutaka. *Ima Akasu Sengo Hishi* [The secret postwar history revealed now]. Tokyo: Sankei Shuppan, 1983.

Sasaki Takeshi, ed. *Seiji Kaikaku 1800 nichi no Shinjitsu* [The truth about 1,800 days of political reform]. Tokyo: Kōdan-sha, 1999.

Sasaki Takeshi and Shimizu Masato, eds. *Zemināru Gendai Nihon Seiji* [Seminar contemporary Japanese Politics]. Tokyo: Nihon Keizai Shimbun-sha, 2011.

Sasaki Takeshi, Yoshida Shinichi, Taniguchi Masaki, and Yamamoto Shūji, eds. *Daigishi to Kane: Seiji Shikin Zenkoku Chōsa Hōkoku* [Lower house members and money: Report of the national survey on political funds]. Tokyo: Asahi Sensho, 1999.

Sassa Atsuyuki. *Hontoni Karera ga Nihon wo Horobosu* [They really will ruin Japan]. Tokyo: Gentō-sha, 2011.

———. *Karera ga Nihon wo Horobosu* [They will ruin Japan]. Tokyo: Gentō-sha, 2011.

———. *Kiki Kanri Saishōron* [On prime ministerial leadership in crisis management]. Tokyo: Bungei Shunjū, 1995.

———. *Shin Kiki Kanri no Nouhau* [New know-hows for crisis management]. Tokyo: Bungei Shunjū, 1991.

Sataka Makoto. *Nihon Kanryō Hakusho* [White paper on Japanese bureaucracy]. Tokyo: Kōdan-sha, 1989.

Satō Akiko. *Watashi no Tanaka Kakuei Nikki* [My diary on Tanaka Kakuei]. Tokyo: Shinchōsha, 1994.

Satō Seizaburō and Matsuzaki Tetsuhisa. *Jimintō Seiken* [The LDP administrations]. Tokyo: Chūō Kōron, 1986.

Sekai Heiwa Kenkyusho. *Nakasone Naikakushi* [The history of the Nakasone cabinet]. 5 vols. Tokyo: Chuo Koronsha, 1995, 1996, 1997.

Sekō Hiroshige. *Jimintō Kaizō Purojekuto 650-nichi* [650 days of the LDP reform project]. Tokyo: Shinchō-sha, 2006.

———. *Purofesshonaru Kōhō Senryaku* [Professional communications strategies]. Tokyo: Goma Books K.K., 2006.

Serita Kentarō. *Nihon no Ryōdo* [Japan's territory]. Tokyo: Chūkō Sōsho, 2002.

Shimizu Masato. *Kantei Shudō* [Initiative of the Prime Minister's Office]. Tokyo: Nihon Keizai Shimbunsha, 2005.

——. *Keizai Zaisei Senki: Kantei shudō Koizumi kara Abe e* [Record of battles over economic and fiscal issues: The Kantei initiative from Koizumi to Abe]. Tokyo: Nihon Keizai Shimbun-sha, 2007.

——. *Shushō no Satetsu: Post-Koizumi Kenryoku no Tasogare* [Setback for the prime minister: Sinking power of post-Koizumi]. Tokyo: Nihon Keizai Shimbun-sha, 2009.

Shindō Muneyuki. *Gyōsei Kaikaku to Gendai Seiji* [Administrative reform and contemporary politics]. Tokyo: Iwanami Shoten, 1986.

——. *Seiji Shudō* [Political leaderhsip]. Tokyo: Chikuma Shinsho, 2012.

——. *Zaisei Hatan to Zeisei Kaikaku* [Financial breakdown and tax reform]. Tokyo: Iwanami Shoten, 1989.

Shinoda Tomohito. "Gaikō Seisaku Kettei Actor to shiteno Ozawa Ichirō" [Ozawa Ichiro as a foreign policy actor]. In *Nihon Gaikō no Naisei Yōin* [Domestic determinants of Japan's foreign policy], 25–69. Tokyo: PHP, 1999.

——. "Hashimoto Gyōkaku no Naikaku Kino Kyokasaku" [Cabinet reinforcement in Hashimoto's administrative reform]. *Leviathan* (Spring 1999): 50–77.

——. *Kantei Gaikō* [Foreign policy led by the Prime Minister's Office]. Tokyo: Asahi Sensho, 2004.

——. *Kantei no Kenryoku* [The power of the Prime Minister's Office]. Tokyo: Chikuma Shinsho, 1994.

——. "Koizumi Shushō no Ri-da-shippu to Anzen Hoshō Seisaku Katei: Tero Taisaku Tokusohō to Yujikanrenho wo Jirei toshita Doshinen Bunseki" [Prime Minister Koizumi's leadership and national security policy process: Concentric circle model analysis on the antiterrorism legislation and the contingency legislation. *Nihon Seiji Kenkyū* 1, 2 (July 2004): 42–67.

——. "Kyōka sareru Gaikō Rīdashippu: Kantei Shudō Taisei no Seidoka e" [Strengthened leadership in Foreign Affairs: More institutionalized kantei's initiative]. *Kokusai Mondai* 558 (Jan.–Feb 2007): 4–16.

——. *Nichibei Domei to iu Realism* [Emerging realism of the Japan-U.S. alliance]. Tokyo: Chikura Shobo, 2007.

——. "Nihon no Taigai Intelligence Community" [Foreign intelligence community of Japan]." *Nihon Seiji Kenkyu* 3, 2 (2006): 92–111.

——. *Reisengo no Nihon Gaikō: Anzenhosho Seisaku no Kokunai Seiji Katei* [Post–cold war Japanese foreign policy: Domestic political process in national security policy making]. Kyoto: Minerva Shobo, 2006.

——. "Seiji Shudō no Dōnatsuka Genshō" [Donut-style political leadership]," *Sekai to Gikai* (February 2010): 4–9.

——. *Sōri Daijin no Kenryoku to Shidōryoku* [The power and leadership of the prime minister]. Tokyo: Tōyō Keizai Shinpō-sha, 1994.

———. "Taigai Seisaku Katei: 'Koizumi Gaikō' ni okeru Seiji Katei" [Foreign policy making: Political process of "Koizumi diplomacy"]. In *Gaku to shiteno Kokusai Seiji*, edited by Tanaka Akihiko, Nakanishi Hiroshi, and Iida Keisuke, 93–111. Tokyo: Yuhikaku, 2008.

Shiota Ushio. *Kishi Nobusuke*. Tokyo: Kodansha, 1996.

———. *Shinban Minshutō no Kenkyū*. [New edition, study on the DPJ]. Tokyo: Heibon-sha Shinsho, 2009.

Shiratori Hiroshi. *Toshi tai Chihō no Nihon Seiji: Gendai Seiji no Kōzō Hendō.* [Urban versus rural in Japanese politics: Structural changes in contemporary politics]. Tokyo: Ashi Shobō, 2004.

———, ed. *Seiken Kōtai no Seijigaku: Chihō kara Kawaru Nihon Seiji* [Political study on power shift: Japanese political changes from the rural]. Kyoto: Minerva Shobō, 2010.

Shiratori Rei, ed. *Nihon no Naikaku* [The Japanese cabinet]. Tokyo: Shin Hyōron-sha, 1981.

Sōmu-chō Gyōsei Kanri-kyoku. *Gyōsei Kikōzu* [Administrative organizational charts]. 1991.

Sugawara Taku. "Chūsenkyokusei to Jimintō Seiken: 55nen Taiseika ni okeru Tanki Hiijōshiki Tōhyō no Keiryō Bunseki" [The medium electoral system and the LDP administration: Quantitative analysis on the impact of the single nontransferable vote under the 55 system]. Ph.D. dissertation. University of Tokyo, 2007.

———. "Kakusa Mondai wa Daini no 'Yūsei' to Naruka." [Will the gap issue be another "postal reform"?]. *Chūō Kōron* (April 2006): 134–43.

———. *Seron no Kyokukai: Naze Jimintō wa Taihai Shitanoka* [Misunderstanding public opinion: Explanation for the LDP's big loss]. Tokyo: Kōbunsha Shinsho, 2009.

Suzuki Kenji. *Rekidai Sōri Sokkin no Kokuhaku* [The confessions of close associates of prime ministers]. Tokyo: Mainichi Shimbun-sha, 1991.

Suzuki Ryōichi. *Wakariyasui Seiji Shikin Kiseihō* [Political fund control law easy to understand]. Tokyo: Gyōsei, 1995.

Suzuki Tetsuo. *Seitō ga Ayatsuru Senkyo Hōdō* [Media coverage on election controlled by the political parties]. Tokyo: Shūeisha Shinsho, 2007.

Suzuki Yukio. *Keizai Kanryō: Shin Sangyō Kokka no Prodyūsā* [The economic bureaucrats: The producers of a new industrial nation]. Tokyo: Nihon Keizai Shimbun-sha, 1969.

Tachibana Takashi. "Kensatsu no Kakumo Nagaki Nemuri" [Such a long sleep for the Prosecutor's Office]. *Bungei Shunjū* (December 1992): 94–109.

Tachibana Tamiyoshi, ed. *Minshutō Jūnenshi* [Ten-year history of DPJ]. Tokyo: Daiichi Shorin, 2008.

Tagawa Seiichi. *Nicchū Kōshō Hiroku* [Secret record of Sino-Japanese negotiation]. Tokyo: Mainichi Shimbun-sha, 1973.

Tahara Sōichirō. *Atama no Nai Kujira: Seijigeki no Shinjitsu* [Headless whale: The truth of political plays]. Tokyo: Asahi Shinbun-sha, 1997.

———. *Kyodaina Rakujitsu: Ōkura Kanryō Haisō no 850 nichi* [Huge sunset: The retreat of MOF bureaucrats for 850 days]. Tokyo: Bungei Shunjū, 1998.

———. *Nihon no Kanryō 1980* [Japan's bureaucrats 1980]. Tokyo: Bungei Shunjū, 1979.

———. *Sōri wo Ayatsutta Otokotachi* [Men who controlled prime ministers]. Tokyo: Kōdan-sha, 1989.

Takahashi Yōichi. *Kangu no Kuni: Naze Nihon dewa Seijika ga Kanryō ni Kussuru noka* [The country of stupid bureaucrats: Why politicians yield to bureaucrats in Japan]. Tokyo: Shōden-sha, 2011.

———. *Saraba Zaimushō* [Farewell to the Ministry of Finance]. Tokyo: Kōdan-sha, 2008.

———. *Shōhizei Zōzei wa Iranai: Zaimushō ga Minshutō ni Oshieta Zaisei no Oouso* [Consumption tax increase is unnecessary: A big lie that the MOF taught the DPJ]. Tokyo: Kōdan-sha, 2010.

Takeda Kazuaki. *Seiken Kōtai: Jimintō Hōkai eno 400-nichi* [Power shift: 400 days to the collapse of the LDP]. Tokyo: Kawaide Shobō Shin-sha, 2009.

Takemura Masayoshi. "Renritsu Seikenka no ano 'Fukushizei' tekkai wa Nani wo Monogataruka" [What does the withdrawal of the welfare tax under the coalition government mean]. *Bungei Shunjū*, July 1997.

Takenaka Harutaka. *Shushō Shihai: Nihon Seiji no Henbō* [The control by the prime minister: The change in Japanese politics]. Tokyo: Chūō Kōron-sha, 2006.

Takenaka Heizō. *Keisei Zaimin: Keizai Senryaku Kaigi no 180 nichi* [Governing the world to rescue people: 180 days of the Economic Strategy Council]. Tokyo: Daiyamondo-sha, 1999.

———. *Kōzō Kaikaku no Shinjitsu: Takenaka Heizō Daijin Nisshi* [Truth of structural reform: Diary of Minister Takenaka Heizō]. Tokyo: Nihon Keizai Shimbun-sha, 2006.

Takeshita Noboru. *Shōgen Hoshu Seiken* [Testimony on conservative administrations]. Tokyo: Yomiuri Shimbun-sha, 1991.

Takeshita Noboru and Hirano Sadao, eds. *Shōhizei Seido Seiritsu no Enkaku* [Development toward the introduction of the consumption tax system]. Tokyo: Gyōsei, 1993.

Tanaka Aiji, Kōno Masaru, Hino Airō, Iida Ken, and Yomiuri Shimbun. 2009-nen Naze Seiken Kōtai Dattanoka [Why power shift in 2009]. Tokyo: Keisō Shobō, 2009.

Tanaka Hitoshi. Gaikō no Chikara [The power of diplomacy]. Tokyo: Nihon Keizai Shimbun Shuppan-sha, 2009.

Tanaka Hitoshi and Tahara Sōichirō. Kokka to Gaikō [The nation and diplomacy]. Tokyo: Kōdan-sha, 2005.

Tanaka Kakuei Kinenkan, ed. Watashi no naka no Tanaka Kakuei [Tanaka Kakuei in my memory]. Niigata: Tanaka Kakuei Kinenkan, 1998.

Tanaka Kazuaki and Okada Akira, eds. Chūō Shōchō Kaikaku: Hashimoto Gyōkaku ga Mezashita "Kono Kuni no Katachi" [Central government reform: The shape of this country that the Hashimoto administrative reform aimed at]. Tokyo: Nihon Hyōron-sha, 2000.

Tanaka Rokusuke. Futatabi Ōhira Masayoshi no Hito to Seiji [Again on the personality and politics of Ōhira Masayoshi]. Tokyo: Asahi Sonorama, 1981.

Tanaka Shūsei. Sakigake to Seiken Kōtai. [Sakigake and political change]. Tokyo: Toyo Keizai Shinpo, 1994.

Tanaka Yoshiaki. "Nihonkoku Kenpō Seitei Katei ni okeru Niinsei Shoan" [Bicameral proposals in the process of making the Japanese Constitution]. Reference (June 2004): 25–48.

Taniguchi Masaki. Gendai Nihon no Senkyo Seiji: Senkyo Seido Kaikaku wo Kenshō Suru [Contemporary Japanese electoral politics: Examining electoral reform]. Tokyo: Tokyo Daigaku Shuppan-kai, 2004.

Taniguchi Naoko. Gendai Nihon no Tōhyō Kōdō [Contemporary Japanese voting behavior]. Tokyo: Keiō Gijuku Daigaku Shuppankai, 2005.

Tase Yasuhiro. Kokka to Seiji: Kiki no Jidai no Shidōshazō [The nation and politics: Leaders in the age of crisis]. Tokyo: NHK Shuppan Shinsho, 2011.

Tatebayashi Masahiko. Giin Kōdō no Seiji Keizaigaku: Jimintō Shihai no Seido Bunseki [The logic of legislators' activities: Institutional analysis of LDP dominance in Japan]. Tokyo: Yūhikaku, 2004.

Tazaki Shirō. Seijika Shikkaku: Naze Nihon no Seiji wa Dame Nanoka [Disqualified politicians: Why Japanese politics is not good]. Tokyo: Bunshun Shinsho, 2009.

——. Takeshita-ha Shitō no Nanajū Nichi [70 days of fierce battle of the Takeshita faction]. Tokyo: Bunshun Bunko, 2000.

Tomita Nobuo. Ashida Seiken 223 nichi. [The Ashida administration 223 days]. Tokyo: Gyōken, 1992.

Tsuda Tatsuo. Zaikai-Nihon no Shihaisha Tachi [The business community: The people who rule Japan]. Tokyo: Gakushū no Tomo-sha, 1990.

Tsuji Kiyoaki. *Shinban Nihon Kanryōsei no Kenkyū* [New edition, study on the Japanese bureaucracy system]. Tokyo: Tokyo Daigaku Shuppan-kai, 1969.

Tsujinaka Yutaka. *Rieki Shūdan* [Interest groups]. Tokyo: Tokyo Daigaku Shuppan-kai, 1988.

Tsutsui Kiyotada. *Ishibashi Tanzan: Ichi Jiyū Shugi Seijika no Kiseki* [Ishibashi Tanzan: Trace of one liberal politician]. Tokyo: Chūō Kōron-sha, 1986.

Uchida Kenzō. *Sengo Nihon no Hoshu Seiji* [Conservative politics in postwar Japan]. Tokyo: Tōyō Keizai Shimbunsha, 1994.

Uchida Kenzō, Hayano Tōru, and Sone Yasunori. *Daiseihen: Hosokawa/Hata Rirē Seiken no Kōseki* [Big political change: The wake of the Hosokawa-Hata relay governments]. Tokyo: Iwanami Shoten, 1969.

Uchiyama Yū. *Koizumi Seiken* [The Koizumi administration]. Tokyo: Chūō Kōron-sha, 2007.

Uekami Takayoshi and Tsutsumi Hidenori. *Minshutō no Soshiki to Seisaku: Kettō kara Seiken Kōtai made* [The organization and policy of the DPJ: From the establishment to the power shift]. Tokyo: Tōyō Keizai Shuppansha, 2011.

Uesugi Takashi. *Kantei Hōkai: Abe Seiken Meisō no Ichinen* [Collapse of the Prime Minister's Office: One year of drift under the Abe administration]. Tokyo: Shinchō-sha, 2007.

Uji Toshihiko. *Suzuki Seiken 863 nichi* [The Suzuki administration's 863 days]. Tokyo: Gyōsei Mondai Kenkyūsho, 1983.

Wakabayashi Aki. *Taiken Rupo: Kokkai Giin ni Rikkōho Suru* [My experience report: Running for the Diet]. Tokyo: Bunshun Shinsho, 2011.

Wakaizumi Kei. *Tasaku Nakarishi wo Shinzemu to Hossu* [Wish to believe that there was no option]. Tokyo: Bungei Shunjū, 1994.

Watanabe Akio, ed. *Sengo Nihon no Saishō tachi* [The prime ministers of postwar Japan]. Tokyo: Chūō Kōronsha, 1995.

Watanabe Tsuneo. *Hanbatsu to Tatōka Jidai* [Factions and the multiparty era]. Tokyo: Sekka-sha, 1967.

——. *Nagata-chō Kenbunroku* [Observation on Nagata-chō]. Tokyo: Sekka-sha, 1980.

——. *Ten'un Tenshoku.* [Destiny and mission]. Tokyo: Kōbun-sha, 1999.

——. *Tōshu to Seitō: Sono Rīdāshippu no Kenkyū* [Party leaders and political parties: Study on their leadership]. Tokyo: Kōbunsha, 1961.

Watanabe Yoshimi. *Kōmuin Seido Kaikaku ga Nihon wo Kaeru* [Bureaucratic reform will change Japan]. Tokyo: Asuka Shinsha, 2009.

——. *Minshutō Seiji no Shōtai* [The truth about DPJ politics]. Tokyo: Kadokawa SSC Shinsho, 2010.

———. *Zettai no Ketsudan* [Absolute determination]. Tokyo: PHP Kenkyūsho, 2009.

Watanabe Yoshimi and Eda Kenji. *Datsu Kanryō Seiken Juritsu Sengen: Kasumigaseki to Tatakau Futari no Seijika* [Declaration to establish an antibureaucracy administration: Two politicians who fight against Kasumigaseki]. Tokyo: Kōdan-sha, 2009.

Yachi Shōtarō. *Gaikō no Senryaku to Kokorozashi* [Strategy and will for diplomacy]. Tokyo: Sankei Shimbun Shuppan, 2009.

Yajima Kōichi. *Kokkai* [The Diet]. Tokyo: Gyōken, 1987.

Yakushiji Katsuyuki. *Gaimusho: Gaikoryoku Kyoka eno Michi* [The MOFA: Road to strengthen diplomatic power]. Tokyo: Iwanami Shinsho, 2003.

Yamada Eizō. *Shōden Satō Eisaku* [True story of Satō Eisaku]. Tokyo: Shinchō-sha, 1988.

Yamada Masahiro. "Kōenkai Seiji no Bunseki Wakugumi" [Analytical framework of Kōenkai politics]. *Hō to Seiji* (March 1997): 15–36.

———. "2009-nen Sōsenkyo ni okeru Seiken Kōtai to Swing Voting" [The power shift and swing voting in the 2009 general election]. *Senkyo Kenkyū* 26, 2 (2010): 5–14.

Yamaguchi Jirō. *Igirisu no Seiji Nihon no Seiji* [British Politics, Japanese Politics]. Tokyo: Chikuma Shinsho, 1998.

———. *Ittō Shihai Taisei no Hōkai* [The collapse of the one-party dominance system]. Tokyo: Iwanami Shoten, 1989.

———. *Naikaku Seido* [Cabinet system]. Tokyo: Tokyo Daigaku Shuppankai, 2007.

———. *Ōkura Kanryō Shihai no Shūen* [The end of the domination by Finance Ministry bureaucrats]. Tokyo: Iwanami Shoten, 1987.

———. *Seiji Kaikaku* [Political reform]. Tokyo: Iwanami Shinsho, 1993.

———. *Seiken Kōtai-ron* [Argument for power shift]. Tokyo: Iwanami Shinsho, 2009.

———. *Seiken towa Nandattanoka* [What power shift meant]. Tokyo: Iwanami Shinsho, 2012.

Yamaguchi Yasushi. *Seiji Taisei* [Political system]. Tokyo: Tokyo Daigaku Shuppan-kai, 1989.

Yamamoto Shichihei. *Habatsu no Kenkyū* [Study on factions]. Tokyo: Bungei Shunjū, 1989.

Yamawaki Takeshi. *Yūsei Kōbō* [Battles over postal reform]. Tokyo: Asahi Shimbun-sha, 2005.

Yan Jiaqi. *Shunōron* [Theory of national leaders]. Tokyo: Gakusei-sha, 1992.

Yano Junya. *Nijū Kenryoku Yami no Nagare* [Dual power, current in the dark]. Tokyo: Bungei Shunjū, 1994.

Yomiuri Shimbun Chōsa Kenkyū Honbu, ed. *Nihon no Kokkai* [The Japanese Parliament]. Tokyo: Yomiuri Shimbun-sha, 1988.

Yomiuri Shimbun "Minshuism" Shuzaihan. *Haishin Seiken* [The betraying government]. Tokyo: Chūōkōronshin-sha, 2011.

Yomiuri Shimbun Seiji-bu, ed. *Bōkoku no Saishō: Kantei Kinō Teishi no 180-nichi* [The prime minister of a collapsed country: The 180 days of the dysfunctional Kantei]. Tokyo: Shinchō-sha, 2011.

———. *Gaikō wo Kenka nishita Otoko: Koizumi Gaikō 2000-nichi no Shinjitsu* [The man who turned diplomacy into fight: The truth about the 2,000 days of Koizumi diplomacy]. Tokyo: Shinchō-sha, 2006.

———. *Minshutō Meisō to Uragiri no 300-nichi* [The DPJ, 300 days of drifting and betraying]. Tokyo: Shinchō-sha, 2010.

———, ed. *Shinkū Kokkai: Fukuda "Hyōryū Seiken" no Shinsō* [Empty Diet: Truth about the Fukuda drifting government]. Tokyo: Shinchō-sha, 2008.

———, ed. *Sōri Daijin* [The prime minister]. Tokyo: Yomiuri Shimbun-sha, 1971, rev. 1972.

———, ed. *Sōri Daijin Nakasone Yasuhiro* [Prime Minister Nakasone Yasuhiro]. Tokyo: Gendai Shuppan-sha, 1987.

Yomiuri Shimbun-sha, ed. *Daihenkaku eno Joshō: Kenshō Shinseidoka no '96 Shūinsen* [The first chapter toward big change: Examining the '96 general election under the new system]. Tokyo: Yomiuri Shimbun-sha, 1996.

Yosano Kaoru. *Minshutō ga Nihon Keizai wo Hakaisuru* [The DPJ will destroy the Japanese economy]. Tokyo: Bunshun Shinsho, 2010.

Yoshida Shigeru. *Kaisō Jūnen* [Memoir of ten years]. Tokyo: Tokyo Shirakawa Shoin, 1957, reprinted 1982.

Yoshida Takafumi. *Seron Chōsa to Seiji: Sūji wa Dokomade Shinyō Dekiruka.* [Opinion poll and politics: How much can we trust numbers?]. Tokyo: Kōdansha Plus Alfa Shinsho, 2008.

Yoshimura Katsumi. *Ikeda Seiken 1575 nichi.* [The Ikeda Administration: 1575 days]. Tokyo: Gyōsei Mondai Kenkyū-sho, 1985.

Zaikai Henshūbu, ed. *Yūsei Kaikaku no Genten: Ikuta Masaharu Nihon Yūsei Kōsha Shodai Sōsai Yonenkan no Kiseki* [The origin of postal reform: First president of Japan Post Ikuta Masaharu's four years]. Tokyo: Zaikai Kenkyūsho, 2007.

INDEX